Working Women, Entrepreneurs, and the Mexican Revolution

The Mexican Experience
William H. Beezley, series editor

Working Women, Entrepreneurs, and the Mexican Revolution

The Coffee Culture of Córdoba, Veracruz

HEATHER FOWLER-SALAMINI

University of Nebraska Press · Lincoln and London

Library of Congress Cataloging-in-Publication Data

Fowler-Salamini, Heather, 1940–
Working women, entrepreneurs, and the Mexican revolution: the coffee culture of Córdoba, Veracruz / Heather Fowler-Salamini.
    pages cm. — (The Mexican experience)
Includes bibliographical references and index.
ISBN 978-0-8032-4371-2 (pbk.: alk. paper) 1. Women coffee industry employees—Mexico—Córdoba (Veracruz-Llave)—History—20th century. 2. Coffee industry—Mexico—Córdoba (Veracruz-Llave)—History—20th century. 3. Córdoba (Veracruz-Llave)—Economic conditions—20th century. 4. Córdoba (Veracruz-Llave)—Social conditions—20th century. I. Title.

HD6073.C6382M646 2013
331.4'83373097262—dc23   2012047431

Set in Arno Pro by Laura Wellington. Designed by A. Shahan.

Contents

ILLUSTRATIONS

MAPS

TABLES

Acknowledgments

This project has led me down many different paths that I could hardly have anticipated when I started. Many people have offered me their wholehearted support on this marvelous journey. I want to first acknowledge the warm and continuous support that I received from so many Veracruzanos in this endeavor. Without their help, I could never have completed this study. As a friend, colleague, and confidant, Adriana Naveda Chávez-Hita, who grew up in Córdoba, has helped me immeasurably from the work's inception, introducing me to many Cordobans as well as explaining to an outsider many of the traditions and customs of her birthplace. Her mother, Isabel Chávez-Hita de Naveda, and her sisters, Beatriz and Christina, opened their homes to me and provided me with valuable personal contacts within the Spanish business community. Javier Domínguez Sánchez, Luis Sainz Pardo López Negrete, Baltazar Sánchez Regules, and Eduardo Alvarez Amieva provided me with valuable information about their Spanish immigrant families. Javier Domínguez Sánchez graciously lent me the unpublished biography of his grandfather, Severo Sánchez Escobio, written by his nephew. Before his untimely death, Aquileo Rosas Juárez lent me a copy of his unpublished manuscript on the Revolution of 1910 in Córdoba. Other Cordobans, including Luis Puig Hernández and Ruben Calatayud, were also extremely generous in sharing time with me. Finally, Reyna Ríos Dominguez, director of the Córdoba Municipal Archive, brought me hundreds of boxes of documents to pore over and placed me in contact with some of my first interviewees. In my search for retired sorters in Coatepec, Soledad García Morales located administrators and coffee sorters for me to interview. Her uncle, Antonio Díaz Sauría, took me to an abandoned plant to explain the entire coffee preparation process and helped me to understand the nature of the sorter culture. In Huatusco, Susana Córdova Santamaría arranged a marvelous interview with the former coffee exporter, Rafael Fentanes Guillaumin. Ricardo Romero introduced me to two family members who had worked in the Orizaba beneficios. I would like to especially thank the fifteen sorters who agreed to be interviewed. Brígida Siriaco García, Delia Ortiz Sarmiento, and Estela Velázquez Ramírez welcomed me every summer into their homes when I returned to pepper them with additional questions.

Olivia Domínguez Pérez, director of the Veracruz State Archives, and her staff went out of their way to make available to me all the documents that I needed, even though at times it was undergoing reorganization. In particular I want to thank José Luis Barradas López for tolerating my incessant requests for more folders from the State Board of Conciliation and Arbitration and to Ana María Salazar, who was in charge of the Matías Romero Library in 1999. Sara Buck generously shared her index of Gobernación y Justicia.

Over the years, I have had the pleasure to work side by side with a distinguished group of Veracruz scholars at the Instituto de Investigaciones Histórico-Sociales of Veracruz University, who enriched my knowledge of the state's history and included me in their social events and excursions into the countryside. They include Rosío Córdova Plaza, Pedro Jiménez, Alberto Olvera, Juan Ortiz Escamilla, and Davíd Skerritt Gardner. Carmen Blázquez Domínguez has been a wonderful colleague, assisting me in tracking down inaccessible archival collections and Veracruzanos with special knowledge of Veracruz history. At the Colegio de México, I would like to thank in particular Javier Garciadiego Dantán, Romana Falcón, Alicia Hernández,

Marco Palacios, Anne Staples, and Gabriela Cano for welcoming me into their vibrant intellectual community during my stays in Mexico City. I want to acknowledge the assistance of a number of Veracruz students in data collection. Gilberto Cházaro García entered data on union membership and created the tables found in chapter 2. Gerardo Ciruelo Torres, Andrés Aguilar y Portilla, and Davíd Ruiz Ramón transcribed my interviews.

The research for this project was originally funded by a Fulbright-García Robles Lecturer/Scholarship in 1998–99 when I lived for a year in Xalapa, Veracruz. I returned almost every summer to continue my research, very often funded by a Bradley University Research Award. In the fall of 2005, I spent a semester in Mexico City writing the first chapter and consulting Carmen Ramos Escandón's wonderful book collection on gender.

Numerous colleagues in the United States have supported me on this long journey. First, I want to thank Mary Kay Vaughan for her unfaltering support of this project from the very beginning. Her advice has been invaluable at every step of this process. Francie Chassen-López read and commented on the first three chapters. I would like to thank Mabel Rodríguez Centeno, whose outstanding work on Córdoba provided me with the framework to understand its coffee economy. John Womack Jr. and Stephen Topik made invaluable comments on chapter 1. I also want to thank the two anonymous readers who helped me to focus the manuscript more clearly on working women and commercial entrepreneurs in a history from below. Others who have read and commented on all or portions of this manuscript include Bradford Brown, Raymond Buve, Teresa Fernández Aceves, Edmund Fowler, Leticia Gamboa Ojeda, John M. Hart, Thomas Miller Klubbock, and Susie S. Porter. I would like to mention the unfaltering support of Friedrich Katz, who was always challenging me to explore the complex relationships between social movements and revolution.

During my years at Bradley University, a number of people made the completion of this project possible. Claire Etaugh, former dean of the College of Liberal Arts and Sciences, was extremely supportive of my research on women and provided funding to cover many trips to Mexico over the years. I want to thank Marina Savoie in the Interlibrary Loan Department, who always found it challenging to search for my obscure requests. Gina Meeks configured all the tables in chapter 1. Duane Zehr photographed and digitized pictures for me. I would also like to thank Bridget Barry and Joeth Zucco at the University of Nebraska Press along with Jeremy Hall for their assistance in preparing this manuscript for publication. My husband, Leonardo, and my two children, Yvonne and Alexey, have always been present throughout this project, offering enduring support and an enormous amount of patience and understanding. This book is for the coffee sorters whose unceasing struggle to support their families inspired me to initiate this project in the first place. The translations from Spanish are my own. Whatever errors remain are my responsibility.

Shorter versions of chapter 2 were published in "Gender, Work, and Working-Class Women's Culture in the Veracruz Coffee Export Industry, 1920–1945," in *International Labor and Working-Class History* 63 (Spring 2003): 102–21 (Copyright © 2003 by the International Labor and Working-Class History Society, reprinted with permission of Cambridge University Press); and in "Gender, Work, Trade-Unionism, and Working-Class Women's Culture in Post-Revolutionary Veracruz," in *Sex in Revolution: Gender, Politics, and Power in Modern Mexico*, ed. Jocelyn Olcott, Mary Kay Vaughan, and Gabriela Cano (Durham NC: Duke University, 2006), 162–80 (reprinted by permission).

The first four sections of chapter 3 were originally published in the *Journal of Women's History* 14, no. 1 (Spring 2002): 34–63 (reprinted with permission by Johns Hopkins University Press).

A shorter version of chapter 4 was originally published in Spanish as "Caciquismo, sindicalismo y género en la agroindustria cafetalera de Córdoba, Veracruz, 1925–45," in *Integrados y marginados en el México posrevolucionario*, ed. Nicolás Cárdenas García and Enrique Guerra Manzo (Mexico City: Porrúa / Universidad Autónoma Metropolitana–Xochimilco, 2009), 205–45.

Abbreviations

ANFER   Asociación Nacional Femenil Revolucionaria (Women's National Revolutionary Association)
BENEMEX   Beneficios Mexicanos del Café (Mexican State Coffee Agency)
BNCA   Banco Nacional de Crédito Agrícola (National Bank of Agricultural Credit)
BSAM   *Boletín de la Sociedad Agrícola Mexicana* (*Bulletin of the Mexican Agricultural Society*)
CEIMSA   Compañía Exportadora e Importadora Mexicana (Mexican Export and Import Company)
CGOCM   Confederación General de Obreros y Campesinos de México (Mexican General Confederation of Workers and Peasants)
CGT   Confederación General de Trabajadores (General Confederation of Workers)
CNT   Confederación Nacional de Trabajadores (National Confederation of Workers)
COM   Casa del Obrero Mundial (House of the World Worker)
CROC   Confederación Regional de Obreros y Campesinos (Regional Confederation of Workers and Peasants)
CROM   Confederación Regional Obrera Mexicana (Mexican Regional Worker Confederation)

CSOCO	Confederación Sindicalista de Obreros y Campesinos de la Régión de Orizaba (Confederation of Workers and Peasants of the Orizaba Region)
CSOCEV	Confederación Sindicalista de Obreros y Campesinos del Estado de Veracruz (Confederation of Workers and Peasants of the State of Veracruz)
CSORM	Confederación de los Sindicatos Obreros de la República Mexicana (Confederation of Labor Unions of the Mexican Republic)
CSUM	Confederación Sindical Unitaria de México (Mexican Unitary Union Confederation)
EXCAXA	Exportadores de Café de Xalapa (Xalapa Coffee Exporters)
FNTIC	Federación Nacional de Trabajadores de la Industria del Café (National Federation of Coffee-Industry Workers)
FROC	Federación Revolucionaria de Obreras y Campesinos (Revolutionary Federation of Workers and Peasants)
FSOCC	Federación de Sindicatos de Obreros y Campesinos de la Región de Córdoba (Federation of Worker and Peasant Unions of the Córdoba Region)
FSOCO	Federación Sindicalista de Obreros y Campesinos de la Región de Orizaba (Federation of Worker and Peasant Unions of the Orizaba Region)
CTM	Confederación de Trabajadores Mexicicanos (Mexican Worker Confederation)
Peasant League	Liga de Comunidades Agrarias y Sindicatos Campesinos del Estado de Veracruz (League of Agrarian Communities and Peasant Unions of the State of Veracruz)
PCM	Partido Comunista Mexicano (Mexican Communist Party)
PNR	Partido Nacional Revolucionario (National Revolutionary Party)
PRD	Partido Revolucionario Democrático (Revolutionary Democratic Party)
PRI	Partido Revolucionario Institucional (Institutionalized Revolutionary Party)

PT Partido del Trabajo (Labor Party)

SDC Sindicato de Desmanchadoras de Café, Córdoba (Córdoba Coffee Sorters Union)

SIOECC Sindicato Industrial de Obreras Escogedoras del Café del Distrito de Córdoba (Industrial Union of Coffee Sorters of Córdoba)

SITCTAC Sindicato Industrial de Trabajadores de Café, Tabaco, Maderas, Destiladores de Aguardiente y Comercio del Distrito de Córdoba (Industrial Union of Coffee, Tobacco, Wood, Sugarcane Distillery, and Commercial Workers of Córdoba)

SODCC Sindicato de Obreras Desmanchadoras del Café de Coatepec: "Union Libertadora" (Coffee-Sorter Union of Coatepec, "Liberating Union")

SOECC Sindicato de Obreras Escogedoras del Café de Córdoba (Union of Coffee Sorters of Córdoba)

Working Women,
Entrepreneurs,
and the Mexican
Revolution

Introduction

In March 1965 the coffee exporters of Córdoba, Veracruz, laid off all the women workers who cleaned their green coffee, and replaced them with electronic sorting machines in their preparation plants (*beneficios*). This decision marked the conclusion of a seventy-year period of enormous expansion and gradual mechanization of the state's coffee agroindustry. As the *Diario de Xalapa* had noted at the onset of mechanization, it "would have repercussions throughout the country owing to the fact that Veracruz has more coffee workers and grows more coffee than any other state."[1] For the coffee entrepreneurs, plant modernization and the success of the labor settlement would ensure future economic profits. For the women workers, it represented the elimination of a relatively secure form of employment and the failure of the labor movement to save their jobs. It also marked the end of an era in which global, national, and regional forces had come together in such a way as to create employment for thousands of working women, foster their unionization, and foment the development of a working women's culture.

My purpose here is to write a history from below. This regional history of Córdoba's coffee economy shows first how it was shaped by national and international forces and how, in turn, it influenced the development of Mexico's coffee agroindustry. The study is about how place matters, because it helps us understand the interrelationships between the region's entrepreneurs, workers, labor movements, gender relations, and culture on the one hand and Mexico's social revolution, immigration, modernization, and the Atlantic coffee market on the other hand. It contends that macrolevel processes helped to shape Córdoba's regional economy, which influenced the development of Mexico's coffee agroindustry and its labor movement.

Regional Coffee-Export Economies in an Atlantic Context

At least three theoretical approaches have influenced the study of the Latin American coffee economies over the past century. Each of them grapples with the constantly shifting interrelationship between macrolevel and microlevel social, economic, and political factors. First, nineteenth-century laissez-faire and certain forms of twentieth-century modernization theory that are based on classic economic theory support the idea that world trade was the engine of regional economic growth. Dependency theory offers an alternative approach, contending that this export model actually made Latin America more and more dependent on foreign capitalism for its markets and its financing and that most profits ended up in the pockets of foreign financiers and import companies rather than smaller native producers and the workers. They also argue that regional coffee elites were complicit in assisting foreign entrepreneurs in the penetration of the weaker underdeveloped coffee economies.[2] A third approach to the study of coffee focuses on commodity chains that "serve as a bidirectional link between producers and consumers worldwide." A modified form of the world systems theory, it argues that the production, financing, transport, preparation, financing, and marketing of coffee has been vertically and sometimes horizontally organized by global capitalism over the course of the last 150 years. It leaves open, however, a large range of possibilities on how the boom and bust cycles impact regional economies and cultures.[3]

Without denying the overall impact of the global market on Latin American coffee economies, I prefer to concentrate on the commercialization of coffee and migration of people within the Atlantic world during the three major coffee booms that occurred between the 1880s and the 1950s. As one Colombian scholar noted, coffee needs to be seen within the context of growing demands for tropical products in industrializing nations of the North Atlantic basin.[4] As Atlantic scholars are now making clear, Atlantic history is not only about "literal points of contact . . . but rather about explaining transformations, experiences, and events in one place in terms of conditions deriving from that place's location in a large multifaceted, interconnected world."[5] Rachel Moore has shown this to be true for Xalapa, Veracruz, which became integrated into the Atlantic community in the eighteenth century. Although it lay forty miles from the coast, it emerged as the linchpin for internal Atlantic trade for the Spanish empire.[6] I will argue that the region of Córdoba began evolving at the end of the nineteenth century from an inward-looking, sugar- and tobacco-producing, postcolonial economy into Mexico's major center of coffee production, preparation, and commerce.

The Latin American coffee economies have largely been studied from the perspective of production and their relationship to land tenure, emerging rural elites, oppressive rural labor systems, and the growers' relationships with merchants, the state, import houses, and the world market.[7] Very few studies have focused specifically on the merchants and exporters who served as intermediaries between regional coffee growers and their domestic and foreign markets and as the preparers of export-grade coffee.[8] Most scholars are in agreement, however, that the coffee merchants, preparers, and exporters served as the key financial brokers stimulating the development of Latin American coffee-export economies in the final decades of the nineteenth century,[9] but what is less well understood is their relationship with coffee growers, the nature of their business and industrial operations, their ties with other regional coffee elites, and the composition of their labor force. William Roseberry argued that these coffee intermediaries occupied "nodal positions within a variety of hierarchical networks," among exporters, foreign import-export companies, and local merchants that varied from region to region.[10] This study aims to explore the nature of these hierarchical networks, in particular between Atlantic import-export companies and local commercial entrepreneurs.

The study of coffee has received far less attention in Mexico than in other parts of Latin America for a number of reasons. In Brazil, Colombia, Venezuela, Central America, and the Caribbean, coffee production was the dominant economic sector. In spite of the fact that coffee remained Mexico's second most important agricultural export for many decades, the country's national economy was based on not one but a number of lucrative exports. As a consequence, the state did not play such a decisive role in its development as in other Latin American countries. What is more, a cohesive coffee elite with strong ties to the national political system did not begin to develop until the late-1940s in part because of the dispersed nature of the regional coffee economies and the lack of a centralized transportation and commercialization structure. For all these reasons, Mexican scholars displayed far greater interest in the multinational companies that invested heavily in more-lucrative export commodities, such as petroleum, minerals, henequen, sugarcane, and cotton.

I have chosen to employ the term "agroindustry" for the production, preparation, commercialization, and exportation of coffee beans, as Mexican scholars do. It is very difficult to disaggregate the producing, commercial, and agroindustrial stages; for they are dynamic, constantly changing constructs across time and place. Furthermore, the nature of this agroindustry varies so much from region to region and country to country in terms of the relationship between these different stages. Some argue that because the coffee beans are not transformed into another product during the preparation process, it should not be called an industry, and there is some merit in this argument. However, the beneficio relies on heavy machinery to prepare (*beneficiar*) the product, and it employs a disciplined workforce that follows a fixed work schedule just like any other consumer or export industry.[11]

To place the evolution of Córdoba's export coffee economy in a broader comparative perspective, I have situated it within regional, state, national, and Atlantic historical contexts. Veracruz's coffee economy was primarily concentrated around five highland towns in Central Veracruz: Coatepec, Córdoba, Huatusco, Orizaba, and Xalapa. Each of their regional coffee economies had unique characteristics and developed at a slightly different pace, although Córdoba's was the most technologically advanced and outpaced the other regions of the state. At the national level, Veracruz dominated the coffee agroindustry through the 1940s. To understand why it was able to maintain this position for so long, I compare its coffee economy with that of Chiapas and Oaxaca. Finally, in the Americas, Mexico's coffee exports were tiny in comparison to those of Brazil, and they always lagged behind those of Colombia and several Central American countries. Yet Mexico's proximity and easy access to the constantly growing U.S. market gave it a distinct cost advantage over other coffee-exporting nations.

The emergence of Córdoba's coffee-export economy was closely tied to the role of transatlantic immigration and the creation of a vibrant Spanish commercial community in the first decades of the twentieth century. I approach immigrant entrepreneurism within the context of broad transatlantic migration patterns rather than Hispanic exceptionalism. Most studies on the Spanish immigrants in Mexico have attributed their economic success to unique Spanish qualities associated with the Hispanic privilege, ethnic superiority, chain migration, patriarchy, entrepreneurism, and family networking.[12] All these factors are important, but this view seems incomplete. José C. Moya's broader analytical framework emphasizes the "complex interplay between the premigration heritage and the host environment, between continuity and change" as they gradually integrated themselves into Buenos Aires society.[13] This is to say, Spanish immigrants benefitted from a constantly shifting transatlantic bicultural and binational culture. Their experiences held much in common with those of members of other European and Middle Eastern immigrant communities in Latin America at this time.[14]

Studies on the predominantly female labor force employed in the coffee beneficios are even scarcer than those on their employers.[15] Nevertheless, nineteenth-century coffee promoters, including Carlos Sartorius, Matías Romero, John Southworth, and Gabriel Gómez, all recognized the essential importance of women coffee sorters (*escogedoras* or *desmanchadoras*) to carry out the sorting, or cleaning, of the beans for export. Their conception of women's work was based on the common perception that rural domestic duties could simply be transferred into the dry preparation plants (*beneficios secos*). Thus, the meaning of women's work for these coffee promoters was always linked to manual, low-paying, and less prestigious work. However, for the subjects themselves, it meant a steady seasonal wage and the opportunity to penetrate previously masculinized public workplaces.

Social Revolution, the Coffee Agroindustry, and Organized Labor

The Mexican Revolution of 1910 brought new challenges to Mexico's coffee economy. Fortunately, the most important regional coffee economies in Veracruz, Oaxaca, and Chiapas were not the major theaters of wide-scale military operations. It will be shown that coffee production was more disrupted than its transportation, trade, preparation, and export. In fact, the collapse of political and economic control during the revolutionary chaos actually created a vacuum for commercial entrepreneurs to engage in windfall profit taking, as Jean Meyer has suggested occurred in many other export industries in Mexico.[16]

The relations between coffee elites and the modern Mexican state were not nearly so congenial as in other Latin American countries, for coffee never played such a predominant economic role.[17] For many years, official Mexican historiography articulated an antiforeign and anticapitalist stance, which fostered the impression that the postrevolutionary Mexican state was more antibusiness than, in fact, it really was. This perception is now being revised.[18] The federal government followed fiscal policies that assisted growers and exporters in weathering downturns in the market, but it did not directly intervene to prop up the coffee exporters until the Second World War. Not until the late 1940s did coffee producers, preparers, and exporters finally take the initiative to organize a nationwide organization that served as a pressure group to lobby for state support. The state rather belatedly embraced their plans for full mechanization in the 1950s as part of its industrialization and modernization policies. Relations between the coffee workers and the postrevolutionary state were much more complex and contradictory.

Labor scholars have tended to view the Mexican state's support of organized labor as being based on the twin objectives of benevolence and control. It intervened and mediated prerevolutionary conflicts on numerous occasions beginning in the mid-nineteenth century with these goals in mind.[19] Populists have tended to downplay the role of the state during the Revolution of 1910–17 in order to emphasize the spontaneity of worker mobilization. As a consequence, they have vilified the oppressive labor policies of both the prerevolutionary and postrevolutionary regimes.[20] On the other hand, revisionists have viewed the revolutionary state's role as manipulative, arguing that it co-opted the labor movement into a patron-client relationship to build a new authoritarian regime.[21] More recently postrevisionists have sought to strike a balance between these two perspectives and to emphasize the importance of worker agency, where strikes and negotiations from below led to a broad range of sociocultural and economic concessions by the state and industry.[22] My sources lead me to similar conclusions. Central Veracruz seasonal coffee workers, both women and men, were, on the whole, unusually successful in negotiating from below to obtain the same worker rights as permanent workers from 1915 on in the new labor institutions created by the revolutionary state.

The recent gender turn has led authors to reevaluate their views concerning the relationship between women workers and the revolutionary state. New studies have revealed that women activists organized women-dominated and mixed workshops with the wholehearted support of the anarchist movement and the revolutionary state during the early phases of revolution. In their struggle for survival, women's economic demands were slightly different from those of men workers. What is more, political alliances forged between radical revolutionary military commanders, politicians, and labor organizers at the local level were as beneficial for working women as for working men.[23] In the states of Jalisco, Michoacán, Yucatán, Tamaulipas, and Veracruz, progressive governors responded to rising protests by all workers regardless of their gender for ideological and, more importantly, for political reasons to calm social unrest and to bolster their own power bases in the 1910s and 1920s.[24]

The state of Veracruz was in the forefront of labor activism, legislation, and prolabor state governments during the revolution. The first municipal industrial-labor boards created in 1915, I contend, concerned themselves with economic rather than gender issues in their handling of grievances. Therefore, these boards became a major mechanism through which women coffee workers could air their demands and have their demands met. Owing to their large numbers and their relatively high level of mobilization, coffee sorters held a relatively strong bargaining position. Moreover, their ability to launch strikes and demonstrations forced state interventions from 1915 through the early 1930s to uphold coffee workers' rights. In short, Veracruz authorities realized that a peaceful workforce and a robust coffee-export sector were critical for the recovery of the state's economy.

The state's positive attitude toward organized women workers began to wane at end of the 1920s with the onset of economic depression, the institutionalization of the labor organization within the official party, and threats from the political right. It began to support social and political stability, endorsement of the family wage, and the denial of suffrage to women.[25] Moreover, the postrevolutionary state started to construct a nationalistic culture, incorporating what Mary Kay Vaughan has termed the "modernization of patriarchy" into its agrarian, labor, and educational projects. Thus, the objectives of the Mexican Revolution became in many respects a male project or patriarchal event.[26] Women workers were also increasingly marginalized by the men-dominated national trade union movements allied with the official party that were determined to impose their control over their memberships.[27] However, the women-dominated coffee-sorter workshops retained some degree of union autonomy and a female leadership, while the formation of a women-dominated boss rule (*cacicazgo*) was not necessarily linked to masculinity.

Once the state launched its industrialization programs associated with the Economic Miracle of the 1940s and 1950s, organized labor found itself increasingly marginalized and even under attack.[28] When coffee exporters decided to fully mechanize their plants and lay off their manual women workers, the state supported their plans. Just as in the textile industry, tortilla shops, and tobacco workshops, women workers played a key role in the transition toward full mechanization, but they were also its first major victims.[29] Before the mechanization process was completed, however, Veracruz sorters had the opportunity to construct a workshop community and culture.

Engendering Working-Class Culture

Like other forms of popular culture, urban working-class culture has been referred to as "the symbols and meanings embedded in the day-to-day practices of subordinated groups."[30] It encompasses the relationship between class and gender, constraint and agency, and contingency and conflict. It is also assumed that there is a continual tension between the subaltern and hegemonic culture.[31] My approach to working-class culture seeks to balance the social historian's focus on class or group formation with a cultural historian's concern with experience and discourse. To uncover the experiences and voices of the workers who labored in the coffee preparation plants, I examine their everyday experiences in the local workplace, at home, and in the community. These work experiences become interwoven at the national and transnational level with the agroindustry, revolutionary politics, and the Atlantic coffee economy. Key to new gendered labor history is the assumption that the history of the everyday, which is implicitly linked to the notion of experience, must include discursive and ideological formations.[32]

European social history has heavily influenced my approach to working people's everyday lives. Geof Eley argues that its practitioners have sought to probe everyday life "by investigating the material circumstances or daily existence at work, at home, at play," while at the same "entering the inner world of popular experience of the workplace, the family and household, the neighborhood, [and] the school."[33] Rather than focusing on the history of oppressed groups, everyday history shows how those who have remained nameless are agents of change by appropriating, while simultaneously transforming, their world.[34] Labor historians can construct a bridge from social to cultural history by conceptualizing worker culture as a social process emerging out of the individual and collective workplace and household experiences, resulting in the formation of a group consciousness to contest elite culture.[35] This interconnection can only be achieved, says Kathleen Canning, if experience is conceptualized as "more than the mere 'living through of events'; the term also encompasses the way in which 'people construed events as they were living through them."[36] However, she makes clear that "to historicize the category of experience itself," it must be situated in "distinct historical eras and processes of transformations."[37]

To understand how workers construed their experience, one must turn to discourse, for it probes the meanings of work, gender, and workplace culture in the minds of the workers themselves. It is from this perspective that I approach the workplace in chapter 2 to show how coffee sorters shared a working experience that profoundly shaped their collective memories of their work, family, workplace, identity, and community.

Until recently, Latin American historians conceptualized workers' culture within a masculinized workplace that obscured or marginalized women workers; the family, workplace, and union culture were viewed through the lens of a masculine value system.[38] With the emergence of studies on gendered working people's culture, it is now being recognized that working women's culture can be quite distinct from that of working men's culture. Therefore, I believe it is important to use the term "woman worker" (*obrera*) to juxtapose with the term "man worker" (*obrero*) to emphasize the gendered nature of workplaces and worker communities. As Susie Porter has pointed out, the term "obrera" is actually not a new one, for it was already being employed in the late nineteenth century to refer to a female wage laborer.[39] My decision to use this term is rooted in Joan Scott's two interconnected propositions about gender; it is a "constitutive element of social relationships based on perceived differences between the sexes, and gender is a primary way of signifying relationships of power."[40]

It was generally assumed that bourgeois gender norms and moral values more often than not trickled down or were imposed by industrialists, government officials, the press, and social reformers on the Latin American popular classes. The upper classes employed the cult of domesticity, moral respectability, and the idea of separate spheres to exercise sociocultural hegemony over working people. This constructed gender ideology sought to visualize the woman within a dichotomized paradigm of the "prostitute and the guardian angel."[41] This meant obreras had the impossible task of struggling to "square the circle," or struggling to adapt to the masculinized workplace.[42]

A new generation of scholars now is advancing the idea that working women exercised much more agency as individuals and created collectively their own working women's culture. In certain respects, working women's union culture was a variation of men's union culture. Low-income women and men more often than not entered into the workplace for the same basic reasons: survival of the family. They shared similar rural origins, migration patterns, and working experiences in paternalist workplaces where exploitation was commonplace. Working men had a gremial and mutualist popular tradition dating back to the colonial period, but female cigarette workers and seamstresses had followed their lead and created their own mutualist societies during the nineteenth century.[43] These experiences had a singular effect of empowering women individually and collectively outside the home; and in so doing, it challenged gender norms.

Susie Porter suggests that women workers developed their own culture in Mexico City's mixed-gendered workplace by negotiating within a masculinized worker culture and a dichotomized virgin/ prostitute discourse to legitimize themselves as honorable working women from Porfirian times. Working women learned to operate "within a discourse of female honor" while still adhering to existing norms of female virtue by the early decades of the twentieth century.[44] For the postrevolutionary period, Teresa Fernández-Aceves goes further by showing the ways in which women workers and teachers took on active leadership roles to confront and create alternative organizations to the male-dominated Guadalajara labor movement.[45]

What I propose to explore here is how work experience and discourse in women-dominated workshops in postrevolutionary Mexico created gender-specific worker communities that developed relatively unhampered from continual male intrusion in Central Veracruz. Women became the real originators of their workplace culture, and their culture seeped out into the streets, union halls, and homes. It was quite distinct from obrero culture not only in terms of how women perceived their work and their work experience but also insofar as how it shaped gender and work identities, social networks, and their worker community.

Sorter culture was gender specific in other respects because these women shared experiences that were different from those of men workers. Their treatment as second-class persons socialized them to have low self-esteem. This everyday experience had economic consequences as they searched for employment. Yet in their all-women workshops, unions, and communities, their individual and collective experiences helped them build a collective sense of community and memory. They continually sought to resist the gender marker that placed them on the lowest rung of provincial society as women of the streets.

Strong women leaders in Córdoba, as well as in Coatepec, were also critical to the development of an alternative working women's community and culture. Leaders were able to build effective patron-client relationships within the rank and file. They also served as effective intermediaries between the rank and file and the national labor confederations. Continuity in leadership, which paralleled patterns in Mexican men's unions, was rooted in strong charismatic personalities, rotation of power within a collective leadership, and the eventual emergence of women's boss rule. While men's trade unionism was based on physical prowess, violence, and authoritarianism, these traits were more muted in women's trade unionism, as we shall see in chapter 4. Sorter leaders became political brokers between the labor movement and the public at large. By courting the neighboring Orizaba labor confederation and remaining loyal official party adherents, they strengthened their legitimacy. These leaders also participated in the body politic as labor officials, municipal councilwomen, and active suffragettes.

They also served as cultural brokers, organizing union dances and theatrical and band performances to create a more cohesive sorter community, while solidifying their own legitimacy. These cultural activities were part of what James C. Scott has called the "hidden transcript," played out offstage with the purpose of resisting official transcripts and regulations.[46] In so doing, they enabled obreras to participate in liberating forms of behavior outside the confines of the household. Sorters could express themselves as actresses, dancers, and musicians in public performances. This alternative culture displayed an amazing amount of variation and ambiguity, at same time supporting and subverting provincial gender norms.

Oral History and Everyday Experience

Oral history is one tool that social historians employ to uncover the hidden transcript, or the voices and experiences of subalterns.[47] It provides us with greater workplace specificity as well as greater understanding of the complexities of experience, whether we are speaking of the textile mills of Brazil or Colombia, the meatpacking plants of Argentina, or the beer breweries of Mexico.[48] It assists us in engendering private and public spaces and revealing how they are interconnected. Early oral histories of obreras were often framed within oppression theory that was premised on the idea that the workplace was simply an extension of the patriarchal household into the workplace.[49] This supposition tends to permeate oral histories exploring masculinity in the workplace, where masculine values and paternalism permeate the workshops, the union halls, strike lines, and the communities.[50]

Feminist anthropologists and historians working in the field of gender studies in the 1980s began altering their oral history methodology to assist them in engendering experience and uncovering hidden transcripts. They embraced an "egalitarian research process characterized by authenticity, reciprocity, and intersubjectivity between the researcher and her 'subjects'" to end the treatment of working women as objects.[51] Employing this equalizing approach, they sought to find a sense of shared empathy for the women's cause. In particular, Ruth Behar, Lynn Stephen, and Florencia Mallon placed individual peasant women center stage in their testimonials, while they themselves served as mediators of the life histories.[52] This empathetic approach and the claim that "horizontal affinity" could actually be achieved has been criticized by Daniel James, among others. He suggests that "unmediated access to subjective historical discourse" cannot be represented "except in terms of the dominant male discourse." The stories of working women, he argues, are really being told with tension and ambiguity "out on the borderlands," where disruption of the central narrative is possible but not available for everyday use.[53] This study tries to show that this is not always the case. I do believe that oral history is still the best tool we have to bring to light women's experience and discourse and to show their centrality in the agroindustrial workplace.

Researching in archives does not provide the necessary information on the everyday experiences of coffee workers or their Spanish employers. In the case of the commercial entrepreneurs, there was little if no official correspondence between them and state authorities because they networked within their immigrant communities. Although I did locate a handful of the immigrants' descendants, many of them showed little inclination to speak with a foreign scholar who wanted to question them about their family businesses. Therefore, I found interviewing elites more difficult than interviewing workers. I also located a small number of beneficio workers who were still alive, although all of them were women. Since all the important leaders had died or were quite aged, most of my information comes from interviews with rank and file workers, whose knowledge about union power was rather limited. Men workers were even more difficult to track down because they seemed to have moved back and forth across urban and rural landscapes as seasonal workers. Cecilia Sheridan Prieto's classic ethnographic case study of Coatepec's escogedoras inspired me to follow a life-history approach in my interviews of their Córdoba counterparts.[54]

Rereading my field notes and interview transcripts, it gradually became clear to me that these life histories were not simply individual histories but parts of a collective history of coffee sorters, for they shared so many common everyday experiences. In short, I envisaged my role as a socially committed scholar, as Susan Crane has suggested, not as "remembering lived experience but rather as witnessing the experiences of others through their testimony, . . . and then speaking of this evidence."[55]

Needless to say, the interviewees had their own agendas several decades after they had stopped working: to cover up the dark side of their daily existence, downplay bitter disputes among rival patron-client groups, and de-emphasize their real lack of economic security. On the whole, they wanted to represent themselves as proud workers and mothers. Their alteration of reality came from their view of the past through the prism of their own experiences as well as the selective memory of the person. Reconstructing their past assisted them in legitimizing it for the interviewer as well as making it more meaningful for themselves.[56]

Organization and Scope

This study analyzes the complex interconnectedness between the entrepreneurial and labor sectors of a regional agro-export economy in the midst of revolution and modernization within the Atlantic community. It is organized into six chapters. The first chapter focuses specifically on how a small group of immigrant entrepreneurs, in large part of Spanish origin, captured control of the financing, preparation, and commercialization of export-grade coffee in the Córdoba region and, in so doing, came to dominate the nation's coffee-export agroindustry. It emphasizes the interplay between external market forces, social revolution, and regional factors from the 1890s through the 1930s. Chapters 2 through 5 focus on the women and men workers in the semimechanized coffee beneficios of Córdoba during the first half of the twentieth century. Chapter 2 presents a broad survey of the nature of the workforce in the coffee plants and the complex interrelationship between gender, work, and workplace in five Central Veracruz towns. Chapter 3 analyzes the ways in which coffee sorters mobilized and unionized into gender-segregated unions to meet the challenges of spiraling inflation and job insecurity during the revolutionary and postrevolutionary periods under the guidance of anarchosyndicalist, tenant, and Peasant League activists. The construction of a collective women's boss rule (*cacicazgo*) that served as an effective mechanism to fight for worker's rights from the 1930s is the subject of chapter 4. Chapter 5 explores the everyday experiences through the collective memory of a working-class women's community during the Mexican Miracle. The final chapter examines the events leading up to the mechanization of the Veracruz coffee beneficios in the 1950s and 1960s and the ways in which the sorter community collectively remembered these events and resisted the harsh reality.

1

Emergence of a Coffee Commercial Elite in Córdoba, Veracruz

When the recent Spanish immigrant Antonio García Menéndez entered into a commercial agreement with a British and a German entrepreneur in Córdoba, Veracruz, to buy, prepare, and export coffee to Europe and the United States in 1895, he created the first major agro-export business that functioned as a commercial intermediary between Mexican coffee producers and the Atlantic community. This venture, which included the construction of a beneficio to prepare export-grade coffee, marked a decisive turning point for Mexico's coffee agroindustry. This chapter seeks to explore the macrolevel and microlevel factors that contributed to the transformation of Córdoba's coffee economy between the 1880s and the 1940s as it solidified its links to the Atlantic coffee market. It analyzes the rise and decline of Córdoba's coffee producers, the penetration of U.S. export-import companies, and the emergence and consolidation of a new immigrant commercial elite. This transformative process would shape Central Veracruz's coffee agroindustry and also that of the nation.

This chapter shows how Córdoba was transformed from an internal-oriented economy to an export-oriented one that shipped to markets along both Atlantic coasts and the contiguous Caribbean Ocean and Baltic Sea. It became a "linchpin" between transatlantic trade and immigration and the interior of Mexico.[1] As Alison Games contends,

"Atlantic history is not only about the literal points of contact (ports, traders, or migrants, for example), but rather about explaining transformations, experiences, and events in one place in terms of conditions deriving from that place's location in a large, multifaceted, interconnected world."[2]

A number of macrolevel and microlevel factors contributed to Córdoba's emergence as the nation's largest commercial center for coffee preparation and commercialization beginning in the 1890s. Most importantly, the enormous increase in demand for coffee and ensuing price increases on both sides of the Atlantic drove foreign and domestic entrepreneurs to invest heavily in the financing, commercialization, and preparation of this commodity in Córdoba, just as in other parts of Latin America. The town's central location privileged it over all other coffee centers. It enjoyed easy access to the coast, lying only sixty miles from the port of Veracruz and at the intersection of two national railroad lines. However, the role of other internal factors cannot be discounted.

Medium-sized landowners who produced sugar, tobacco, and coffee for the domestic market spurred the initial phase of coffee commercialization and preparation in the Córdoba region. By the 1880s, they had developed an unbounded confidence in the idea that coffee production and export could drive national development. This process paralleled what was occurring in other Latin American coffee regions at the same time.[3] However, a major shift occurred as agro-industrial operations moved from the coffee farm (*finca*) to the urban exporting firms (*casas de exportación*). Two groups of immigrant merchants altered the urban landscape by establishing family businesses that would finance the basic infrastructure for Córdoba's future Atlantic-oriented agro-export industry. Meanwhile, large U.S. coffee-export-import companies began to enter the region and compete in the region's coffee market. Their coffee profits spurred urban modernization, cultural projects, but also socioeconomic inequality as the Porfiriato came to a close.

Córdoba's coffee exporters were able to adapt far more easily than its growers to the external challenges of overproduction, social revolution, and depression that buffeted the region between 1906 and 1940.[4] In the midst of political and economic upheaval, the second group of Spanish immigrants began to emerge as the region's key coffee traders, financiers, and preparers. They organized their export firms around family-based entrepreneurial strategies that allowed them to respond and adapt with greater alacrity to the boom and bust cycles of export commodities than the growers. As the second coffee boom reached its height in the mid-1920s, the immigrant entrepreneurs developed different power relationships with the growers, the predominantly female labor force, and foreign buyers. They came to hold shifting "nodal positions within a variety of hierarchical networks."[5]

How can we explain the extraordinary success of this new commercial elite? The *Cordobeses*, the term applied to the emerging coffee exporters by Veracruzanos, built their businesses around their traditional patriarchal family structure, which concentrated social and economic power and wealth in the hands of a founding patriarch. They shared this tradition with other immigrant groups, such as the Lebanese immigrant entrepreneurs of the Yucatán.[6] Moreover, their transatlantic movement across the Atlantic was "a series of movements that included permanent and temporary settlement, return, back-and-forth traveling between sending and receiving societies, and relocation from one destination to another outside the place of origin."[7] This process led to constant renewal and growth of the Spanish immigrant community.

"A México! A México! A sembrar café!"

Situated at approximately 800 meters above sea level on the eastern slopes of the Sierra Oriental, the Córdoba region was much more suitable for growing sugarcane and tobacco than high quality mountain-grown coffee, which grows between 1,200 and 1,500 meters.[8] From the colonial period, the crown regarded its rich volcanic soil, relatively plentiful water supply, and subtropical climate as ideal for the development of a commercial agricultural center. The Spanish state first encouraged colonists to establish haciendas in the lowlands to the south and east of the town early in the seventeenth century to grow sugarcane to meet the colony's needs. Sugar planters developed medium-sized slave plantations ranging from 200 to 1200 hectares (1 hectare = 2.47 acres) in size that were highly profitable. These growers also tried growing tobacco on the hilly and outlying sections of their properties by the eighteenth century. When the crown designated the Orizaba-Córdoba region as the primary site for tobacco production for its state monopoly in 1765, Córdoba once again benefited from Spanish imperial economic policies. Two other regional factors influenced its agricultural development. It lay on one of the two stagecoach routes between Veracruz and Mexico City, so it developed into a key supplier of agricultural produce for the interior towns of Puebla, Oaxaca, and Xalapa. Moreover, a tightly knit merchant-planter community, composed of both Spaniards and creoles, began to emerge and take control of its regional economy and politics by the end of the colonial period.[9] This elite would come to play a critical role in the transformation of Córdoba into one of Mexico's most important coffee-producing regions. What factors explain Córdoba's transformation from a sugarcane- and tobacco-based economy oriented toward the domestic market to a coffee-export economy by the end of the nineteenth century?

Enterprising Spaniards and Frenchmen brought the coffee plant to the colony of New Spain in the final decade of the eighteenth century from Cuba. A growing market in Europe seemed to augur well for cultivation of this new stimulant. Most probably, coffee was first planted in Central Veracruz, for records show it began to be exported from the port of Veracruz in 1802.[10] Its cultivation in the Córdoba region dates from the 1810s. According to Córdoba's chroniclers, Juan Antonio Gómez de Guevara, a Spanish landowner, planted coffee seeds purchased in Cuba on his hacienda in Amatlán de los Reyes, a village on the outskirts of the town. After the postindependence governments adopted laissez-faire trade policies, massive imports of cheap

Caribbean sugar forced many planters into bankruptcy, while others began to think twice about cultivating sugarcane any longer. To make ends meet, they began planting coffee trees with the help of free labor alongside their tobacco on the hillsides. Scarcely a decade after coffee's introduction, Veracruz (*porteño*) merchants were purchasing Córdoba beans at twelve pesos a *quintal* (46 kilos or 100 U.S. pounds), the same price they were paying for Cuban beans.[11]

As wealthy Europeans became more and more enamored with the custom of sipping coffee at a nearby café every afternoon, their countrymen residing in Central Veracruz began to foresee the potential for hefty profits from coffee production and trade. Carlos Sartorius, the German landowner and entrepreneur, planted a small number of coffee trees on his Huatusco hacienda, El Mirador, during the 1840s. By the mid-1860s, he was predicting that coffee, not sugarcane, would be the crop of the future. It could be easily and cheaply grown, he argued, and then sold in the port of Veracruz for a 100 percent profit. It was the ideal crop for the small landowner or *ranchero* (medium-sized landowner), who could care for fifteen thousand trees along with his subsistence crops. "Coffee is like cash," he wrote. As an avid proponent of the privatization of communal lands, he saw coffee production as a way to civilize the Indian, whom he thought had little incentive to farm unless he could farm his private land.[12] Córdoba's coffee must have been served in Paris by this time, for a businessman had opened the Café de Córdoba there in the 1840s. The Frenchman, Juan Pedro Duhalt, was the first foreign entrepreneur to operate a dry preparation plant in Córdoba, exporting five or six classes of coffee during the 1860s. Most coffee was still being prepared by the rudimentary "dry process." The beans were dried on terraces and then pounded in wooden mortars to remove the outer shell. This ordinary coffee (*café corriente*) was neither depulped nor washed, so it was only sold in the domestic market.[13]

The 1870s and 1880s were transition years in the development of the coffee agroindustry in Mexico, as well as in the rest of Latin America. External factors contributed to the beginning of the first coffee boom. Increased demand on both sides of the Atlantic triggered a steep rise in prices, spurring hacienda owners (*hacendados*) and rancheros to plant more coffee trees and install small wet beneficios to prepare parchment coffee (*café en pergamino*) on their properties. Meanwhile, in the United States the Arbuckle Brothers had started experimenting with different roasting processes and packaging techniques to bring ready-to-use coffee beans to the corner grocery store and into the home.[14]

In Mexico the ambitious railroad projects of Presidents Benito Juárez, Miguel Lerdo de Tejada, and Porfirio Díaz facilitated the transport of coffee, as well as other export commodities, from the producing regions to Mexico's ports and the U.S. border. Coffee producers in Oaxaca and Puebla could ship their coffee to Córdoba for preparation, and then its merchant-preparers could send it on to the North, Mexico City, and the port of Veracruz.[15] In 1873 the completion of the Mexican Railroad (Ferrocarril Mexicano) between the capital and Veracruz, through Orizaba and Córdoba rather than Xalapa, provided a strong economic stimulus to both towns. When Córdoba's merchants discovered that the nearest station would be built two kilometers away from the downtown, two Spanish entrepreneurs quickly took the initiative in building an urban rail line (*ferrocarril urbano*) to transport freight and passengers in mule-drawn wagons back and forth to the main line (see photograph 1). Córdoba now found itself only fifty-seven miles (ninety kilometers) from the port of Veracruz by rail, and merchants could easily ship their merchandise in a matter of hours for a fraction of the mule-train cost to the coast.[16] The northern Xalapa-Coatepec coffee region would have to wait almost two decades for the completion of the Interoceanic Railroad (Ferrocarril Interocéanico), which ran from Mexico City to Veracruz via Xalapa. This gave Córdoba a twenty-year head start in the development of its coffee agroindustry. A third railroad line, the Veracruz and Isthmian Railroad (Ferrocarril de Veracruz al Istmo) finished in 1903, connected the Mexican Railroad with the Isthmian Railway (Ferrocarril del Istmo) at Córdoba. This line provided coffee growers of the

1. Coffee transport on urban streetcar, 1900. Reprinted from Ukers, *All about Coffee*, 264.

isolated regions of Zongolica and Oaxaca's Sierra Mixteca and Pluma Hidalgo regions more direct access to Córdoba's preparation plants.[17] Thus, Córdoba's strategic location at the intersection of two national railways, the Mexican and the Isthmian lines, was one of the key reasons entrepreneurs chose to build their coffee beneficios there. The local link to connect the Interoceanic and Mexican railway lines in Central Veracruz was projected to run south from Xalapa to Córdoba, but it was never entirely completed. Instead, a narrow-gauge railway was constructed heading south from Xalapa to Teocelo and north from Córdoba to Coscomatepec.[18] The failure to complete this north-south line meant that two separate coffee regions developed in Central Veracruz: the Córdoba-Orizaba-Huatusco subregion in the south and the Xalapa-Coatepec one in the north (see map 1).

Like many other towns along the railway, Córdoba was soon "discovered" by Mexican and foreign travelers and tourists as a favorite place to visit and reside because of its pleasant subtropical climate and its luxuriant flora. Its poet José Sebastián Segura described it as "the Garden of Eden," the place where Adam and Eve lived before they were cast out of paradise, or the "mansión eterna de la primavera."[19]

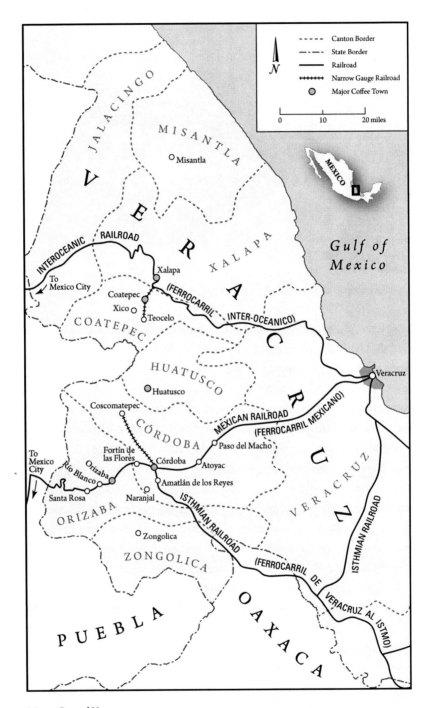

Map 1. Central Veracruz

Its agreeable climate was just one reason why the population of the canton of Córdoba increased more than threefold during the Porfiriato (1876–1910) from 26,000 to 91,000. It almost surpassed the population of the canton of Xalapa.[20] For Matías Romero, the former minister of development and the treasury, Córdoba held another attraction. After having assiduously studied coffee cultivation throughout Mexico and Asia, he reached the conclusion that Córdoba's coffee economy should become the model for the rest of Mexico. Romero had started cultivating coffee in Soconusco, Chiapas, after temporarily withdrawing from politics in the 1870s and had written effusively about its virgin soil, cheap land, and low labor costs; but he came to recognize that very few fincas properly prepared export-grade beans.[21] After visiting Michoacán, Colima, Jalisco, Oaxaca, and Veracruz, he began to see the potential of the Córdoba region: "People will come to understand that the coffee agroindustry is growing rapidly there and soon will reach full development. Due to this industry Córdoba is becoming an important commercial center." His hope was that it "will serve as a stimulus for other districts of the Republic [and that they will] follow the waves of Córdoba."[22] It had two distinct advantages over other coffee regions. Its geographical location provided it with easier access to the port of Veracruz, and its coffee planters were true entrepreneurs, technologically far more advanced in their cultivation and preparation of coffee than anywhere else in the republic.[23] The French Latour brothers were the first Europeans to recognize Córdoba's potential as a preparation center and to install a U.S.-made hulling machine in the early 1880s with the capacity to hull two hundred quintals of parchment coffee a day to prepare café verde. Their dry preparation plant was most likely the largest in the nation.[24]

As the domestic price of coffee doubled between the 1877–78 and the 1888–89 seasons, Mexican landowners started planting more trees than ever before. National production increased to 8.3 million kilos by 1889.[25] In just ten years Mexico's contribution to world production increased from 2 to 4 percent. Its mild Arabica coffee was selling for 19.75 cents a pound, or two cents higher than the less-well-prepared Brazilian variety on the New York Coffee Exchange.[26] Governor Juan Enriquez y Enriquez stated in his 1890 annual report that production for the state of Veracruz had reached 87,400 quintals (4,020,400 kilos) with a value of 1.7 million pesos, which was approximately half of Mexico's production. Although the canton of Córdoba reported producing slightly less than 1 million kilos, the governor estimated that its coffee farmers (*finqueros*) were actually producing more than 3 million kilos and grossly underreporting their yields to avoid the steep taxes. He also reported that the port of Veracruz had exported almost 9 million kilos, the majority of which was grown in the state and 97 percent of which was headed for the United States.[27]

In 1889 Licenciado Rafael Herrera, the owner of the El Corral rancho, was writing euphorically about Córdoba's exceptional coffee agroindustry. The increase in the level of production and the adoption of more technologically advanced preparation procedures led foreign firms to pay higher prices. "All the Monte Blanco [hacienda] harvest has been sold more than a month ago at 24 pesos per quintal, with the advance of its total value to be repaid next March." Two other large producers were able to bargain with German agents or directly with the major Hamburg company to sell their crop for twenty-six to twenty-seven pesos a quintal.[28] Soaring coffee prices had reached sixty centavos per kilo by 1892–93, spurring Herrera to write his famous *Estudio sobre la producción del café* (*Study of Coffee Production*) for the Development Ministry.[29] In his concluding section entitled "A México! A México! A sembrar café!" he urged Mexico to begin a major campaign to plant coffee trees. He cited major structural weaknesses in the Brazilian coffee economy, in particular free labor scarcity and landowner indebtedness, to explain why it would be unable to produce as much coffee as it had in the past.[30] His boundless optimism revealed a fundamental lack of understanding of the resiliency of Brazil's coffee economy as well as the relative inelasticity of demand and supply of coffee. Moreover, as a good Porfirian liberal, he believed commodity exports and free trade would be the engine for the modernization of Mexican society. Like Sartorius, he thought that the distribution of vacant lands to the dispossessed Indians to grow coffee would save the nation. It was the only way to civilize and regenerate the Indian race that had fought so bravely for independence and the Liberal reforms.[31]

By the early 1890s most of Córdoba's larger coffee growers had heavily invested in imported machinery to prepare export-grade green coffee. Growers in Coatepec, Xalapa, Orizaba, and Huatusco lagged far behind Córdoba in terms of their level of investment.[32] At this time, Veracruz producers were primarily shipping to New Orleans buyers, although they were also selling to New York and Piedras Negras firms. Growers preferred to borrow from local lenders at the beginning of the season, because their interest rates were lower, rather than from regional banks. The National Bank (Banco Nacional) ran a branch office in Veracruz that charged at least 11 percent on short-term loans, while local merchants advanced credit at the beginning of the growing season and simply subtracted two to five pesos from every quintal of harvested coffee at the time of sale.[33]

In the early 1890s, finqueros were already beginning to borrow money as never before and to sell their entire crop in advance to foreign import enterprises through their consigners in Veracruz. Mexican promoters considered this development extremely positive, for it seemed to suggest a growing demand and popularity for Córdoba coffee. A writer for the *Boletín de la Sociedad Agrícola Mexicana* (BSAM, *Bulletin of the Mexican Agricultural Society*) wrote, "According to one newspaper, the canton of Córdoba, Veracruz, has acquired such an importance as a center of coffee production that various important U.S. firms have sent their agents there to contract for the largest amounts of coffee beans, and even to make advanced payments without any interest on the next harvests."[34]

Córdoba was thus playing a decisive role in the development of the national coffee agroindustry during the first export boom. It was producing at least 4.4 million kilos of coffee in 1900, which was more than any other Veracruz canton. Veracruz was producing approxi-

TABLE 1: Mexico and Veracruz Coffee Production, 1897–1907

Canton	1897 (kilos)	1900 (kilos)	1907 (kilos)
Coatepec	4,000,000	2,760,000	2,708,186
Córdoba	2,871,858	4,400,000	5,610,881
Huatusco	3,000,000	3,000,000	3,002,000
Orizaba	3,128,000	1,000,000	2,470,994
Xalapa	——	57,000	197,560
Veracruz	14,302,714	12,492,654	32,962,467
Mexico	19,059,900*	21,088,128	50,113,450

Sources: Figueroa, *Guía general descriptiva de la República Mexicana*, 690; Secretaría de Fomento, *Anuario de la República Mexicana de 1900*, 459–60; and Secretaría de Fomento, *Anuario de la República Mexicana de 1907*, 520–21, 534.

* Secretaría de Fomento, *Anuario de la República Mexicana de 1895*, 826.

mately 60 percent of total national production (see table 1). Although the value of coffee exports never compared with that of minerals or henequen, it was an important product in the "export basket." In the 1880s and 1890s foreign coffee sales were significant enough to stimulate and define the nature of the first Mexican export boom before it took off. In 1894 sales had risen to 16 percent of the value of Mexican exports, although they would taper off to 10 percent, where they would remain until 1929.[35]

Unfortunately, Mexican growers and Porfirian officials seemed oblivious to the fact that they could not control world prices. As Steven Topik has succinctly put it, the market was under the domination of "the dozen European and North American exporters who had access to superior capital and credit, information on foreign markets, and stock abroad, and used these advantages to impose an oligopsony."[36] This became abundantly clear when Brazil embarked on one of the most dramatic initiatives in new coffee cultivation, more than doubling the number of trees in production in the Santos region between 1894 and 1900. Brazil was once again supplying two-thirds of the world's production, and supply was outpacing demand. The problem was that "coffee trees will not stop producing simply because the market situation is unfavorable."[37] As a consequence, prices fell dramatically from 17.2 to 7.9 cents per pound on the New York exchange between the 1893–94 and the 1897–98 seasons.[38]

Preparing Coffee for Export

Beginning in the 1870s Mexican coffee growers began to install machinery on their fincas to prepare export-grade green coffee so that they could sell in the Atlantic market. The process involved simply the removal of the outside skins of the coffee cherry (*café en cereza*), so it is more accurate to refer to it as "coffee preparation," which is closer to the Spanish term *beneficio del café*, rather than "coffee processing." Romero was the first coffee promoter to study extensively coffee preparation in Ceylon, Guatemala, and Chiapas and to urge Mexicans to abandon the traditional dry method for the wet method, saving time, labor, and money, and to produce an export-grade commodity. He was also an early proponent of sorting or cleaning (*escogida* or *desmanche*), the coffee to remove the discolored and fragmented beans, which were referred to as the waste coffee (*mancha*). He also endorsed the classification of the beans into five classes based on size, shape, and color.[39] In the late 1890s Gabriel Gómez, an official in the Development Ministry, described the steps for the preparation of export-grade coffee based on reports written by Córdoba growers to encourage the adoption of the wet method using water-, steam-, and gas-powered machinery. He described in detail the depulping, washing, fermenting, drying, hulling, polishing, winnowing, classifying, and cleaning, which took place in the wet and dry beneficios.[40] Seventy years later, very few technological advances had been introduced to alter the manner in which these processes were carried out.

Coffee preparation began almost as soon as the harvesting had ended each day, because café en cereza starts to ferment ten hours after it is picked. The cherries were transferred to the wet beneficios where they were immediately submerged in water to prevent any spoilage. They first passed through the depulpers (*despulpadoras*), which removed the thick outer skin. The outer skins, which made up the bulk of the cherries, were usually dumped into a nearby brook or river. For this reason wet beneficios were built on the banks of rivers, because they needed large quantities of water to run their depulpers and to dispose of the refuse. The coffee was next transferred through water ducts to fermentation tanks, where it would remain for ten to forty-eight hours, so that the mucilaginous layer under the outside skin could be loosened. It was then moved to another set of tanks where it was stirred to remove the mucilage from the beans. After the beans had been thoroughly washed, they were spread out on drying terraces (*asoleadoras*) or placed in cylindrical dryers with multiple air holes (*secadoras*), which were heated and rotated by a furnace for at least twenty-four hours.[41] The parchment coffee (*café en pergamino*) was now ready for the second stage of coffee preparation in the dry beneficio, for it was still surrounded by two closely fitting layers: the thin parchment layer and the silver skin. Sometimes these two stages were combined together in mixed beneficios, but it was more common for the wet preparation to take place on the finca and the dry preparation to occur in an adjacent building or in urban centers.

In the dry beneficio, the five remaining operations took place: the hulling, polishing, winnowing, classifying, and cleaning. The huller (*descascadora, morteadora, majadora,* or *trilladora*) removed the parchment and silver skins. After the beans were run through polishers (*pulidoras*), large fans winnowed out the remains of the thin skins. The beans were then transferred to separators or classifying machines (*separadores* or *clasificadores*), which were cylindrical containers with many different sized holes that separated the beans according to size and shape into distinct classes. The large single bean, or peaberry (*caracolillo*), was considered the most valued bean, followed by the largest flat bean (*planchuela*). The final stage, cleaning or sorting, removed "the defective or broken grains, as well as whatever foreign object or waste," and was "work generally performed by women and children."[42]

Herrera's and Gómez's descriptions of the imported machinery used in Mexican beneficios relied heavily on information supplied by Córdoba coffee growers. They seemed to have been the pioneers in investing in imported machinery to prepare green coffee for export in the 1880s and 1890s. John Gordon, a British firm, manufactured the best depulpers, while English, U.S., and German companies produced the most popular hullers. More-sophisticated English and U.S classifiers were introduced in the 1880s and 1890s to separate the peaberry from the first- and second-class coffee grades. In one day a man, who earned approximately fifty centavos, could classify four to six quintals with these machines.[43] In their excitement to extol the efficiency of the newest imported machinery, coffee promoters and government officials never discussed the beneficios' labor system.

The Coffee Boom and the First Wave of Foreign Entrepreneurs

Coffee commercialization was directly tied to the technological and economic organization of coffee preparation, which included the control of the dry beneficios and the distribution of credit to growers.[44] Up until the mid-1890s Córdoba's medium-sized growers operated wet and dry beneficios on their estates and sold their coffee directly to agents who worked for foreign import-export companies. When the coffee boom reached its height in the mid-1890s, these trade patterns began to change. Between 1895 and 1913 six merchants of European origin constructed or acquired dry or mixed coffee beneficios in the town of Córdoba and the neighboring village of Amatlán de los Reyes. They quickly emerged as the first group of major traders and exporters of Veracruz coffee. They began as local dry goods merchants, trading groceries and the canton's three major commodities: coffee, sugar, and tobacco. Gradually they expanded their business operations to become regional creditors, preparers, and coffee exporters. Apparently, they were much more willing to take higher risks than local hacendados and rancheros in their extension of credit to small, medium, and large growers. Firmly convinced that they could make higher profits from the preparation and commercialization of coffee, they sold their land and practically ceased growing coffee.[45] This shift in control over coffee commercialization from the growers to urban merchants was a gradual process, which culminated only after the worldwide Depression. We will focus on six of these entrepreneurs, who followed slightly different trajectories in Córdoba's nascent coffee export economy (*caficultura*).

The Spaniard Antonio García Menéndez, who was mentioned earlier in this chapter, first appears in Córdoba's public records when he entered into a business partnership with another merchant in 1882.[46] By the early 1890s, he had created his own business, Menéndez and Company, extending short-term credit to small coffee and tobacco planters.[47] By the time he dissolved his business in 1895, he had accumulated 466,000 pesos in assets and another 83,000 pesos in merchandise and property. In the same year, he entered into a joint-stock partnership (*sociedad en comandita*) with the British entrepreneur Bryan Edward Tomblin and with Theodore Krap, a German agent for the Hamburg Import Company. The new company, which retained the Menéndez name, had the stated purpose of buying and selling commodities on commission for overseas export. The commercial agreement did not specifically mention coffee by name, but Tomblin began immediately constructing a large mixed beneficio several blocks from Córdoba's central plaza on Eleventh Street and Seventh Avenue. Menéndez and Tomblin contributed 40,000 pesos and 60,000 pesos, respectively, for a total of 100,000 pesos in capital to the business, making it one of the largest companies in the canton. Krap contributed no money but agreed to work as financial manager and export agent. In its first year, the firm lent modest sums, between 500 and 1,500 pesos, to small coffee growers guaranteed by mortgages on their trees, land, and buildings.[48] Shortly after the dramatic fall in coffee prices during the 1896–97 season, Krap pulled out of Menéndez's firm to start his own coffee business, while Tomblin remained in the partnership through 1904.[49]

In 1905 Menéndez reorganized his company once again, taking on two local coffee growers as new partners. He contributed 100,000 pesos, while his two associates agreed to run the business for 150-peso monthly salaries. As manager, Menéndez received an annual five thousand–peso salary. Two years later, he opened his own mixed beneficio in the 400 block of Third Avenue, just a few streets down the hill from the main square, Constitution Plaza. The year before, the town council had extended him permission to build his own water main from the town's new water system, so he could convert an old pasta factory into a beneficio. Since the town had just installed electricity, he was also able to install electric rather than gas motors to run his machinery. During the early 1900s most of his loans to local producers were not extremely large, ranging from three thousand to six thousand pesos. In 1910 he acquired another wet beneficio from one of his bankrupt customers in Tepatlaxco for sixteen thousand pesos.[50]

In 1891 Menéndez's major partner, Bryan E. Tomblin, had formed his first business partnership to sell merchandise with Francisco Rebolledo de Cuevas, a prominent hacienda owner and coffee grower. Within months, he purchased from his cash-strapped partner part of his hacienda and proceeded to sell off his portion in small lots to pay off his debt. Throughout most of the 1890s Tomblin loaned money to small- and medium-sized coffee and tobacco producers who were renting or sharecropping outlying parcels of neighboring haciendas.[51] Tomblin also extended credit to farmers outside the municipality in San Andrés Tuxtla, Cosamaloapan, Tuxtepec, and Amatlán.[52] When he entered into partnership with Menéndez and Krap, his cash contribution went toward the construction of the new beneficio. He also purchased a magnificent two-story stucco building on Ninth Street, where he opened his business office and took up residence. These two buildings are still standing today in downtown Córdoba. Menéndez extended to him the right to purchase coffee, tobacco, and rice; and Tomblin, in turn, delegated to his own local agents the same authority. Over the course of the next five years, Tomblin began to concentrate more and more on his coffee business, gradually abandoning his earlier financial ventures in real estate and coffee production.[53]

The business activities of the third member of the Menéndez company, Teodoro Krap, are more difficult to trace because he was an agent for a foreign company. We know that he disassociated himself from Menéndez's firm in 1899 and established his own company to purchase and sell coffee, rice, and tobacco. The year before, he had acquired a dry beneficio in Amatlán to hull rice and coffee, where he paid high prices for premium quality coffee to export to the more discerning European consumer. To raise additional capital, he entered into a partnership with the well-established Spanish hardware store owner and entrepreneur Manuel Abascal.[54] In 1911 Krap collaborated with three other coffee traders: David González Rojas, Leonardo Penagos, and landowner José Antonio Marquez Hoyos. Together, they opened a local café, El Emporio, to promote local coffee consumption. He served as the first president of its board of directors,[55] but unfortunately this enterprise did not flourish once the revolution disrupted the economy.

The remaining three immigrant coffee merchants did not center their activities entirely in the canton. Manuel Sainz Gutiérrez opened a grocery store in Peñuela, a settlement on the outskirts of Córdoba, soon after his arrival from Spain in the 1880s. At first, he extended credit to small coffee tenant farmers or sharecroppers who were cultivating outlying parcels of nearby haciendas.[56] In the late 1890s, he repossessed the pulping and hulling machines of one of his clients. Unlike the other five entrepreneurs, Sainz Gutiérrez tended not to enter into partnerships, and his business activities remained largely confined to Amatlán. In 1902 he found himself in such desperate financial straits that he had to mortgage his machinery to Tomblin to pay off his debts.[57] The fifth merchant, Pedro Díaz, began loaning money in the mid-1890s to medium-sized coffee growers in the region. He invested a good part of his profits in urban real estate, frequently under his wife's name, in Córdoba and the port of Veracruz. In the early 1900s, he acquired a beneficio for hulling both rice and coffee.[58] Finally, Pedro Candaudap Quemard, who appears to have been a naturalized citizen of French origin, began extending loans for coffee cultivation with his brother Juan to rancheros in the 1890s. He also engaged in other financial transactions and served as a financial broker in Huatusco, Zongolica, Veracruz, and Soyaltepec, a tobacco-producing region in Valle Nacional.[59] Like the other members of this new urban commercial bourgeoisie, he was more interested in land speculation and export commodities than landownership. In 1902 he became the sixth entrepreneur of immigrant stock to acquire a coffee beneficio in the Córdoba-Amatlán region.[60]

Córdoba preparers and exporters had no local financial institutions to rely on until after the turn of the century. Menéndez and Sainz Gutierrez opened accounts with the Veracruz branches of the Banco Nacional Mercantil (National Mercantile Bank) and the Banco Agrícola e Hipoteca de México (Mexican Agricultural and Mortgage Banks) respectively, while Tomblin preferred to hold his accounts in Mexico City, managed by the Banco de Londres y Mexico (Bank of London and Mexico). The Banco Central Mexicano (Mexican Central Bank) did not open a branch in Córdoba until the first years of the new century. When the Bancaria Cordobés (Córdoba Bank) opened its doors in 1906 with 100,000 pesos in capital, it became one of the major lending institutions for local coffee entrepreneurs.[61] Undoubtedly, most producers preferred, however, to take out short-term loans with the beneficiadores themselves rather than with the banks because the beneficiadores charged lower interest rates. As one can see, financing coffee cultivation brought these merchant-exporters into all types of interlocking power relationships with small, medium, and large growers just as it did in two important Colombian coffee-producing regions, Medellín and Bogotá, during the same time period.[62]

By 1907 Córdoba was producing 5,610,881 kilos of coffee, which was equivalent to one tenth of national production (see table 1). In sum, four large urban dry beneficios were operating in the town, not including the two in Amatlán. They annually prepared approximately 2.7 million kilos of coffee with a value of 934,000 pesos. These four plants employed 132 men in such jobs as machinists, carpenters, and loaders and 420 women as coffee sorters (see table 2). We will discuss

TABLE 2: Córdoba Coffee Beneficios, 1907

Owner	Year	Amount (kilos)	Value (pesos)	Workers (M) (W)		Wages (centavos) (M) (W)	
Pedro Díaz	—	466,666*	154,000*	2	—	50	—
Bryan Tomblin	1895	690,000	210,000	70	200	100	50
Antonio Menéndez	1901	644,000	210,000	50	180	100	50
Pedro Candaudap	1902	920,000	360,000	10	40	100	50
Totals		2,720,666	934,000	132	420	2	—

Source: AMC, box 310 (1908), file "Estadísticas."

*Díaz's rice and coffee hullers prepared 1.4 million kilos altogether, which was valued at 225,000 pesos. I estimated that 30 percent was coffee, and then I based the value on the kilo/value ratio of the other plants (33 percent).

the nature of this labor force in greater detail in the next chapter. Córdoba had become by this time the nation's leading preparation and export center. Moreover, the canton was producing more coffee than any other in Veracruz, and for that matter in the republic. In many respects, it was the linchpin between Mexico's coffee economy and the Atlantic market. However, this pioneering Córdoba group soon found itself facing stiff competition from U.S. and European coffee import-export firms eager to reap huge profits.

U.S. and European Investment and Economic Crisis

Foreign investment in Veracruz's coffee agroindustry during the first coffee boom was stimulated by a series of external factors, including U.S. monetary policy and the Porfirian state's development policies to attract foreign capital. The United States' return to the gold standard in 1900 precipitated a sharp decline in the value of the peso, which severely hurt the domestic economy while simultaneously stimulating foreign investment. Meanwhile, President Díaz's land and commercial policies facilitated property acquisition and the importation of foreign machinery, prompting foreign entrepreneurs to invest in numerous agroindustries.[63] At the state level, Governor Teodoro Dehesa left no stone unturned to give special tax exemptions to foreign export-import companies and to publicize the investment opportunities existing in Veracruz.[64] He hired the well-known British promoter of Mexican foreign investment John R. Southworth to author a study of the state's natural and human resources. In his bilingual, illustrated book, Southworth extolled, among other things, Veracruz's agricultural potential, trumpeting the virgin lands ready for coffee cultivation: "Millions of acres of land suitable for coffee production are yet in their virgin condition in the State of Veracruz. These lands can be purchased at reasonable figures and present good opportunities for investment to persons of ample capital. In regard to the prices at present ruling in the markets for Mexican coffees, the present system of imperfect cultivation usually returns large profits. With proper cultivation it should be an easy matter to improve upon present prices."[65]

The two largest foreign companies to invest in Central Veracruz's coffee economy at the turn of the century were the Arbuckle Brothers and the Hard and Rand Company, which were both headquartered in New York City. While German and French companies also invested heavily, the size of their operations was far smaller. In the 1860s, John Arbuckle and his brother, Charles, had created the Arbuckle Brothers Company, which soon became the largest U.S. coffee importer, roaster, and packager. By the 1890s, the Arbuckles dominated the Brazilian coffee market,[66] and they soon began to purchase coffee in other Latin American countries. Their firm emerged as the most important coffee financier (*aviador* or *habilitator*), buyer, and preparer in Mexico. They described their operations in their claim to the U.S. and Mexican Special Claims Commission in 1925 in the following terms: "For many years prior to and until about the end of the year 1914, the Arbuckle Brothers' business in Mexico consisted in buying and selling coffees, exporting the same, habilitating, supplying and furnishing coffee growers with money and capital for the fomenting, development and cultivation of their coffee plantations."[67]

According to John Hart, the Arbuckles "worked with the most experienced and powerful Mexican entrepreneurs in the New York financial community."[68] Before the revolution, they extended over $1.5 million in mortgage loans to Veracruz growers. Their shipping agents, the Agencia Comercial y Maritima (Commercial and Maritime Agency), shipped their coffee directly to their roasting plant and merchandising offices on Front Street in New York City.[69] The Arbuckle Brothers' two most active areas of investment were to the north of Córdoba in Misantla and Xalapa-Coatepec, where they held over six hundred accounts. In the Córdoba region, the Arbuckles extended loans to forty growers, including Silvestre and Miguel Aguilar, before 1916. They also supplied credit to at least three of the first group of coffee entrepreneurs—Sainz Gutierrez, Pedro Candaudap, and Antonio García Menéndez.[70] The Arbuckles became directly involved in coffee preparation in Coatepec around 1908, when they purchased a beneficio and installed imported machinery. In the following year, they purchased land and built a large wet beneficio next to Córdoba's railroad station. A dry beneficio was added soon afterward.[71] Before the Revolution of 1910 erupted, they had opened offices in Veracruz, Coatepec, Xalapa, Teocelo, Cosautlán, Xico, and Córdoba. Production peaked during the 1912–13 season, when they purchased 1,123,644 kilos of coffee from their growers.[72]

The second U.S. corporation, the Hard and Rand Company, entered the Mexican coffee market in 1897, when their agent, Louis Hewlett, arrived in Veracruz. He opened its main office in Córdoba, where it acquired a preparation plant on Fifth Avenue. A branch office was subsequently established in the port of Veracruz. Most of its coffee was shipped to New Orleans because of its cheaper steamer rates. We know that Hewlett bought coffee in Orizaba, Córdoba, Coatepec, and Xalapa. In 1913 Hard and Rand moved its national headquarters to Mexico City. Other U.S. companies and investors invested in southern and central Veracruz, where poorer quality coffee was cultivated at lower altitudes, alongside sugarcane and rubber extraction.[73] All these companies collaborated closely with members of the local elite. Prominent Porfirian landowning families began entering into financial agreements with foreign companies to cultivate coffee as well as sugarcane and tobacco. By the turn of the century, this form of collaboration had increased dramatically as new companies entered the canton.[74]

All was not well in the international coffee market by this time. In 1906, coffee growers and merchants heard the shocking news that Brazil was harvesting a bumper crop of coffee. To maintain prices, the Brazilian state had to intervene. It raised 15 million British pounds to keep excess coffee off the market by selling bonds on the international market, which actually relinquished more control of the market to the "great international coffee trust." As one Mexican observer wrote, the trust "was gradually taking control of the coffee trade away from national producers and exporters."[75] The collapse of coffee prices was compounded by the 1906 world economic crisis, whose real impact did not hit Mexico until two years later. While Mexico's coffee production reached an all-time high of 50,115 metric tons (1 metric ton = 2,240 pounds) in 1907, coffee exports declined dramatically.[76] How did this set of events affect Córdoba's coffee economy?

The level of financial activity in Córdoba remained relatively stable during 1906 and 1907, although a large number of property sales took place, which included the sale and the division of a number of haciendas. This suggests that landowners were feeling the effects of the coffee crisis as well as the internal economic crisis.[77] Large coffee producers were not alone in being affected by these crises. Menéndez, who was heavily in debt to the Arbuckle Brothers, was rapidly heading toward bankruptcy. Beginning in 1908 his luck began to fail, but he remained undeterred and continued borrowing large sums of money from the company. In 1912 he failed to meet a payment to the Arbuckles' New York bank, and he was forced to put another lien on his machinery, buildings, and his 300,000 coffee trees in Cuetzalan, Puebla. In 1914 he was forced into bankruptcy with debts of over 163,000 pesos, and his creditors seized his plant and his machinery.[78] Sainz Gutierrez also began to run into hard times as early as 1902. By 1905 his debts to Tomblin had ballooned to 37,500 pesos. To cover his losses, he was forced to mortgage the coffee machinery that he had purchased in 1897 and to divest himself of numerous coffee parcels in Amatlán. By 1909 his business seemed to have turned around, as coffee prices began to climb again.[79]

In short, by 1913 the first group of coffee commercial entrepreneurs was rapidly disappearing from the scene. Two of the six had experienced severe financial difficulties. Díaz, Candaudap, and Tomblin had died.[80] Sainz Gutierrez and Krap remained in the coffee-export business but only as minor players. The era of the precursors had come to an end due to the vagaries of the coffee cycles, financial instability, and their own mortality. None of their children displayed much interest in carrying on their family businesses. However, these pioneering entrepreneurs had built the first urban beneficios and set up the financial networks for the emergence of a new urban commercial bourgeoisie.

Córdoba's Coffee Culture

The first coffee boom transformed Latin American regional coffee economies into vibrant enclaves of export capitalism, and they generated profits that dramatically reshaped their culture. It spurred economic development and urban modernization, while at the same time it increased the divide between town and countryside as well as between rich and poor.[81] Although the coffee culture did not impact Mexico's economy, politics, and society to the same degree as it did in Brazil, Colombia, and Central America, it heavily influenced certain regional economies and cultures.[82] The coffee boom particularly affected the coffee-growing regions of Veracruz, Chiapas, Michoacán, and Oaxaca during the second half of the Porfiriato. It has been estimated that eight thousand laborers were working in national coffee production and preparation at this time.[83] Although we have no accurate information on the profits of these coffee entrepreneurs, there is broad evidence to suggest that the urban commercial entrepreneurs invested heavily in infrastructure, public works, and cultural facilities. Furthermore, the state and municipal revenues generated from taxation funded the construction of roads, schools, and municipal buildings.

The canton of Córdoba region entered into a period of sustained prosperity beginning in the early 1890s primarily due to its lucrative coffee production and trade. Its revenues nearly doubled between 1894 and 1896 from 134,000 pesos to 210,000 pesos due to steep taxes collected on coffee- and tobacco-producing properties and on trade.[84] Its booming agricultural economy attracted thousands of migrant workers from the sierra states seeking employment, who were drawn by the high daily rural wage that was expected to top seventy centavos in 1894.[85] The number of inhabitants in the town of Córdoba also increased; it jumped from 4,122 to 10,295 between 1872 and 1910, which represented a 250 percent increase. This was not surprising given Córdoba's proximity to two major railroad lines, which provided sierra migrants with the means to escape their impoverished villages in the interior. Córdoba was not alone in experiencing this level of demographic growth. The other four Central Veracruz coffee-producing regions also experienced sizable population increases.[86]

The immigrant entrepreneurs were only gradually accepted into Córdoba's upper class, which was made up of a traditional landowning and professional creole elite that had controlled regional politics and culture since colonial times. The continued presence of the Cevallos, Gómez Vargas, and Márquezhoyos families was still clearly visible to the stroller who walked by their lavish mansions under the main plaza's colonnades. They continually celebrated their shared Spanish and French heritage and traditions to set themselves apart from the rest of Córdoba society. "They were a very cohesive group, unified around what they called the [birthplace,] 'patria chica,'" with a real reluctance to allow newcomers into their circle.[87] Lineage still played a prominent role in marital relations among these families. You needed to be white and have a good family name to marry into this provincial elite. Louis Panabiere described Cordoba's upper-class society at the turn of the century in these terms: "The neighborhood around the plaza was the high lineage neighborhood, where the notables would meet. . . . Two or three generations resided in the same mansion. Although the children married, they continued to reside around the patriarch of a closed family circle."[88] Newcomers inserted themselves with difficulty into this closed group. "Few Spaniards, except those of the first generation, . . . could live up to these prescriptions and criteria of *status*, although other foreigners somehow managed to do so."[89] A few foreigners could enter into the creole elite through marriage. For example, the wealthy U.S. entrepreneur Tomas Braniff Jr. married Elena Amor de Escandón, whose family owned the large Monte Blanco hacienda.

Although immigrant exporters had not yet been accepted into the creole elite's social circles, they began to loan money to its members and to participate in the expansion of the city's infrastructure, which in one way or another benefited their own business interests. The introduction of water and sewage systems, electricity, telephones, paved streets, and the construction of municipal buildings were all directly or indirectly financed by local coffee growers and merchant-exporters. These projects radically transformed the town's center and were visible symbols of Porfirian progress and modernization at work.

Potable water had been on the minds of Cordobans ever since the postindependence era, when they drew up plans to build a water main from the Metlac River to the town. Early efforts to raise the funds failed, so a number of hacendados had already acquired their own private water concessions from the federal government.[90] In 1904 the cantonal prefect (*jefe politico*) took the initiative to bring together the town's wealthiest merchants, including Tomblin, Menéndez, Leonardo Penagos, and José Tresgallos, to discuss a potable water proposal. Although Governor Dehesa denied their request to levy an additional tax on coffee and tobacco to cover the costs, he agreed to float bonds through the Banco Mercantil (Mercantile Bank) for the water project. The potable water and sewage systems were completed between 1905 and 1907. Coffee beneficiadores were among the first to benefit from the town's new water system. They could draw large quantities of water to operate their depulpers and their fermentation tanks, and they could empty their waste into the sewage system.[91]

The introduction of electricity and telephone service were two other critical technological advancements that helped to modernize the coffee agroindustry. Once again, the precursory group played a key financial role in their completion. In 1895 Pedro Díaz formed the Empresa Córdoba de Luz Eléctrica y Energía Motriz (Córdoba Electric Light Company) with an initial 300,000-peso investment. He forthwith entered into a service agreement with the municipal council to convert all the streetlights to electricity. By 1906 Tomblin, Krap, and Severo Sánchez Escobio, a recent Asturian immigrant, had introduced electricity into their urban beneficios, along with the owners of the San Francisco y Toxpan and the San Miguelito sugar mills.[92] A telephone system was also desperately needed by coffee growers and brokers to remain in constant contact with their consigners and buyers in Veracruz and abroad. By 1898 nine local landowners and merchants had installed their own private lines, connecting their homes and businesses with the urban transit system, town hall, and major coffee-producing haciendas. They included Díaz, Tomblin, Candaudap, and the Penagos and Fernández Company. Both Tomblin and Candaudap had installed direct lines from their offices to nearby coffee-producing haciendas.[93] This extensive private telephone network suggests that coffee merchants had access to one of the most sophisticated telecommunication networks in Central Veracruz.

Menéndez seemed particularly keen on displaying his newfound wealth and winning the acceptance of respectable townspeople (*gente decente*). He constructed an elegant mansion with the latest electrical fixtures, which was considered one of the most elegant houses in the entire state. In addition, he became a founding member of two of Córdoba's most distinguished social clubs, the Casino Español and the Casino Cordobés. In 1910 his prominence as a successful businessman and community leader helped him to win the presidency of the Casino Español. For the centennial celebration of Mexico's independence, he represented the Spanish community in welcoming the Spanish delegation to the city.[94]

Coffee revenues contributed to the construction of a new town hall.[95] In 1905 the colonial administrative buildings with their wooden roofs were torn down and replaced with a neoclassical Florentine building topped with zinc and sheet metal cupolas. La Parroquia, the main church, underwent extensive renovations, which included the construction of an elegant wall around the courtyard. Among the contributors to this project were all the well-known members of the regional economic elite, including prominent landowners and two coffee merchants, Tomblin and Candaudap.[96] Another display of their benevolence was Pedro Díaz's decision to construct a magnificent one thousand–seat neoclassical theater, which bore his name. It became the major venue of elite culture after its completion in 1895.[97] To this day it remains the principal site of civic, educational, and cultural events in downtown Córdoba.

Overreliance on an export economy model came, however, with a heavy price. It brought many economic and social contradictions associated with the modernization process, including the increased marginalization of major segments of society. The concentration of wealth in the hands of local elites and foreign entrepreneurs began to take its toll. Certain Córdoba coffee and tobacco merchants began to actively collaborate with Porfirian officials and foreign investors in the seamy side of coffee and tobacco speculation in Valle Nacional. They contracted workers into slavish conditions in the tobacco and coffee plantations of the Tuxtepec region. The streets of Córdoba soon became filled with young men arriving by rail from the interior with high hopes of finding salaried work, only to be bundled off to Valle Nacional as contract laborers.[98] Moreover, the precipitous drop in coffee prices in 1897 seems to have contributed to serious fiscal problems for the canton and its municipalities. The cantonal seat was forced to take out loans from the Banco de Londres and the state in the early 1900s to cover its expanding public expenditures for its new prison and hospitals. The mayor blamed the shortage of funds, in part, on ballooning social costs, due to the alarming influx of what he termed "sick people" with the opening up of the Veracruz and Isthmian Railroad. A surge in prostitution likewise stretched the scarce resources of the new women's hospital to the limit.[99]

In sum, coffee had dramatically transformed Córdoba's urban landscape in the 1890s and 1900s. Coffee was now outpacing sugarcane and tobacco production and emerging as its most lucrative agricultural commodity. Córdoba had now truly earned its title as the City of Coffee Groves (*la ciudad de los cafetos*). In contrast to the Xalapa-Coatepec, Huatusco, Chiapas, and Central American coffee economies, Córdoba's agroindustry experienced an early transference of preparation and commercialization from the countryside to the city. As the plantation system broke down and was replaced by medium-sized multicrop haciendas, ranchos, and subsistence farms (minifundios), a separation took place between coffee production and commercialization. This evolution more closely resembled early stages of Medellín's agroindustry. As Marco Palacios has emphasized, "the marketing of coffee became separated from its production as the hacienda gave way to other new units of production."[100] What is more, Córdoba's emerging commercial entrepreneurs followed preparation strategies that closely resembled those of the native Medellín commercial bourgeoisie, who began building urban beneficios in 1902.[101] The rise of the urban merchant had begun even a decade earlier in Cundinamarca, Costa Rica, and Venezuela.[102] Yet there are some significant differences between the Antioquia and Córdoba cases. The native Antioquia merchants invested their urban profits at first in large coffee haciendas, and then they diversified into textiles and entered into politics.[103] This did not occur in Córdoba primarily because the immigrant merchants had more limited profits and smaller financial networks, so they concentrated their efforts on their regional family businesses and infrastructural projects.

Coffee, Rural Rebellion, and Revolutionary Politics

The outbreak of social revolution in 1910 did not cause as much disruption to Mexico's coffee agroindustry as might have been expected. The production level remained relatively stable from 1910 to 1917, averaging 43,700 metric tons annually, until it suddenly dipped in 1918. Approximately one half of the national coffee production was exported during these years. Coffee exports fluctuated much more widely from 10,542 to 24,385 tons during the same period, if the year 1914 is excluded, when the U.S. marines occupied the port of Veracruz.[104] A number of regional factors contributed to the relative prosperity of the coffee regions. Veracruz, Chiapas, and Oaxaca were not theaters of major military conflict. Moreover, as Jean Meyer has suggested, export enclaves remained relatively untouched or accelerated their growth during the revolution because local strongmen frequently collaborated with foreign corporations.[105] What is also clear is that local producers, merchants, preparers, and foreign export-import companies collaborated closely, no matter what their nationality, to export their coffee to the Atlantic community.

In Veracruz, military conflict was primarily limited to small-scale skirmishes between rival armed bands. No sustained grassroots popular movement rocked the Córdoba region, which might have brought the agroindustry to a standstill. Although Porfirian state and municipal officials were initially replaced with the overthrow of Porfirio Díaz, the political and economic elite gradually regained control of the political apparatus. Local supporters of Francisco I. Madero and Venustiano Carranza, leaders of moderate political reform, seemed more intent on consolidating their power, disarming ranchero-led rebels, and political pacification than embracing sweeping social and economic reforms.[106] Geopolitical factors also played a pivotal role in the rapid reconstitution of military and political authority under the stewardship of General Cándido Aguilar in Central Veracruz. For the most part, his political, military, and economic strategies favored the coffee merchants and exporters of his hometown, except during the turbulent year of 1915.

While Madero's Revolution of 1910 brought the resignation of Governor Dehesa and the replacement of cantonal prefects and municipal authorities in Veracruz, former Porfirians and conservative Maderistas soon reestablished political order and marginalized more radical military leaders in Central Veracruz. In Córdoba, the gente decente welcomed General Victoriano Huerta's overthrow of democratically elected president Madero in February 1913, because he offered greater political and economic stability. This turn of events forced Cándido Aguilar, the native son of Córdoba who had launched the initial Maderista uprising, to flee northward to join Carranza's Constitutionalist forces. He did not return until June 1914 at the head of the Division del Oriente (Division of the East), when he marched south from the Huasteca to liberate Central Veracruz from the Huertistas.[107] In September 1915 as provisional governor Aguilar moved the state capital from Veracruz to Córdoba, where it would remain until May 1920, except for a brief period when it was located in Orizaba. The town was militarily and economically strategically situated. Its two railroads permitted the transport of sugar, coffee, and tobacco out of the Papaloapan Valley, Oaxaca, and even Chiapas to the port or capital; and they facilitated the movement of troops from Central Mexico to the South as well as to the Northwest via Salina Cruz. As governor Aguilar became the town's favorite son, he gradually built a strong political following there. To consolidate his power base, he placed family members and former Porfirian officials in key military and political positions. His uncle, Miguel Aguilar, became the region's military commander and later served a number of times as provisional governor during his long absences from the state. In short, Aguilar made sure that the governorship was always in the hands of his loyalists.[108]

Although Aguilar spent a good part of his four years as governor (1917–20) out of the state serving as President Carranza's secretary of foreign relations, he remained closely engaged in Veracruz politics. Undoubtedly, his marriage to the president's daughter in September 1917 was one important reason why the Carranza wanted to keep him close by his side as a loyal confidant. However, at the same time, he developed into a homegrown version of Carranza's military proconsuls.[109] He shared common goals with other Carrancista commanders, who were early progressive social reformers. He upheld the principles of nationalism, anticlericalism, worker rights, and agrarianism that Governors Salvador Alvarado, Francisco Múgica, Heriberto Jara, Pablo González, Francisco Múgica, and Jesús Agustín Castro followed.[110] As we shall see in chapter 3, he promulgated labor legislation in 1914 and 1918 to improve working conditions and wages. Meanwhile, he worked to stabilize socioeconomic conditions and restore political order that benefited the entire coffee agroindustry.

Coffee production and export in Veracruz was not seriously affected by the revolution until the end of 1915 when the Carrancistas gained control of the state. In fact Mexico exported more coffee in 1913 than any other year between 1870 and 1928, with 60 percent destined for the United States. The Arbuckles, who had loaned over 1.5 million dollars to Veracruz coffee growers in the final decade of the Porfiriato, viewed it in a slightly different light; "it was common knowledge that the coffee growing industry . . . was in a flourishing condition on or about the end of the [growing] year 1913–4, and that had it not been for the revolution and the acts of armed forces, . . . Veracruz coffee planters . . . would have been able within a few years to repay with their crops what the Arbuckle Brothers had invested."[111] However, the conditions deteriorated during the 1914–15 season, "and in the crop year 1915–6 no further coffees were delivered to them by the coffee growers." They blamed the Constitutionalist, Convention, and Zapatista armies for this precipitous decline in coffee production. Between August 1914 and the middle of 1915, the Arbuckles claimed that Aguilar's troops had even forced the company's clients to suspend coffee cultivation in the Misantla region because the forces were stealing all their stores.[112]

The revolution did actually open up new spaces for coffee entrepreneurs to buy land, invest in coffee preparation machinery, and expand their coffee trade in Central Veracruz. They were aided and abetted by both sides; Huertistas and Carrancistas alike made overtures to producers and merchants to stimulate coffee production and coffee exports. For revolutionary armies who were short on cash, exports yielded much-needed customs revenue for the purchase of arms and ammunition. For instance, when the state's Cámara Agrícola appealed to the Huertista governor to lift the onerous export tariff in 1913, he consented in order to spur exports.[113] Two years later the Carrancistas went out of their way to show their political support for the coffee exporters of the Xalapa-Coatepec region. When Governor Aguilar celebrated in Xalapa Alvaro Obregón's victory over Francisco Villa at Celaya in March 1915, he invited prominent members of the coffee elite to the festivities. As one Mexican scholar has phrased it, "the economic crisis . . . favored one faction of the bourgeoisie, in this case, the coffee sector, for General [Aguilar] opened the doors to the free trade of the aromatic bean."[114] The Spanish immigrant Justo Fernández González, who had married into the well-known Felix López landowning family in 1910, even began to speculate on the coffee market, extending credit in inflated paper currency and requiring repayment in gold or U.S. dollars. He then bought up properties of his bankrupt clients.[115] He was essentially imitating the financial strategies of Porfirian commercial coffee brokers. In Chiapas, Carranza made similar overtures to the German coffee producers, preparers, and exporters to keep production stable and sustain coffee exports while imposing a twenty-five centavo tax on every one hundred kilos produced.[116]

Revolutionary strife did temporarily disrupt coffee production and exports in the Córdoba region beginning in 1914. During the first four years of the revolution, production remained relatively high. In 1910 the municipality of Córdoba produced 2.8 million tons, which was very close to its record level of 1889. Although production declined in the following year, it remained remarkably stable until 1914. Córdoba merchants continued to ship most of their coffees to the United States and Canada without much difficulty during these years. The prefect even reported increased exports to the latter country in that year. Unfortunately, no figures exist for the following years. Rodríguez found no major structural changes in land tenure occurring during the revolutionary years. No haciendas changed hands, and only one large rancho was sold. Landowners seem to have maintained their solvency simply by temporarily abandoning their crops and moving into town. Only a few anti-Spanish acts of retribution occurred in Córdoba, in contrast to the Federal District, Puebla, Morelos, and the North.[117] The Arbuckles had to cut back their operations during the hostilities, for it issued only a handful of contracts in Córdoba. Unlike Xico and Xalapa-Coatepec, where the land market was relatively active, Córdoba experienced a greater circulation of urban properties.[118] More than likely, the presence of many civil servants and military personnel in the state capital explains why well-connected landowners preferred to invest in the urban real estate market and postpone the planting of new coffee trees.

The outbreak of World War I on the other hand did have major repercussions on both sides of the Atlantic for the coffee agroindustry. The German ports could no longer handle freight ships due to the British blockade, so demand for coffee dropped by late 1914. Export shipments were not seriously affected until 1917, when German U-boats began attacking merchant ships on the high seas. New York coffee prices, which had peaked during the 1912–13 season at 16.0 cents a pound, began to steadily drop after this, bottoming out at 9.6 cents in 1915–16. In the face of overproduction, low demand, and slumping prices, the Brazilian government was forced to step in for a second time to protect its growers and exporters in 1918. By the following season, prices had rebounded. Mexican export prices fluctuated just as widely as New York prices between 1915 and 1919.[119]

The disruption of exports to Europe and the United States' entrance into the war benefited Mexico's coffee agroindustry more than other Latin American countries. Beginning in 1917 the U.S. Army began to place large orders for coffee, which could be shipped relatively safely by sea or by land because of Mexico's proximity to the world's largest market. The Arbuckle Brothers and Hard and Rand profited from this situation, for they already had established trade routes to two U.S. ports. Coffee exporters' earnings increased as well. Regional factors likewise favored Córdoba over other coffee regions in Veracruz, Chiapas, and Oaxaca.

While Córdoba served as state capital, coffee beneficiadores enjoyed a modicum of security, and their businesses flourished. Coffee preparation plants operated almost continuously in the town's center throughout the revolution, while most rural ones had to suspend operations when the peasants occupied the haciendas or rebels destroyed their machinery. Only the haciendas of La Defensa, Santa Margarita, Santo Tomás, and Peñuela continued to operate their beneficios in the countryside. At some point after 1914 the Arbuckles' plant near the station temporarily suspended its operations. In February 1915 the urban beneficiadores petitioned the municipal government for a permit to operate their beneficios all night rather than suspend operations at the designated ten o'clock shutdown time, despite the complaints of the townspeople. Severo Sánchez, who had installed a wet beneficio on the banks of the San Antonio River in 1905, could claim that the urban beneficios had "saved" the agroindustry during a period of instability in the countryside.[120] The coffee exporters had less control over random rebel attacks on the Mexican Railway. At one point, Hard and Rand filed a complaint against the Zapatistas, who had burned 5,200 kilos of coffee while en route to Veracruz in 1917.[121] On the whole, coffee preparation and transport to Veracruz were not severely interrupted during the revolutionary years, although there were occasional attacks by local rebel groups.

One nagging problem confronting coffee exporters, however, was the continual depreciation of the peso following the massive printing of paper money by the Huerta, Carranza, and Villa governments. By December 1913 inflation was so severe that the peso had lost 32 percent of its value.[122] Needless to say, a weak peso made coffee exports cheaper for the U.S. consumer. Coffee exporters could resolve this problem for themselves by carrying out all their transactions in gold or U.S. dollars. Even this method of circumventing the use of paper money was not entirely satisfactory for handling large transactions. A better strategy was to open bank accounts overseas. Sánchez established an account at the National City Bank in New York with the assistance of his buyer, José Zardain Monteserín, who directly deposited payments for his parchment coffee there.[123]

The Arbuckle Brothers and Hard and Rand continued to extend credit in Córdoba, Huatusco, and Xalapa producers throughout the revolutionary years, albeit at a lower level. Casimiro Muñoz, a Coatepec coffee producer, served as the Arbuckles' office manager and plant supervisor in Córdoba from 1913 until 1922, as well as their principal buyer in Huatusco. Hewlett headed its Xalapa office.[124] The two U.S. corporations capitalized on their ability to use the favorable exchange rate to their advantage in purchasing coffee at low prices. The Arbuckles remained Veracruz's major coffee exporter in 1918, with almost all its shipments going to New York. The second largest exporter, Hard and Rand, was now shipping more of its coffee to New York than to New Orleans. Córdoba's Olavarrieta Brothers were the third largest shipper, and they sold to the Westfield Brothers in New Orleans as well as to mining companies in northern Mexico. Two smaller Córdoba beneficiadores, Manuel E. Marenco and Davíd González Rosas, were shipping to A. E. Hegewisch in New Orleans.[125]

Certain coffee entrepreneurs became victims of their risky borrowing strategies, which they had entered into with the Arbuckles during the Porfiriato. Menéndez, whom we encountered earlier, was the biggest loser. Somehow he recovered from bankruptcy in the early years of the revolution. But he still owed the Arbuckles $25,000 in 1916, and his properties were heavily mortgaged.[126] The wealthy ranchero and merchant Nestor Cuesta, who had been one of the most active lenders to small and medium coffee producers on the eve of the revolution, also entered into bankruptcy when he could not repay his outstanding loans to the Arbuckles. He had borrowed large sums of money through their agent, the wealthy ranchero Arcadio Guerra, and mortgaged his properties in Tepatlaxco, San Juan de la Punta, and Huatusco before the revolution. After some of Cuesta's properties were occupied by revolutionary forces, he was unable to deliver his coffee shipments or fulfill his contract obligations. The Arbuckles therefore forced him to foreclose on some of his properties.[127]

The disappearance of some Córdoba commercial entrepreneurs from the urban landscape coincided with the appearance of new ones.

The Olavarrieta brothers, who had been engaged in the coffee trade since the Porfiriato, acquired a beneficio in the center of town. Meanwhile, the Mexican González Rosas, who had opened his coffee trading business in 1913, accumulated sufficient capital to purchase the old Menéndez beneficio on Third Avenue in 1919. Manuel Olmos was hulling both coffee and rice at his rice mill (Molino Arrocero), while he also operated the Marure huller on the Buena Vista hacienda. In 1913 another newcomer, the Spaniard Pedro J. Silva, bought the rice mill El Fénix, which could also hull coffee.[128]

Córdoba's coffee entrepreneurs were in a very favorable position to assist German coffee merchants, who found themselves in difficult circumstances after the United States declared war on Germany. Under the U.S. Trading with the Enemy Act of 1917, Germans as well as non-German merchants who were trading with the enemy were blacklisted. The U.S. consul in Veracruz, Francis Stewart, was instructed to send lists of German merchants in his district to Washington. The State Department also ordered the consul to oversee all coffee shipments scheduled to sail from Veracruz. Export firms wishing to ship their produce to the United States were required to petition in advance for the consulate's approval. Guillermo Boesch, the well-known merchant and exporter in Orizaba and Coatepec, was a prime target. The U.S. consul's informants related how Boesch and the Vivanco family were collaborating to ship coffee out of the country. He was even selling some of his coffee through intermediaries in Córdoba. Fernando Balmori and the Zardain Brothers were reselling his coffee to Hard and Rand. One informant wrote, "The Zardain Bros. (Spaniards) claim to be Pro-Allied, but this transaction shows that they are only acting as a cloak for the Germans." Informants also recommended that Krap be put on the War Trade Board's blacklist. Stewart and the British vice-consul labeled the Dutchman Leon Zeevaert, the Austrian Max Schaefer, the Zardains, and González Rosas all as German collaborators.[129] Even the Arbuckle Brothers came under suspicion because their agent, George Bergman, was of German origin. The State Department labeled "the entire Arbuckle crowd very pro-German," for they were "flirting with firms on the enemy trading list through Bergman." To discourage any further collaboration between the Arbuckles and the Germans, the State Department ordered the firm to fire three lower-level employees stationed in Veracruz, reassign Hewlett back to the New York office, and require Bergman to apply for a new passport before he reentered Mexico in the fall of 1918.[130] Profits were just too irresistible for foreign export-import firms and regional exporters not to try to test the United States' ability to enforce its extraterritoriality.

Córdoba's municipal council was not willing to let the coffee entrepreneurs be the sole beneficiaries of this spike in coffee revenues. It proceeded to raise taxes in 1917 on businesses using the public water supply. Monthly bills more than doubled for some beneficiadores, for they needed large amounts of water to operate their wet beneficios. To further aggravate them, the municipality decided to charge its water rates in silver pesos because President Carranza's new stabilization polices gave the states the right to collect taxes in gold or its equivalent after June 1916. Some plant owners were so irate over this change in tax policy that they complained vociferously to the city council.[131]

In the spring of 1918 Stewart wrote a wide-ranging report on what he considered were the gloomy economic conditions in the entire Veracruz Consular District since the outbreak of the world war. His pessimistic assessment glosses over a much more complex economic and commercial scenario due to his rather shortsighted objective, the return to prewar production and export levels. He had little statistical information at his disposal, so he garnered information from U.S. company informants and detailed shipping records. He observed, "The effect of the European War has been but gradually felt. Even in the shipping industry the internal conditions in Mexico have been a factor of greater immediate importance than the War." The U.S. occupation of the port of Veracruz in 1914 and the Mexican decision to temporarily cut its railroad service had measurably decreased shipping even further for a time. But when German, British, and French ships ceased to arrive, he noted, U.S., Spanish, and Cuban ships had picked up the slack. By admitting that the European war had not seriously hurt the export of agricultural goods, he was implying that the United States was still buying large quantities of coffee. He was particularly pessimistic about coffee production. Many plantations had been abandoned, with their owners seeking refuge in the larger towns: "Coffee trees are being choked by overgrowths of brush, . . . all because of the internal disturbances." In his mind, "the export trade has not been influenced so much by the demand as by the supply, and the supply has constantly been diminished due to revolutionary disturbances in this state." Furthermore, he argued, railroad transportation was as risky as muleback transport because of the frequency of rebel attacks. The Veracruz banking infrastructure was also in shambles owing to the closing of the regional banks of issue in 1914. The only bright spot in the coffee economy, he noted, was that all large properties had remained intact and had not been affected by agrarian reform since 1914.[132] Although he saw a rupture in coffee production brought on by revolutionary disturbances, coffee exports had actually remained remarkably resilient, primarily due to the port of Veracruz's ideal geopolitical location, the low level of military activity, and the pragmatic strategies of the second group of immigrant entrepreneurs.

The rebound in coffee prices in 1918 with the end of European hostilities facilitated the emergence of a new coffee elite in Córdoba. The Spanish immigrant Manuel Zardain Monteserín decided to move his business operations from his hacienda to downtown Córdoba in 1918. He had originally emigrated from Pola de Allande, Asturias, in 1904 at the age of nineteen. His two younger brothers, José and Ventura, soon followed him. They had first traded tobacco and coffee in partnership with fellow Asturian Severo Sánchez, for it was the custom to trade in multiple commodities. When the Zardains made their first windfall profits in tobacco, they purchased part of La Defensa hacienda, which had its own coffee beneficio, around 1906 in Paso del Macho. In 1910 Manuel and José created the firm the Zardain Brothers. They installed their offices on the corner of First Street and Second Avenue and purchased imported hulling equipment. The Zardain Monteseríns and the Sánchez Escobios were two of the five new Spanish families intimately associated with the burgeoning of Córdoba's coffee-export economy after 1918. We will meet the other three later in this chapter. The other coffee merchant to take advantage of rising coffee prices at the end of the First World War was González Rosas, who set out to refurbish Menéndez's old plant. Following the Zardain brothers' lead, he petitioned the municipality's Sanitation Board for permission to install threshing machinery in Menéndez's old plant on Third Avenue.[133] These entrepreneurs would play crucial roles in Córdoba's trajectory as the nation's linchpin for coffee commercialization, preparation, and export.

The Coffee Boom of the 1920s

The twenties were the second golden age of coffee in Latin America. Strengthening demand after the world war brought soaring prices and widespread euphoria. Coffee prices doubled on the New York Coffee and Sugar Exchange during the 1919–20 season, skyrocketing to 24.8 cents per pound, only to sink back to 10.4 cents per pound during the 1920–22 seasons. They reached another high of 24.5 cents during the 1925–26 year. Mexican export prices followed these same cyclical patterns.[134] With the return of stable political and economic conditions, Mexicans planted more trees. Unfortunately, just as national production peaked at 53,021 metric tons in 1928, prices began plummeting in New York and Europe due to Brazil's overproduction.[135] How did Veracruz *cafetaleros* (the term often applied to both coffee growers and exporters) respond to these cyclical swings? Who benefited most?

During the early 1920s the Veracruz U.S. consular district, which included most of Chiapas as well as parts of Oaxaca, sent home reports that did not forecast a very rosy future for Mexico's coffee agroindustry. The continuing insecurity in the countryside was still of grave concern. U.S. corporations were still investing considerably

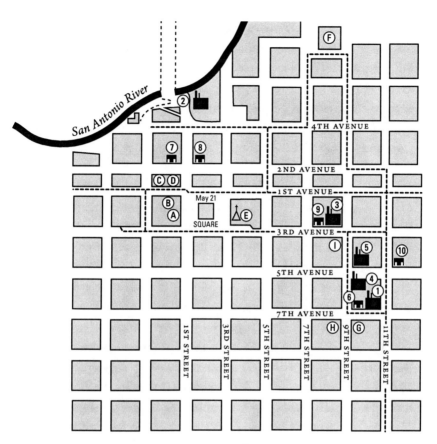

Municipal Landmarks

A. Municipal Palace
B. Pedro Díaz Theater
C. Preparatory School
D. District Public School
E. Church of the Immaculate Conception
F. Market
G. San Sebastián Church
H. Madero Park
I. Bank of Córdoba (Marenco)

----- TROLLEY LINE

Coffee Beneficios

1. Ezequiel González-La Garza
2. Severo Sánchez-San Antonio
3. David González
4. Hard & Rand-El Cañon
5. Sainz Pardo

Exporter Businesses

6. Ezequiel González
7. Severo Sánchez
8. Zardain Brothers
9. David González
10. Arbuckle Brothers

Map 2. Coffee beneficios of Córdoba, Veracruz, 1930. Adapted from Herrera Moreno, "Plan de la Ciudad de Córdoba, 1892," in *El cantón de Córdoba*.

more money in sugarcane than in coffee. Crop estimates for coffee throughout the entire consular district ranged from 20 million to 25 million pounds, which was half the prerevolutionary level.[136] However, by the mid-1920s, growers were rushing to expand new acreage and plant more trees to take advantage of soaring prices. By 1929 Frank Meehan, the manager of Hard and Rand, estimated that the Córdoba-Orizaba-Huatusco region alone could harvest 330,000 quintals that season.[137]

Consular reports provide relatively little information on the operations of the two U.S. corporations during the 1920s. Hard and Rand seems to have become much more active than the Arbuckles in the Córdoba region by this time. Its beneficio, which was the second largest plant in the state, handled approximately one quarter of the entire Veracruz crop. Although Meehan conservatively valued the company's property, equipment, and household and office furniture at only $25,000 in 1927, he reported that his company had "a large amount of money invested annually in crops through advances to Indian farmers." They were also advancing credit to hacienda owners in return for payment in kind after the harvest. Hard and Rand contracted the Ward Steamship Line to handle its weekly shipments to New York, while the Cuyamel Fruit Company and the Standard Fruit and Steamship Company shipped Hard and Rand's coffee to New Orleans.[138] Consular reports had such scanty information on the Arbuckles that one has to presume that they were now handling their affairs through their Mexico City headquarters. In January 1920 they did ask for permission to build a large warehouse near the Córdoba station to store coffee, most probably next to their enormous beneficio. Meanwhile, they continued to advance loans that averaged two thousand pesos to small producers. Its main Veracruz office remained in Xalapa, although it continued to operate agencies in Huatusco, Orizaba, and Oaxaca.[139]

The U.S. companies soon began to encounter considerably more difficulty operating under postrevolutionary regimes than they had under the Porfiriato. After the military revolt of 1923, both Bergman and Meehan complained to the U.S. embassy concerning Governor Adalberto Tejeda's (1920–24) insistence that they pay their state and municipal taxes over again after they had been forced to pay under the rebel occupation.[140] When Governor Heriberto Jara (1924–27) decided to levy a new export tax on coffee exports in January 1925 to finance road construction in the face of declining petroleum revenues, Meehan expressed his frustration once more with these fiscal impediments: this "confounded tax which is still pending has everyone up in the air." Meanwhile, the Arbuckles had filed a claim with the Mixed Claims Commission to recover $1.5 million of prerevolutionary investments plus 6 percent interest.[141] Finally, the two companies became the target of organized labor. As chapter 3 explains, the Confederación Regional Obrera Mexicana (CROM, Mexican Regional Worker Confederation) began organizing their women workers and succeeded in pressuring the companies to sign collective contracts in the mid-1920s. The militancy of postrevolutionary labor organizations was just one more factor explaining these companies' decision to move their operations out of Mexico. The waning U.S. presence in Central Veracruz's coffee economy coincided with growing involvement of Spanish immigrant entrepreneurs, who dramatically transformed Central Veracruz, particularly in the Córdoba region.

The coffee agroindustry became increasingly concentrated in the hands of five Spanish families' firms, who emerged as the second group of the commercial bourgeoisie. Although the municipality of Córdoba boasted fourteen coffee plants in 1921, Spaniards owned the largest ones, with the exception of the two U.S. plants.[142] The number gradually declined as the wealthier entrepreneurs bought the older plants and consolidated their operations. By the middle of the decade, only eleven plants remained in the downtown (see table 3). Four of the five families had acquired or built their own beneficios by the mid-1920s. The eldest member of this group, Severo Sánchez, continued to operate a wet beneficio within the city limits, while his business office was on First Street, across the street from the Zardains. The Zardain Brothers, led by Manuel, were fast emerging as Córdoba's

TABLE 3: Córdoba Coffee Beneficios in the mid-1920s

Firm	Nationality	Type	Location
Arbuckle Bros.	United States	dry beneficio	11th Ave. and 27th St. (railroad station)
Nestor Cuesta Lix	Mexican	rice/coffee beneficio	238 Independencia
David González Rosas	Mexican	dry beneficio	149 3rd Ave. and 9th St.
Ezequiel González López	Spanish	mixed beneficio	La Garza 7th Ave. and 11th St.
Hard and Rand	United States	dry beneficio	El Cañon 5th Ave. and 9th St.
Manuel Olmos y Cia.	Mexican	rice/coffee beneficio	Molino Arrocero 2nd Ave. and 15th St.
Manuel Sainz Pardo	Spanish	dry beneficio	156 5th Ave. and 9th St.
Severo Sánchez	Spanish	wet beneficio	San Antonio
Pedro J. Silva	Spanish	rice/coffee beneficio	El Fénix
Justo Sobrón	Spanish	dry beneficio	1st Ave. and 8th St.
Zardain Bros.	Spanish	dry beneficio	4th Ave. and 1st St.

Sources: *Blue Book of Mexico*, 100, 104–5; and AMC, box 395 (1929), file "Sanidad."

major coffee preparers and exporters. Three remaining Spanish businesses—those of Manuel Sainz Pardo and his two brothers, Ezequiel González López and Ricardo Regules Baranda—were founded in the 1920s and 1930s. Although other Spanish coffee entrepreneurs traded, prepared, and exported coffee, these five families would soon surpass all the others in terms of the amount of credit extended to growers, trade, preparation, and exports. Their economic successes not only influenced the regional export economy, but also that of the state and the nation as well.

Manuel Sainz Pardo had arrived in 1901 at the age of twenty-four to work for his uncle Manuel Sainz Gutierrez, who operated a dry goods store in Peñuela. He came from a cattle-ranching family in Villar de Soba, Santander. Since his uncle was heavily involved in coffee production, preparation, and commercialization, Manuel immediately began to learn the coffee trade. During the early days of revolution Sainz Pardo struck out on his own, opening his own dry goods store in a neighboring village. To keep his business within the family, he convinced his two much younger brothers to emigrate and work for him. Ceferino arrived when he was ten in 1905, while Tirso followed later when Ceferino was seventeen years of age.[143] After the Olavarrieta Brothers entered into bankruptcy in 1923, Manuel bought their beneficio. Ezequiel González López, the fourth member of this group, arrived at sixteen from Santander in 1912 and bought Tomblin's La Garza in 1928.[144] The last member of this new commercial elite, Ricardo Regules Baranda, did not arrive until 1916. He came from a family of impoverished shepherds living in the tiny hamlet of Espinosa de Los Monteros, Burgos. When he arrived in Córdoba, the Spanish owner of Leones grocery store immediately hired him on as a clerk.[145] He would eventually buy this store and become involved in the coffee trade, but he did not acquire a beneficio until the 1930s.

The eleven coffee beneficios became permanent fixtures of the city's commercial landscape, so it was not surprising that municipal authorities disregarded citizen complaints about the noise and pollution generated by these plants. They were creating major environmental and health hazards for the local population, although no one seriously considered at the time their impact on their workers. Townspeople demanded that González Rosas not be given a permit to install larger machinery because vibrations, dust, and noise emanated from these buildings around the clock during the harvest season. One letter of complaint called his plant "a grave danger and nuisance. In the first place, the dust that the machines emit when they are functioning fills our houses, which is dangerous to the health of our families . . . ; in the second place, the constant noise of the movement of the machinery is very annoying."[146] González Rosas responded by saying he was just simply moving equipment, which he had used since 1919, to the adjoining house. His hullers, polishers, and separators all had vents that collected dust and shunted it into an adjoining room that was hermetically sealed and cleaned each day. Despite the warnings of the health inspector that this kind of machinery should not be located in residential districts, the town council did not take any action against González Rosas. Its rationale for this decision reveals its probusiness orientation. Since the 13 men and 120 women workers who worked all day in the workshop had experienced no harmful effects, the council argued, it saw no need to alter the city's regulations regarding urban beneficios.[147]

Two of the five coffee beneficiadores, Sainz Pardo and González López, established their businesses and residences in the 1920s on Fifth and Seventh Avenues, several blocks down the hill from the main square. The Zardains and Regules would open beneficios in the same neighborhood in the early 1930s. Thus, a Spanish business and residential community began to take shape. It was a very convenient venue, to say the least, for these ambitious beneficiadores. The Hard and Rand beneficio was already located there. What is more, the urban trolley passed right in front of most of their plants (see map 2). It also abutted the creole elite's preferred commercial and residential address, which stretched from Seventh to Ninth Streets on Third Avenue.[148] A good address was considered important for an up-and-coming immigrant merchant. They attended the same parish church, San Sebastián; sent their children to the same schools; and interacted socially at the Casino Español. All these factors contributed to the cohesiveness of this northern Spanish community. This residential pattern would continue through the 1930s, at which time the Zardains and the Sainz Pardo brothers bought residences in the capital.

This community was built on a shared transatlantic culture. They originated from the same northern Spanish provinces. The first member of each family to arrive was a young man with no immediate family. Much like the Xalapa group, the name Anne Beaumond gives to the five Xalapa-Coatepec coffee beneficiadores, they came from relatively humble social origins.[149] In addition, they constructed family businesses that were based on gender and age hierarchies, family- and community-based financial networks, male chain migration, and a binational Hispanic culture. As José Moya has argued, this transatlantic culture "included permanent and temporary settlement, return, back-and-forth traveling between sending and receiving societies, and relocation from one destination to another outside the place of origin."[150] These Spanish immigrants displayed the same type of dualistic transatlantic immigrant identity, or double identity, that Armando Paredes Cruz found among the Barcelonnettes, the French immigrants who spurred Mexico's industrial and financial development. They constructed a transatlantic collective memory, which drew on a biculturalism as well as collective success.[151]

The second coffee boom, like the first one of the 1880s and 1890s, spurred the Mexican state to undertake a massive study on the coffee agroindustry. The Mexican Secretaría de la Economía Nacional (SEN, Ministry of National Economy) published a study, *El café: Aspectos económicos de su producción y distribución en México y en el extranjero*, that was in many respects quite critical of the agroindustry's lack of efficiency. It serves as an invaluable source of statistical information and provides a comparative perspective on the nation's agroindustry at the end of the 1920s. It demonstrates the continuing dominance of Central Veracruz, although it foreshadows Chiapas's imminent emergence as the nation's premier coffee zone.

The republic had a total of 311 beneficios in 1929, of which 193 were wet plants while the remaining 133 were either mixed or dry (see table 4).[152] More than one half of the plants, specifically 182, were located in Veracruz, while Chiapas followed with 93. Veracruz plants prepared 53.55 percent of Mexico's export-grade coffee, and Chiapas was still far behind. The report compared the amount of coffee production prepared by the traditional dry method and the modern wet method. Only 72 percent of the republic's total coffee production of 39,124,657 kilos was prepared in wet beneficios. The study attributed the low level of wet preparation to the small growers' inability to pay for preparation.[153] While Chiapas reported that it wet processed 99 percent of its coffee, which was quite unrealistic to say the least, Veracruz re-

TABLE 4: Mexican Coffee Production and Preparation for Export, 1929

State	Plants	Coffee production (kilos)	Prepared coffee (kilos)	% Prepared	% of national production
Chiapas	93	11,740,392	11,623,774	99	41.02
Oaxaca	26	3,095,209	991,156	32	3.50
Puebla	4	——	228,713	—	—
Veracruz	182	18,144,674	15,176,207	83	53.55
Other States*	6	——	319,186	—	1.10
Mexico	311	39,124,657	28,339,036	72	100.00

Source: Adapted from Secretaría de la Economía Nacional, *El café*, 133–38.

*Colima, Michoacán, Nayarit, and San Luis Potosí.

ported that it did so for 83 percent of its coffee. Part of this disparity between the two states can be explained by the fact that more than half of Veracruz producers were small, and they could not afford to purchase machinery to wash their coffee. There were other regional differences between Veracruz and Chiapas. Although Veracruz had more beneficios and prepared more coffee than any other state, its plants were older and less efficient. Chiapas had fewer, but more efficient, dry beneficios.[154] It also had higher levels of investment, lower fuel costs, and lower labor costs.[155] At this time, coffee was Veracruz's fourth most valuable commodity with a value of 10,700,631 pesos, behind textiles, sugar and sugarcane alcohol, and petroleum.[156]

According to this study, the coffee agroindustry employed only 2,836 men and women workers nationwide. However, the next chapter will show that Veracruz alone employed this many women workers. Central Veracruz had higher wages than Chiapas or Oaxaca, which was a reflection of the abundance of cheap labor in the latter two states. If we look at the profile of the 220 Veracruz beneficios owners, the majority were Mexicans—26 were Spaniards, 7 were U.S. citizens, 10 were Italians, 9 were Germans, and 4 were either French or British.[157] However, foreigners owned all the largest and most

TABLE 5: Mexican Coffee Beneficios in Selected States, 1929

State	Plants	Workers	Daily wage (pesos)	Machinery investment (pesos)	Coffee production (kilos)	Coffee preparation (kilos)
Chiapas	**93**	**1,326**	**1.22**	**1,187,187**	**72,443,375**	**11,623,774**
Cacahotaan	22	222	1.45	—	12,070,185	1,366,107
Huixtla	5	201	1.30	—	13,286,000	1,522,382
Tapachula	9	457	1.48	—	28,951,800	5,614,148
Union Juárez	26	637	1.12	—	5,332,650	953,432
Oaxaca	**26**	**187**	**1.00**	**133,736**	**10,478,238**	**991,156**
Veracruz	**182**	**1,065**	**1.51**	**1,087,774**	**171,885,505**	**15,176,207**
Córdoba	22	494	1.98	—	42,124,650	6,855,675
Coatepec	22	102	1.63	—	29,444,550	1,546,607
Huatusco	12	98	1.18	—	7,028,075	851,810
Xalapa	3	9	2.08	—	6,369,250	1,520,756
Mexico	**311**	**2,836**		**2,507,676**	**261,671,968**	**28,339,036**

Source: Adapted from Secretaría de la Economía Nacional, *El café*, 127–29, 131–32, 143–44.

modern plants. While Córdoba's coffee was exported to the same destination as the Xalapa group—that is, New York, New Orleans, Hamburg, Le Havre, Santander, and Bremen—its domestic market was centered in northern Mexico rather than the Federal District.[158]

The SEN report included valuable information on the number of plants and level of production at the municipal level. The municipality of Córdoba listed twenty-two wet, dry, and mixed plants. It prepared coffee not only from local growers but also from the surrounding regions of Orizaba, Huatusco, and Zongolica. Its plants prepared 45 percent of the state's coffee production, or 6,855,675 kilos, while Coatepec's twenty-two plants, combined with those located in Teocelo, Cosautlán, Xico, and Xalapa, prepared only 3,704,488 tons, or 24.4 percent of the state's production. While Córdoba's plants were more efficient than those in Coatepec, the Orizaba plants, owned by Guillermo Boesch and Juan Echenique, were rated the most efficient in the state.[159] Córdoba also prepared more coffee than Tapachula, the Chiapas center of coffee preparation.

Preparation costs were overall higher in Córdoba than in Chiapas. Córdoba had the second highest daily wage in the state, averaging 1.98 pesos (see table 5). Tapachula's wage was 1.48, which was the highest for Chiapas but considerably lower than in Veracruz.[160] The cost of preparing one quintal of café verde in Córdoba was broken down into six steps: depulping, fermentation, washing, drying, hulling, and sorting, taking into account labor costs, amortization, and indirect costs.[161]

Depulping:	0.25
Fermentation:	0.05
Washing:	0.15
Drying:	0.80
Hulling and Polishing:	0.80
Classification and Sorting:	0.90
	2.55 pesos

It is worth noting that the final stage, the manual classification and sorting of the beans performed by women and children, was the most costly part of the entire operation.

By the end of the 1920s Veracruz was still growing more coffee than any other state in the republic.[162] Its commercialization, preparation, and export of coffee were concentrated in two major centers: Córdoba and Xalapa-Coatepec. Although the latter region produced higher quality coffee because it was mostly grown between 1,200 and 1,500 meters, its transport costs were higher. It was more difficult to ship coffee out of the Coatepec region, where mule transport was cheaper than rail. Córdoba exporters had a definite cost advantage because of the town's location on the railroad line. On the other hand, their machinery was aging, and they were having difficulty keeping up with the Soconusco region in Chiapas, where land and labor were considerably cheaper and the plants were more modern.

Producers and Exporters Confronting Hard Times

The structural imbalance between a rapidly growing supply of coffee and stagnant demand finally resulted in a major crisis in the Atlantic coffee market. During the last week of October 1929, the Rio de Janeiro and Santos coffee exchanges closed because Brazil's state agency could no longer afford to pay growers to keep their coffee off the market. The impact of this decision was devastating. The price of coffee plunged from 22.1 cents to 13.2 cents per pound by the 1930–31 season.[163] A second crisis rooted in the collapse of the U.S. financial system occurred simultaneously, resulting in lower demand for coffee and decreased overseas investment. Were the entrepreneurs or the growers affected more by these two crises?

Mexico suffered considerably less from the Depression than most other Latin American coffee-producing countries. Its more diversified agricultural system made it less susceptible to severe fluctuations in commodity prices and to the world depression. Lorenzo Meyer maintains that, although "the world crisis constitutes a very important element that cannot be left out of any analysis of Mexico in the

1930s, its specific influence must be calculated with much care; the fact that the majority of the population sustained itself through traditional agriculture meant Mexico was less affected than other countries of the region."[164] Moreover, Mexico was much less dependent on coffee exports than Central America, Colombia, or Brazil because its petroleum, silver, mineral, and grain exports were much more important. In his study on the impact of the 1929–32 crisis in Colombia and Costa Rica, Mario Samper Kutschbach likewise downplays the negative short-term effects of the coffee crisis of 1929 on non-Brazilian coffee economies, for they had a variety of ways to compensate for these lost revenues. These two countries maintained or increased their production to counteract the severe and prolonged drop in coffee prices.[165] The Mexican coffee agroindustry followed the same course. In 1929, coffee production was approximately 52,500 metric tons, but it dropped to 41,000 tons in 1932. It rebounded to a new high in 1936, as the trees planted four or five years earlier reached maturity. Exports also dropped from 29,800 metric tons in 1929 to 20,048 in 1932, only to rebound again to 42,800 tons in 1936. Unfortunately, export prices remained depressed, and their value never reached 1928 levels again.[166]

Commercial entrepreneurs weathered the low coffee prices better than the growers in part because of the devaluation of the peso. The peso had stood at 2.12 to the U.S. dollar in 1930, but its depreciation accelerated in the following years, reaching 3.53 to the dollar in 1933. The devaluation privileged exporters and large growers, who bought their coffee from small producers in pesos and sold their green coffee to their consigners in dollars.[167]

Córdoba's continued dominance of the Mexican coffee-export sector during the depression years is best revealed in Veracruz's customs records for coffee shipments (*salidas de café*) leaving the two major coffee regions, Córdoba and Xalapa-Coatepec, for the 1932–33 season. Needless to say, this year is not an ideal year to examine because of the effects of the world overproduction and the world depression, but it is the only year that records are complete (see table 6). According to shipment records, Córdoba exporters shipped 10,039,157 kilos of green

TABLE 6: Coffee Shipments from Córdoba and Xalapa-Coatepec, Veracruz, 1932–33

Exporter	Coffee (kgs.)
Córdoba	
Zardain Bros.	4,532,118
Mario Fernández	2,073,046
Sainz Pardo Bros.	1,974,999
Davíd González	995,109
Agrícola Francesa	133,011
Arbuckle Bros.	80,730
Ricardo Regules	13,602
Ezequiel González	8,314
Others	227,328
Subtotal	**10,039,157**
Xalapa-Coatepec	
Severino Cortizo	2,289,285
José J. Grayeb	1,547,925
Rosaura L. Vda. de Fernández	624,036
Samuel Teplow	488,727
Miguel Alfonseca	427,340
Fertilizadora y Exportadora	314,354
Juan E. Martínez	237,277
Alejandro C. Sloss	170,959
Arbuckle Bros.	6,681
Others	57,293
Subtotal	**6,163,877**
Total	**16,203,034**

Source: AGEV/ACG, 1926–33, boxes 1–3, file 31.4, "Salidas de café."
This data does not include 57,436 kilos of parchment coffee shipped by Guillermo Boesch from Córdoba and 34,846 of parchment coffee shipped by Arbuckle Brothers and José J. Grayeb from Xalapa-Coatepec.

coffee between October 1, 1932, and September 31, 1933. This amount is considerably higher than the amount shipped by Xalapa-Coatepec exporters—6,163,877 kilos—during the same season. If the data is broken down based on its final destination, we learn that Córdoba exporters shipped 8,171,594 kilos or 81.4 percent of their coffee by rail to the port of Veracruz for export overseas. The second most important destination was northern Mexico, which received 1,533,713 kilos. Most consigners were located in towns or seaports close to the border, such as Manzanillo, Mazatlán, Mexicali, El Paso, Ciudad Obregón, and Nuevo Laredo, where they could ship to the United States. Much smaller amounts headed for the mining and industrial centers of Torreón, Monterrey, and Chihuahua City. Less than 350,000 kilos remained in Central Veracruz or was shipped to the Federal District. The Xalapa-Coatepec exporters shipped 99 percent of their coffee to the port of Veracruz, destined primarily for New Orleans and New York.[168] What percentage of Mexico's total coffee exports did Veracruz exporters prepare and ship? If we average INEGI export statistics for the years 1932 and 1933, we estimate that approximately 30,700 metric tons, or 30.7 million kilos, were shipped out of the country during the 1932–33 season.[169] Thus, Córdoba exporters were shipping approximately 32.6 percent and Xalapa-Coatepec exporters, 20.2 percent of Mexican exports for this year, or the equivalent of half of all Mexican coffees.

Table 7 reveals two changes unfolding by the early 1930s in the Veracruz coffee export economy. The presence of foreign corporations has dramatically diminished. It appears that U.S. corporations were withdrawing from Veracruz, finding it no longer an ideal environment for their business operations because of high labor costs, antiforeign and prolabor governors, and a militant labor movement. Hard and Rand closed its plant in 1933, and the Arbuckle Brothers were shipping out very small quantities of coffee, which primarily came from its Oaxaca finca, Maria Luisa. Even the size of the French Agricultural Company's (Companía Agrícola Francesa) shipments pale in comparison with those of the Spanish entrepreneurs. This same pattern is found among Xalapa-Coatepec exporters, where the Arbuck-

TABLE 7: Coffee Shipments of Córdoba Exporters, 1932–33

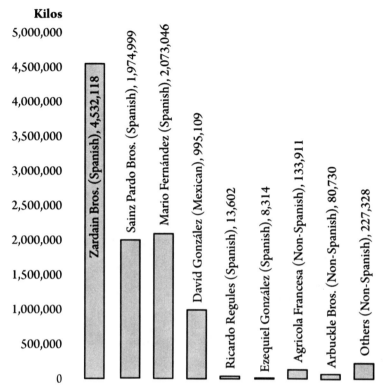

Source: AGEV/ACG, 1926–33, boxes 1–3, file 31.4, "Salidas de café."
This data does not include 57,436 kilos of parchment coffee shipped by Guillermo Boesch from Córdoba and 34,846 kilos of parchment coffee shipped by the Arbuckle Brothers and José J. Grayeb from Xalapa-Coatepec.

les are no longer the principal exporters. The collapse of coffee prices therefore seems to have had a much larger impact on foreign export-import corporations than on local export firms. Second, almost all Córdoba exporters are now Spanish immigrants. The Zardain Brothers, who shipped a total of 4.5 million kilos, are by far the largest exporters. Mario Fernández, the Sainz Pardo Brothers, and Davíd González Rosas (the only Mexican exporter) shipped smaller quantities. The two other important Spanish immigrants, Ricardo Regules and Ezequiel González, are far behind.

TABLE 8: Major Coffee Consigners of Córdoba Exporters, 1932–33

Kilos

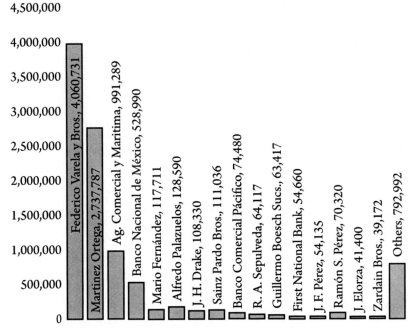

Source: AGEV/ACG, 1926–33, boxes 1–3, file 31.4, "Salidas de café."
This data does not include 57,436 kilos of parchment coffee shipped by Guillermo Boesch from Córdoba and 34,846 kilos of parchment coffee shipped by the Arbuckle Brothers and José J. Grayeb from Xalapa-Coatepec.

Another way to understand the extent of the Córdoba's dominance over the state's coffee trade, and to a lesser extent the national coffee trade, is to examine the origin of the coffee that they were preparing and exporting. Almost all of the coffee shipped out of Córdoba came from the southern part of Central Veracruz, which included the former cantons of Córdoba, Huatusco, and Orizaba in descending order. At the end of the harvest, much smaller shipments arrived from Esperanza (Puebla), San Geronimo (Oaxaca), Tabasco, and even Misantla.[170]

The interlocking relationships between exporters and their consigners in the port of Veracruz and in the North appears to have been quite close, for they sold their coffee through a handful of firms (see table 8). Exporters were dependent on these financial intermediaries to transport the coffee to Atlantic markets. The two major consigners for the Cordobeses in the port of Veracruz were the Federico Varela Brothers and Martínez Ortega. The Agencia Comercial y Maritima and the Banco Nacional de México (Mexican National Bank) handled smaller amounts, with the latter shipping mostly through the North. The Arbuckles also worked through the Agencia Comercial. Some exporters, including the Zardain Brothers, the Sainz Pardo Brothers, Mario Fernández, and the inheritors of the Guillermo Boesch estate, acted at times as consigners themselves.

Coffee financing and trade became increasingly concentrated in the hands of a few commercial brokers, or intermediaries, in the years after the depression. As a consequence, economic tensions between exporters and growers continued to rise in Central Veracruz, just as they did in Colombia and Costa Rica.[171] However, producer resistance was much more muted in Veracruz than in these other two countries. In the Córdoba region, the small- and medium-sized growers never attempted to organize against the urban agribusinesses. On the other hand, in Coatepec the relationship between exporters and producers was more conflictive. Large coffee producers were more likely to be also the preparers and exporters, and they systematically blocked every attempt at the formation of a farmer organization. However, these repressive tactics backfired, for the Banco Nacional de México stepped in to provide financial assistance for the creation of a producer cooperative and the purchase of a preparation plant in 1932.[172] Perceptions of the increasingly oligopolist strategies practiced by coffee exporters began to seep into contemporary discourse. State officials started using the term *acaparador*, or monopolist, to refer to an exporter. One federal agent, assisting in the formation of the Coatepec farmer cooperative, even referred to the large exporters as a "social plague."[173]

One of the ways that coffee beneficiadores weathered low prices and relatively stagnant exports during the 1930s was by keeping labor costs low. This will be discussed later. However, it is quite clear that despite the implementation of the Labor Code in 1931 and the creation of a state agency to enforce the minimum wage, entrepreneurs made few efforts to raise the piece-rate wage above the minimum wage during the depression years. Moreover, coffee firms fought hard to challenge efforts by their seasonal workers to gain worker benefits.

Undoubtedly one of the most aggressive strategies to weather economic uncertainty and to expand operations into other regions was to merge companies. The consolidation of the Zardain and the Sainz Pardo family businesses in October 1934, which created the Beneficiadora (Companía Beneficiadora y Exportadora del Café SA), is a case in point. The principal objective of the two patriarchs—Manuel Zardain and Manuel Sainz Pardo, who oversaw the merger—was to expand their operations to Mexico City so as to capture a larger share of the national market. In addition, the eldest brothers had decided to leave Córdoba and return to Spain with their Spanish wives. The restructuring of their family businesses secured their control over a major portion of the company's stock and the right to remain silent partners. In this way, the two secured for themselves a steady income for life.

The consolidation process actually began a year earlier, when Manuel Sainz brought his younger brothers, Ceferino and Tirso, into the family business to purchase, prepare, and export coffee. According to the company's statutes, Manuel contributed 70 percent, or seventy thousand pesos, of the capital and was to receive 40 percent of the profits, while Ceferino and Tirso furnished 20 percent and 10 percent of the capital, respectively, and were to receive 35 percent and 25 percent of the profits. In short, the age hierarchy among the siblings served as the framework for the financial structure of the family business, just as for the Zardains. None of their wives ever participated as stockholders in their firms. For the time being, Manuel was to serve as business manager, operating his old plant on Fifth Avenue until the reincorporation was completed. He then moved his family over to the corner of Seventh Avenue and Eleventh Street, where the two families had bought a large lot to build a new beneficio, offices, and residences (see map 2).[174]

In anticipation of this merger, Manuel and José Zardain also restructured their family firm, dissolving their old company and reincorporating it with the inclusion of their younger brother, Ventura. At the time of its dissolution in October 1933, it was valued at 568,935 pesos. Their inventory included two wet beneficios, one in Atoyac and the other on the Hacienda Zapoapita, with a combined value of thirty thousand pesos. They also declared forty thousand pesos' worth of urban properties as well as ninety thousand pesos in merchandise. They still owned the largest movie house in Córdoba, Teatro Zardain, which they had built a few years earlier; a large apartment house; numerous urban properties; and their residence at Seventh Avenue and Eleventh Street.[175] Over the course of less than three decades, these first-generation immigrants had become Córdoba's wealthiest coffee entrepreneurs. They would retain this position for at least the next ten years.

The statutes of Beneficiadora set out sweeping objectives for the firm: to purchase, prepare, and export coffee produced in all parts of the republic and to engage in other commercial activities for eight years. The six brothers brought into the joint-stock company two minority partners, Mario Fernández and Pío Pérez, who resided in the Federal District. With 500,000 pesos, they issued 500 shares valued at 1,000 pesos apiece. The Zardain family controlled 225 shares, while the Sainz Pardos held 163 shares. José Zardain and Ceferino Sainz Pardo became president and vice president, respectively, of the new company. The two other brothers, Ventura and Tirso, became members of the executive board (*vocales*), while the two oldest brothers became silent partners. To expand operations to the national scale, they established two separate branches. The Sainz Pardos would operate the Córdoba branch, while the Zardains would operate the new branch from their Ixcatepec plant in the Federal District. José and Ceferino served as the managers of their respective branches.[176]

Beneficiadora's operations now dwarfed all the other Córdoba companies. Just one month after its formation, the firm contracted their fellow compatriot Ezequiel González as an agent to buy coffee berries, parchment, or ordinary coffee for the 1934–35 season. Fernández seems to have withdrawn entirely from the Córdoba region in order to establish his own offices in Coatepec, where he collaborated with Justo Felix Fernández until 1943. In the 1930s the Sainz Pardo Brothers expanded their operations into Huatusco, appointing Manuel's brother-in-law Pedro Pardo Zorrilla to run the plant.[177] At the end of 1939 the Zardains decided to close their business operations altogether in the Córdoba region. They sold all their shares to the Sainz Pardos and relinquished control of their two theaters.[178] José then moved to Mexico City to focus his attention on his own new company that prepared and exported coffee from Puebla, Oaxaca, and Chiapas. He also opened a coffee-roasting company.

The pioneer of the second group of the Cordobeses, Severo Sánchez, suffered a serious financial crisis in the early 1930s. He had been much less diversified in his holdings, because he had followed more conservative business strategies since his family had suffered economic misfortunes in the past. His concentration on only one stage of the preparation process put him in a disadvantageous position between the growers and his compatriots who owned dry beneficios. Therefore, he was forced to sell off a number of his properties.[179]

The last of the five Spanish merchants to enter the agroindustry was Ricardo Regules Baranda. Five years after arriving in Mexico, Ricardo entered into a partnership to operate a dry goods store in 1921, which included trading coffees and tobaccos. He rented his first beneficio in Amatlán in 1932.[180] Two years later he entered into a partnership with Mario Fernández, who owned a coffee-export firm on Seventh Avenue across from Madero Park. In 1936 Regules acquired El Cañon, the old Hard and Rand beneficio.[181] Despite all the economic uncertainties of the 1930s, Regules's business seems to have prospered, for he entered into another business venture with 100,000 pesos in November 1936 with Manuel Albo, who operated in Soconusco. The following fall, he was already exploring new ways to expand his operations. He decided to rent the old Sainz Pardo plant, which had stood vacant for three years. Rather than handling merely three carloads of coffee each week, he could now handle six in his two plants, and he increased his workforce to 10 men workers and 200 women sorters. By the late 1930s he had expanded his operations into the Huatusco region, renting a coffee plant from José Sanfilippo Parlatto, who had previously worked for Davíd González Rosas before he went bankrupt.[182]

Up to this point very little has been said about the role of the postrevolutionary state in protecting coffee producers or exporters. It did not intervene directly in the coffee sector, neither subsidizing prices nor stemming the expropriations of the medium-sized coffee landholdings. Despite the producers' continual complaints about their dire economic circumstances throughout the 1930s,[183] a strong state response was not forthcoming. On the other hand, neither growers nor beneficiadores seemed to have had a particularly close relationship with state or federal authorities. In their minds, the state continued to see the agroindustry as a lucrative revenue source to fund education, roads, and infrastructural projects. The major exception to this minimalist policy was the efforts of Governor Tejeda on behalf of the small-scale growers during the depression.

Tejeda came to the assistance of coffee producers by attacking the out-of-state coffee brokers. In his last annual report before leaving office in December 1932, he pointed to the major problem facing the coffee agroindustry: the stranglehold exercised by national and international coffee "monopolists" over Veracruz producers. They were reaping huge profits at the expense of local growers. Before leaving office, he initiated the first steps in the creation of a state-funded producer cooperative, for he believed that such an organization would be able to sell coffee directly to European and North American firms and bypass the coffee brokers. For him, it was a question of social justice to protect the small coffee producers from speculators and monopolists who had absconded with most of the coffee profits.[184] Unfortunately, the governors who succeeded him, Gonzalo Vázquez Vela

(1932–36) and Miguel Alemán Valdés (1936–40), took little real interest in the coffee agroindustry.

Coffee growers and merchants did agree on at least one issue: the exorbitant federal, state, and municipal taxes levied on them since the Porfiriato. These fees continued to be levied throughout the post-revolutionary era to raise much-needed revenue for public services. At the end of 1930 the federal government temporarily lifted the 2.70-peso export tax on 100 kilos of green coffee for three months in the midst of a slump in coffee prices. It temporally suspended the tax once again in December 1931 when the price of coffee fell below the threshold of 90 centavos per kilo. In February 1932 when the exemption on the tax was lifted, U.S. and Spanish exporters in Córdoba wrote to President Abelardo Rodríguez asking him to extend the exemption because the price of coffee still remained below 90 centavos.[185] In 1936 the Treasury Ministry issued another temporary exemption when prices slumped again. When the economy turned sour after the expropriation of the oil companies in 1938, the federal government imposed a new 12 percent ad valorem export tax to raise additional revenues to purchase grains, machinery, and equipment for farming and the newly expropriated oil industry. This was a new blow to coffee exporters, who pleaded for an exemption once again from what they considered a very arbitrary tax. The 1938 export tax so infuriated the Cordobeses that they even persuaded their workers to go out on strike unless the export taxes were reduced and to call on their fellow workers throughout the country to join them. Coffee planters were so enraged with the excessive production tax they decided to challenge the state in court.[186]

Throughout the 1930s the state saw little reason to adjust its taxes on coffee production or exports, for coffee remained its most valuable agricultural export commodity. In the face of the collapse of coffee prices between 1929–32, however, it made some concessions to protect the agroindustry. It juggled conflicting interests by resorting to ingenious fiscal measures to cause the least amount of pain for growers and exporters.[187] Ramón Fernández y Fernández claimed that Veracruz had the highest level of taxation on coffee in the republic; there were municipal, state, and federal taxes on growers and traders as well as port loading fees, which the agronomist said could add up to twenty pesos (U.S.$3.35) per quintal.[188]

The state did even less to prop up the struggling agroindustry in the late 1930s when the problem of overproduction raised its ugly head again. Brazil still continued to have two-thirds of the world's oversupply, even after it destroyed a good portion of its 1937 and 1938 crops.[189] Coffee prices remained significantly below 1929 prices on the domestic and external markets. Although Mexico was exporting more coffee in 1938 than in 1929, its value was considerably lower. Thus, the entire market remained depressed.[190] In the wake of Brazil's decision to abandon its policy of holding its surplus coffee off the market in 1937, the federal government hastily organized a national convention of coffee producers in Mexico City on April 19–24, 1937, to search for new ways to provide financing. Little concrete action came out of this meeting. President Lázaro Cárdenas even called for an international conference to formulate measures to regulate production and commerce, but this never materialized.[191]

At the end of the 1930s, Fernández y Fernández, who worked for the Banco Nacional de Crédito Agrícola (BNCA, National Bank of Agricultural Credit), painted a rather sober assessment of the Veracruz coffee agroindustry. He laid most of the blame on the commercial brokers. Exporters strenuously denied his allegations and argued that they too were suffering hard times. It was true, he argued, that Veracruz's large preparers had not purchased any equipment in the 1930s with the sole exception of the Sainz Pardos in Córdoba. Too many small, inefficient wet and dry beneficios still remained in operation, so Chiapas was now able to prepare twice as much café verde as Veracruz. Fernández singled out other obstacles, such as the link between the commercial entrepreneurs and politicians. However, he was most concerned with the conflictive relationship between growers and beneficiadores that had grown worse over the past decade. "There exists an intermediarism that can best be qualified as excessive, for the intermediaries obtain the major portion of the profits."[192] Dry beneficio owners entered into price-fixing arrangements among themselves in regions like Huatusco, where the Zardains exercised almost a complete monopoly.[193] Fernández's solution to the ills of the coffee agroindustry was prescient of what would actually occur a decade later. The state should intervene as an intermediary between the grower and the preparer to keep prices high.[194]

This chapter has examined four interlocking themes related to the transformation of the Córdoba coffee agroindustry between 1890 and 1940. It argues that a series of concomitant regional factors contributed to the emergence of this town as Mexico's foremost center of coffee commercialization, preparation, and export. Its location at the southern end of Central Veracruz's coffee producing region meant that it had immediate access to large amounts of coffee. Moreover, its strategic location at the intersection of two railroads linking it with other coffee growing regions in Puebla, Oaxaca, and Chiapas as well as to the port of Veracruz spurred its development as the linchpin between interior producers and the exporters. Moreover, the town already boasted a well-established and flourishing small Spanish merchant community that embraced the two groups of transatlantic migrants. Place matters in explaining why Córdoba—not Orizaba, Huatusco, Xalapa-Coatepec, or Tapachula—became the nation's primary coffee agro-export center.

Second, the interlocking relationship between regional coffee growers, urban commercial entrepreneurs, and foreign import-export companies changed dramatically over the course of this fifty-year period. In effect, the coffee agroindustry passed through three stages. During the first stage, medium-sized landowners, who produced coffee for the domestic market, initiated investment in imported machinery to prepare export-grade coffee. At the end of the nineteenth century, U.S. and European export-import corporations became the largest traders and preparers. Finally, coffee preparation, financing, and trade passed into the hands of recent Spanish immigrant entrepreneurs who worked and lived in downtown Córdoba. Shifting power relationships between commercial entrepreneurs and producers characterized this period of cyclical fluctuations and social revolution.

Third, two groups of Spanish immigrants arrived in Córdoba, and they employed business strategies that were linked to transatlantic immigrant culture. They were willing to take greater risks, to enter into partnerships within their Spanish networks and with Atlantic community corporations, and to diversify their commercial ventures to trade in multiple commodities. The Menéndez multinational firm was the exception to the rule. The Mexican Revolution of 1910 privileged Córdoba's urban coffee entrepreneurs because Aguilar moved the capital to his hometown. The exporters could take advantage of a relatively secure urban environment for coffee preparation and easy access to the railroads. While the two coffee booms pushed these coffee entrepreneurs to expand their preparation capacity and invest in new machinery, the busts that followed forced them to devise strategies to adjust their power relationships with growers, their labor force, and their international buyers.

Finally, Córdoba's coffee agribusinesses survived the turbulent postrevolutionary instability and the depression remarkably well. They were actually enabled by two external factors: the coffee boom of the twenties and the withdrawal of two major U.S. corporations from the region. Their strategic reliance on financial resources from within the immigrant community rather than from the postrevolutionary state was critical. Their decision not to fully mechanize and to retain a large labor force proved fortuitous in the long run. Now we must turn to the workforce that these coffee entrepreneurs employed in their beneficios. These workers played an integral role in the development of a vibrant coffee economy and a well-organized coffee-worker labor movement.

2

Work, Gender, and Workshop Culture

The semimechanization of coffee preparation in the 1880s and 1890s in Central Veracruz's highland towns necessitated the hiring of a new labor force to remove the inner skins, dry, polish, classify, and sort the beans to prepare the green coffee for export. Since no machine had been invented by then to sort or clean coffee, women and children were brought in from the countryside to carry out this manual labor. What was the gendered nature of this new workforce that labored in the dry beneficios of five Central Veracruz towns in the first half of the twentieth century? What was their work experience, and how were these workers transformed by their experiences? In particular, how did gender shape women workers' sense of identity and workplace culture in a female-dominated workshop?

This chapter argues that Mexican labor history has slighted agro-industrial seasonal workers and focused almost exclusively on permanent workers of traditional industries. It constructs a profile of the coffee women and men workers of the 1930s and 1940s in Veracruz to show how they were formally integrated into this agro-export industry. In the past, Mexican women workers were often characterized as passive objects in the workplace, unable to modify or resist oppressive working conditions, low pay, gender segregation, and marginalization within the workforce.[1] Recent studies on Mexican women textile, garment, tortilla, and rural workers have begun to dispute this stereotype and uncover obrera agency, which developed within the historical context of modernizing processes during the revolutionary era. Through their working experiences, many were able to transform themselves as individuals and as a collectivity, challenging stereotypical views of women workers.[2]

Mexican ethnohistorians have studied coffee sorters in the past relying heavily on oral history because official records were so incomplete and fragmented.[3] I adopted the same approach, employing a life-history format in my interviews of former sorters, who entered the beneficios primarily in the 1940s and 1950s, to flesh out how they perceived their workplace, work experiences, and the meaning of work. They were also able to shape their own workshop community. I find Jeffrey Bortz's concept of "layered communities" particularly useful for analyzing working people's culture. He has suggested that working-class communities are shaped by three factors: social class, represented by the concept and meanings of the obrero, inclusive of the obrera; interlocking social relationships between family, workplace, and community; and finally ideas, or ideology.[4] While he relied on labor reports to tease out the layered communities of textile workers, I employ life histories to construct women workers' everyday experiences and their perceptions of themselves as obreras, as women and mothers, and as members of a women worker community. These histories are invaluable in discovering the subjective meanings underlying social reality.

I analyze the nature of the women's work from the perspective of the worker herself as well and how she perceived the gender dynamics and power relationships in the workshop. The escogedoras represented themselves as workers as well as wives and mothers, but they had to search for ways to juxtapose and justify these contradictory roles. It is clear that their interaction on a daily basis with their coworkers and their bosses (*patrones*) contributed to a new sense of self-worth and self-awareness. Thus, identity for these women workers was about the "experience of women as they traverse the borders between family and wage work."[5] In constructing a dual identity, they were also challenging provincial gender norms and conceptions of work held by working men and the upper classes.

Maurice Halbwachs's notion that collective memory is intimately related to an individual's lived experience applies well to their life histories. This can be done, Susan Crane argues, by relocating collective memory "back in the individual who articulates it" and by attending to "the ways individuals experience themselves as historical entities."[6] The sorters' life histories, which recount their everyday experiences, help to construct a collective memory of their working women's community within the context of postrevolutionary Mexico.[7]

The final section explores how escogedoras forged an alternative workplace culture that varied from that of working men and the provincial bourgeoisie. Work-related experiences that included social interactions with their work companions and bosses in public spaces were major factors in the formation of a new set of values, understandings, and practices that questioned provincial norms of paternalism, patriarchy, and worker communities. Thus, work, gender, and workplace culture were inextricably intertwined. In a manner of speaking, escogedoras were reconfiguring their gender and work relationships inside and outside the workplace.

Profile of the Veracruz Coffee Agroindustry Workforce

The true size of the coffee agroindustrial workforce is rather difficult to determine from official documents because seasonal workers were generally not included in census data. When skilled seasonal workers were included in industrial data collection, manual workers were not.[8] Municipal archives more often than not have the most detailed information on seasonal women workers. We know that, in the nineteenth century, coffee pickers and sorters were recruited from the hacienda workforce.[9] As we have seen, the first coffee boom spurred the Central Veracruz commercial entrepreneurs to invest heavily in imported machinery and to hire hundreds of workers to work in their new urban beneficios. By the first decade of the twentieth century,

Córdoba coffee preparers employed 420 women and 123 men in their four beneficios, or the equivalent of four women for every man (see table 2). Approximately 340 sorters were employed in the neighboring town of Orizaba; and another 200, in Coatepec.[10]

By the mid-1920s during the second coffee boom, the number of sorters working in Córdoba's plants had risen to over 500. Two of the largest exporters, the Arbuckle Brothers and Davíd González Rosas, were each employing 200 women. These numbers continued to increase into the early 1930s, driven by high coffee production fueled by the boom of the 1920s. Although union membership lists are notorious for being padded with extra names, they still are the only statistical records available on coffee workers. They reveal that by the early 1930s, Córdoba beneficiadores combined with those of neighboring Peñuela were employing 1,500 sorters. The figures are considerably lower for the other four coffee towns. Coatepec had 496 unionized sorters, while the Boesch Brothers and the Lartigues family employed 200 workers in Orizaba.[11]

By the mid-1930s, the twenty-two dry beneficios in the five coffee towns employed 2,942 unionized escogedoras (see table 9). This number does not include those working in smaller towns such as Misantla, Jalacingo, and Zongolica or the coffee sorters laboring on small farms. Most likely for every unionized escogedora, there were two or three times as many women working on family holdings or neighboring ranchos for little or no pay. Another way to understand the large size of this female workforce is to compare it with that of the Veracruz textile and garment industry. In 1930, 346 out of the 7,679 textile workers were women, but 2,680 women worked in garment workshops, which were concentrated in the Valley of Orizaba.[12] This is to say, the number of unionized coffee sorters in the five coffee towns was almost as high as all the women textile and garment workers employed in the entire state. While the sorters' numbers were increasing, the number of obreras working in the textile, garment, tortilla, and tobacco industries was contracting. This downward trend was due to lower demand, greater mechanization, and increasingly rigid gender

TABLE 9: Unionized Coffee Sorters in Central Veracruz, 1936

Towns	Beneficios	Coffee sorters
Coatepec	6	409
Córdoba	6	1,402
Huatusco	2	197
Orizaba	2	400
Xalapa	6	534
Total	**22**	**2,942**

Source: AGEV/ACG, 1936, boxes 386–87, file 502-13, "Sindicato Union Libertaria de Obreras Desmanchadoras de Café"; file 502-21, "Coatepec; Sindicato de Obreras Desmanchadoras Diversos Trabajo Pro-Ursulo Galván (Huatusco)"; file 502-24, "Sindicato Carlos Marx de Obreras Desmanchadoras de Café (Xalapa)"; and file 502-14, "Sindicato de Obreras Escogedoras de Café de la Región de Córdoba."

norms that developed during hard economic times to protect positions for men workers.[13] What accounts for the continued growth of the female labor force in the Mexican coffee agroindustry? While Brazilian and Colombian preparers began introducing large conveyor belts to accelerate the coffee cleaning process and reduce the number of women workers during the late 1930s, Mexican beneficiadores preferred to continue hiring cheap women workers. More than likely, they were reluctant to risk large capital investments when the U.S coffee market was so unstable.[14] Women were still simply "cheaper than machines."[15]

What was the gender composition of the workforce in Córdoba's coffee agroindustry in the 1930s? Men held the skilled positions as machinists, carpenters, furnace stokers, as well as the unskilled positions of sackers, stirrers (*graneleros*), loaders (*cargadores*), and truck drivers. Córdoba's largest dry beneficios hired between five and ten permanent men workers to run the machinery and an additional twenty temporary unskilled employees. Thus the gender ratio was approximately one man for every seven to ten women. The Union Sindical de Trabajadores y Similares en General de las Casas Benefi-

TABLE 10: Age Distribution and Marital Status of Córdoba Male Coffee, Tobacco, and Commercial Workers, 1938

Marital status		Number	%
Married		23	11.33
Single		179	88.18
N/D		1	0.49
	Total	203	100.00

Age		Number	%
14–19		5	2.46
20–24		29	14.29
25–29		49	24.14
30–39		89	43.84
40–49		23	11.33
50–59		7	3.45
60–69		1	0.49
	Total	203	100.00

Source: AGEV/ACG, 1938, box 539, file "Union Sindical de Trabajadores y Similares en General de las Casas Beneficiadores de Café, Tabaco y del Comercio de la Región de Córdoba, Veracruz."

ciadores del Café, Tabaco y del Comercio de la Región de Córdoba, Veracruz (Union of Workers of the Coffee, Tobacco, and Commercial Businesses of the Region of Córdoba) had only 203 members in the late 1930s (see table 10). Not even all members of this union worked in the coffee beneficios, but the majority did. Truckers and loaders tended to move back and forth between coffee, tobacco, and commercial businesses depending on seasonal demands.

Most Veracruz first-generation coffee workers in Córdoba, Orizaba, and Coatepec came from peasant stock. They originally migrated from the surrounding countryside or from the more impoverished sierra states of Oaxaca, Michoacán, and Puebla during the early twentieth century. In many cases, their mothers arrived as the primary breadwinners of female-headed households, having lost their husbands in the revolution or to another woman. In other cases, entire families migrated in search of work, because the revolutionary armies had destroyed their houses and properties. Many escogedoras had worked as coffee harvesters before entering the beneficios.[16] I was unable to locate any former men workers to interview, but their origins were similar to those of women workers. The second and third generations of the women workers had become urban dwellers. On the other hand, most temporary workers who were recruited each year came from rural origins, or they were former domestic servants or street vendors. A former resident recollected that domestic servants were very difficult to find when the beneficios initiated their operations in October or November in the late 1930s.[17]

To develop a general profile of the coffee sorter, I created databases from the 1932 and the 1944 membership lists of the Sindicato de Obreras Escogedoras del Café de Córdoba (soecc, Union of Coffee Sorters of Córdoba). The wide diversity in the ages of the Córdoba workers seems to suggest that many women sorted coffee for a good part of their lives and not simply for a few years before they married. The ages of the sorters range from fourteen years to the mideighties (see table 11). One might have expected most workers to come from the twenty–to–twenty-nine age group. However, this is not the case. In 1932 the largest age group was the thirty- to thirty-nine-year-olds, who made up 40 percent of the sorters. The twenty–to–twenty-nine age group was slightly smaller, comprising 36 percent.[18] By 1944 there was a decrease in the two largest age groups, but it was more significant for the twenty–to–twenty-nine group. This group dropped to only 25 percent of the labor force. The largest percentage of workers still fell within the thirty–to–thirty-nine age group. What is particularly striking was the rise in the forty–to–forty-nine age group. This suggests that many women workers did not fit the traditional stereotype of the woman worker, who was young, childless, and single.[19] Sorters generally remained in the plants to support their families over a relatively long period of time.

TABLE 11: Age Distribution and Marital Status of Córdoba Coffee Sorters, 1944

Age	Single	%	Married	%	Widowed	%	Total	%
14–19	32	91.43	3	8.57	0	0.00	35	2.13
20–29	317	77.51	92	22.49	1	0.00	409	24.91
30–39	433	74.02	152	25.98	21	3.59	585	35.63
40–49	297	72.44	113	27.56	20	4.88	410	24.97
50–59	123	71.93	48	28.07	14	8.19	171	10.41
60–69	21	70.00	9	30.00	4	13.33	30	1.83
70–79	1	0.00	0	0.00	0	0.00	1	0.00
80–89	1	0.00	0	0.00	0	0.00	1	0.00
Total	1,225		417		60		1,642	

Source: AGEV/JCCA/S, 1932, box 33, file 18, membership list of Sindicato de Obreras Escogedoras de Café de Córdoba, 1944.

Three-quarters of the escogedoras listed their marital status as single, which most likely included a significant number living in free union. This is not at all surprising, given the high level of common-law relationships present among the rural and urban lower class. Most sorters never took wedding vows, due to the instability of their sexual relationships, uncertainty of their economic livelihood, as well as the costs of a religious ceremony. Another group of workers represented in this category are those women who had been abandoned by their partners, leaving them to run female-headed households. This explains why less than one-quarter of all the workers who were thirty years of age or older were or had been legally married.[20]

The men workers fell primarily within the same thirty–to–thirty-nine age group, but their civil status was more likely than the women to be single. Table 10 shows that 44 percent were in their thirties and that a surprising 88 percent were single. For married male workers, seasonal work was certainly less desirable, for it was more difficult to support a family on a six-month salary. More often than not, the sea-

TABLE 12: Age Distribution and Dependents of Córdoba Coffee Sorters, 1944

Age	# Sorters without dependents	# Sorters with dependents	% Sorters with dependents
14–19	24	11	0.75
20–24	36	56	3.83
25–29	56	264	18.05
30–39	75	532	36.36
40–49	31	398	27.20
50–59	18	169	11.55
60–69	3	31	2.12
70–79	0	1	0.07
80–89	0	1	0.07
Total	**243**	**1,463**	**100.00**

Source: AGEV/JCCA/S, 1932, box 33, file 18, "Sindicato de Obreras Escogedoras de Café de Córdoba."

sonal workers were peasants or day workers during the regular growing season who tried to make ends meet by working during the winter months in the beneficios.

When age and dependents are cross tabulated for the women workers, one finds that the thirty–to–thirty-nine age group supported the largest number of dependents (see table 12). They are followed by the workers in their forties. This evidence lends even more credence to the argument that many sorters were primarily working in order to feed and clothe their large families. Table 13 shows that when marital status and dependents are cross tabulated, the data show that single and widowed workers make up almost two-thirds of the workers with dependents.

Other factors might have contributed to the predominance of middle-aged workers by the 1940s. Once workers gained a permanent position (*de planta*), they were loath to give it up, particularly during the depression. These guaranteed positions almost always went to

TABLE 13: Civil Status and Dependents of Córdoba
Coffee Sorters, 1944

Civil status	% with dependents
Single	61.47
Married	21.89
Widowed	3.44
No Dependents	13.19

Source: AGEV/JCCA/S, 1932, box 33, file 18, "Sindicato
de Obreras Escogedoras de Café de Córdoba."

the women with the most seniority or to loyal union members. In
fact, the unions' continual struggle to obtain as many permanent positions as possible in their collective contracts reaped many rewards.
Another factor explaining the aging of the labor force was most likely the lack of alternative employment opportunities for manual wom-
en workers during the depression and war years.

The Gendered Workplace

Although beneficios were not industrial factories, their workers followed workday schedules and workshop regulations, which bore a
striking resemblance to those existing in the factory system. Therefore, in many respects, work experiences and identity resembled those
of the industrial worker. Their gendered work identity in the workplace reflected how women and men viewed and performed their
work and the multiple meanings they derived from and imparted to
their work. Canning characterizes textile-worker identity as "the ways
men and women related to their work sphere, encompassing their
machines, the products of their labor, and their ethics of work, the
social networks that divided or united the shop floor, and even the
physical space of the mill."[21]

In the first half of the twentieth century, coffee beneficio work, like
industrial work, was still largely determined in terms of two interlocking gendered social patterns in Mexican rural society: patriarchy and

the gendered divisions of labor in agriculture. Coffee preparation in urban beneficios by and large replicated the gendered division of labor for traditional dry preparation on family farms and haciendas. Owing to their greater physical strength, men removed the outer layers of the dried coffee cherries with a pestle in a large wooden mortar. The practice of cleaning and grading the beans had always been "women's work," or an extension of rural domestic work.[22] When coffee finca owners began to build dry beneficios alongside their wet ones so they could also remove the two inner skins, men were hired as skilled laborers to operate and maintain the machines, while women and children were hired to perform the unskilled manual work of cleaning and classifying.

Work in the mixed and dry beneficios was organized around gender-segregated tasks and spaces. Mixed beneficios were generally two-storied structures enclosing a cement patio, which often served as a drying terrace and contained a tall chimney for its furnace.[23] The depulping machines for removing the outer shells; the hulling machines, used to remove the two thin inner layers of the coffee bean; the polishers; and the classifiers—all took up the space on the ground floor, where the machine operators and furnace stokers labored. The male loaders would then carry the café verde upstairs in sacks to a large workshop (salón or sala) lined with windows or to a smaller workshop (taller) attached to the end of the building, where the sorters worked.[24]

How did the escogedoras characterize the organization of the workshop and their work in the beneficios? The Coatepec sorter Ana María Hernández described the process to Olivia Domínguez Pérez in the following manner:

> The workshop was very large; there were 600 to 800 women, including temporary workers; they had not created the category of permanent worker [at this time]. On one side were 10 tables and on the other were 6 to 11 tables with enclosed edges. There was a scale and several chutes where you emptied your coffee

after it was weighed, so it fell down into a covered passageway.
. . . Here male workers stirred the heaps of coffee on some movable platforms; they came and went; there was a chute for the discarded coffee and another for the cleaned coffee, and below the men waited to pile it in heaps on canvases.[25]

The sorting process removed the undesirable beans that did not conform to the specific bean grade in terms of form, weight, and color, plus the remaining impurities. The term *desmanchadora* is derived from the word *mancha*, the waste that was removed from the coffee bean. While this term continued to be employed in the region, once sorters began to unionize, they began to employ a second term, *escogedora*, which was considered less demeaning. The term *desmanchadora* was more frequently used in the smaller, remote coffee towns of Coatepec and Huatusco. The task that they performed required a high level of finger dexterity, good concentration, and considerable patience because it was monotonous work. At first, women performed this work while standing or sitting outside at long tables in the finca courtyards (see photograph 2).[26] When the sorting process was moved inside, the beneficio introduced smaller tables (*mesas a metro*) that were two or three meters long with partitions to separate six or more workstations (see photographs 3 and 4). By the 1930s most large Veracruz beneficios had introduced pedal machines (*máquinas* or *mesas de pedal*), which resembled pedal sewing machines. A foot pedal moved a tiny cloth-covered conveyor belt carrying the coffee beans toward the escogedora (see photograph 5). Aldegunda Montaño described to Domínguez Pérez the cleaning process in these terms:

> There were some pedal machines; in the lower part there were some small containers where the discarded and the cleaned coffee went. The machine had a small chute like the coffee depulper which would let the coffee drop out. . . . To begin, we sat on a bench and worked the machine with a foot pedal which was down near the floor. . . . As you moved your feet, the belt moved

2. Porfirian coffee sorters. Reprinted from South-worth, *El Estado de Veracruz-Llave*, 42.

3. Coatepec sorters at long tables, 1920s. Reprinted from BENEMEX, *BENEMEX, su evolución, 1956–70*, 18.

4. Coatepec sorters at long tables, 1930. Courtesy of the AGEV.

forward, and it raised and lowered a lid in the neck of the chute, letting the coffee drop [onto the belt], where we cleaned it according to [each worker's] ability.[27]

Once the sorter had filled her basket with an arroba of cleaned coffee, she would hoist it onto her hip and carry it to the front of the workshop and empty it onto a large table (*burra*) where the receiver (*recibidora*) would inspect it. If the receiver considered her coffee not clean enough, the sorter would have to clean it again. Once the receiver had approved the quality of the work, the checker would weigh the coffee and/or the waste, note down in his ledger the number of arrobas of cleaned coffee, and give the sorter a stamped voucher. Then she would walk over to the large bin at the front of the workshop, pour more uncleaned coffee into her basket, and return to her table.

5. Sorter pedal table, Hacienda Cocuyos, Huatusco. Photograph by author.

A worker could clean, on average, eight to ten arrobas a day, depending on how fast she could work and the dirtiness of the coffee. Depending on her skill and dexterity, she could remove from 75 to 150 kilos of waste a week.[28]

The sorters' wages in Córdoba were equivalent to or higher than rural wages. In 1907 they were earning fifty centavos, or double women's 1898 rural daily wage, while men took home .50 to 1.00 peso, which was also slightly above the man's rural wage.[29] By the 1910s the sorters were being paid by the piece-rate, which was less advantageous. At ten centavos per arroba of cleaned coffee, they could only earn .80 to 1.00 peso if the coffee was quite clean.[30] The piece-rate returned to the prerevolutionary level in the 1920s, after a period of hyperinflation. During the 1926–27 season, the Arbuckles were still paying ten centavos per arroba in Coatepec, which was equivalent to .80 to 1.00 peso a day. This was still slightly above the rural daily wage, which ranged from .60 to 1.00 peso.[31] Although coffee prices were significantly higher in the 1920s, beneficiadores were not passing their lucrative profits on to their workers. This was one of the principal reasons coffee workers began to organize, which will be explored in more detail in the following chapter.

By the early 1930s the piece-rate had risen to twenty to twenty-five centavos per arroba of cleaned beans in Coatepec and Xalapa. However, sizable differences existed in the wages of individual workers due to their varying skill level and their motivation. Daily wages actually ranged from sixty centavos to 3 pesos; however, the vast majority earned less than 1.65 pesos.[32] In Córdoba, sorters were paid based on the amount of waste that they removed from the coffee, which meant that they could earn more when the coffee was very dirty but less when it was clean. Escogedoras received thirty centavos for every kilo of waste, plus an additional centavo for the union's social fund. If a sorter was able to clean eight to ten arrobas of coffee, removing approximately half a kilo of waste from each arroba, she could earn 1.24 to 1.55 pesos a day. This was roughly equivalent to the one and a half peso rural minimum daily wage set by the Labor Department for Córdoba in 1933. Was this sufficient to feed a family if the worker was the head of a household? According to the 1933 cost-of-living statistics, it cost 2.07 pesos a day to sustain a family of five, which meant a sorter could support herself but not single-handedly her entire family.[33] In Huatusco the renters of the Regules and Sainz Pardo–Zardain beneficios paid the same rate as in Córdoba. However, one beneficiador actually lowered the piece-rate to seventeen centavos per kilo in 1935 because of the mid-decade crisis in the coffee market.[34] These wages seem rather low because the minimum wage served as both the floor and the ceiling for wages. However, Susan Tiano and Linda Lim have argued most Mexican women workers, and for that matter men workers, outside the export-processing sector even in the 1980s were still earning less than the minimum wage. In actuality postrevolutionary state regulation obliged beneficiadores to pay the legal minimum wage; they were actually earning more than rural workers, where the minimum wage was not enforced, and many service workers.[35]

The wages of the men workers were higher than women workers because of the gender-segregated occupations and gendered perceptions of work. In 1931 the three or four white-collar workers in the large beneficio received between 100 and 230 pesos a month, while the skilled machinists were making 4 pesos a day. The sackers were paid eight to ten centavos to fill, tie, and carry seventy- or ninety-two-kilo sacks to and from the beneficio.[36] If they filled and carried twenty sacks a day, they could earn 2.00 pesos at a ten-centavo piece-rate, which was considerably more than the escogedoras.

The depression years were not particularly kind to coffee workers. In the second half of the 1930s, the piece-rate for loaders had inched up only one or two centavos.[37] Sorters were earning approximately the same piece-rate wage as they had a decade earlier.[38] By the end of the decade wages were on the rise. In Huatusco, José Vallejo agreed to pay a total piece-rate wage of thirty-three centavos per kilo of waste: twenty-seven centavos per kilo of waste or per fourteen-kilo bucket of cleaned coffee, plus five centavos to cover Sunday pay and one centavo for the sickness compensation. These wages were carefully pegged to approximate the minimum rural daily wage. At thirty-five centavos per kilo of waste, Córdoba's wages were slightly higher, but the higher cost of living meant that this difference was meaningless.[39]

Working conditions varied considerably from one dry beneficio to another, depending on their size and the owner's financial resources and sensitivity to the well-being of his workers. Unfortunately, very few labor reports exist detailing the actual working conditions.[40] In the small, less mechanized plants of Coatepec, Xalapa, and Huatusco, the workshops were little more than sheds attached to the back of the beneficio, where workers had to stand in front of their tables in wooden shoes, cleaning for four or five hours at a time without resting. After pedal machines were introduced, the low but monotonous clicking noise of the foot pedals permeated the workshop space. Poor lighting, inadequate heating, and dust pollution were common complaints that were mentioned in the union's complaints (*quejas*). While the machine operators began to wear masks to protect themselves from the coffee dust by the 1940s, this precautionary measure was never extended to the women workers. To keep their clothes clean, the sorters wore aprons over their dresses. There were bathrooms for both sexes in the beneficios, although Orizaba worker Maria del Carmen Ríos Zavala told a tale that linked the quality of the drinking water to workshop violence. The bathrooms made her sick to her stomach, so she never used them, "and I went to get water from the tap to drink, and it had a black piece in it, like a piece of a black person's hair. . . . They said that a man had been killed in the filtration system and this was part of his remains. . . . Never did I return to drink water there."[41] To explain the reason for the foul tasting water, she was telling a tale of violence that seemed to implicate the owner. At the end of the day, the sorters had to sweep up the fine layer of dust that covered the entire workshop floor. In the majority of my interviews, the interviewees did not volunteer any complaints about the working conditions. Yet poor working conditions were the norm in any developing country, and workers had little choice but to accommodate themselves to them. When the interviewees were questioned about the dust, they said it led to all sorts of respiratory problems and even death.[42]

The receiver was responsible for quality control and workshop discipline on the shop floor. She was chosen for her sorting ability, her capacity to discipline workers, and her popularity among the workers. Up through the 1920s, receivers worked under an individual contract with the owners. The receivers rather than management were responsible for training young new workers who came into the beneficio. Once the workers obtained collective contracts, the receivers' daily wages were determined through collective bargaining. Bound to the closed-shop provisions of the workers' contracts, she was required not to accept coffee sorted by nonunion workers. This seldom occurred because by the late 1920s and early 1930s the larger unions had won the right to control the hiring and firing of additional workers.[43]

The semiskilled manual work performed by seasonal coffee sorters in the coffee agroindustry bore some resemblances to the work performed by women permanent garment workers in the 1920s and 1930s. They worked in gender-segregated workshops, which were separated from the machinery rooms. The specific task that they performed was always considered "women's work." Sorting coffee required less training and fewer skills than making shirtwaists or underwear, and therefore it was more accessible to low-income women. However, these seasonal workers were earning similar wages and working under harsher working conditions than Córdoba's shirtwaist workers.[44] In short, the seasonal coffee sorters had been integrated into the formal sector of capitalism by being guaranteed a minimum wage under the law.

"The Best Husband Is Work"

Work had a different meaning for women than men. For women, work was simply a means to an end: family survival. For men, too, work was a means to achieve family survival, but it was also closely related to their gender identity, as the primary breadwinner and patriarch of the family. This led Mexican society and men workers to belittle women's work outside the home as temporary, less skilled, less secure, less prestigious, and morally scandalous. Women tended to view themselves as temporary workers, which made it more difficult for them to use their work as the foundation for constructing self-identity.[45] In spite of this gendered mentality, sorters were able to construct, for the most part, a positive work identity based on their common work experiences, their capacity to earn a living wage, and their ability to traverse boundaries between family, wage work, and community.

To confront this discrepancy and to come to terms with her identity as a working woman, Mexican women in general, and sorters in particular, had to resolve two basic contradictions embedded in social norms concerning the relationship between gender and work. First, it was bound up in the conflictive interrelationship between gender and class. Deborah Levenson-Estrada has maintained, men could quite easily conflate class and maleness for themselves. However, "the tension between representing unions, militancy, and class as male and the reality that unionism, militancy, and class were both male and female could not be eradicated." She suggests that the only way Nicaraguan society could recognize a woman as an important labor leader was to masculinize her.[46] However, it was not always necessary to masculinize militant women. Porter has suggested another way that Mexico City women workers dealt with this seeming contradiction. Women workers could construct their own distinct identity based on middle-class notions of respectability and honor, which intertwined gender and class in manners different from bourgeois norms and those of lower-class men. Poor working women were generally represented through two paradigms: industrial paternalism and middle-class norms of femininity. Both shared the idea of female vulnerability. These paradigms separated honor as a private virtue for women from honor as a public virtue based on family reputation and economic status for men. To win respect as disciplined workers and retain their wage-earning capacity, obreras "sought to separate honor as a private virtue from honor as a social precedence." This is to say, to represent oneself as a committed worker rather than a sex object was enough to qualify them as honorable.[47]

The second contradiction in societal norms confronting women workers was the bourgeois notion of separate spheres—that is, the assumption that the private sphere of the home did not overlap to any noticeable degree with the public sphere of work and politics. As we have suggested, provincial upper-class women were raised to perform only domestic work within the household. Family members strictly monitored women's movements outside the home. They seldom ventured outside their homes alone, except to buy food or to run errands. To do so threatened their reputation as "honorable" women and their desire for "respect" as loyal daughters, wives, and mothers.[48] Some working men were influenced by these gender norms to the point that they discouraged and even punished their working wives and daughters for leaving the house unaccompanied or talking to people on the streets.[49] However, this separation of spheres did not reflect the reality of poor women's everyday experiences, for it was imperative for them to work outside the home. Therefore, obreras always had to reconfigure their work identities based on the varying rhythms of their work experiences, their family lives, and their sorter community.[50]

In their testimonies, most sorters strove to represent a flexible dual identity to society at large, as hardworking women intent on supporting their families but also as good providers, faithful mothers, maintainers of the household, and morally upright wives upholding gender norms of respectability and honor. In so doing, they continually challenged provincial society's representation of them as street women (*mujeres de la calle*). Former sorters seemed to recognize the inherent contradictions between the reality of their private lives and the bourgeois ideal of the good housewife. They saw their work experience as an integral part of their role as sustainers of the family. In the past, scholars have explained this contradiction in women workers' life histories by emphasizing the persistence of the patriarchal domestic model. The perception that the women considered themselves women first and workers second suggests that the traditional household—where the values of submission, sacrifice, silence, and resistance prevailed—was only being played out once again in the workshop.[51] This interpretation seems to downplay the ties between work, experience, and agency.

When asked whether it was more important for them to be a worker or a housewife, they volunteered varying responses. Needless to say, their responses were influenced by the fact that they were now grandmothers and their family roles had diminished considerably. Their answers were almost always linked to a twofold identity. For Brígida Siriaco García the two roles could not be separated; they were completely intertwined. "I loved my work." She was so enchanted by her work that she had even dropped out of school. She liked to come to work so much as a child that she would arrive at the beneficio gates a half hour early so that she could mingle with the other workers. It was not so much the work or the workplace itself that she liked, she admitted, but the experience of working and socializing with other women. "I feel so emotionally moved," she said, almost in tears as she reminisced about her working years. In her case, work was at first an escape from school, where she had been struggling because of her health problems. Although she did not frame it in these terms, the opportunity for a gregarious young woman to socialize with other girls and women must have been very appealing. It was most probably an escape from the patriarchal household where she was destined to play a subordinate role. She did stop working to bear her first child. But when her partner (*compañero*) abandoned her, she returned to work to support not only herself and her child but also her parents, which was her social responsibility as the youngest daughter. Very often she had to take her young children to work to breastfeed them during the day.[52]

How did women justify their need to work in their life histories? Women workers almost always expressed their need to work in terms of "necessity" or the need to "help" their families rise out of poverty.[53] In almost all cases, they began to work as children to "supplement" the family income. In the larger provincial towns of Córdoba, Orizaba, and Xalapa, their partners were usually urban workers: tailors, bakers, drivers, textile workers, day laborers, or even an occasional musician from a well-off family. In Huatusco and Coatepec, they were generally rural day workers. Other times, their husbands or partners had abandoned them or had become alcoholics, and they were left to manage female-headed households with multiple dependents. Inés Reyes Ochoa's mother, Juana, had lived in an unstable relationship for years, which forced her to leave the house to go to work. Guadalupe López Osorio had graduated from primary school and had married before she started to work in the beneficios. However, her husband was unable to find work in the midst of the depression, so she entered the workplace at the age of sixteen in 1930 to help pay the bills. María Elena Serna's mother had started working in the 1920s because her husband, who was a telegraph operator, could not earn enough money to support their six children.[54] What often began as a temporary job for a child, a single childless teenager, or a married woman with children very often developed into an occupation (*oficio*). Since the welfare of the family always came first, sorters often brought their daughters, sisters, or cousins into the beneficio to supplement family income. Two- and three-generation sorter families were quite common. This employment pattern mirrored family practices in the textile industry.[55]

Why did these women prefer working in a coffee beneficio to a farm? They associated work in the coffee-sorting rooms with making something of oneself; or as Ann Farnsworth-Alvear has called a desire "to make something of oneself" (*progresar*), or acquire greater social mobility.[56] Work in the coffee beneficios was far more desirable than hard manual labor on the coffee fincas because of the better working conditions and higher pay. The work was less strenuous, cleaner, more congenial, and indoors; for no one liked to work in inclement weather. In addition, the work was more secure, because you were assured a wage for four to six months of the year if you were a permanent worker. A temporary worker who worked approximately one week a month during the coffee harvest and the remainder of the year as a rural day laborer or a street vendor explained her preference for beneficio work in the following terms: "You earned good pay. It was nice work and better than in the country or domestic work, where they paid you less."[57] The coffee sorters perceived beneficio work as a definite improvement in their lives in terms of their ability to support themselves and their families and the attainment of a somewhat higher sociocultural status.

Respect and happiness are two dominant themes that run through most life histories of Latin American obreras, whether they were Argentine meatpackers, Mexico City or Bajío textile workers, or Veracruz sorters. Just like men workers, women workers took considerable pride in their accomplishments as workers and their ability to support their families. They expressed genuine satisfaction in their achievements and in the respect they received for being good economic providers for the family.[58] Cecilia Hernández de Huerta felt "proud to be able to earn enough to buy food each day" and to support her ten children after her husband abandoned her. The orphan Isabel Romero Serrano was so "pleased when Saturday arrived and I was paid . . . my twenty-five pesos, [that] I came home with such enthusiasm, to say [to my grandmother], 'here is my pay.'"[59] Estela Velázquez Ramírez, a married sorter with nine children, articulated the same sentiments: "It gives me pride even today . . . because . . . I raised my children honorably . . . with much pride because the work allowed me to gain experience and more education; just think, work never honors a person; it is the person who honors the work."[60] Brígida expressed it in terms of how work and her earnings gave her a sense of independence from her husband: "I like to work. Never did I like to rely on a man."[61]

Although these former sorters portrayed their work outside the home as an economic necessity, they seemed to recognize the built-in contradiction between the reality of their working lives and the good housewife they wanted to represent to society at large. Therefore, they legitimized their work within the context of the "good" housewife. As a consequence, they constructed an identity that encompassed both roles to downplay this tension between the two. In so doing, they were creating a gender identity, which glossed over the seeming contradictions between these two roles. Enriqueta Salazar Báez legitimized women's work by comparing it to a good husband: "The best husband is work." She wanted to be remembered as a superwoman (*supermujer* or *madrona*), a woman who could bring home the paycheck and also be a responsible housewife and mother. She represented herself in front of her husband as a strong woman who, like working men, did not want to be crossed.[62]

Underneath the representation of themselves as proud, conscientious, capable mothers and workers was the contradictory one of the exploited worker. Some former union leaders even recognized how they had been exploited. "They worked like little animals," recalled Alicia Limón, the Coatepec union leader. Her use of the impersonal pronoun "they" allowed her to distance herself from the bad experience and to show that this treatment was also experienced by all workers. She was articulating an individual memory of a collective experience. This theme most frequently surfaced among temporary workers. Maria del Carmen Ríos Zavala, a single mother, was even more disillusioned with her work experience in Orizaba as a temporary worker. "Well, I feel like mother and father—this is what I feel because . . . well, as a coffee sorter, now I feel nothing . . . because when they brought in the machines, I received nothing . . ."[63] In many respects, temporary workers were the bottom layer of the sorter community, with very few rights.

The final contradiction in their representation of themselves was that they downplayed the sacrifices they made in their triple workday as workers, partners, and mothers. It is possible that over the years, they had forgotten some of the drudgery of domestic life and remembered the good times spent with their compañeras. They did, however, describe the difficulties of juggling all three roles with minimal help from their male companions. Before and after work, there was always child care, food procurement and preparation, cleaning, ironing, and satisfying their companions' needs from dawn until far into the night. Three to five hours sleep was simply a normal part of their

6. Coffee sorters in the Ezequiel González beneficio, 1932. Courtesy of the AGEV. Photograph by Villanueva.

everyday lives.[64] They had come to accept this lifestyle because family came first.

Constructing Women's Workshop Culture

Mexican workshops in the first half of the twentieth century were not simply hierarchically structured communities that closely resembled extended patriarchal families. They were also layered, gendered communities. Undoubtedly, their bosses acted as paternalistic figures, providing work for employees while also protecting and assisting them in times of unexpected family misfortune or external threats. Since workers brought family members into the plants, interactions and tensions with each other and with supervisors on the shop floor were often closely linked to family matters.[65] On the other hand, workshop culture had different meanings for women and men. Women developed new social relationships with their female coworkers that gave them the opportunity to build an alternative working women's culture. Moreover, in the female-dominated workshops, interactions between sorters and their peers and their bosses led to constantly shifting vertical power relationships. For example, in Ezequiel González's commissioned photo of La Garza's sorter workshop, González, interestingly enough, represents his workers as respectable and well dressed, while he himself is seen only at the rear of the room. This photo in some ways represents more closely how the women workers would have liked us to envision them. In short, new working experiences allowed escogedoras to cross boundaries and to adapt to, circumvent, and even challenge paternalism, patriarchy, and masculinity. In their collective memories, the cohesive workshop community became a special place outside the bounds of their immediate families.[66]

Paternalism on the shop floor dates back to the nineteenth century, where hacendados tried to bring rural patron-client relations into their textile factories, sugar mills, or coffee beneficios located on their estates. Paternalism on the shop floor is generally viewed as a hierarchical relationship between the boss and his workers, where the boss tries to create a culture based on personalism, fatherly benevolence, and authority to keep his workers contented but under his control. This practice was soon extended to urban plants to maintain discipline but also to look after the well-being of the workers and their families well into the twentieth century. Bringing Catholicism into the workshop through the erection of a chapel or a statue to the Virgin of Guadalupe reinforced this male-dominated culture.[67]

The continuity of paternalist labor relations in Monterrey, Atlixco, and Tlaxcala factories in postrevolutionary Mexico has been well documented. Michael Snodgrass has shown how, in Monterrey, the Garza Sada family, in their beer factory, "shared, judging from their words and actions, a sincere and heartfelt concern for their workers' well-being," and the workers felt "reverential gratitude" in return. Factory owners established personal bonds of obligation in order to create paternalistic systems of control. Owners and administrators consistently imposed paternalistic societal values in the workshop to keep workers compliant and to discourage unionization, despite worker resistance.[68] The patrones "forged rank-and-file loyalty toward the company by making the workers feel as a part of a family."[69] Paternalism's success depended on the owner's ability to minimize the social distance between themselves and their women as well as men workers. It relied heavily on a personal style: "The owners visited the plant frequently, saluting the operatives, lending a hand, and inquiring about their families." It was not uncommon for the boss to slap women brewery workers on the back, just as they did to men workers, and shout out, "*Ándale muchachas*" ("Come on girls").[70]

Yet paternalism also had a gendered dimension. Owners' held different attitudes concerning manliness and womanliness. Women's labor was often considered more expendable and temporary, so they could be paid less. Young single women were traditionally preferred over married women, who might become pregnant and therefore were considered less reliable workers. Owners sometimes intentionally segregated women and men by occupation to minimize the importance of tasks performed by women so as to treat them as more sexually vulnerable and to weaken their solidarity. These gender biases have been observed in Latin American as well as U.S. factories.[71] Paternalism was further reinforced in Mexico by the postrevolutionary state and the national labor confederations, which often represented the obrera as compliant, maternalistic, and domestic, primarily to safeguard jobs for men.[72]

In the Veracruz beneficios, paternalist labor relations continued to predominate up through the 1960s, yet worker-management relations in the semimechanized agroindustry were far less rigid and more informal than in more-mechanized industries. The rhythm of work in the sorters' workshop was driven in part by the individual worker's abilities and motivation rather than by the machines. On the other hand, owners did establish deadlines on some occasions for the completion of some coffee contracts that had to be met by the women workers collectively. This meant working far into the night for all the women in the workshop. In spite of these hierarchical power relationships, beneficio work brought provincial women into new heterosexual workspaces hitherto off limits to them. Former Córdoba coffee sorters constantly recalled an informality in their relations with their male patrones and plant managers. By characterizing their relations with their bosses in these terms, they sought to reconfigure their representation of themselves as respected women, wives, and workers. Another instance where the growing empowerment of the obrera in the workshop can be seen was in the increasing influence of the receiver over the years.

Until the 1930s, owners appointed a trustworthy employee (*empleada de confianza*) to serve as receiver, to inspect all sorted coffee before it was sent down the chutes to the stirrers. This practice continued for much longer in the smaller workshops in Huatusco and Xalapa, where the unions were weak. The receiver worked under an individual contract, and the manager had the right to fire her if he was not satisfied with her performance. By the early 1930s, the CROM had organized the sorters into strong unions in Córdoba and Coatepec, and the workers had won the right in their collective contracts to choose their own receivers. They also elected their union shop stewards (*encargadas*) after the passage of the Federal Labor Law of 1931. Union members would elect two well-respected union leaders for each large beneficio. Former encargadas considered it a great honor to be elected to this position, for they enjoyed the support of the rank and file. By the late 1930s the position of shop steward had become essential for workshop discipline, and it was reflected in the collective contracts. They were earning between 2.50 and 3.00 pesos a week, which was the equivalent to the wages received by the machinists and furnace stokers.[73]

Once the union shop stewards and work committees had gained control over enforcement of work regulations on the shop floor, the paternalistic authority of the beneficio owner began to erode in the larger plants. The escogedoras were no longer directly under the supervision of the patrón or administrator (*gerente*) but rather one of their own compañeras. The lessening of strict authority on the workshop floor gave women more room to maneuver and engage in different forms of informal resistance. For instance, owners insisted that the workers not engage in small talk while they were working so that they could concentrate better on their task. The sorters remember how their favorite union leaders used to ask them not to talk loudly or sing while on the job; but they continued to do so, albeit in muffled tones, despite their warnings. They did not have harsh words for their beloved leaders who were required to enforce discipline. Needless to say, if a sorter were to flirt with one of the men workers, the administrator, or an owner, they knew that this was a serious infraction, and they would be severely reprimanded for inappropriate behavior.[74] In certain respects, owner paternalism was being supplanted on the workshop floor by a form of godmotherhood (*madrinismo*) constructed by their leaders.

Undoubtedly, Mexican workers themselves contributed to the continuation of paternalism in the workshop because they believed they were benefiting from owner beneficence. Paternalism was partially "built upon working-class traditions of mutual aid and tapped into labor's historic aspirations for self-improvement."[75] Therefore, sorters tried to be accommodating toward plant owners. In their testimonies, the sorters represented the plant owners as their principal benefactors, and they often emphasized the fluidity of their relationship with these male authority figures. The permanent workers recalled their interactions with managers as harmonious and nonconfrontational. They constantly mentioned how the owners treated them with respect. Respect for their ability to be hard workers was one of the dominant themes in the sorters' narratives, just as it was for men workers. In other words, obreras tried to represent themselves as equally qualified as men workers to legitimize their work outside the home. The women accepted the paternalistic environment as part of the economic reality, for the workers felt that the owners looked after them. "There were no clashes," a number of Córdoba workers recalled. Don Ricardo Regules "knew how to treat the sorters well" and was a great fatherly person (*padrote*). Regules "talked with them," making them feel that he genuinely cared about their livelihood. The workers usually associated the Regules family with good wages: "The Reguleses were good to us. Humberto, Ricardo, and his father paid us well." Others made a distinction between Don Ricardo and his two sons: "The sons did not behave well. When they inspected the coffee, they always found some bad coffee beans." The workers had less kind words for Tirso Sainz Pardo and his nephew, Julian, who were described as "demanding" and at times "hard-hearted."[76] In Coatepec, Adelina Téxon and Alicia Limón echoed these same sentiments, reiterating that the owners treated them with respect.[77] Owners were characterized as good or demanding, but in general they were not described in negative terms.

The sorters' representation of the beneficiadores was influenced to some degree by a collective memory of the not-so-distant past, when the owners and managers shared a similar socioeconomic status with the workers. Their grandmothers and mothers had passed down to them stories about how these Spanish immigrants had arrived from northern Spain without a peso to their name and almost illiterate. Stories still circulate about the affairs some of them had had with sorters, street vendors, and rural women. Before he became wealthy, Ricardo Regules Sr. had even married a working-class woman.[78] Thus, in their everyday memory the sorters could relate to these self-made former shepherds and small farmers. For example, the gregarious Brígida Siriaco recalled conversing on the shop floor with Ricardo Sr. on numerous occasions, using the familiar "tu" instead of the formal "usted" pronoun.[79] Nevertheless, such memories of the past did not fundamentally alter the unequal power relations between the workers and their bosses, and the escogedoras clearly recognized their dependence on the owners' goodwill for their economic livelihood.

The sorter workshops, where hundreds of women sat side by side for hours performing monotonous work, were quite conducive to the transgression of paternalist authority. The intrepid Inés Reyes, who loved to sing and act in her spare time, was notorious for bursting forth in song. One time, Tirso Sainz Pardo was so irritated by her behavior that he sent her across the street to La Garza, where the shop steward was stricter. However, Inés continued to sing, without being disciplined further.[80] Because she was a respected union leader, management could not afford to have her fired. In short, coffee sorters seized everyday opportunities to resist the paternalistic discipline of the workplace and to assert their own individuality.

In her study of Colombian textile workers, Ann Farnsworth-Alvear argues that "doing factory work meant being in close proximity to persons outside one's family circle for most of the day, and more than the 'vertical' relationship to a mill-owner or administrator, it was this 'horizontal' relationship to large numbers of other women and men that made mill work different."[81] The same is true for coffee sorters. They recalled with great fondness their new social relationships with the nonfamily compañeras but not with their compañeros.

There appears to have been a minimum of cross-gender affinity in the beneficios. The sorters characterized their relationship with the obreros as professional but cordial. They definitely wanted to give the impression that there was a distance between the two genders to uphold their moral respectability. Management always saw the men workers as a distraction, for they disrupted the women's work routine. It continually discouraged workers from entering into the other gender's space, striking up conversations, or flirting.[82] Nevertheless, they came from similar socioeconomic origins, so sorters were bound to strike up conversations, enter into affairs, and even marry their fellow workers. Since they emptied their baskets of cleaned coffee down the chutes to the stirrers below, the sorters were more likely to develop close relationships with these unskilled workers than with machine operators.[83]

On the shop floor, they developed new and strong friendships with their coworkers as they chatted over the click-click of the foot-pedal machines. The gender-segregated workshop provided them with horizontal spaces to develop their own sorter community. This contrasted with the workshops of textile workers and tortilla workers, who had to be constantly attentive to the rhythm of their machine, the danger of getting their clothing or limbs caught in the machinery, and the continual confrontations with the male workers. More than likely, the sorters remembered more of the good experiences of bantering with their compañeras than the bad experiences of petty rivalries. This in part explains the difference in the responses of the escogedoras and the textile obreras, who encountered a more contentious working climate in mixed workplaces.[84]

In their collective memory, the sorters were creating an alternative community to their domestic one. They sang boleros and ranchero songs together, shared notes on family problems and boyfriends, and developed a special camaraderie based on their everyday experiences. Cecilia Sheridan Prieto discovered this same type of social intercourse among sorters in Coatepec: "The women sorters succeeded in creating their own space: 'their workshop,' one could call it. As they sat next to each other with their attention fixed on the conveyor belt carrying the coffee, there were no communication barriers."[85] While they performed their monotonous work, they told each other off-color jokes and swapped stories about their personal lives, tragedies, illnesses, abortions, births, and husbands. Brígida described it in the following terms: "Almost the majority of them passed the time talking. . . . But the hands were working. . . . You are talking to your compañera who was on one side of you, or the other side of you, and here comes the belt. . . . Many times we talked about our domestic problems, . . . pregnancies, boyfriends, husbands, about everything we talked, and one or the other of them would make comments."[86]

These newfound friendships led many single workers to spend some of their leisure time together before and after work. Kathy Peiss's observations about New York City single women workers holds true for the escogedoras. They "experienced the rhythms of time and labor more similar to man's than married women's, and shop-floor cultures reinforced the notion that leisure was a distinct realm of activity to which workingwomen could demand access."[87] Sorters walked to work and returned home together, ate lunch together, bought drinks together, went to the movies together, and attended union meetings and dances with one another. They learned all the gossip of the neighborhood (*barrio*) in the workshop. When they married, they became each other's godmothers (*comadres*), shared babysitting chores, and stepped in to assist their compañeras when family tragedy struck.[88] Their interaction with their fellow workers on and off the shop floor represented a significant change from the ideal vertical male-female gender dynamics found in most working-class households. Workplace culture seemed to be spilling out into the streets; strengthening ties among women workers; and in so doing, subverting patriarchal domesticity.

Although partnered women had little time to socialize outside of their workplace because of their myriad domestic chores, their common work experiences were reinforced when they met at their weekly union meetings, dances, Labor Day marches, and pilgrimages to the Virgin of Guadalupe. They distinctly remember leaving their husbands or companions at home and holding hands while walking in groups to the union hall for these organized activities, sometimes returning home alone late at night. In these public places, they continued their conversations about home, work, and love; their complaints against the plant managers; and the local gossip of the neighborhood. This newfound sociability led to the evolution of their own jargon. One former administrator spoke of the ways in which sorters developed their own banter, streetwise behavior, greater independence from their family responsibilities, and greater self-worth. In a sense, he said, they became "liberated."[89] They were subverting the conception of workers' culture as exclusively male—organized around cantinas and sports—by constructing an alternative female one.

The sorters' domestic and workplace lives were much more intertwined than those of men workers in part because they were tied to food procurement and preparation. They often brought snacks from home to munch on. After working a couple of hours, they would eat a small taco or sandwich roll (*pambaso*) that they had secretly brought into the beneficio and then would continue working until one o'clock. If their homes were close by, they would dash home in the middle of the day to prepare dinner for their family and to eat a quick meal. Other workers who had traveled a long distance loitered around the beneficios with the men to eat on the sidewalks or in the nearby parks, where they ate their lunch (*itacate*). They then would return to the beneficios at two o'clock for three more hours of work, after which they would rush home to prepare the evening meal.[90]

The more-entrepreneurial workers used their ingenuity to find alternative ways to supplement their meager wages. Some surreptitiously sold snacks—such as fruit or seeds—and clothing, inside or outside the plants throughout the day, employing a voucher system so that workers did not have to pay in cash. On payday they would send one of their children around to each workshop to collect on their bills. To make ends meet, they also sold clothes or washed clothes on weekends. If they were really strapped for cash, they would work a second shift, as bartenders or prostitutes in the local brothels or in the red-light district. During the offseason (*el tiempo de guayaba*), they would return to their street vending or set up stalls in the local marketplace. Temporary workers usually returned to their former positions as domestic servants, tobacco strippers, or rural workers.[91] They engaged in survival strategies to work in multiple formal and informal forms of employment. In short, the meaning of work was not entirely defined by one occupation.

To the gente decente, women who left their home to work represented a direct threat to patriarchy and their moral value system. Its members still embraced nineteenth-century bourgeois gender norms that advocated separate spheres, inferring that women did not belong in the workplace. Porter asserts, "The factory represented a potentially threatening space within which employers, overseers, and workers might violate norms of femininity."[92] Women's penetration of public spaces frequented by men—whether it was in the workplace, the market, the union hall, the dance hall or the cantina—created a stigma on the reputation of an honorable woman. As soon as a Mexican woman abandoned her children to enter the factory or to work on the streets, she was identified as a loose woman.[93] Working alongside men each day seemed to threaten traditional gender roles. Moreover, the fact that some sorters frequented bars and even worked as prostitutes to make ends meet simply reinforced this image. The Friday- and Saturday-night union dances, where the women went unaccompanied by their male family members, led to even more raised eyebrows.

Plant owners and townspeople employed gender ideology to question the workers' morality as honorable women, when the Coatepec sorters went out on strike for higher wages and the right to organize in the late 1920s. In so doing, they sought to cast aspersions on the credibility of their economic demands. Townspeople yelled at them in the streets, calling them dark-skinned she-goats or sexpots (*chivas prietas*). The sexual and racial connotations of this term simply reinforced stereotypes of these working women. Moreover, devout Catholics could even use the term "chivas prietas" to insinuate that the sorters were religiously disoriented women seeking to challenge trade-union anticlericalism. Priests went so far as to threaten to excommunicate any obrera who tried to join the union. Over the decades, the attitude of Coatepec townspeople toward sorters did not change appreciably. Sorters still have strong memories of the townspeople's disdain for them.[94]

To well-off townspeople the sorters were social deviants or sexually promiscuous women who had strayed far from proper womanly behavior. For this reason, they were frequently referred to as "street women." Priests and owners, the two most powerful authority figures in these towns, continually admonished them not to stray from the fold. María del Carmen remembered bitterly how an Orizaba priest admonished a group of sorters before their December 12 pilgrimage to the statue of the Virgin of Guadalupe: "Even the priest told us: don't go and cave in to the reputation that you have. Behave yourselves! We were doing nothing wrong because many of the women had brought their children, their grandfathers, and their grandmothers along. We were nothing more than that for the townspeople. We were all bad, and I was only a young girl. . . . I did not even know what movies were. We grew up in a world of hypocrisy, and this is the way

I was judged."[95] Again and again, sorters returned to the same phrase: "We were not street women."[96]

In conclusion, women made up the vast majority of the workforce in the semimechanized coffee agroindustry from its inception in the 1890s. By the 1930s and 1940s the number of unionized sorters working in the five major Veracruz coffee towns had risen to equal the number of women working in Veracruz's textile and garment industry. A large proportion of these women were middle-aged heads of households, supporting numerous dependents, which deviates from the commonly held assumption that primarily single women worked outside the home. They were earning wages that were higher than most rural women workers and comparable to nonunionized women in the service sector as well as unionized women in the textile and garment industries. In spite of the seasonal nature of their work, the sorters with permanent status had, in fact, been formally integrated into the capitalist export sector.

Their collective memory preserved the memory of their shared lived experiences.[97] In their life histories, rank-and-file sorters revealed a dual identity as wives and mothers and as workers. To legitimize these two roles, they linked their conception of work with the need to sustain the family. They constructed their meaning of work around the family's need for a primary wage earner, where private and public spheres had to be intertwined in family survival strategies. In spite of the provincial perception of them as loose women, these former sorters exhibited a relatively high level of job satisfaction in their collective memory. They were proud of their ability to perform their work well and to earn enough money to support their families. Finally, they developed an alternative working-class women's culture stemming out of their close-knit workshop community. They shared horizontal and vertical relationships with nonfamily members on the workshop floor. In this new heterosexual public space, they adapted to, circumvented, and at times challenged their bosses' benevolent paternalism. Their new relationships with the women and men who were not family members challenged patriarchy, paternalism, and bourgeois gender norms. In building a genuine sense of women's camaraderie, they were reconfiguring provincial conceptions of work, gender, and class. The next chapter analyzes the ways in which these women and men coffee workers mobilized themselves into labor organizations during the revolutionary and postrevolutionary years.

3

Sorters' Negotiations with Exporters and the State

The political and socioeconomic chaos and insecurity brought on by the Mexican Revolution of 1910 opened new spaces and opportunities for Veracruz seasonal workers to organize, take to the streets, and demand rights. In certain respects, they enjoyed more opportunities for mobilization than any other coffee-producing state. Veracruz had larger exports, the nation's major port, and a long history of labor militancy. The collapse of the central state in 1914 contributed to the widespread urban unrest and worker mobilization over the next twenty years.

This chapter explores the interrelationship between organized labor, the state, and gender in Veracruz's coffee agribusiness during revolutionary chaos and subsequent postrevolutionary institution building. It seeks to address a number of questions concerning the nature of labor organization in the 1910s and 1920s from a gendered perspective. What were the major reasons for coffee-worker unrest, and did it have a gendered dimension? Were women and men coffee workers able to organize themselves independently or did they receive outside assistance? How successful were their strikes and protests in resolving their grievances? How did the institutionalization of the labor movement advance or impede the renewal of their demands in the 1920s, and how did women workers in particular respond to the increasingly male-dominated regional and national labor federations? Finally, how did organized labor reconcile the contradictory roles of women as mothers and wives and as wage workers?

The evidence suggests that the greater the depth and intensity of worker mobilization during periods of instability or revolution, the more involved and visible working women become.[1] Women workers mobilized primarily for economic or class-based reasons, but gender-specific reasons were intertwined. Following Temma Kaplan's lead, John Lear has suggested that Mexico City women workers' major reason for taking to the streets in 1916 "represented a gender-specific defense of the working-class community." Men, on the other hand, "struggled with their employers over the terms and remuneration of employment, supported political candidates in elections, or joined the different military factions."[2] This chapter presents new evidence to support these gendered dimensions of labor mobilization.

Veracruz was one of the most important laboratories of revolution in the republic for both women and men workers. In collaboration with anarchosyndicalist activists, coffee sorters resorted to collective action against the beneficiadores in the midst of revolution to demand the same workers' rights as men. This chapter begins by examining three ad hoc petitions sent between 1915 and 1918 by coffee-sorter unions in Córdoba, Xalapa, and Orizaba to the newly created local and state industrial-labor boards. The official documents reveal how women workers under the guidance of external organizers carved out new public spaces in three coffee regions embroiled in military and political turmoil.

The emerging revolutionary state became more sensitive to the demands of women workers when it realized that they played such a strategic role in the coffee preparation and export. The Carrancista state had to make concessions to their unions to keep the Veracruz coffee economy afloat at the height of the military strife. It, therefore, did not use gender as a means to deter obreras from presenting their demands to the state-sponsored industrial-labor boards. As Gilbert Joseph and Daniel Nugent have argued, the dynamics of Mexican state formation was "the quotidian process whereby the new state engaged the popular classes and vice versa" in order to regain control of the population.[3] In this case, women workers were an integral part of these popular classes.

The interrelationship between labor mobilization and gender became more complex after hostilities ceased; for a variety of social organizations vigorously competed to mobilize women as well as men workers during the 1920s and 1930s. Most scholars contend that the postrevolutionary era was marked by the marginalization of women workers in the workplace and within the labor movement.[4] In the case of the female-dominated coffee workshops of Central Veracruz, this was not necessarily true.

The second half of this chapter analyzes the role of anarchosyndicalists, tenant unionists, organized labor, social reformers, agrarians, and communists in the mobilization of Central Veracruz coffee workers in the 1920s and early 1930s. Sorter mobilization followed different patterns in each coffee town, depending on the regional nature of the shifting sociopolitical coalitions. The CROM played a key role, however, and aggressively negotiated to win union recognition and collective contracts for seasonal women workers in Córdoba, Xalapa, and Coatepec. Progressive state governors were also particularly instrumental in creating openings for women workers to mobilize during these years when Veracruz politics remained largely outside the long arm of the federal government. In the waning years of the twenties, however, the external intervention of the Liga de Comunidades Agrarias y Sindicatos Campesinos del Estado de Veracruz (League of Agrarian Communities and Peasant Unions of the State of Veracruz; abbreviated as "Veracruz Peasant League" from here on) to seize control of Córdoba's sorter union in the long term only weakened its political autonomy and feminist leanings. Finally, the men's unions followed an entirely different evolution due to their relatively small membership.

Veracruz as a Laboratory of Revolution

The Mexican Revolution was not a social revolution carried out by urban workers, but they did contribute to the destabilization of the

Díaz regime by challenging its proindustry policies in violent demonstrations and strikes beginning in 1906.[5] Veracruz transportation, textile, and tobacco workers were particularly militant between 1900 and 1910 and played a critical role in challenging the Porfirian economic and political structure, supporting the presidential candidacy of Francisco Madero in 1910 and contributing to the eventual resignation of Governor Dehesa.[6] Once Madero had assumed the presidency, his political movement slowly disintegrated in Veracruz, as rival military leaders quarreled among themselves over the political spoils or left the state on military assignments. As a consequence, the entrenched landowning, commercial, and industrial elites quickly reasserted control over state and local politics with the acquiescence of the president himself. When the federal government finally collapsed with the resignation of President Huerta in July 1914, Veracruz became increasingly engulfed in the civil war between the three major revolutionary movements, respectively led by Emiliano Zapata, Francisco Villa, and Venustiano Carranza.

When Carranza and his armies were forced to abandon Mexico City in November 1914 and retreat to the port of Veracruz with Zapata and Villa's armies on the verge of descending from the sierra in hot pursuit, Veracruz became one of the last Constitutionalist strongholds. With his back to the gulf, Carranza was reluctantly persuaded by his more progressive generals to make major concessions to the peasantry and labor to attract popular support away from his two more popular opponents. In a desperate attempt to regain momentum, Carranza issued his famous agrarian decree of January 6, 1915, promising to create a state agency to restore and grant land to landless peasants. A month later he signed a pact with the leaders of the Casa del Obrero Mundial (COM, House of the World Worker)—who favored collaboration with the Constitutionalists—in which he pledged to support the just claims of workers and to permit them to organize unions throughout the republic. In return, the COM pledged to recruit worker battalions, which would join his faltering Constitutionalist forces in their struggle against the Zapatista-Villista coalition forged at the Convention of Aguascalientes.[7] In his increasingly weakened military position, the First Chief temporarily extended to provisional military governors the right to exercise considerable discretionary powers to construct a proworker, propeasant, promunicipal, anticlerical revolutionary project to win the support of the populace. This political strategy spawned social laboratories for the construction of new revolutionary states, temporarily opening up new spaces for negotiation from above with the peasantry, organized labor, and women's groups. Simultaneously, it created an environment for coalition building among popular groups to negotiate from below for socioeconomic demands. Carrancista generals in Veracruz, Yucatán, Tabasco, Puebla, Jalisco, Federal District, San Luis Potosí, and other states took the initiative to issue the first labor and agrarian decrees to woo popular groups.[8]

Soon after capturing control of most of the state, provisional governor Aguilar began issuing a series of social reform measures in the fall of 1914 not only to satisfy popular demands but also to preempt the agreements made by the Conventionist forces. They included an anticlerical decree, which would expel all foreign priests, and an agrarian law that called for the division of large private properties.[9] His October 1914 labor decree stated that "work dignifies man and cooperates with capital for the progress of the people. . . . The state must dictate rules whose objective it is to establish the just equilibrium between the economic interests in general and the individual in particular." Thus, the Veracruz state assumed an interventionist position and left open the possibility for direct negotiations between employers and workers. The labor decree also called for a nine-hour day with flexibility in working hours to be determined by owners and workers, obligatory rest on Sundays and national holidays, nearby lay primary schools, a one-peso minimum rural wage, and fines for the violation of these provisions. Even workers paid by the piece-rate wage were included in these provisions. What was most progressive in the labor law was the granting of power to enforce this decree to two new state institutions: a state labor inspection system and the provisional municipal councils (Juntas de Administración Civil). At the local level, labor inspectors were given the authority to levy and collect fines on those owners who violated the law, while the municipal committees were given the right to hear and resolve disputes and the obligation to pass on to the inspectors the complaints of workers and industry. Barry Carr has argued that Aguilar's labor law was the most effective in the republic for it gave labor inspectors the right to oversee its implementation.[10] In many respects, the new provisional municipal boards assumed some of the same functions exercised by Governor Alvarado's regional military tribunals in Yucatán. Both institutions would address the social problems of labor, the poor, the helpless, and women. They allowed the "revolution's entrance into the lives of many Yucatan women."[11]

The COM leadership, which had left the capital and moved to Orizaba in March 1915, created the Central Office of Revolutionary Propaganda, which acted in loose coordination with the Constitutionalist's Department of Information of Propaganda under the minister of interior, who was based in the port of Veracruz. In the spring of 1915 the Central Office of Revolutionary Propaganda began to send out organizing committees throughout the state and the nation to organize unions.[12] They were instructed to proceed to the principal squares when the local orchestras were playing, stand on street corners to deliver speeches, or write articles on the objectives of the Constitutionalist Revolution. One of its directives gave the following instructions:

> If the region is agricultural the theme of the discussion will be the resolution of the agrarian problem: (improvements for the day worker or rural peon, division of the land, irrigation, etc.). If the region is industrial, the themes related to worker problems will be developed: (implementation of the eight-hour day, formation of unions, protection of women and children who work in the workshops and the factories, laws for work-related accidents, sanitary conditions, and an increase in wages, etc.). If the

region is quite fanatical, the theme will be why this is an anti-clerical, but not an antireligious campaign. . . . Note: This program captures the fundamental idea, but it can be adapted given the circumstances.[13]

Meanwhile, the state's Office of Development and Agriculture in collaboration with the COM's affiliate, which controlled the chamber of labor (*cámara del trabajo*) in the port of Veracruz, began to send its labor inspectors out into the countryside to inspect and report on working conditions on haciendas and in factories. These paid state employees were committed COM organizers, intent on reporting violations of Aguilar's labor law. They simultaneously performed the role of spies, supervisors, and propagandists for the governor's new state apparatus. One Veracruz labor inspector, Mateo Rodríguez, circulated a flyer that explained that his immediate role was to help rural and urban workers improve their working conditions. However, he also explicitly stated his larger political objective: "the workers of the world" must know that they will be avenged not by Villa or Zapata but by the "triumphs of the glorious Constitutionalist revolution."[14]

Over the course of the next year and a half, Veracruz's military commanders, who were also serving as provisional governors, issued a series of decrees that established the functions of labor inspectors and the provisional municipal councils to define their decision-making authority in labor conflicts. Tripartite information-gathering committees were established at the factory level with representatives from labor and capital that were presided over by the state labor inspector. If these discussions failed, the case would be sent to the second level, a tripartite Junta Municipal de Conciliación (Municipal Conciliation Board) presided over by the labor inspector. In the final instance, a tripartite Municipal Arbitration Board overseen by the municipal president would issue a decision on the conflict that was binding on all parties.[15] The Constitutionalist governors, Aguilar, Agustín Millán, and Heriberto Jara Corona, had now laid the foundation for a state mechanism to resolve disputes between labor and capital at the municipal level, which gave the municipality independent authority in theory to oversee the resolution of labor disputes and implement its final decisions. These decrees would serve as the foundation for the Veracruz Labor Law of 1918. However, the Aguilarista industrial-labor system would probably never have been fully implemented without the active collaboration of another set of actors, the COM organizers.

The Casa and Gender

The COM was not founded until the Madero period, but its antecedents stretch back to the nineteenth century. Under the influence of Greek, Spanish, and Italian exiles, Mexican anarchists adopted an ideology based on the emancipation of the individual; the creation of a libertarian union between man and woman; self-management of artisan shops; and the elimination of the patriarchal family, church, state, and private property. While anarchists sought to organize at the workshop level, anarchosyndicalists advocated worker management in the industrial sector and the international unification of the workers of the world. In their minds, mobilization and syndicalization of women workers was one strategy to create a more just, classless society where gender equality would prevail. Putting into practice their beliefs on class conflict, working-class consciousness, education, and direct action, anarchosyndicalists had already organized both men and women in the tobacco, textile, garment, printing, and cigarette trades in Mexico City by the fall of 1914.[16]

Among COM goals were gender issues: the liberation of men, women, and children from all forms of exploitation, in particular the emancipation of women from any kind of oppression that had hindered their lives. Much like their anarchist predecessors, most COM members thought that women's oppression was caused by economic oppression of the capitalist system. They were far more interested in achieving the simultaneous liberation of women and men through the overthrow of the bourgeoisie. Women's liberation within the domestic sphere was of secondary importance and would occur only as a result of the elimination of private property.[17] This gender ideology prevailed among its members not only in Mexico City but also in Veracruz.

Central Veracruz had been a bastion of militant labor organizing from the 1890s. Under the leadership of Cuban anarchists, men and women in the tobacco industry had formed mixed and gender-segregated unions and struck for better working conditions and higher wages in San Andrés Tuxtla and Xalapa beginning in 1896.[18] In the strikes and riots that exploded in the Valley of Orizaba in 1906–7, textile workers of both genders influenced by anarchist and mutualist traditions protested side by side to obtain improved working conditions, higher wages, lower prices in the company stores, and the right to organize. When President Díaz sent in the army, the troops arrested men and women and shut down their labor organizations.[19] Once the revolution erupted, the port of Veracruz became one of the principal hotbeds of anarchist and anarchosyndicalist activity. The Confederación de los Sindicatos Obreros de la República Mexicana (CSORM, Confederation of Labor Unions of the Mexican Republic) was founded in early 1912, months before the COM. Once the COM shifted its strategies to organizing labor unions in the provinces as well as the capital, the CSORM became one of its principal affiliates. By late 1914, the CSORM's organizing activities in the port intensified after former members of the state's worker battalions returned to the city. In collaboration with foreign anarchists, they began actively mobilizing artisans, electrical workers, trolley car operators, and stevedores.[20]

While almost of all the CSORM and COM labor inspectors who operated in Veracruz were men, some of them showed a genuine sensitivity for gender equity. For example, Rafael Alcalde complained in his report to the governor that the U.S. company, the Arbuckle Brothers, was not even paying coffee sorters on their Coatepec finca the one-peso minimum rural wage required by state law. If they cleaned five to seven arrobas of the dirtiest grade of coffee in one day, they only earned between fifty and seventy centavos. As a result, the sorters were often forced to engage in other "shameful occupations." Alcalde then proceeded to give a rationale for why these women should receive the equivalent of the minimum rural wage: "They do not have the same strength of a man nor can their work be considered indispensable, but their tasks are just as important as the men's tasks. . . . There is no reason to believe that a man because he is stronger is capable of sorting more coffee."[21] The inspector's reasoning about the importance of coffee sorting might have been somewhat exaggerated, but his pledge to fight for equal rights for women workers is noteworthy. Whether his attitude was typical of other COM organizers is not certain, but his remarks reveal a determination to fight for pay equity so that women could support their families and not have to resort to prostitution. In short, when the CSORM's Propaganda Committee arrived in Córdoba to organize workers, it was ready to mobilize all the workshops regardless of gender.

Mobilizing Córdoba Coffee Sorters and Tobacco Workers

At six o'clock in the evening on January 26, 1915, Cayetano Sánchez, Agustín Arrazola, and Spanish anarchist Pedro Junco, members of the porteño Cámara del Trabajo's Propaganda Committee, opened a meeting in Córdoba attended by women coffee sorters and tobacco workers. Sánchez called on the "emancipated" men and women workers to organize themselves in order to achieve complete human progress. He asked them if they wanted to affiliate with the Veracruz chamber, and they yelled back "of course." This was the first step in the creation of the Sindicato de Escogedoras de Café y Obreras Tabaqueras (Union of Women Coffee Sorters and Tobacco Workers), which became the first Córdoba branch of the CSORM-controlled Veracruz chamber. The coffee sorters most probably represented the largest group of agroindustrial workers in town and, therefore, were one of the first groups targeted. Although this union seems to have been organized from the outside, its first elected officers were all women. Ana Herrera, who was chosen for its first secretary general, articulated the rationale for organizing a union: "Everyone is complaining because they earn so little and everything is so expensive."[22] Within weeks, the CSORM activists had also organized the male bricklayers, bakers, carpenters, mechanics, beer workers, and coffee and tobacco loaders and sackers.[23]

Ten days after the founding of the predominately female coffee-sorter and tobacco-worker union, a letter on small notepaper in the handwriting of a woman arrived at the town hall. In that letter, the union's officers set forth their economic and social demands in quite strident language: "This union . . . decided by unanimity to send the following message with the objective of informing you of the conditions under which the coffee and tobacco workers of this city will continue working." The terms included union recognition, the use of only unionized workers, the right of the union to supply additional workers, an eight-hour day, a one-and-a-half-hour break for the midday meal, a daily wage of 1.25 pesos, double pay for extra days, and the continued payment of trolley fare to the Arbuckle Brothers' plant outside of town. No worker could be unjustifiably fired without an investigation by the new Municipal Conciliation Board. They insisted on no work on Sundays, national holidays, and May 1. If the owners or their overseers violated any of these clauses, the union threatened to file a grievance with the appropriate authorities. Their petition closed with the anarchist motto, "*Unión y Emancipación.*"[24] These socioeconomic demands closely paralleled those of the men's organization, the Sindicato de Cargadores y Enfardeladores del Comercio de Café y Tabaco (Union of Loaders and Sackers of Coffee and Tobacco), which arrived at the town hall a month later. The major difference was that the loaders asked for a two-peso daily wage, almost double the women workers' demand.[25] CSORM leaders seem to have accepted the gendered division of work and a two-tiered wage system for manual labor. The underlying assumption still was that women's work was less important than men's work for the survival of the family.

The decision to seek union recognition and the right to a closed shop was very radical for the time. Their demand for a daily wage in an occupation where conventionally the form of payment was a piece-rate wage likewise represented a dramatic departure from the prerevolutionary norm. Perhaps the strong Cuban anarchist tradition among tobacco-worker organizations of San Andrés Tuxtla had served as an inspiration for some of these workers. In Córdoba it was not unusual at all for women to work in both tobacco and coffee plants.[26] In any case, the formation of the Córdoba women's union definitely demonstrated the CSORM's commitment not only to organize seasonal women workers but also to seek essentially equal workers' rights for their women and men followers.

The union's letters to the JCCA contained numerous references to economic necessity and the inability of the workers to earn a living wage in times of revolutionary upheaval. As mothers, wives, and sisters, they were concerned with the price of food and clothing so as to be able to preserve the family. Women often participated in collective action in cases of human need or for defense of the household. These issues are often categorized as consumption issues, which are closely tied to family and community survival.[27] Since the responsibility for buying food and household items fell on the shoulders of women, men were less likely to be concerned with the prices of primary necessities in their demands. In response to the sorters' demands, the local authorities couched their arguments in proworker language that included women workers. In contrast, foreign companies came to the table with a different set of priorities and sought to represent the women's unions in a disparaging way. More often than not, they framed their arguments in terms of company profitability.

When the mayor did not attend to the sorters' petition immediately, the union resorted to direct collective action, which was the most common anarchosyndicalist strategy. They asked for and received permission from the town council to hold a public meeting in the main square, where the town hall was located. When public protest did not convince the coffee- and tobacco-company owners of the seriousness of their demands, the women went out on strike in the first week of February 1915, at the height of the coffee-export season. Within two days, the two U.S. firms, the Arbuckle Brothers and Hard and Rand; the British inheritors of the Bryan E. Tomblin beneficio;

and the tobacco firms had caved to all the union's demands. The smaller Spanish and Mexican casas were not included in this contract for
some reason. In sum, the firms consented to recognize the union and
to hire only its members between the ages of thirteen and fifty. In return, the union agreed that the owners had the right to hire whom-
ever they wanted as long as they were union members. The owners
accepted an eight-hour day as long as they could set the work schedule. All of the workers' wage demands were met, as was their request
to designate Sundays, national holidays, and May 1 as days of rest.
Shortly thereafter, the Municipal Conciliation and Arbitration Boards
approved Córdoba's first agreement.[28] This agreement between the
beneficio owners and their workers was probably the earliest collective agreement or contract for women workers, much less seasonal
workers, in the republic. Upon learning of the simultaneous resolution of the strikes in Córdoba by the female-dominated coffee sorters
and tobacco workers and by the male urban transit workers, the governor sent a telegram effusively congratulating the mayor "for the triumph of the working class."[29] The governor made no distinction between the two unions, even though the women's union was comprised
of seasonal women workers.

Why did the companies capitulate so rapidly? At least two reasons
might explain this astonishing result: the state's prolabor policy and
the timing of the strike. CSORM-organized unions were in a particularly strong position at this moment because the struggling Constitutionalists desperately needed their support. Veracruz's minister of
internal affairs had sent a telegram to the mayor during the strike in
which he had made clear that the state would not welcome a disruption of the strike by the owners. In other words, local authorities
would not send troops to support the companies as it had done in
the past, and in so doing, they strengthened the position of the striking workers.[30] The other explanation hinges on the fact that the sorters struck at the height of the coffee preparation season, when the
beneficios were operating day and night at least six days a week. The
exporters were in an extremely precarious financial position. They

could not sack their coffee for shipment to the port of Veracruz unless the coffee was sorted. If they could not make the scheduled departures of the steamships to New Orleans and New York to fulfill the contract obligations of their overseas buyers, they faced substantial losses in revenues as well as the threat of losing future contracts.

The same rapid resolution of women workers' demands also occurred in Orizaba. After the COM activists from Mexico City descended in early March, the "mundialista" (COM adherent of world revolution) spring continued. In April they organized two hundred seamstresses and called a strike in La Suiza, where army uniforms were being made, which was supported by twelve other seamstress workshops. In this case, the governor, the local military commander, and the Carrancista head of the Labor Department all intervened to pressure the owners to sign an agreement as quickly as possible and raise their wages.[31] The newly formed escogedora union also negotiated successfully a collective agreement. These rapid settlements with women's unions suggest that the Carranza state was desperately seeking to stymy the intense mundialista campaign and keep the Veracruz economy functioning. The gender of the striking workers was immaterial. In short, women unions were vital elements of a restless labor movement that had to be kept under control. This had not been the case a few years earlier nor would it be a few years later.

After winning its contract in February, the Córdoba sorter union continued to collaborate with the CSORM in campaigns that attacked the local merchants for extorting consumers and chastised the Catholic Church for spreading religious fanaticism. They organized food cooperatives with other unions to fight the exorbitant prices charged by merchants. Ana Herrera played an active role on the committee organizing these demonstrations. She also took to the streets to support the bakers in their demands for higher pay and no night work. Armed with a pistol, she even accompanied bakers to destroy their ovens. In March all the recently organized Córdoba unions asked the governor to take possession of five churches and to turn them over to the CSORM for the "progress of the working class." Within two weeks the Constitutionalist troops had occupied all five churches. San Sebastián, which was around the corner from La Garza beneficio, was probably where coffee sorters held their meetings.[32] Union meetings in churches must have seemed quite unusual for former rural folk, or for that matter for women, but the labor organizers must have convinced the women and men workers that such places should not be reserved only for the elites.

A year later the union petitioned again for further wage adjustment because of "the pressing circumstances in which the women workers find themselves at the moment, due to the depreciation in the value of the Constitutionalist paper money." This depreciation stemmed from the large quantities of worthless paper money that had begun circulating. The two pesos that every worker now earned did not suffice to pay for "the articles of primary necessity, which [were] being sold at such high prices."[33] The women workers related their plight directly to the reality of everyday experiences. Thus the women's discourse seems linked to the survival of the household. In other words, women's union leaders were thinking less in terms of a subsistence peasant household economy and more in terms of an urban household economy, where the family had to adjust its consuming and spending habits to the spiraling market prices.[34] In Mexico City, Lear also argues that women workers were more likely than men workers in 1915–16 to organize and become involved in collective action around the defense of home and community rather than working conditions. The women workers were at the forefront of the food riots and general strike of July–August 1916, when the demand for payment in gold was uppermost in their demands.[35]

In November the coffee-sorter and tobacco-worker union petitioned provisional governor Jara for their wages to be paid in hard currency and for the creation of factory-level information-gathering committees called for in the 1914 labor law. Upon the advice of their advisors, the union had seized the opportunity to reopen the wage issue and seek the assistance of the new state institutions to fight for their rights in the midst of economic chaos, just as other Veracruz workers were doing. Even the Huatusco coffee sorters and harvesters formed a union under the guidance of anarchosyndicalist labor inspectors to demand higher wages.[36] Although the Córdoba coffee exporters, just like the owners of the textile factories in the Valley of Orizaba, never agreed to pay their workers in silver or gold, this did not signify that the sorters' union had given up airing their grievances. The union formed a committee composed of five women and an advisor to represent them before a Municipal Arbitration Board hearing.[37]

Women workers had become empowered by social revolution. They had crossed a number of spatial, institutional, and cultural boundaries, as they joined unions, participated in public meetings and strikes, sent repeated demands to their bosses and state agencies, and collaborated with other unions to confront exploitive businessmen and to win their economic rights.

Raising the Ante in Xalapa

The COM organizers arrived in Xalapa as peace was returning to the state in the fall of 1915. They had already organized the textile workers, but now their sights were focused on the bakers, tobacco workers, and coffee sorters. Under the watchful eye of Mateo Rodríguez, the Sindicato de Escogedoras de Café (Union of Women Coffee Sorters) was formed. Within days the union, in collaboration with some women matchmaker workers, presented its demands to the inspector and the U.S. Pan Mexican Coffee Company, couching their plea in terms of humility by asking for help for this "humble working women's union." They linked their economic demands to consumption issues: "The articles of primary necessity are too expensive, and the clothing that covers us is too costly." They asked for Rodríguez's help because they were fearful that the U.S. company would not listen to them: "We understand that they will not give us the time of day, and if they do not respond, we will find ourselves forced to suspend our labors." Their petition began by complaining about the workers' inability to support a family on their pitiful earnings, which suggests once again that many sorters were the primary wage earners: "Given the circumstances that the women workers are experiencing, due to the scarcity of articles of primary necessity as well as the low salaries, which are insufficient for us to survive on, this union, a lover of civilization and progress, is making the following demands, with the hope that within twenty-four hours of receipt [of this petition] you will name a committee to begin negotiations."[38]

The union's proposals, which had been approved by the porteño Cámara and Aguilar's Department of Development and Agriculture, were strikingly similar to those made by their Córdoba compañeras six months earlier, although they demanded even higher wages. They asked for union recognition, the hiring of only union workers, national holidays and Sundays off from work, and an eight-hour workday. In particular, they demanded that a three-peso daily wage replace the piece-rate system. Like the Córdoba sorters, they wanted to abolish the exploitative practice of calculating wages on the basis of the amount of coffee cleaned because it penalized a worker when the coffee was very dirty. There are several possible explanations why the union's demands were more strident and called for higher wages than in Córdoba. Inflation had reached 2,000 percent for some products by the end of 1915, which particularly affected low-income workers. What is more, the sorters were quite possibly in a stronger position in Xalapa because other obreras working in the match, brush, and tobacco industries were already organized.[39] Finally, their demands had already been approved by the Aguilarista state.

Their last demand was to be paid one hour before they left the workshops on Saturdays "to avoid being out on the streets at night." The issue of street safety introduces a new women's issue concerning access to public spaces. In the countryside, women's social space centered around the home, family plot, and church, while men occupied and dominated public spaces, primarily through control over family resources and enforcement of cultural norms. Once women began to leave the house to work as salaried wage earners, private and public spaces became increasingly blurred. One of these new spaces was the street, which women used to go back and forth to work. Coffee sorters still felt threatened on the streets of Xalapa when they took their weekly pay home each Saturday, and they believed that the owners could do something to guarantee them greater personal safety if they paid them earlier in the day. Thus the workplace was changing these women's perspective toward their identity both as women and as workers, for now they felt comfortable demanding free and safe access to the streets.

The company's response to these demands was to try to bluff the union into backing down from its demands. Its representative informed the union that sorting operations would be moving back to their New York City headquarters at the beginning of the next season, where the sorting would be done by American workers in the company's own workshops. Therefore, there was no need for the company to recognize the union or to take heed of its other demands.[40] Upon being informed by the labor inspector that the company was threatening to fire all the coffee sorters in the next season, Governor Aguilar and his secretary general intervened directly in support of the women workers. To the labor inspector, Aguilar's subordinate wrote, "This government is disposed to use its influence so that the cleaning of coffee performed by the Xalapa workers is not taken away from them." He continued the next day, "It would be convenient if the quotas are fixed so no skilled woman worker earns less than 2.50 pesos a day."[41] The state wanted not only to ensure that the coffee sorters would not lose their jobs but also to secure a daily wage for them equal to the rural minimum wage. This stance by the state authorities represents strong support for the seasonal obreras' plight, which was highly unusual.

Pan Mexican was forced to back down for at least two reasons. The one hundred or so coffee sorters had refused to go to work, bringing most operations in the beneficio to a standstill at the start of the preparation season. This can be surmised from a second letter sent by the company's manager to provisional governor Millán. Without acknowledging that he had suspended operations, the manager suggested that the "work stoppage" had hurt the one hundred women workers and their families more than the company itself. The suffering of the workers was a more important concern than the loss of profits for Pan Mexican. For this reason, he wanted to arrange a satisfactory solution to this conflict quickly. He made it clear, however, that the company could not afford to pay a daily wage. It was not economically feasible given the fact that not all workers worked at the same rate.[42] The other reason the company caved in was that Aguilar, who was not in the state at this moment, had very probably instructed the provisional governor, who was in Xalapa and was most likely negotiating with both parties, to intervene directly in the dispute on the side of the workers.

The agreement that was signed six weeks later, on December 15, between the coffee sorters and the company was an obvious triumph for the workers, for they won almost all their major demands. The company recognized the union and agreed to hire only union workers. However, it stood firm against shifting from a piece-rate system to a daily wage. Over the course of the negotiations, the owners had twice increased the piece-rate for cleaning two arrobas of medium-grade, number-four coffee beans from the old rate of fourteen centavos to forty and then to fifty centavos. At this rate, if a woman sorted ten arrobas a day, she could earn 2.50 pesos, which was the wage that the state authorities had wanted in the first place. Sorters would receive an additional 2.50 pesos for each two arrobas of waste they separated out. The receivers and weighers had their daily wage increased from 1.25 to 2 pesos.

As a COM militant, Rodríguez was determined to use this precedent-setting agreement to serve as a model for the other foreign Xalapa coffee agribusinesses. He proceeded to invite the two other firms, which were owned by Italians, to enter into the negotiations with their sorters. In the end, they agreed to join Pan Mexican in signing the collective agreement with the union.[43] With the active collaboration of their COM comrades as well as with state authorities, women sorters won major wage increases, union recognition, and an eight-hour day from all three foreign-owned firms. In the face of revolutionary chaos and tremendously unstable socioeconomic conditions, women had organized themselves and won significant economic concessions from powerful foreign companies.

These two case studies illustrate what Stephanie Smith has also found in the Yucatán: "Women were not simply pawns of the revolutionary state," for these "everyday women" were able to enter into complex negotiations with their bosses and the revolutionary state to win their demands.[44] The weak, embryonic Aguilarista state was willing for very pragmatic reasons to support women and men workers who were protesting. State authorities were eager to keep the coffee-export industry in operation. Meanwhile, foreign-owned companies lost ground during these revolutionary times. They faced a rising militancy among their female-dominated workforce; anarchosyndicalist collective action; and a state that, for the time being, was willing to intervene actively on the side of labor.

Pushing the Beneficiadores to the Limit

To what length would the women sorters and their COM advisors go in their demands to secure their socioeconomic well-being? With its 35,000 inhabitants, the municipality of Orizaba had a much stronger working-class tradition than the other two smaller towns. Textile workers had been actively organizing and making labor demands in the Valley of Orizaba long before the outbreak of the revolution.[45] After the promulgation of the 1918 Labor Code, union officials were eager to bring seasonal workers under its provisions. The Orizaba case demonstrates just how far trade-union activists would push their demands for seasonal women workers.

The Sindicato de Desmanchadoras de Café de Orizaba (Orizaba Union of Coffee Sorters) had been organized shortly after the Córdoba one in May 1915 and had also gone on strike that spring. The sorters were able to win rapid union recognition and a 65 percent wage increase.[46] The new state labor law of January 14, 1918, granted new workers' rights, but they had to be implemented. Orizaba was the obvious town to start testing them. Its 206 articles spelled out new areas of labor law that were so progressive that they became models for other states. The law codified and systematized all the previous state decrees and established the tripartite Junta Central de Conciliación y Arbitraje (JCCA, State Board of Conciliation and Arbitration), which took authority away from the municipal boards to arbitrate industrial-labor conflicts. The law also guaranteed workers the right to organize unions, a "collective" contract, an eight-hour day, sick pay, compensation for being fired for joining a union, and profit sharing. It called for equal pay for equal work (Article 93), provided maternity leave with half pay (Article 91), and protected women from performing night labor or dangerous work. In the following years, labor organizers would struggle to win owner compliance of all these provisions.[47] The sorter case tested whether seasonal workers under contract could demand the same rights as permanent full-time workers, although they were not specifically covered under the law.

On March 19, 1918, the textile leader Pedro Sosa, of the Federación Sindicalista de Obreros y Campesinos de la Región de Orizaba (FSOCO, Federation of Worker and Peasant Unions of the Orizaba Region), wrote a letter of complaint to the municipal president on behalf of the coffee sorters working on the Lemaistre Brothers' coffee finca. At this juncture, the anarchosyndicalist-dominated FSOCO controlled almost all rural and urban unions in the entire Orizaba region.[48] The Lemaistres did not abide by the contract they had signed a month earlier with the women, the plaintiff contended. In early March the sorters and the Lemaistres had negotiated an agreement, with the principal municipal judicial officer (*primer síndico*) serving as mediator. The firm had agreed to pay the women 1.25 centavos per kilo of cleaned coffee. Sosa claimed that they were now only paying them .77 centavos. The federation threatened that if the firm did not live up to its contract, the women would "take to the streets" to uphold Articles 72 and 99 of the recently issued state labor law.[49]

The response to this complaint is missing from the records, but the sorters did enter into a short-term contract with the Lemaistre Brothers on May 28 to sort three hundred quintals of coffee. The owners agreed to pay the workers according to the type of coffee they sorted. They would pay 1 centavo per kilo for cleaning type A coffee, 1.5 centavos for type B, 2 centavos for type C, and so on. This piece-rate pay scale remunerated the workers more for sorting the expensive grades of coffee than under the older system, which was based simply on weight. The company won an important concession, however. Every worker would have to meet a daily quota. The contract also called for an eight-hour workday running from seven thirty in the morning until five o'clock in the afternoon with a one-and-a-half-hour break for the midday meal.[50] The Orizaba beneficiadores never felt compelled by union pressures, unlike the Córdoba owners, to abandon the piece-rate system for a daily wage.

A little over one month later, the Lemaistre Brothers notified the sorters at the end of the week that they would be laid off in two days. The secretary general of the union, Trinidad Hernández, immediately protested to the municipal president. She wrote that the workers had been "inopportunely suspended" from their work without the proper period of notification in violation of the new labor law. "We do not feel that it is just that we have been dismissed today in a brusque manner after we have worked so honestly. All of us have four to seven years of service working on this coffee finca, and for this reason we think it is only right that the owners pay us just compensation."[51] Most probably the Lemaistres had been hiring female members of their resident peon or sharecropper families to work as sorters each year. These women workers were more than likely hired under contract every November and then laid off in February or March. In this particular year, they had been rehired in May under a special, short-term contract. The women were now claiming that they had worked continuously at the dry beneficio for many years.

In accordance with the 1918 law, the Municipal Conciliation Board was convened to mediate the dispute. The women chose two officers of the FSOCO, Ernesto de la Fuente and Pedro Sosa, to represent them in the grievance process. At the opening hearing, the Lemaistre representative contended that the suspension of the in-house work had occurred because there was no more coffee to sort, so the contract was no longer in effect. De la Fuente agreed this was in fact correct, but he argued that the workers had worked for many years for the finca owners and that the owners had laid them off without giving them the required twenty-one day notification. According to Article 33, paragraph 7, workers who had worked for one year for an employer were entitled to a gratification in the form of a share of the profits or the equivalent of one month's salary. Since they had worked approximately six months, they should have at least received fifteen days' salary. The Lemaistres' advocate refused to accept this demand and countered that the company had fulfilled its obligations under the short-term contract. What is more, he added, since the law had only come into effect on January 18, the workers had worked less than a year under its provisions. Because the dispute remained unresolved at the local level, it was forwarded to the newly created JCCA located in Córdoba.[52]

In the opening arguments presented to the state board, de la Fuente reduced his demands for financial compensation for the sorters. While the Lemaistre Brothers had clearly violated the law, he argued, it would be asking too much for the owners to pay one month's compensation to seasonal workers. However, the company should at least provide these women with enough compensation so they could "feed themselves." He asked instead for seventy-five pesos for travel expenses, so each worker could move to another location to find work as stipulated in Article 33. When the company refused to accept this demand, the case was sent to arbitration.[53]

The owners' lawyers decided to change their strategy this time and present an antiunion position. They presented the union as a troublesome organization that disrupted the smooth operations of their beneficio. Since the plant had opened its doors, the owners argued, the coffee sorters had given them constant difficulties. They contended that the union had approached the local authorities in the first place to "intervene" in the drawing up of the contract. The May contract had been signed between the two parties to complete a specified task:

the sorting of three hundred quintals of coffee. The work was completed, and all the terms of the contract had been met. The company argued that the workers had only worked a little over one month under this contract, and it requested the workers drop these unwarranted demands.[54]

The chief of the Department of Labor, who chaired the JCCA, handed down the final decision in favor of the Lemaistres. The state ruled that the workers had not been "inopportunely suspended without the required notification period." The workers were demanding that Article 33, which stipulated full-time workers should receive one month's compensation after completion of one year's work, be enforced. Even though the women had worked a number of years for the Lemaistres, the workers had not been employed under this short-term contract for an entire year. Therefore, the union held an untenable position, for the owners had fulfilled their part of the contract. To make the case not appear a complete defeat for the union, the Labor Department recommended that the company give each woman a letter of recommendation to help her find work in "other states" as stipulated in the law. This minor concession simply recognized the precarious condition of seasonal laborers in the agroindustry. The state board refused to treat the sorters as permanent residents because they were working under a short-term contract and therefore were not eligible for comparable employment as displaced workers under the law.[55]

This particular case holds little in common with the other hundred-odd disputes brought before the JCCA during 1918. It appears to be one of the only ones initiated by a women's union, or for that matter by seasonal workers, in that year.[56] However, its very uniqueness makes it ideal for gaining insight into the gender and class contradictions in the COM and the state's strategies. What does this case demonstrate about the conflict between gender and class issues within trade-union leadership as the labor movement and revolutionary state became more institutionalized? Why would the male activists of the FSOCO take up the seemingly hopeless case of these women seasonal workers?

The coffee sorters most probably chose two men to represent them because of union politics and hierarchy. They felt that experienced FSOCO leaders were familiar with the legal procedures and could present their case in a more convincing manner. The Orizaba leaders might have decided to press this case before the Veracruz conciliation and arbitration boards to test how broadly state authorities would extend the provisions of Article 33. Were these peasant-worker women simply the "straw women" to be sacrificed for the future of trade unionism? In other words, were gender issues sacrificed for a male working-class agenda? Given this highly unusual demand, it is entirely possible. Labor activists wanted to test the limits of Article 33 in a laboratory where an emerging revolutionary state was willing to negotiate and bargain with mobilized working-class groups.[57]

Coffee-worker mobilization seems to have subsided after 1918, or all records after 1919 are missing. It is not known whether their unions were taken over by the Confederación Regional de Obreros Mexicanos (CROM, Mexican Regional Workers Confederation) soon after it was founded in 1918. The CROM's principal leader, Luis Morones, developed strong ties with Alvaro Obregón and was more willing to cooperate with the state than the anarchosyndicalists. In the meantime, militant petroleum workers, port workers, and textile workers emerged as more-serious threats to Veracruz industrialists. A second window of opportunity for escogedoras did not present itself until the 1920s, when two progressive governors, Adalberto Tejeda Olivares and Heriberto Jara Corona, took up the cause of the workers.

Veracruz's Postrevolutionary Caudillos and Organized Labor

When Colonel Tejeda assumed the governorship of Veracruz in the final days of 1920, observers assumed that he would continue to follow his activist agrarian policies, but few predicted that he would become almost inadvertently an advocate of the workers and a key player in the struggle for workers' rights. His position toward organized labor has most frequently been characterized from a corporatist perspective, for he often served as a mediator or intermediary between the national leadership and the workers, whom he manipulated from above for his own political purposes. His seeming disinterest in labor affairs was primarily attributed to his rural upbringing and a real passion for resolving agrarian problems. His handling of labor disputes was characterized most frequently as a case-by-case approach. Therefore, some scholars have argued his primary contribution was simply to promote workers' rights by sponsoring and passing legislation to implement the radical provisions of the 1918 labor law.[58] More recently it has been suggested that the political relationship between Tejeda and organized labor was not so hegemonic as originally envisioned and that he was often pressured from below to take action. The militant labor protests, strikes, and demonstrations that rocked the port of Veracruz and Orizaba in particular forced him to ally himself with organized labor to sponsor legislation and to intervene on the side of labor during fierce labor conflict.[59] Both of these interpretations contain elements of truth.

Tejeda had no background as a labor leader, unlike Heriberto Jara. Jara had participated in the Orizaba riots of 1906 and issued a number of labor decrees as provisional governor of Mexico City and then Veracruz. However, the historic militancy and autonomy of the state's labor movement made it difficult for both governors to exercise much influence over these disparate unruly movements that caused disruption of operations in the northern Huasteca oilfields, the central cities of Orizaba and Veracruz, and southern Minatitlán oilfields.[60] In 1923 in the port of Veracruz, the labor movement became hopelessly divided between three distinct ideological factions, each following varying strategies: anarchosyndicalism, CROM reformism, and a libertarian communism. Unable and perhaps unwilling to become involved in trade-union politics, Tejeda preferred to collaborate closely with two emerging, progressive labor politicians: Rafael García Auly and Martín Torres. The stevedore García emerged as the leader of the Liga de Trabajadores de la Zona Maritima (League of Maritime Workers) in the port, while Torres, a textile worker, would serve for many years as secretary general of the Confederación Sindicalista de Obreros y Campesinos de la Región de Orizaba (CSOCO, Confederation of Workers and Peasants of the Orizaba Region), which was allied with the CROM. Both won election as mayor in their respective urban strongholds in the early 1920s. Meanwhile, Tejeda increasingly distanced himself from Luis Morones, the national leader of the CROM. He sharply disagreed with the latter's willingness to make concessions to industry and to collaborate with Presidents Obregón and Plutarco E. Calles.[61]

Tejeda had to face numerous violent strikes, inter- and intraunion conflicts, and urban demonstrations throughout 1922 and 1923.[62] While he almost always supported the workers' cause, whether they were men or women, he was forced, in many cases, to intervene as a mediator between labor and industry to reach negotiated settlements and, at times, to arrest provocateurs to end public violence. The tenant movement was one occasion that really tested his skill as a negotiator and as an upholder of public order. Tejeda's inability to exercise any measurable control over the tenant movement or to challenge the CROM's grip over the textile unions in Orizaba might explain in part his decision to shift his attention to the organization of the Veracruz Peasant League in collaboration with former tenant leaders in early 1923.[63]

During Tejeda's first administration (1920–24), organized labor orchestrated massive work stoppages to push industry to comply with the most progressive provisions of Article 123 of the 1917 Constitution and the Veracruz Labor Law of 1918. His early support of organized labor is illustrated by his decision in his first weeks in office to send the draft of the Ley de Participacion de Utilidades (Law of Profit Sharing) to the state legislature. It called for companies to share 10 percent of their profits with its workers. But industrialists and merchants immediately blocked the governor's efforts by appealing directly to President Obregón and mobilizing the state's chamber of commerce (cámara del comercio) on their behalf. The bill was never passed. He was more successful in winning passage of the Ley de Enfermedades Profesionales y No Profesionales (Law on Work-Related and Nonwork-

Related Illnesses) in 1923. In this case, the president grudgingly accepted Tejeda's scaled-back version of the bill in order to retain his critical worker support in the Valley of Orizaba. Thus, Tejeda's legislative endeavors during his first term in office were only partially successful due to the continued strength of the business community and his unwillingness to anger his patron, President Obregón.[64] Another important step he took was to create a Department of Labor and issue a regulation on the duties of state labor inspectors.[65]

Neither Tejeda nor his successor, Heriberto Jara, showed any particular inclination to improve the status of the obrera, although they both were proponents of equal rights for women. Rather, they strove to create a proworker environment to encourage widespread labor mobilization for all working women and men. The postrevolutionary governors—Tomás Garrido Canabal, Francisco Múgica, Lázaro Cárdenas, Felipe Carrillo Puerto, Guadalupe Zuno Hernández, and Emilio Portes Gil—were far more concerned with the mobilization of rural and urban women to create a large popular base before they formed their own political parties.[66] These regional caudillos supported women's leagues (ligas femeninas), women's unions, and auxiliary branches of their state peasant leagues and labor confederations in order to integrate women into the body politic through their antialcohol and anticlerical campaigns. However, neither Tejeda nor Jara chose to follow this strategy in the 1920s.

In the meantime, Veracruz anarchosyndicalists and libertarian communists continued to take up the cause of the obrera. Herón Proal and Úrsulo Galván, who were both members of the Antorcha Libertaria (Libertarian Torch), collaborated with the leaders of the Sindicato de Obreras Molineras de Nixtamal (Union of Tortilla Mill Workers) in the port after they were fired for their organizing efforts in 1919. Three years later these two leaders became even more involved in the organization of the Sindicato Revolucionario de Inquilinos (Revolutionary Union of Tenants). When Proal called for tenants to take their anger into the streets, irate prostitutes were the first to take up the challenge. One contemporary sympathizer of the renters' strike characterized it as the "rebellion of the women."[67] Although Proal did not give women leadership roles in the union, except for his partner, he encouraged their active participation.[68] By June 1922 the tenants' strike had escalated into a general strike supported by most labor organizations throughout the port. Governor Tejeda sought to resolve the dispute by drawing up the new Ley de Inquilinato (Tenancy Law) to restore rents to their 1910 levels with an additional 10 percent to cover inflation. However, his legalistic approach failed, primarily because internecine quarrels broke out within the union's leadership. He reluctantly acquiesced to Obregon's demand that federal troops intervene to stamp out the violence. The arrest of its major leaders, including ninety male and fifty female members, quelled the shedding of any more blood.[69]

Heriberto Jara's short and unfortunately tempestuous gubernatorial administration did little to further the cause of the obrera directly, although he did continue to uphold Tejeda's prolabor policies. Most importantly, Jara championed the creation of autonomous trade unions that sought to challenge the politically opportunistic policies of the CROM's national leadership.[70] During Jara's administration, the CROM's local Orizaba branch initiated its own well-organized campaign to mobilize Córdoba's workers, including the coffee sorters.

Coffee Sorters Reorganize

The refounding of Córdoba's coffee-sorter union in February 1925 occurred against the backdrop of a vibrant grassroots mobilization carried out by a local tenant movement, a militant local baker union, and the CSOCO's concerted campaign to mobilize the largest contingent of agroindustrial workers in the town. The smaller and weaker Xalapa and Coatepec sorter unions followed slightly different trajectories due to local labor politics.

In early 1922 the tailor Gonzalo Hernández Rojas and other Córdoba labor activists traveled to Veracruz to consult with Proal, Galván, and Manuel Almanza about the possibility of organizing disgruntled tenants against the Spaniard landlords, who owned most of the tenement housing (*patios de vecindad*), dwellings where worker families would rent out rooms surrounding a central patio. In April, tailors, bakers, office workers, tobacco workers, peasants, street vendors, and coffee sorters began meeting to protest Córdoba's high rents. Coffee sorters became involved because some landlords had entered into agreements with the Arbuckle Brothers to rent out rooms to their workers. Two future sorter union leaders, Margarita Bolloa and Virginia Sánchez, rented rooms adjacent to the beneficios, and they actively participated in this protest movement. When police tried to block a public meeting in Madero Park next to the major beneficios, the protesters refused to be intimidated and retreated to a barbershop to organize their own Union of Tenants. Adopting the red and black banner and slogans of the port's movement, they organized at least twenty-three patios and convinced tenants to stop paying rent. The union renamed their patios with revolutionary names, took landlords to court, strung up strike banners, and organized frequent outside demonstrations. Events even turned violent when some Spaniards began shooting at demonstrators from the rooftops of their shops. Landlords, who had made housing arrangements with the Arbuckles, even asked the company to represent them in court to fight the tenant's demands for lower rents.[71]

In the following year, the CROM's Orizaba branch sent organizers to Córdoba to unionize tailors, office workers, shoemakers, and rural unions as part of a systematic campaign to form the regional confederation, the CSOCO.[72] The Cromistas did not concern themselves with organizing the escogedoras at this time. But two years later in 1925 under the guidance of former tenant leaders—Bolloa, Sánchez, Hernández, Leopardo Z. Burgos, and Miguel Velasco Muñoz, the baker and future Communist Party leader—the Sindicato de Desmanchadoras de Café (SDC, Union of Coffee Sorters) was constituted. Within months of the refounding of this sorter union, it had ninety members, and it surpassed all Córdoba unions in size except for that of the bakers. The sorters elected Margarita Bulloa as their first secretary general. Rather than adopt the CROM motto, the SDC chose that of the feminist anarchosyndicalists, "Por los derechos de la mujer," following in the footsteps of the porteño tortilla makers. Months later the sorters participated with other newly organized Córdoba unions in the founding of the Federación de Sindicatos de Obreros y Campesinos de la Región de Córdoba (FSOCC, Federation of Worker and Peasant Unions of the Córdoba Region).[73] The SDC was not the first coffee-sorter union to reorganize in Central Veracruz, for CROM activists had already reorganized Xalapa sorters in José Tanos's plant in 1922. However, the SDC became the largest and most powerful sorter union in Mexico.[74]

As soon as the harvest began in the fall of 1926, the SDC entered into negotiations with the beneficiadores to obtain its first collective contract in many years. The owners followed a well-known strategy to block the union by conspiring to split it in two, offering positions to the nonunionized temporary sorters (*libres*). This conflict took on some of the trappings of the cultural wars playing out at the national level during the Cristero Rebellion (1926–29). The local chamber of commerce backed up the plant owners in their union-busting campaign, writing to the president and claiming that the SDC did not have the required twenty members to form a union or to sign a contract.[75] In spite of the obstructionism on the part of the plant owners and the business community, it won its first collective contract in late November 1926 with the two U.S. coffee importers, the Arbuckle Brothers and Hard and Rand.[76] Why the first legal collective contracts were signed with the foreign firms rather than with the Spanish beneficiadores is not entirely clear, but the Spaniards had put up stiff resistance to the SDC's demands for a contract and continued to hire nonunion workers. The SDC retaliated by expelling these "traitors" from the plants in accordance with their closed-shop policy. The libres then appealed to President Plutarco Calles and complained about their loss of employment. Other proindustry actors began to intervene on their behalf. The municipal president, representatives of the federal government, and state labor inspectors tried, to no avail, to dissuade the SDC from insisting on a closed shop.

The union leaders proceeded to go on the offensive to blacken the name of the owners by accusing them of financing the celebration of the Virgin of Guadalupe in the workshops, which violated the new anticlerical ordinances that forbade religious ceremonies in public spaces. In their letters to the government officials—including Tejeda, who was now Calles's minister of internal affairs—Virginia Sánchez and Luz Vera accused the owners of manipulating the twenty-eight libres, who represented only a fraction of the five hundred–member union, in an attempt to divide the organization. They claimed that these libres had been encouraged to yell "*Viva Cristo Rey*" ("Long live Jesus Christ") in the workshop and that they had been forced to accept a lower piece rate: twenty-five centavos per kilo of waste instead of the agreed upon thirty-five centavos. Vera also accused the military of interfering in the conflict by pressuring the SDC to accept the libres back into the workshops. All these obstructionist tactics by outside forces failed to mollify the CSOCO and Córdoba's militant unionists, who forced the Spanish and Mexican exporters to finally sign a new collective contract in October 1927.[77]

The CROM displayed relatively little interest in organizing men workers in the coffee agroindustry until the Federal Labor Law of 1931 required employers to sign collective contracts with all their workers, regardless of whether they were unionized or not. What is more, it had less incentive to unionize the men because only thirty men worked in the largest beneficios. When the CSOCO finally unionized the men, it brought together loaders, truck drivers, sackers, machinists, and other workers in several industries into the Sindicato Industrial de Trabajadores de Café, Tabaco, Maderas, Destiladores de Aguardiente y Comercio del Distrito de Córdoba (SITCTAC, Industrial Union of Coffee, Tobacco, Wood, Sugarcane Distillery, and Commercial Workers of Córdoba). Its multi-industry membership meant it never became a strong union. Membership fluctuated between two hundred and three hundred workers during the 1930s. It signed its first collective contract with the five largest Spanish companies and the two U.S. companies in 1931.[78]

The Coatepec sorters were the last of the three women's coffee unions to organize in the 1920s. Communist and anarchosyndicalist textile workers affiliated with the PCM and the Confederación General de Trabajadores (CGT, General Confederation of Workers) assisted the Coatepec sorters in their efforts. In 1926 the sorters had complained to Arbuckle Brothers that the piece-rate of ten centavos per arroba of cleaned coffee was not a living wage. The company tried to buy the women off by raising the piece-rate and by forming a company union (*sindicato blanco*), but the sorters refused to cave in. For three years the sorters struggled to organize themselves without much success. They faced an unsupportive community and a local clergy who, from their pulpits, called them Bolsheviks and dark she-goats and who threatened to excommunicate them if they joined the union. Finally, in 1929 the San Bruno and La Purissima textile workers helped them to form the Sindicato de Obreras Desmanchadoras del Café de Coatepec: "Union Libertadora" (SODCC, Coffee-Sorter Union of Coatepec, "Liberating Union"). As in the case of Córdoba, the Coatepec men workers did not unionize until 1931. In the same year, both unions signed separate contracts with the three major coffee firms: the Arbuckle Brothers, Carlos Polanco, and Guillermo Boesch. The escogedora contract guaranteed a certain number of permanent positions and an eight-hour day and stipulated the piece-rate wage.[79] By the end of the 1920s Veracruz sorters had unionized in Córdoba, Xalapa, and Coatepec. Unfortunately, their struggle to maintain some form of autonomy within the labor movement would become almost as daunting a challenge as gaining union recognition.

As Morones's power ebbed in the Federal District after his alleged involvement in the assassination of president-elect Obregón in 1928, Orizaba's regional confederation began to eschew the CROM's centralizing and hierarchical tendencies and expand its own regional power base. The CSOCO's strategy shift created fresh problems for Córdoba coffee sorters. The CSOCO had never really wholeheartedly embraced the right of women to work. In Orizaba's newspaper, *Pro-Paria*, articles on feminism in the 1920s counseled obreras to be "la madre Mexicana" and to concentrate on their education to improve their own status and prepare themselves for raising children.[80] Instead of promoting equal rights for working women and men, csoco affiliates tended to promote maternalism in their statutes. Unlike the anarchosyndicalists, the csoco employed class and patriarchal ideology to marginalize working women from skilled work and leadership roles and to promote the middle-class cult of domesticity.[81] One sign that the sdc was increasingly unable to maintain some political autonomy was the substitution of its feminist motto with the crom's more ambiguous one, "Salud y Revolución Social."[82]

The sdc's tense relationship with the csoco was further complicated by the decision of the Communist Party's trade-union affiliate, the Confederación Sindical Unitaria de México (csum, Mexican Unitary Union Confederation), to open a branch in Córdoba. In an effort to resist this intrusion, the csoco decided to create the Confederación Sindicalista de Obreros y Campesinos del Estado de Veracruz (csocev, Confederation of Workers and Peasants of the State of Veracruz) and to hold its first convention there in September 1928.[83] However, the csoco would have serious difficulties consolidating its control over Córdoba's obstreperous labor movement because its labor militants had strong ties to Governor Tejeda, to the Peasant League, and to the Partido Comunista Mexicano (pcm, Mexican Communist Party).

In 1930 the sdc's relationship with the csoco deteriorated even further because its local federation, the fsocc, became heavy-handed in the oversight of union elections and administration of the sorter's social fund. The conflict was exacerbated by plunging coffee prices, which put many coffee workers out of work. A midnight meeting on March 1 highlights the high level of anti-csoco sentiment that had developed among union members. Three outspoken leaders—Luz Vera, Luz Romero, and Inés Reyes—complained vociferously about the sdc executive committee's failure to deposit the quotas deducted from workers' paychecks into the union's social fund or provide any financial assistance to ill workers. They were also unhappy with the local federation's campaign to single out workers and force them to sign an agreement to support a national boycott being carried out by CROM unions. Sorters accused the FSOCC of violating the union's autonomy and its internal regulations. In response to the SDC's uppitiness, federation leaders raided its offices and stole its archives. In a letter to Governor Tejeda, the SDC's secretary general asked for guarantees: "We declare our autonomy and free ourselves from the arbitrary tutelage of the Federation leaders."[84] The labor inspector, who was supporting the seven hundred sorters, calculated how much money should have been going into the social fund each year and how much was being embezzled. He concluded the SDC executive committee had been coopted and corrupted by male federation leaders who wanted to administer the fund themselves. He attributed the women leaders' naiveté to their gender: "The leaders of the union—because of their sex and lack of culture—have very distinct social relations with the leaders of the Federation, who have always manipulated them."[85] Federation leaders struck back by accusing the SDC of allying itself with the Communists, led by Gonzalo Hernández, Eduardo Valverde, and Leobardo Z. Burgos, who had marched around the Juárez Market continually waving red flags.[86]

The dispute between the SDC and the FSOCC was finally resolved but not before the sorter leaders had resorted to a discourse that intertwined traditional gender values and the championing of the respectability of the obrera. The secretary general wrote that certain provisions in the federation's regulations governing relations with its local unions would need to be abolished because they threatened the obreras' legitimate rights: "If we are weak because of our sex, we must be strong [in supporting] our rights . . . we are looking for complete autonomy . . . without the intervention of MEN." She went on to ask that the sorters not be required to participate in all worker parades, except for May 1, "because the woman's place is at home and not participating in other activities." She then added, "We likewise want to be respected in terms of our private lives and our liberty, so that criticisms and comments do not injure female honor and sensitivity and [ignore] the necessity to work." Therefore, from then on, she continued, only the union would negotiate future contracts, except in extreme circumstances when it would ask the federation to intervene. "We appear to have been deceived by our goodwill and incapacity to defend ourselves."[87] Her defense of the union's political autonomy is laced with the seeming contradiction between sexist trade unionism and the rights of the obrera. As Porter has pointed out, women frequently found the space to legitimize themselves by falling back on traditional gender morality: "It was precisely based on conceptions of female virtue that Mexican working women legitimated a place for themselves within the public sphere."[88] Hierarchical, androcentric trade-union practices were threatening the political autonomy of Córdoba's sorter union. To legitimize its resistance to the FSOCC's encroachment on its autonomy, the SDC's leadership felt it was necessary to couch its discourse in terms of female respectability and honor.

Coffee-Sorter Unions and Peasant League Politics

The CSOCO was not alone in wanting to take control of the coffee-sorter unions in Veracruz. Since its inception in 1923, the Peasant League had the objective of organizing urban as well as rural workers. Its principal leaders, Úrsulo Galván, Manuel Almanza, and Sóstenes Blanco, adhered to an ideology that called for the mobilization of both the urban and rural proletariat.[89] In the mid-1920s a contingent of libertarian communists, agraristas, and anarchosyndicalists moved to Córdoba from the port and the Federal District to establish a new base of operations for radical worker mobilization with local labor activists. Galván, the shining star of the Peasant League and a prominent member of the PCM, decided to run for Córdoba's state deputy in 1925. By the end of the 1920s, Córdoba had attracted a small contingent of Communist activists, who traced their roots back to either the tenant movement or the bakers' union. Former tenant leader Gonzalo Hernández had a particularly close relationship with Galván and regularly attended league meetings in Xalapa, while the baker Miguel Angel Velasco Muñoz became active in both the CROM and the PCM. In 1929 these *rojos* (reds) invited Manuel Díaz Ramirez and Rafael Carrillo, prominent PCM leaders, to speak for Córdoba's May Day celebrations.[90]

Under the watchful eye of Galván, the league formed its own federation of urban and rural day workers. It operated in Huatusco, which was the birthplace of Galván and Almanza, but it also began to aggressively organize rural worker, peasant, and commercial employee unions beginning in Córdoba in 1927.[91] Despite their radical agenda, they displayed, at first, little interest in gender issues or organizing working women.

The league's campaign to mobilize Córdoba's coffee sorters began in earnest around 1930. Following Galván's untimely death, tenant and agrarista leaders founded the Centro Social "Úrsulo Galván" (Úrsulo Galván Social Center) with the objective of unifying autonomous workers and peasant groups in the Córdoba region. The Tejedistas began their organizing activities in the coffee beneficios of Peñuela, in the neighboring municipality of Amatlán. The BNCA had created an agrarian cooperative of small farmers, which had acquired its own dry beneficio. In the midst of the economic depression, the BNCA and Amatlán's mayor hammered out an agreement to pay the sorters a wage that was ten centavos lower than the Veracruz Labor Department's stipulated thirty centavos per kilo of waste. With the assistance of a Tejedista labor inspector, some disgruntled sorters created a rival sorter union affiliated with the Peasant League rather than with the CROM. The SDC reacted immediately to what it saw as the league's incursion into its sphere of influence. It dispatched its organizers to woo the sorters back into a CROM-affiliated union. One of these young workers recruited by Luz Vera was Eufrosina Moya, whom we shall meet in the next chapter. The SDC was able to woo 170 of the 280 workers back into the fold. The labor inspector tried valiantly to coax the two groups to unify so as to give all workers equal access to the jobs, but outside political interests made this impossible. Moreover, the Cromistas resorted to a discourse that linked the rival union not to the Peasant League but rather to the right-wing Catholic women's association that had supported the Cristero Rebellion against the Calles government. In her letters to the governor, the SDC's secretary general accused the upstart Peñuela union of slanderous acts, which included following the orders of the Unión de Damas Católicas (Catholic Women's Union) and flagrantly disobeying the government's anticlerical policies. This interunion labor conflict eventually was sent to the JCCA for resolution.

Both sides appealed to Governor Tejeda for support, but he preferred to stand on the sidelines and have the JCCA, which he probably controlled, make the final ruling. Its resolution called for the two unions to cooperate with each other in order to keep the remaining one hundred positions that had been cut during the collapse of coffee prices. However, it did not rule on whether the union should affiliate with the CROM or the Peasant League.[92] The struggle between the Cromistas and the agraristas over Córdoba's coffee sorters would continue for three more years, as will be explained in the next chapter.

In conclusion, revolutionary and postrevolutionary turmoil opened public spaces and political opportunities for Veracruz seasonal workers to mobilize in the coffee agroindustry between 1915 and 1931. Over the course of this sixteen-year period, sorter unions emerged at some time in all five of the major Central Veracruz coffee towns, although the Córdoba union was the largest in size and the best organized to fight for the women workers' cause. Although men workers organized in the heady days of 1915, they did not reconstitute their unions until after the promulgation of the 1931 Labor Code.

Anarchosyndicalists and anarchists of the COM were far more willing to organize women workers in consumer and export industries than the reformist Constitutionalists. They believed that economic issues were just as important for women workers as they were for men workers. In 1915 in the midst of revolutionary strife, the coffee-sorter unions of Córdoba, Orizaba, and Xalapa negotiated collective contracts with the assistance of mundialista labor inspectors and the tacit support of the state. No other seasonal workers in Mexico, or for that matter in Latin America, won these kinds of concessions from their owners. Social revolution and militant trade unionism had opened up spaces for mobilizing women workers to fight for equal worker rights as never before. Although the CROM took a leading role in organizing sorters in the 1920s, it increasingly employed a discourse based on masculinity as a rationale for protecting patronage positions for male breadwinners and implemented policies that sought to eliminate the autonomy of women's as well as men's unions.

Mobilization of Veracruz coffee sorters had some gendered dimensions. Women's motivation for organizing seems to have been more closely linked to the preservation of their families and their communities than for men workers. There was a noticeable shift in the ways in which sorters viewed themselves as workers and within the labor force during this period. At first, their rhetoric referred to their union as "humble," and they fought for simply a living wage. But by 1929 they wanted men to stay out of their union's affairs and no longer advise them. In Córdoba during the 1920s, sorters adopted mottos that championed women's rights, fought for more political autonomy, and won collective contracts long before the men workers. They elected their own leaders, who wrote letters, albeit with the assistance of their male labor advisors, to governors, presidents, and state and federal officials. At times, they even appropriated the Cromista anticlerical rhetoric to attack the Catholic Women's Union in order to show their loyalty to the Mexican state and its religious policies.

Finally, gender and the revolutionary state intersected when the revolutionary and postrevolutionary state intervened to uphold almost the same worker rights for working women as for working men. In times of political crisis, the Constitutionalists had to embrace equal rights for men and women workers in order to keep worker discontent to a minimum. In the postrevolutionary era, the Veracruz state created the conditions for greater mobilization of obreras as an integrated part of the workforce and the labor movement, although it did little to support women's issues per se. The efforts of Veracruz's postrevolutionary governors to pass labor legislation protected the rights of seasonal women and men workers as never before.

4

Caciquismo, Organized Labor, and Gender

If you were to enter the headquarters of the local federation of the CROM in Córdoba, Veracruz, you would find a plaque, installed in 1972, with the names of the six most outstanding union leaders of the region. Two of the names are those of escogedoras, Inés Reyes Ochoa and Sofía Castro González. These two leaders, along with a dozen others, dominated the leadership of Córdoba's coffee-sorter union for five decades. This chapter shows how these sorters gradually built a collective leadership during the 1930s, not unlike those created by men union leaders, by serving as effective intermediaries between the rank and file and the national labor movement, setting the stage for the development of a women's collective cacicazgo.

How could these women workers establish a union cacicazgo when the workplace and union hall were conceptualized as masculine spaces? This chapter begins to answer this question by examining the relationship between trade unionism, leadership, gender, and the state in Córdoba's coffee agro-export industry during the 1930s. A number of national, state, and regional factors contributed to the rise of a women-led cacicazgo. At the national level the emerging modern state willingly cooperated with many hybrid and malleable forms of caciquismo that evolved in the postrevolutionary era. The relatively fluid political milieu opened up opportunities for both women and men labor leaders to emerge as powerful powerbrokers or intermediaries and to gain and maintain power in an exclusive manner. As part of the centralization process, the state created and sponsored industrial-labor boards that played an important role in giving women leaders an equal voice in presenting their claims against their employers. The Orizaba–Córdoba corridor continued to remain a CROM enclave, strong enough to block the penetration of rival Tejedista- and Cardenista-sponsored labor movements but still fragmented to the extent that it allowed workers a certain level of autonomy in controlling their own unions. In the case of Córdoba's coffee-sorter union, a number of factors contributed to the formation of an all-women collective leadership: a female-dominated workforce, the intervention of competing rural and urban social movements that galvanized support for union leaders, and the leaders' use of gender-neutral and gender-specific strategies to gain and maintain authority and legitimacy.

I contend that women union leaders established a flexible and adaptable cacicazgo, which blended traditional and new elements of boss politics. The mechanisms of patron-client relationship, exclusion, and intermediation that they employed to concentrate power in their own hands should not be exclusively linked to masculinity. Their successful employment of a mixture of mobilization strategies demonstrated that the relationship between gender and caciquismo was in transition.

Caciquismo, Revolution, and Gender

Classic or traditional Latin American caciquismo has been characterized as a form of personal and informal political leadership. It is generally associated with male leadership patterns, but women cacicazgos have existed since preconquest and colonial times.[1] "As products of the incongruous union of 'modern' politics with 'traditional' society," says Alan Knight when referring to twentieth-century Mexico, "conceptually, they are representatives of patron-client systems, which embody hierarchies of authority, involving actors of unequal status and power, who are linked by bonds of reciprocity and patronage (also unequal)."[2] Traditional caciques distribute their favors personally, or informally; and they generally do so in an unequal manner. In return for the wealth, labor, and political positions they grant to the members of their power bases, they expect them to reciprocate with their personal services and loyalty. Normally they also exploit family and kinship ties to construct a loyal group of agents who practice violence or the threat of violence to control various political, economic, and social domains.[3] In some respects caciques are Janus figures in the sense that they must cultivate "upward" or external linkages with outside organizations and "downward" or internal linkages within their organization. Acting as intermediaries or brokers, they seek to reconcile the specific demands of their clientele with the broader objectives of regional and state leaders.[4]

Mexican caciquismo experienced a significant transformation as modernization and revolution fomented dramatic social, economic, and political disruptions in the first decades of the twentieth century. Caciques found themselves forced to become more flexible and adaptable to changing power relations. Although caciquismo would survive and flourish during the years of revolutionary strife, Presidents Calles and Lázaro Cárdenas Ríos made serious advances in disarming, subjugating, or eliminating most traditional rural caciques in the postrevolutionary era.[5] Only the more nimble caciques who could adapt "to the new rules of the game, integrating themselves as gears into mass organizations, unions, and associations linked to the [the official party]," survived as what Raymond Buve has termed gatekeepers.[6]

Labor leaders, whether they were men or women, had to start building patron-client systems from the bottom up within the new postrevolutionary trade-union organizations. Wil Pansters argues that unions, just like other postrevolutionary institutions, "constituted platforms for the emergence of a refurbished, institutionally underpinned caciquismo, as relations of clientelism and personalistic practices colonized them."[7] During the transition to the stabilized development of the 1940s, caciques actually fused personalist and institutional principles of social organization that demonstrated the adaptive capacity of caciquismo.[8] Therefore, the fundamental commonality of postrevolutionary caciquismos is not in the nature of their political practices or their common characteristics—such as machismo, personalism, clientelism, or violence—but rather in the systemic function of the mechanisms of intermediation and exclusion that permitted control over scarce human and financial resources.[9] What I hope to show is that these mechanisms are not exclusively linked to gender identity.[10]

It makes good sense, therefore, to rethink the relationship between caciquismo and gender. Since caciques are shapers of power, cultural phenomena such as gender, religion, ethnicity, violence, and family relationships must be taken into consideration.[11] Union caciquismo has generally been closely associated with masculinity and unequal gender relations in the workplace. The use of violence, manipulation of power, nepotism, and physical and mental intimidation was often extended into the union hall. Within this context it was generally assumed that women could or would only infrequently exercise leadership positions. Therefore, they were more or less excluded from positions of power within the labor movement.[12] Although these generalizations certainly hold true where men dominated the workforce, they need to be reevaluated due to the increasing feminization of the workforce and in light of new studies on women and power.

Women's rise to positions of power occurs more frequently during periods of military disruption and political instability or in situations where formal political structures are weak. For instance, Francie Chassen-López argues that it is precisely the informal nature of caciquismo that allowed Juana Catarine Romero, a Zapotec street vendor, to become a rich Porfirian merchant in the Isthmus of Tehuantepec. She gained socioeconomic power not only through her business acumen and social networking but also through her skill in transforming it into traditional political power in a region where the state government did not have a strong presence.[13] During the Revolution of 1910–17, even more chaotic and insecure conditions existed, which created opportunities for women to join the ranks of the Zapatista and Villista armies. Women attained the rank of officer and commanded women and men on the battlefield, and on their own merits became local cacicas. They were able to achieve this status primarily because the federal army had disintegrated, and the revolutionary armies had not been professionalized into hierarchical institutions. For a time, military leaders felt no need to stifle women's passion to fight or to lead on the battlefield in the name of socioeconomic justice.[14]

In the postrevolutionary period, the formation of women cacicazgos was somewhat easier in urban as opposed to rural regions. Urban movements had a slightly higher chance of being organized around liberal or anarchist ideologies that gave women more opportunities to lead. The grassroots beginnings of new urban organizations therefore provided women workers with greater access to power. María Teresa Fernández-Aceves has clearly shown this to be true in the political trajectory of Guadalupe Martínez Heliodoro, a Jalisco schoolteacher who became a political and cultural intermediary for men and women workers, labor leaders, the official party, and the state between the 1920s and the 1990s in Guadalajara.[15] Her women's political action organization fought for the rights of both urban middle class and working women. After Martínez allied herself and subsequently married a powerful male trade unionist, she helped to forge a family cacicazgo that endured for decades. It was never a completely equal political and personal alliance, for Martínez had to abandon her teaching career and her feminist activism to adapt to the patriarchal and paternalist style of her husband. However, they created the perfect match or the perfect team, each controlling their own separate clienteles.[16] In this case, Fernández-Aceves challenges the belief that men leaders always marginalized and excluded women leaders from positions of power within trade union hierarchies.

When women make up the majority of the labor force in the semi-mechanized agro-export industries, there is an even greater possibility that women will emerge as leaders and even cacicas. In the Córdoba and Coatepec coffee agroindustries where large numbers of women worked, all-women leadership and cacicazgos were bound to develop in the beneficios. What strategies did these leaders adopt to construct a women's collective leadership within the masculine hierarchical structure of trade unionism? Were their strategies gender neutral or gender specific or both? Did the women's union respond differently than men's unions to hostile takeovers from the outside? How could these leaders forge a sense of union solidarity in the 1930s, a period of continual economic and political insecurity? Finally, what success did these emerging leaders have in addressing the workers' economic demands in front of the industrial-labor relations boards?

Construction of a Women Collective Cacicazgo

Córdoba's coffee-sorter union would never have evolved into such a unified organization or have won consecutive collective contracts during the 1930s and 1940s if it had not been for its talented leadership. The systemic dimensions of the caciquismo, the mechanisms of intermediation and exclusion, were critical as they constructed their power base. After they had built clientelist systems within the rank and file, they served as the union's brokers between the union and the CROM's regional and state confederations and in so doing protected the economic and political interests of the membership. During the thirties, Córdoba's sorter union leadership evolved through what Wil Pansters has termed the first stage of caciquismo: "the construction of leadership and the transformation of a leadership into a cacicazgo," which "requires obtaining decisive political, economic, and social control of a particular geographic area or community, the capacity to use or threaten with violence and the acknowledgement and legitimation of the cacique as the only leader of his [sic] realm."[17]

Córdoba's sorter union emerged as the strongest labor organization in this coffee town, or for that matter in Central Veracruz, during the 1930s. In accordance with the new 1931 labor law, the Córdoba sorter union registered itself under a new name, the Sindicato de Obreras Escogedoras de la Ciudad de Córdoba (SOECC, Sorter Union of the City of Córdoba). Over the next decade, it maintained a membership that ranged between 1,200 to 1,700 escogedoras. If each sorter supported three dependents, which was usually the case, the coffee-sorter community made up somewhere between 12 and 17 percent of the municipality's thirty thousand inhabitants.[18] Only the regional sugarcane-worker union might have had a larger membership. The SOECC operated with a certain degree of autonomy before 1933 due to a number of specific regional factors. Most importantly, the region lacked an industrial base, so national labor organizations seem to have paid less attention to the integration of its labor force into their membership, in sharp contrast to the neighboring industrialized Valley of Orizaba. As a consequence, the SOECC's evolution differed markedly from that of its Orizaba counterpart, the Sindicato "Emancipación" de Escogedoras de Café de Orizaba (Orizaba Emancipation Coffee-Sorter Union). After its reorganization in 1931, this union remained completely under the domination of the textile workers of the CSOCO. Its women leaders never emerged, because textile leaders continually served as its secretary generals. As a result this union was inhibited from exercising very much autonomy.[19]

On the other hand, Córdoba and Coatepec sorter leaders created their own forms of women cacicazgos. In Coatepec, where the union was considerably smaller, one leader was able to consolidate her power by the end of the thirties. Amparo Ortiz came to dominate by means of corruption and intimidation over another prominent leader, Belem Carmona. Ortiz's control over the union treasury and her constant verbal threats against individual workers made it possible for her to hold on to power for eleven years before she was ousted as secretary general.[20] In Córdoba no leader seems to have been able to monopolize power singlehandedly, in part because of the large size of the union. As Knight observes, when leaders recognize their inability to exercise exclusive control over their bases or when they want to avoid internal dissent, they turn to resisting challenges collectively. In so doing, they can produce a form of informal power sharing that can be labeled a "collective caciquismo."[21] This seems to have been the case in Córdoba.

The SOECC leaders slowly built their own personal clientele systems, while they simultaneously worked to limit the participation of the rank and file in union politics. In his discussion of Mexico in the 1960s and 1970s, Salvador Maldonado Aranda has argued that although the state had created laws and regulations that governed the creation and functioning of labor unions, it was not strong enough to enforce them. Thus, the "relative autonomy of the labour unions and the state's flexibility in enforcing labour laws have combined to allow the emergence of labour union caciques." The power of these postrevolutionary caciques rested on three factors: control over internal election procedures, the ability of individual leaders to negotiate the workers' demands with the state, and the quotas of power that the official party granted to the union leadership in return for their political and electoral support.[22] In Córdoba the leadership learned to control internal elections by simply rotating executive committee positions among themselves. In this manner, a small clique retained control over the union, but it did so by following the established "rules of the game." They abided by the guidelines of the 1931 law by holding union elections regularly every six months, but they gained control of the nomination process, which allowed them to uphold the legality and legitimacy of their leadership. Moreover, the state's official recognition of their election conferred added authority on them and further legitimized their hegemony.[23] Fortunately, intelligent, charismatic, and politically savvy women initially rose to the top leadership positions. Before explaining how they legitimized their leadership continuity (*continuismo*), it is important to compose a collective profile of these leaders and to furnish some examples of their longevity in power.

The members of this SOECC leadership shared a good number of personal characteristics. They almost always had working-class origins, and they had risen out of the rank and file. Essentially, they were fine examples of Antonio Gramsci's "organic" leaders. Many had not finished primary school, but very often they empowered themselves by finishing their education in night school or by teaching themselves. Most of them excelled as eloquent and powerful public speakers who were able to win the confidence, support, and loyalty of union members. As strong, charismatic leaders, they were not afraid to speak frankly and to publically confront plant owners or the local priest. Rank-and-file members remembered them as rebels and confrontationists, agents of change who had no difficulty acting in a nontraditional manner to challenge the status quo inside and outside the plants. All these figures displayed exceptional leadership qualities, which won them the respect and admiration of the rank and file.

While the longevity of men labor cacicazgos is well documented,[24] this characteristic also held true for the members of this collective cacicazgo. Luz Vera Hernández was the first dominant leader to emerge during the union's early years. As a founding member of the SDC, she could claim more legitimacy than any other leader for many years. It is said that she was the wife of a doctor, but after his death she became a sorter. Not much else is known about her origins. She was elected secretary general at least six times between 1929 and 1939. Other leaders were elected more than two times during the 1930s. For example, Luz Romero Vargas and Sofia Castro, both of whom were barely literate, were elected at least two times to preside over the union between 1936 and 1943. Eufrosina Moya (Sarmiento), nicknamed la Negra Moya, occupied many different posts in the executive committee starting in 1933, and she headed the executive committee in 1937. Nevertheless, a certain amount of flexibility still existed in the internal electoral process until this point in time.

In the June 15, 1937, general assembly meeting, eleven different candidates were nominated for secretary general. It appears that in a previous meeting the rank and file had become dissatisfied with leadership continuity and had voted to disqualify all those who had held positions on the executive committee on three previous occasions. This action was taken to provide greater opportunity for more sorters to hold office. As a consequence of this resolution, four out of the eleven candidates had to withdraw their nominations. However, this was the last time that the SOECC's minutes mentioned contentious nominating processes or registered complete election results. From then on, the leadership would present one slate of candidates for the executive committee. In the following years, the minutes only noted the number of votes the winner received. For example, Inés Reyes seems to have won the secretary generalship for the first time with 338 votes in 1942, but the number of votes received by other contenders was not recorded.[25] The defeated contenders more often than not received the remaining positions on the executive committee as payoffs for their political cooperation.

Once a leader became a member of the executive committee, she started to actively construct her own power base through her control over scarce financial and human resources and her ability to build personal networks. Her right as a union official to hire and fire workers, obtain access to the union's treasury and social fund, and control the issuance of medical vouchers for doctor's appointments facilitated the growth and maintenance of her patronage system. Leaders also followed the practice of enforcing the closed shop, or the union's exclusive right to sign a collective contract and hire only union workers in the workshop. They enforced this practice through an exclusion clause that allowed the leadership to expel dissidents from the union, thus depriving them of the right to work. They likewise manipulated worker recruitment not only through the drawing up of the first and second lists of permanent workers, which they revised every year, but also through the recruitment of occasional workers, who were called up on a week-to-week basis. If a sorter had not worked for some time after giving birth to a child, she would have to approach her madrina to make some form of promise or to give a present to get back her job again. If she needed medical attention, she also went to her patrona to obtain a letter of recommendation or a voucher. In this manner, a leader built her own clientelist system around the sorters whom she had hired, protected, and given financial assistance to.[26]

The emerging cacicas fostered solidarity and imposed discipline among the rank and file through obligatory participation in union activities and stigmatization of inappropriate and rebellious behavior. They likewise exploited the mechanism of exclusion to marginalize upstarts. Attendance was obligatory at the weekly Tuesday afternoon meetings. If a worker did not attend regularly, she was publicly reprimanded and then docked several days' work. The minutes of every meeting listed the names of members who had excuses for their absences and those who did not. Thus, the threat of losing a week's pay or a job was employed as a form of intimidation, or one might say it was a form of economic violence. The possible loss of steady employment for a barely literate provincial woman was a strong incentive to support the union leadership. Other forms of indirect control were employed to keep the rank and file in line. In the weekly meetings, efforts were made to control or limit debate. The secretary generals chose authoritarian compañeras, including Castro or Moya, to preside over the general assembly meetings and to censor obstreperous speakers.[27] They also required union members to participate regularly in official party and union events.

Undoubtedly, direct access to the CROM's state and national leadership was a critical factor in the development of a leader's power base, just as for any emerging cacique. Eucario León López, the Santa Rosa textile leader and cacique of the CSOCO who was elected secretary general of the Moronista CROM for the period of 1932 to 1934, was the kingpin. After the CROM lost the political and financial support of President Calles and his official party (the Partido Nacional Revolucionario [PNR, National Revolutionary Party]) in 1929,[28] the CSOCO and its affiliated unions enjoyed less political access to public officials. The SOECC seems to have been far less involved in labor politics in the 1930s than Xalapa's and Coatepec's sorter unions, which were located in or next to the state capital and became closely affiliated with the Confederación de Trabajadores Mexicanos (CTM, Mexican Worker Confederation). No direct evidence has been found to show that the CSOCO pressured the SOECC to support particular political candidates, but it assuredly did take place. In Coatepec the Cardenista-controlled CTM ordered the SODCC to participate in political demonstrations in Xalapa in 1936 and vote in favor of their gubernatorial candidate in the PNR's first primary elections. They were threatened with the loss of their jobs if they did not abide by this directive.[29]

The SOECC's incipient cacicas also cultivated practices that were not usually associated with masculine trade unionism. They did not use violence or physical force when they were reprimanding or disciplining their members. Instead, they preferred to use psychological and economic threats, such as the loss of work or the levying of penalties, to discipline workers within or outside the workshop. Reyes and Castro were particularly well-known for their iron hand.[30] Brígida Siriaco remembered Castro as a tough disciplinarian "with a big mouth"; but she added that Castro had "a good heart" and that "she taught me how to obey [*cumplir*]."[31] Their union activism had other gendered dimensions, which extended into the working-class community. Some leaders became heavily involved in Catholic movements, literacy campaigns, antialcohol campaigns, and neighborhood projects. Only when intraunion disputes erupted did the cacicas personally resort to physical force against nonunion members to demonstrate their determination to protect their members' right to work.

Kinship is usually considered an important factor in the construction of rural and urban cacicazgos,[32] but family ties appear to have played a minor role for these emerging cacicas. Needless to say, family networks were critical for gaining access to work in the beneficios, just as in other workshops. Sorters would bring their daughters into the workshop when they were adolescents, teach them how to clean the coffee, and then pressure the leaders to give them a permanent position, as we shall see in the case of Inés Reyes. However, these leaders did not practice nepotism to the same degree as most union caciques in the thirties, who regularly handed out union positions to their relatives. Since many of these young leaders were single, separated, or widowed at this time, perhaps they still felt greater class and gender affinity with their compañeras than with their own families.

The political practices of authoritarianism, paternalism, violence, and machismo generally associated with union caciquismo were far less common among the SOECC leadership. Union bosses who controlled important labor organizations in Atlixco, Guadalajara, and Monterrey continually employed these hegemonic strategies. They often presented themselves as paternalistic figures similar to traditional hacendados, owners of textile mills, and military leaders. Furthermore, they emphasized the masculine identity of the worker and promoted the view that the male head of the family was the primary breadwinner. In this manner, they legitimized the exclusion of women workers from the workplace. Very often, they resorted to violent, abusive behavior to intimidate their workers.[33] Emerging SOECC leaders exercised their power in a more subtle and flexible manner. Let us examine the lives of Sofía Castro and Inés Reyes here as two different types of cacicas.

Sofía Castro González (c. 1904–90) came from peasant stock. She had separated from her peasant husband before bearing any children; and once she moved into town, she became heavily involved in union affairs. She was known for her exceptionally strong character and hardheadedness. In her later years, she adopted certain masculine behaviors, but she was the exception to the rule. She was known for carrying a pistol during street brawls, but other union women did the same. She brought it to the Saturday-night dances to prevent men from disrupting the fiesta. On at least one occasion, she was not loath to use it; she fired at a worker's foot because he had refused to pay the admission fee.[34] Union men sometimes masculinized her by referring to her as a "machona" because she wore men's clothing and boots. This transformation of the concept of the *macho* into *machona* was a form of transgendering by masculinizing a strong woman leader.[35] Most probably, Castro assumed a more masculine behavior because it suited her domineering personality, brought greater respect and loyalty from her compañeras and male activists, and gave her greater access to power.

The second emerging cacica, Inés Reyes Ochoa (1911–98), exercised her power in an entirely different manner. She was much more politically ambitious than Castro.[36] She was a third-generation sorter. When her grandfather had been drafted into the Porfirian army and never returned, her grandmother and her adolescent daughter, Juana, were forced to migrate from Chocamán to Córdoba and to find work in the tobacco and coffee preparation plants around 1910. Migration to the city was not always a liberating experience for women. Juana was raped, and she bore a daughter whom she named Inés. As a consequence of this unwanted pregnancy, Inés never enjoyed a very close relationship with her mother. At the age of eleven or twelve, she entered the coffee beneficios to work with her grandmother at the beginning of the 1920s. Reyes only finished three years of primary school, but through pure willpower, she later finished her primary education at night school. Meanwhile, she blossomed into a talented actress and singer and performed on numerous occasions at the magnificent Pedro Díaz Theater. The plant owners considered her a rebel because she violated factory rules by singing in the workshop.

Reyes was raised in a family where coffee sorting and trade unionism were long-standing traditions. Her mother had been one of the founding members of the SDC, although she had never occupied a leadership position. At seventeen Inés became involved in Cromista politics. She was recruited by the CROM to upset the balloting process to prevent the reelection of Obregón in 1928 by throwing chili in the faces of the election officials and overturning the ballot boxes. Throughout the following decade, she dedicated a good portion of her time to union activism, in part because she remained single until 1941. She was also a very talented speaker and showed no compunction about expressing her opinion. As one union leader put it, "she had no qualms about speaking her mind."[37]

Reyes had an extraordinary knack for building a patronage system, employing the human, financial, and political resources that were at her disposal. In the thirties, she developed a clientele composed of numerous sorters by providing them with work. As most caciques or cacicas, she was unusually adept at winning popular support based on merit. Her ability to meet worker demands and solve their grievances brought steadfast loyalty among the rank and file.[38] Between 1933 and 1937 she was elected to the positions of secretary of agreements, treasurer, secretary of internal affairs, and secretary of external affairs; and she had traveled widely as the union's representative to numerous regional labor conventions. At twenty-six she was already overseeing the union's treasury, which had over 3,600 pesos in its coffers. However, when she was nominated for the position of secretary general in 1937, she was forced to withdraw because she had already served too many times on the executive committee. Six months later, she was nominated again. Although she did not win the secretary generalship at this time, she was reelected to the executive committee.[39] In spite of the membership's attempts to prevent Reyes and other emerging cacicas from dominating the executive committee, it was never able to block her political ascendency.

Reyes became very involved in a number of gender-specific activities. She developed a keen interest in the expansion of her workers' community, Miguel Hidalgo. After she had put down an eighteen-peso security deposit (*abonos*) to buy an urban lot on which to build a house, she encouraged many other workers to do likewise. In her spare time she pressured the city authorities to open a preschool in a local hospital. In the 1940s and 1950s she became very involved in two important women's social movements: social Catholicism and antialcoholism. She was an extremely devout Catholic and always carried a rosary with her. She attended mass regularly, unlike many of her compañeras. As an active member of the Obreras Guadalupanas Nacionales (National Workers of the Virgin of Guadalupe), she sought to revive public pilgrimages to Virgin of Guadalupe shrines. Her fervent beliefs involved her on more than one occasion in heated disputes with the local priest, who refused to reestablish these pilgrimages given the hostile anticlerical climate in Veracruz. Religious services actually remained suspended in Córdoba until the late 1930s.[40]

A few SOECC leaders networked with and married fellow activists within the labor movement. If their husbands were affiliated with the CROM or the CTM, they generally supported their wives' union activism. Reyes's husband was a taxi driver who became a local CTM leader before becoming incapacitated by diabetes. The very talented Luz Romero was also married to a union leader.[41] Nevertheless, the other principal leaders, including Luz Vera, Castro, and Moya, did not marry union men. Thus, it is fair to say that marital relation with a union man was not a prerequisite for becoming an SOECC cacica. These women were born leaders, and their innate aptitudes do more to explain their ultimate success than their husbands' union networks do.

Finally, these emerging cacicas served as important brokers between the SOECC and the regional CSOCO. Once León was elected the CROM's national secretary general, he established close relationships with Castro and Reyes. In fact, he became their patrón until his death in the late 1950s.[42] Reyes served as a key intermediary between the union and León. Because of her dynamic speaking abilities, he regularly invited her to CROM regional and state meetings and to celebrations throughout the state. Thus, by the end of the thirties, she had gained the reputation as an effective regional cacica.

Female Caciquismo and External Intervention

In their attempts to build and expand regional power bases, postrevolutionary governors sought to capture control of popular labor and peasant movements. Unfortunately, these practices generated brutal interunion and intraunion struggles between rival groups, which threatened the local autonomy that these regional and local organizations had struggled so hard to win in the 1920s. The ability of the SOECC's leadership to confront a hostile takeover by the Peasant League depended in large part on their skills as leaders and the mechanisms they used to confront these challenges.

The 1931 labor law created a new set of rules that actually facilitated caciques' ability to block challenges to their power base. The law did not prohibit closed-shop clauses in labor contracts, which became one of the most effective mechanisms for blocking dissident leaders from forming rival unions and in this manner perpetuated cacicazgos.[43] Moreover, caciques and cacicas could exploit the high level of insecurity among the rank and file because their jobs were threatened, so they used forms of exclusion to throw dissidents out of the union. As a consequence, the rank and file most frequently supported continuismo, which allowed them to retain their employment and further strengthened cacicazgos.[44]

Militant labor activism was an essential element of the SOECC's response to intraunion conflicts. Leaders and the rank and file alike displayed courageous and aggressive behavior in their use of vulgar language, engagement in hand-to-hand combat in the streets, and occupation of their workplace to confront their bosses and rival unions. Their activism was not shaped specifically by either masculinity or femininity.[45] Although Matthew Guttman has argued that extraordinary heroism and courage in public spaces has been associated with the "masculine in the nonsexist sense,"[46] this was not always the case with shifting gender identities of postrevolutionary Mexico. Although their behavior violated provincial bourgeois norms, women leaders and rank-and-file members felt obliged to engage in militancy for economic survival.[47]

In 1932 Governor Tejeda's key sociopolitical power base, the Peasant League, accelerated its efforts to wrest control of Córdoba's rural and urban labor unions away from the CROM. Since the CROM faced major internal divisions after Morones fell out of favor with Calles and the three provisional presidents that followed him in office, the league took advantage of this opening to make inroads in the Tejedista-dominated Córdoba region. This strategy was part of the governor's overall campaign to create a strong regional power base and to remain independent from the increasingly centralizing influence of Calles's official party. As Córdoba's largest union, the SOECC was chosen as one of its primary targets.

Discontent among the SOECC's rank and file was rooted in long-term economic conditions and internal union politics. Many sorters had been laid off during to the depression, and they were disenchanted with the lack of turnover in the union's executive committee. The common trade union practice of continuismo had set in. Certain leaders, in particular Luz Vera and Luz Romero, had monopolized the secretary generalship since the union's refounding in 1925. Dissidents decided to take matters into their own hands and sought the outside support of the newly "elected" Tejedista mayor Eduardo Valverde and councilman Gonzálo Hernández, both of whom enjoyed close ties with the Peasant League. The league's Córdoba affiliate, the Úrsulo Galván Social Center, had already been aggressively campaigning to capture control of the CROM's unions for coffee workers, sugarcane workers, rural teachers, and musicians since 1931.[48] What appeared to be simply an internal union conflict over leadership continuity was in fact a power struggle between the Cromistas and the Tejedistas for control over the SOECC. The same political conflict occurred in Coatepec for control over the SODCC.[49]

After more than half the SOECC's 1,200 members dutifully "reelected" Luz Vera to the post of secretary general in January 1932, 406 dissidents met separately and voted to suspend her and her close confidants on account of her poor level of performance and her inability to resolve the sorters' economic woes. The dissidents agreed to sever all ties with the CROM, claiming that they wanted to win back their autonomy. They contended that the CROM had collaborated too closely with the Mexican state and announced they would follow a more "revolutionary" orientation as a proletarian organization. They then proceeded to elect a new set of officers.[50] By breaking with the officially recognized SOECC, the dissidents immediately lost their jobs, for their 1931 collective contract had given the union the right to a closed shop.[51]

Thrown out of work, the dissidents, most likely spurred on by local Tejedistas, stationed themselves on February 1 at the entrances of the plants to prevent Cromistas from entering the beneficios, thus paralyzing the coffee-export industry. For days, the blockade continued, while the two groups of women screamed and cursed at each other in the streets. The dissidents also raided the recently opened regional CROM headquarters in collaboration with Tejedista municipal authorities, hoping to find documentation necessary to win the Labor Department's official recognition. The JCCA finally issued a resolution to end the dispute by supporting the officially registered SOECC. However, the board's resolution was not considered legally binding, so the dissidents refused to abandon their occupation of the plants.[52]

When the state labor inspector intervened and proposed that the two groups meet amicably in a joint assembly, the leaders of both factions refused to cooperate. On February 12 the dispute escalated further. The rival factions confronted each other in front of the plants, throwing punches and hurling stones that they had torn up from the streets. After the fifteen-minute melee showed no signs of diminishing, the municipal police, followed by the federal army, intervened to break up the fighting. Twenty sorters were arrested, and three were badly injured. The dissidents refused to give up their struggle. In the ensuing days, they proceeded to attack and injure Vera.[53] With the conflict within the SOECC no closer to settlement, Governor Tejeda personally intervened, calling for the reintegration of the two factions so the dissident minority could regain their jobs. Neither side accepted this solution, which only papered over the underlying rivalry between Tejedistas and Cromistas for control over Veracruz's largest women's union.[54]

As the conflict dragged on, the Cromista-controlled union asked for assistance from the CSOCO and pleaded for Rosendo Pérez Velasco, secretary general of the Cromista state confederation, to come as quickly as possible to Córdoba. Upon his arrival, he tried to call a meeting to reorient all SOECC members. But the dissidents continued receiving the strong support of the Úrsulo Galván Social Center led by Gonzalo Hernández and Leopardo Burgos. Meanwhile, the Peasant League's campaign to extend its control over all rural and urban unions in the Córdoba region continued unabated. By the fall of

1932, the Úrsulo Galván Social Center claimed to have won the affiliation of the tenant movement, worker colonies, sugarcane workers, teachers, office workers, sackers, street vendors, and two coffee-sorter unions: the Majority Group in Cordoba and its counterpart in the neighboring village of Peñuela.[55]

By December of 1932 Tejeda had completed his second term in office, and his peasant organization and armed state militia were about to be disbanded by the federal government. To block his political aspirations to run for the presidency in 1934, Calles, the national strongman, instructed the provisional president Abelardo L. Rodríguez to disarm the state militia and create a rival peasant league.[56] However, Tejeda's followers continued to organize at the grassroots level. The SOECC dissidents decided to make a last ditch attempt to regain their jobs by forming their own organization, the Grupo Mayoritario de Escogedores de Café y Tabaco de la Ciudad y Región de Córdoba (Majority Group of Coffee and Tobacco Sorters of the City and Region of Córdoba) and to elect Carmen Hernández as their new leader. They also decided to adopt the anarchosyndicalist motto, *"Emancipación de la Mujer Organizada"* ("Emancipation of the Organized Woman").[57] They petitioned for official certification once again in mid-December. This time they were successful, most probably because Manuel Almanza, the president of the Peasant League, still exercised enough influence over the JCCA to win a favorable decision.

Within days, Luz Vera sent an irate letter to President Rodríguez, protesting the JCCA's decision and demanding his personal intervention. Finding itself under increasing political pressure, the JCCA reversed its ruling.[58] Unhappy with this reversal, Majority Group members vented their frustrations by taking to the streets of Córdoba once again, throwing the Cromista president of the Municipal Conciliation Board into the fountain in the central plaza. On February 2, with the support of the Úrsulo Galván Social Center and municipal council members, the Tejedistas stationed themselves for a second year at the doors of the five largest beneficios to prevent workers from entering the premises.[59] To avoid further confrontations, the owners decided to lock the workers out, appeal for police protection, and terminate their contract with the SOECC.[60]

The sorters' blockade of the plant entrances continued for seven days, from February 2 to February 8, during which time several bloody clashes broke out between escogedoras of the two rival unions. Meanwhile, loyal Cromista unions from around the state flooded into Córdoba, sent angry letters to the JCCA, and insulted the Tejedistas. They stigmatized the boycotters by accusing them of causing the division. The newly elected Cromista leader of the SOECC even threatened to seize the plants: "We are ready to take control of the beneficios by force and take justice into our own hands." When the municipal police tried to break up the protests, the sorters yelled insults and tried to disarm them. As tempers flared, the police shot a worker, and the dissidents retaliated by wounding a policeman. Order was not restored until February 7, when the state's minister of internal affairs, who had arrived to personally resolve the conflict, asked the federal army to intervene and disarm the municipal police loyal to the Tejedista mayor and to restore order around the plants. Twenty sorters were arrested and many others were sent to the hospital.[61] The next morning, the federal troops set out to dislodge the Tejedistas from the plants, but the dissidents decided to abandon their posts peacefully. Immediately thereafter, the Cromistas reentered the plants, and the machines started operating again. To find employment for the seven hundred Tejedista workers, Governor Gonzálo Vázquez Vela convinced the Hard and Rand Company, which probably had a separate collective contract with the union, to hire these workers.[62]

The military resolution of the Córdoba sorters' intraunion conflict represented one of many defeats suffered by Tejeda in early 1933, as the federal government dismantled his power base. It allowed the CROM to reestablish its hegemony over the SOECC, while simultaneously setting back the union's struggle to retain some level of autonomy from the CSOCO. It also revealed the inability of the rank and file to replace its entrenched Cromista leadership. The union achieved one important victory, however. Vera's protégée, the young charismatic leader Eufrosina Moya (Sarmiento), was appointed to the executive committee of Córdoba's regional federation.[63] Most probably the CROM recognized that it could no longer afford to deny SOECC representation in the labor bureaucracy. This conflict illustrates clearly how obreras will resort to disruptive, aggressive, and at times violent behavior; attacks on popular leaders; and foul language to protect their jobs.

The SOECC's leadership—under the steady hand of Luz Vera and Luz Romero and with the collaboration of two future leaders, Inés Reyes and Eufrosina Moya—had successfully prevented a hostile takeover by Tejedistas through the use of a number of mechanisms of cacicazgo construction. It demonstrated the leadership's determination to retain its hegemony over the union and to forge real cohesiveness within the sorter community. As Norberto Elias has argued, "exclusion and stigmatization of the outsiders by the established groups were . . . powerful weapons used by the latter to maintain their identity, to assert their superiority, keeping others firmly in their place."[64] Leadership continuity was formally sanctioned with the reelection of Vera and Romero as secretary general and secretary of internal affairs.[65] They were now in the first stage of consolidating a women's collective cacicazgo, albeit under the tutelage of León's cacicazgo in Orizaba.

The political dispute between the CROM and the Tejedista Peasant League for control over the SOECC illustrates how the leaders and the rank and file resorted to militant labor activism that should not be associated necessarily with masculinity. Just as in Chile, women workers employed heroic public action simply to save their jobs, "demonstrating both symbolically and practically that labor militancy was not exclusively masculine."[66] They used physical attacks on authority figures, vulgar language, and the hurling of rocks and stones at their erstwhile compañeras to defend their right to work and to resist external intervention. The leaders were also negotiating with the state from below. They sent delegations to Xalapa and to Mexico City to meet with administration officials, and they addressed numerous letters to the governor and the president to ask for their intervention.[67] In short, they exercised their authority to retain control over their union and to safeguard their leadership position in the same manner as men leaders. They had evolved into labor activists and agents of change, as they began to strengthen their collective cacicazgo.

Men Cacicazgos and External Intervention

By way of contrast, Córdoba's men's union was neither a cohesive nor a disciplined organization, nor was it blessed with such talented, unified leadership. Thus, the Cromistas were unable to thwart its hostile takeover by Cardenistas in late 1933. SITCTAC's lack of cohesion was in large part due to its extremely heterogeneous membership. Most of the loaders were communal farmers (*ejidatarios*), small rancheros, or day workers during the growing season who simply supplemented their rural income by working in the beneficios from October to May. Since there were so few men working in each beneficio, the CROM had brought together coffee, tobacco, sugar distillery, wood, and commercial workers into a multiindustry union. Two skilled workers, the mechanics Juan González and Abundio Torres, and the coffee brush clearer Lorenzo Nieva dominated the union leadership from its inception in 1931 until the end of the decade. Although Torres came from peasant origins, he had already emerged as an important CROM leader by the late twenties.[68]

In October 1933 Vicente Lombardo Toledano, the former Cromista and Moronista leader with close ties to presidential candidate Lázaro Cárdenas, arrived in Córdoba with the intention of unseating the FSOCC's Moronista leadership and replacing it with his own. In a large assembly at the Pedro Díaz Theater, workers voted to withdraw their affiliation with the Moronista-led CROM and to affiliate with the Lombardistas. In a matter of days, the Lombardistas formed their own new national organization, the Confederación General de Obreros y Campesinos de México (CGOCM, Mexican General Confederation of Workers and Peasants). This external intervention did not at first lead to any violent confrontations between the two rival groups. However, the Lombardistas had to legitimize themselves by forming new unions in each industry and wooing workers away from the Cromista ones. They quickly reorganized the men workers into the Sindicato de Trabajadores y Similares Generales de las Casas Beneficiadoras de Café, Tabaco, y del Comercio de la Región de Córdoba, (Union of Coffee, Tobacco, and Commercial Workers of the Region of Córdoba). This multiindustry union had difficulty legitimizing itself in part because the mayor continued to support the well-entrenched Moronista organization. When the Lombardistas applied for official recognition from the JCCA, the Moronistas went on the attack. The indomitable SOECC leader Luz Vera was one of many Cromista leaders who wrote to the JCCA and demanded that it deny their application. Since the Cromistas still wielded considerable political influence on the JCCA, it promptly rejected the Lombardista request.[69] The following year the entrenched Cromista SITCTAC was still powerful enough to persuade the largest beneficio owners to renew their 1931 collective contracts with them rather than with the Lombardistas.[70] When the owners, in accordance with the 1934 contract, laid off all their Lombardista loaders in February 1935, bloody confrontations broke out between the rival unions in front of three plants. The JCCA issued a decision supporting the officially recognized Cromista union and its 1934 contract, but work stoppages ensued all over the state in support of both sides.[71] The Lombardistas were not so easily persuaded to back down. They refused to accept the JCCA decision as legally binding and sent their petition to the Supreme Court. The court upheld the JCCA resolution and argued that the 1934 contract could not be annulled. However, it reiterated what it had said in earlier decisions: the closed shop was not obligatory. Therefore, the Lombardistas could not be expelled from the beneficios.[72]

After the Lombardistas reorganized the CGOCM into the CTM in 1936, they launched a statewide campaign to capture control of all coffee-worker unions. Abundio Torres became its point man in Córdoba, after he had shifted his allegiance to the CTM. He played an instrumental role in the negotiation team to win the first CTM contract for the men workers at Córdoba's seven largest plants.[73] In July 1938 Vidal Díaz Muñoz, the sugarcane-worker leader and head of the CTM's state confederation, organized the statewide coffee-worker union, the Sindicato de Trabajadores en General de la Industria del Café (Union of Workers of the Coffee Industry). Córdoba's Lombardista men's union became one of its affiliates. However, this statewide organization was a real potpourri that included both urban and rural coffee workers: some Coatepec, Huatusco, and Xalapa sorters; small coffee producers; day laborers; harvesters; and some loaders.

Córdoba's Cetemista and Cromista rival men's unions continued to spar through the end of the thirties. With approximately two hundred members each, neither one of these unions was cohesive enough to take control of the other.[74] They were both dominated by petty caciques who discouraged any leadership rotation. As the decade drew to a close, the Cetemistas proceeded to launch a series of initiatives to capture control of the SOECC, and they enlisted the local men's union to carry out this assignment. In 1938 and again in 1939, violent confrontations broke out between Cetemista obreros and Cromista obreras in front of the Sainz Pardo plant. Once again, sorter leaders spurred the rank and file to resort to aggressive actions against both men and women workers to defend their jobs and their union. Vera and Reyes were both injured in these scuffles. Meanwhile, they used their skills as intermediaries between their union and the political authorities to block all the CTM's maneuvers and to retain what little autonomy they still could garner under the decrepit Moronista CROM. Vera appealed to both the governor and President Cárdenas to intervene on their behalf to require the CTM to back off. In fact, she even asked for an interview with the president "in the name of the 5000 sorters of the state" to resolve this conflict.[75] Whether these entreaties led to any presidential response is not clear, but the SOECC did not have to confront serious CTM political machinations again. While the men's weak unions were mired in constant interunion disputes, the SOECC managed to come through the decade relatively unscathed with a collective leadership that continued in power and its Cromista affiliation as secure as ever.

The identical CTM campaign to seize control of the Coatepec sorter union between 1936 and 1938 played out in an entirely different manner. The conflict that ensued was even more violent than the Córdoba one, because the Cetemista headquarters were in nearby Xalapa and the state and municipal government supported their hegemonic strategies. In this case, the intraunion conflict, orchestrated from the outside, precipitated the rise of rival women cacicazgos. The Cetemistas courted the support of the opportunistic leader Amparo Ortiz, while the Cromistas or Autonomists, guided by Purissma textile workers, backed Adelina Téxon. The conflict began when Amparo tried to switch the affiliation of the SODCC from the CROM to the CTM without the authorization of the rank and file. Her maneuvers were supported by the CTM, which orchestrated a work stoppage or political strike that paralyzed eight plants for three months. Armed violence broke out between the Cetemista and its factions and led to the death of both men and women. This schism within the SODCC was so intense it pitted family members against each other and disrupted everyday lives. When the Cetemista sorters finally went back to work, the Autonomists blocked the plant doors, put up Cromista banners, and refused to allow the Cetemistas to leave the beneficios. Male Cetemista leaders even resorted to sexual aggression as a form of attack. When they attacked the Autonomists, they stripped Adelina and threw her out of a second floor window. This prompted the Autonomists to appeal to Governor Alemán for his intervention. He simply delegated to the municipal president the right to resolve the conflict. As a result of this aggressive CTM campaign, the SODCC passed under the control of the CTM. In 1938 the CTM won new labor contracts, and it threw the Autonomist minority out of the SODCC. Its members were forced to travel to Xalapa to find work in its CROM-affiliated workshops.[76]

The SOECC collective leadership bolstered by its newly acquired legitimacy and authority found additional ways to solidify its power.

It sent complaints (*quejas* or *demandas*) to the tripartite, state-sponsored conciliation and arbitration board to fight for the worker rights of the escogedoras.

Female Collective Cacicazgos, Workers' Rights, and the State

The 1931 labor law federalized the industrial-labor board system that had only operated in four states before then. It created the Federal Conciliation and Arbitration Board to serve as the final board of appeal, which preempted much of the ultimate authority of the state boards. In the past, it has been argued that the federal law really changed very little in Mexican labor law except that it provided the framework for solidifying the hegemony of the revolutionary state.[77] Kevin Middlebrook contends, on the other hand, that the creation of new state and municipal labor boards in states where little or no labor legislation had previously existed empowered the national labor movement because it removed worker-employer conflicts from the jurisdiction of the judicial system. The new state boards resolved more labor disputes and "increased the labor movement's ability to translate growing political importance into workplace gains."[78] There is no doubt that the local and state boards heard more cases than ever before after the promulgation of the 1931 Labor Code, but the Supreme Court had ruled as early as 1924 that the decisions of these tripartite boards were not legally binding. This loophole permitted each side to appeal to the federal courts for reversal of an unfavorable decision or at least an *amparo* (a stay of execution).[79] Factory owners were much more likely to have the financial resources to follow this option.

In Veracruz, where municipal boards had been in operation since 1914, the number of cases that labor unions brought before the boards increased dramatically after 1931. Needless to say, the strong petroleum, textile, teachers, bakers, sugarcane, electrical, and port unions brought far more claims to these boards than the coffee-worker unions, but the number of cases brought by these workers was surprisingly large. Coffee sorters were one of the major beneficiaries of this expansion of Veracruz's labor bureaucracy. Their leaders sent written communiqués and presented oral grievances before these tripartite boards and, in so doing, employed these boards as avenues for airing women's collective economic grievances. They were also demonstrating their effectiveness as leaders to their rank and file and, in this way, won worker loyalty and bolstered their own legitimacy.

The labor law was open to enumerable interpretations, for ambiguities existed over definitions and the jurisdiction of the industrial-labor boards. Labor caciques regularly manipulated certain provisions to solidify their legitimacy and the legality of their positions. The lack of clarity on the question of the closed shop and the supervision of internal elections are cases in point. The state and municipal boards, organized by the state's Labor Department, most probably provided greater opportunities for women leaders to articulate their demands than they had within the male-dominated national labor confederations. Córdoba and Coatepec leaders, who had created cohesive unions by now, employed these avenues much more frequently than their compañeras in Orizaba, Huatusco, and Xalapa.

Undoubtedly, the JCCA's resolutions were influenced by difficult economic and political times. The low price of coffee in the early 1930s weakened the bargaining power of the coffee-worker unions. Veracruz's coffee entrepreneurs likewise had to adjust to these economic challenges. As we have seen, some filed for bankruptcy, others weathered the storm through consolidation, and a few new firms emerged in the mid-1930s after prices began to rebound. To cut labor costs, some beneficiadores refused to abide by their labor contracts, shipped coffee out of state to be cleaned by nonunion sorters, reduced the size of their labor force, and kept wages stable or in some instances even lowered them.[80] Thus, coffee workers found themselves in a particularly precarious position in terms of their job security and take-home pay. We also know that coffee workers found that their union autonomy was more and more circumscribed by the centralizing tendencies of the CTM and the official party (PNR-PRM) during the governorship of Alemán.[81]

The SOECC leadership focused its attention on gaining the economic rights and benefits guaranteed under the 1931 law for permanent workers. Like the sorters unions in the other four Veracruz coffee towns, the Córdoba sorters union fought for recognition of their collective contracts, maintenance of a certain number of permanent positions, retention of the exclusion clause, receipt of sick pay, and the right to Sunday and holiday pay. They were not able to use the strike to fight for their demands as did the stronger railroad-, electrical-, and oil-worker unions, who had the backing of President Cárdenas.[82] However, they did win some of their cases. By the end of the decade, they had won most of the workers' rights guaranteed for permanent workers under the law, and they were able to increase the size of their membership. These gains were still limited in scope, for they did not address the critical questions of subsistence wages, the number of permanent as opposed to temporary positions, and the unhygienic working conditions. However, for seasonal workers, these gains were unprecedented in Mexico and, for that matter, in Latin America.

The SOECC leadership had to grapple continually with the semantic problem of how to define "seasonal work." The 1931 labor law's definitions of temporary and seasonal work did not accurately fit their specific occupation. Article 26 defines seasonal work as domestic work, farm work, and "occasional and temporary work not exceeding 60 days." These three categories of work did not require a written contract.[83] Because Córdoba's coffee sorters had been working under collective contracts with an eight-hour day and wages equivalent to the minimum rural wage since the mid-1920s, they were in a particularly privileged position in comparison with other seasonal workers. The occupation of coffee sorting was even more complex because their first collective contracts recognized a two-tiered labor system: the permanent worker, who was guaranteed work based on seniority and placement on the union list, and the temporary or occasional worker, who was called on a week-to-week basis according to the supply of coffee needing to be sorted. Both union leaders and exporters manipulated the ambiguity between these two categories to their advantage. Plant owners would characterize all sorters as temporary workers, while the union representatives argued that all full-time workers, and even at times occasional workers, were permanent and therefore entitled to full worker benefits guaranteed under the 1931 law. The SOECC filed the same types of quejas against the beneficia-dores as the men's union, except they were in far greater numbers. I will concentrate on the SOECC quejas because they had greater mean-ing for the construction of a women cacicazgo. Although these coffee workers did not win everything they wanted, the level of agency and the number of their successes must be measured against the even more frustrating experiences of other seasonal workers in the 1930s.

The implementation of Articles 78, 80, and 93, which covered Sun-day and holiday pay, was a critical issue for coffee-sorter leaders. Since sorters usually did not work between May and October, many ben-eficiadores believed it was unnecessary to pay for these nonwork days during the slow season. To force owners to pay wages for September 16 and May 1 at a time when the beneficios were usually not operat-ing was a bitter pill for owners to swallow. In Córdoba, coffee export-ers must have abided by the law, for there were no grievances filed on this particular issue. But in other coffee towns, exporters sometimes intentionally suspended work before December 25 or May 1 to avoid paying the holiday wage, arguing that they had exhausted their sup-plies of café verde. For example, Coatepec's Belem Carmona filed a complaint against the Arbuckles for their failure to pay wages for May 1. The company argued that it did not have enough coffee to sort by late April, so it had suspended operations several weeks before the holiday. Since the workers had not worked up to the holiday, the com-pany contended it was not obliged to pay. The JCCA upheld the work-ers complaint in accordance with Article 80. The Arbuckles hotly contested this ruling and eventually took their case to the Supreme Court.[84]

The right to Sunday pay, addressed in Article 93, was one issue the SOECC cacicas fought hard for. In 1935 the SOECC filed complaints against both Ezequiel González and Davíd González Rosas for failing to pay wages for the seventh day as stipulated in their 1934 contracts. In 1936 when González entered into bankruptcy, he asked for judicial liquidation, which would have allowed him to rescind his 1934 labor contract and not pay back wages for Sundays. When his assets were eventually turned over to Enrique Galván y López and his wife, Esther Marenco, Eufrosina Moya, the new secretary general, called for the new owners to honor the old contract. She sought one month's salary for each worker, or a total of four thousand to six thousand pesos for breaking the contract.[85] By 1937 the JCCA had still not ruled on either case. The SOECC leadership threatened to ask for an amparo in the federal courts if the JCCA ruled against them. The union argued that González had never really entered into bankruptcy proceedings, for all his goods were still listed in the public registry; he had simply passed his properties over to Ester Marenco. In the following year, the JCCA upheld the union; and when Galván y López took his case to the Supreme Court, he lost again. The workers were awarded 7,800 pesos to be taken from the owner's liquidated holdings. Unfortunately, the exporter filed for bankruptcy in 1939, and Alemán intervened and blocked the implementation of the court's ruling.[86] Thus, the governor overruled the JCCA decision in the name of economic exigency.

The closure of a major beneficio presented even a greater challenge to the SOECC leaders, for it could bring a sizable reduction in the number of jobs. When the two U.S. corporations, Hard and Rand and the Arbuckles, did not open their plants in 1933, the SOECC leadership demanded that their properties be embargoed and sold to reimburse the workers for the loss of three months' work, or a total of six thousand pesos.[87] Their advisor, Abundio Torres, also wrote an appeal on their behalf. The JCCA rejected their petition and supported the U.S. companies' argument that nothing in their original contract of 1926 had required the plant owners to supply annual work to the workers.[88] They based their argument on the fact that the owners called up workers only during the harvesting season, and therefore they were not offering the workers full-time employment.

The cacicas always sought to prevent jobs from being transferred to other towns, but it was often difficult to block the beneficiadores' strategies. In November 1935 the Zardain branch of Beneficiadora Exportadora opened a new plant in Ixcatepec outside Mexico City. The Zardains had already closed their older plant on Fifth Avenue and moved their operations to the capital. When it was rumored that twenty-five sorters' tables had been removed from the shuttered beneficio, the SOECC filed a complaint with the JCCA. José Zardain reassured the leadership before the JCCA that the old plant would soon reopen under a new owner, Ricardo Regules, and that no positions would be lost. He also argued that no Córdoba coffee would be sorted in Mexico City; the new workers would be cleaning coffee coming exclusively from Oaxaca and Puebla. The SOECC representative, Inés Reyes, then demanded that the JCCA send Orizaba and Mexico City labor inspectors to ascertain whether the tables had been moved to Ixcatepec. The inspectors reported back to the JCCA that they had only found forty small tables, which were not in use.[89] The SOECC leadership was doing everything in its power to use the state board to protect the loss of permanent jobs. In fact, Regules soon did reopen the beneficio and rehire two hundred sorters.

Another strategy employed by the Córdoba exporters was even more difficult to block. Beneficiadores sometimes shipped green coffee to plants employing nonunion workers to cut labor costs. The Orizaba exporter Guillermo Boesch was well-known for buying coffee from the Cordobeses, preparing it with nonunion labor in his plant in Fortín de las Flores, and selling it there where the price was higher. This practice was discussed in the SOECC's general assembly, but no direct action was ever taken to block the shipments to Fortín. The Cordobeses did not usually follow this strategy or attempt to insert a clause into the collective contracts to permit this practice, for they knew the SOECC was too powerful to allow this to become a regular practice. However, the weaker Xalapa and Huatusco unions found it much more difficult to block the shipment of café verde to other locations for sorting.[90]

The SOECC leadership went on the offensive when the large Arbuckle beneficio finally closed its doors for good in July 1938 but failed to give the required ten-day notification to its workers. The SOECC leaders organized a sit-in to protest the violation of the labor law. They instructed their rank and file to remain in the plant and to refuse to turn in their cleaned coffee. At the Municipal Conciliation Board meeting, the general manager argued that he had given his notification according to "long-held customs and precedents that existed when the sorting process ended each year." This refusal to provide notification not only contravened the law, but it also reflected management's arbitrary behavior toward its workers. Under pressure from the JCCA, the company was forced to back down, pay ten pesos to each worker before the plant closed, and recompense the workers thirty-five centavos per kilo of waste for the coffee they had cleaned. Under this agreement, the sorters ended their occupation of the plant. A second complaint was also filed with the JCCA when the Arbuckles tried to sell their tables to Regules. The state board sent a labor inspector to the site to prepare a complete inventory of the property and to assess its value for the bankruptcy proceedings. When he found most of the tables still there, the SOECC dropped its complaint.[91]

The leadership's most comprehensive demands are found in its 1941 proposal for a new contract when the coffee prices were on the rebound. It was sent to the five major coffee exporters: Ezequiel González, Enrique Galván y López, Tirso Sainz Pardo, Ricardo Regules, and the Arbuckles. It is not clear whether the women's leaders themselves or their male Cromista advisors authored this document, but it did contain some new gender-specific demands. As always, the union wanted its workers to be treated as permanent workers, so it chose to use the term *operaria* (industrial women worker) rather than escogedora to emphasize their entitlement to job security, union-selected floor supervisors, paid holidays, a paid vacation, sickness compensation for illnesses contracted in the workplace, better working conditions, worker housing, and a sliding piece-rate scale based on the coffee grade. To secure a living wage, the proposal called for a wage that would guarantee a stable income.[92] It also demanded a guaranteed date for the commencement of plant operations. Work would have to start between October 15 and November 15, or the companies would have to pay compensation to the workers for loss of pay. The SOECC also requested 250 permanent positions every year. These workers would come from the union's first list. In terms of the piece-rate wage, the proposal called for the introduction of a tiered scale based on the amount of waste in the coffee. If one arroba contained up to one hundred grams of waste, the worker would be paid twenty-five centavos per arroba; and if the coffee contained three thousand grams, the workers would be paid at the rate of 1.35 pesos.[93]

The contract proposal also sought the enforcement of new revisions to the labor law. It called not only for Sunday pay but also for five national holidays, which included January 1. Furthermore, the piece-rate wage, it was argued, should no longer be pegged to the rural but rather to the urban minimum wage, and no distinction should be made between the wages of permanent and occasional workers. This sweeping proposal called for a seven-day paid vacation and 10 percent of the company's annual profits. The union sought insurance to cover all its workers for both professional and nonprofessional illnesses.[94] Owners would be obligated to pay a death benefit equal to one month's wages to cover funeral expenses. Obviously, the leadership wanted to phase out the paternalist practice whereby the patrón would make a voluntary seven- to eight-peso contribution to the family of the deceased.

This contract proposal addressed for the first time the lack of hygienic working conditions and maternity benefits. The leadership asked for an eight-day paid maternity leave before the birth of the child and one month for postpartum recovery. In addition, it asked for a designated place where the women could breastfeed their babies. Bathrooms should have proper ventilation systems, and water fountains should be installed for the exclusive use of the women workers. The women's workshop should be separated from the machine room and the warehouse, where the men worked. The union complained about unhealthy working conditions in the workshops: "If present conditions continue, workers will be adversely affected and will become sick from the dust that they inhale during the work-day."[95] They asked that the workplace have proper ventilation and enough light, so they could more easily and safely sort the coffee. Finally, the company should build houses for its operarias to house 10 percent of their workforce and charge a monthly rent equivalent to .5 percent of the property's assessed value, as specified in Article 111. In essence, the coffee sorters were making the same demands as unionized men workers, the aristocracy of Mexican labor, plus additional maternal provisions. A month later the secretary general, Concepción Rodríguez, sent a revised version of the proposal, showing the seriousness of the leadership's intent to get a new contract with extensive revisions. When the owners refused to enter into contract negotiations, the union called for a strike. A month later the strike order was rescinded because the SOECC was unable to persuade the owners to accept their demands.[96]

At the end of the decade, the SOECC's collective leadership began to pursue another important objective: the acquisition of a union hall. Vera, Romero, and Castro headed a delegation to buy a two-story building on the corner of Third Avenue and Eleventh Street for five thousand pesos. They raised enough funds through a hefty 2.50-peso weekly deduction from each sorter's paycheck. This financial strategy allowed the leadership to pay off their mortgage in three annual installments.[97] Needless to say, the loss of one day's wage was a tremendous sacrifice for the rank and file. But never again would the SOECC have to hold its meetings in the beneficios or the cramped Cromista federation headquarters. The collective leadership had initiated one more strategy to retain local autonomy and fiscal independence.

In 1939 the SOECC's executive committee gathered for an official picture, which was another means to legitimize their authority to the sorter community and the public at large (see photograph 7). The

7. Executive committee of the SOECC, 1939. Standing, left to right: Luz Vera, Francisca Rodríguez, Elodia Belloa, Eufrosina Moya, Sofía Castro, Inés Reyes. Sitting, center: Luz Romero (secretary general). Sitting: Jacinta Vázquez and Guadalupe López. Courtesy of the APIRO.

nine women sedately standing or sitting in formal poses are firmly intent on representing themselves as respectable and honorable labor leaders. Their seriousness and sense of self-confidence exudes from their portraiture. This picture beautifully captures the continuity of leadership from Luz Vera, its founding leader, to Luz Romero, the present secretary general, to the emerging younger generation, Inés, Sofía, and Eufrosina. At the same time, the leaders represent themselves in different ways from the humble Luz Romero with her sandals to the chic Inés with her two-piece dress and heels. Eufrosina with her frills is shoulder to shoulder with Sofía in a formal black dress.

In conclusion, the gendered dimensions of caciquismo need to be included in analyses of postrevolutionary social movements and their leadership. The emerging Córdoba coffee-sorter cacicazgo resembled men's labor cacicazgos in many respects. The factors that led to the emergence of this cacicazgo did not depend on the gender of the leaders. They built a cacicazgo based first and foremost on an informal patronage system, where the godfather (*padrino*), or in this case the godmother (*madrina*), controlled access to human, fiscal, and political resources within the union hierarchy. Their labor activism demonstrated a subtle and flexible exercise of power, where economic threats and psychological manipulation predominated. Physical violence was resorted to only during intra- and interunion conflicts where jobs were at stake. They preferred to use negotiation and manipulation to achieve their objectives. In this early stage, emerging cacicas of the SOECC seemed to have relied more heavily on their own compañeras than on family networks for support.

They employed the mechanism of intermediation to negotiate with those above them in the labor bureaucracy to secure access to financial resources and meet the needs of the rank and file. They also resorted to exclusion in the union's membership to prevent challenges to their political authority by the rank-and-file rebels and to confront external challenges to their authority. As mechanisms of cacical power, brokering and excluding do not necessarily have to be linked to masculinity. In the Veracruz coffee agroindustry, women leaders were actually much more successful than their male counterparts in shaping cacicazgos not only because their unions were significantly larger but also because these women exercised singular leadership skills and courage in public venues. Although courage is often associated with masculinity, it is also a behavior exhibited when the downtrodden are fighting for their very economic survival.

SOECC leaders found their voice in the state-sponsored, postrevolutionary conciliation and arbitration boards. In spite of their seemingly weak bargaining position, they presented their cases and succeeded in negotiating collective contracts, eight hour days with lunch breaks, holiday pay, and wages comparable to the rural minimum wage. If these achievements are compared with those won by the Colombian coffee sorters,[98] Veracruz sorters were very well served by their collective cacicazgo and the postrevolutionary state. Rather than marginalized seasonal workers of the labor movement, their continual involvement in the national conflicts between rival labor confederations made them, for better or for worse, constitutive members of Mexico's organized labor movement.

Córdoba's collective union cacicazgo differed markedly from Jalisco's family duo, or dual cacicazgo. However, the dual and collective cacicazgos seem to suggest that caciquismo can take many forms, which should not be necessarily linked to masculinity. Already, a variety of union cacicazgos among and across genders were beginning to appear. The following chapter explores the sorters' union culture that these cacicas helped to construct.

5

Everyday Experiences and Obrera Culture

When the anthropologist Julio de la Fuente observed that the escoge-doras were one of the key social groups in Córdoba's emerging work-ing class in the early 1940s, he was highlighting their singular impor-tance among the city's working poor.[1] Understanding the nature of this women-centered community involves exploring the interrela-tionships between their everyday experiences in the workplace, the home, and the union halls. According to Lüdtke everyday life centers "on the actions and sufferings of those who are frequently labeled 'ev-eryday, ordinary people.'" It pertains to the "life and survival of those who have remained largely anonymous in history—the 'nameless' multitudes in their work, and 'trials and tribulation,' and 'festive joys.'"[2] To understand this in terms of culture, Norberto Elias notes that the representation of the everyday (*lo cotidiano*), or everyday culture (*la cultura cotidiana*), cannot be understood without putting it into the context of the non-everyday (*lo no-cotidiano*), or the dom-inant culture.[3] If everyday conscience was the incarnation of experi-ence and of ideological, ingenuous, nonreflexive, and even, at times, false thoughts, its opposite is the correct, truly authentic (i.e., domi-nant or bourgeois) conscience.[4] Thus, the interplay between the ev-eryday and the non-everyday is essential in understanding both con-cepts. Undoubtedly, the study of everyday life is about small social groups, but it allows historical subjects to use their own self-will to reappropriate social practices that are not bounded by hierarchical conditioning factors.[5]

Everyday experiences in the workplace influenced sorters' way of thinking and behaving in the streets, churches, and union halls and, in so doing, gave them a new collective sense of identity, comradeship, and citizenship. This obrera culture included emancipatory qualities, for it challenged domestic and workplace patriarchy. It was a multilayered community and culture. Nurtured within women-centered spaces, escogedora culture emerged and flourished alongside and in constant negotiation with that of the coffee elite. At times, it affirmed traditional beliefs about the family, entrepreneurial paternalism, trade unionism, and the state. Other times, it challenged prevailing gender norms and power relations through the discourse and activism of its members in civic and cultural events.

The private sphere has generally been considered predominant over the public sphere in the everyday lives of working women.[6] This chapter shows that the sorters' working experiences, however, did influence their domestic experiences, for they had to continually negotiate with family members for time and space to continue working and participating in union activities. This chapter begins by focusing on their everyday domestic experiences of sorters during the 1940s and 1950s, drawing on interviews conducted in Córdoba, Coatepec, and Orizaba. Since no written records exist on the sorters' domestic lives, I have relied heavily on fifteen oral histories conducted over the past decade. These life histories reveal a striking number of common experiences. These shared experiences allowed the women to forge a collective memory with their coworkers, for "collective memory maintains the lived experience of individuals within groups . . . because that individual experience is never remembered without reference to a shared context."[7]

The sorters constructed an alternative working women's culture around three union-organized social activities: dances, military bands, and theater. Although escogedoras were economically and socially marginalized in provincial society, the cacicas found ways to organize union activities not only to reinforce their own authority and legitimacy over the rank and file but also to gain wider acceptance for women workers within the labor movement and provincial society. As sorters became active social agents at organized civic and social events with other women workers, they transgressed provincial gender norms. In their collective memory, these women recalled gaining a new sense of self-worth, individual autonomy, community cohesiveness, trade-union solidarity, and citizenship. They also exhibited xenophobic feelings, similar to those displayed in other Mexican worker cultures. The sorters clearly understood and conveyed in their interviews the underlining tensions between the emancipatory and clientelist nature of their working women's culture. This culture was, however, always circumscribed by the patriarchal norms of their families, unions, beneficio owners, politics, and the community at large.

Domestic Experiences of Coffee Sorters

The profiles of the fifteen sorters interviewed in Córdoba, Coatepec, and Orizaba reveal a striking number of commonalities they shared with other poor working women.[8] Almost all the interviewees were born into impoverished families during the 1920s and 1930s. More than half of their mothers, and even some grandmothers, had worked in the beneficios before the interviewees were born. Third generation sorters were especially proud of their family's multigenerational obrera tradition. The remaining mothers were recent immigrants from Oaxaca, Michoacán, or neighboring villages around these three coffee towns. A large percentage of the interviewees had grown up in female-headed households, where the fathers had either died or abandoned the family. In other cases, both parents had died. This explains why so many started working before they had finished primary school. The vast majority of them entered into the workplace in the forties or early fifties during the third coffee boom. They still proudly remember the meager wage they brought home their first week of work, which demonstrated their budding sense of identity as a pro-

8. Brígida Siriaco García with her band photo, 2005. Photograph by author.

ductive family worker. In general, they did not talk very much about
their sexual relationships or their childbearing roles and how those
had influenced their working experiences. They began working out
of economic necessity, not because they were simply entering their
teenage years and needed pin money. Most had their first sexual relationships as adolescents, but these were usually not long-lasting relationships; Brígida Siriaco García and Delia Ortiz Sarmiento were

two cases in point (see photograph 8). They usually had more-fulfill-
ing relationships later in life. At the other end of the spectrum were
the sorters whose marital or common-law relationships endured
throughout their entire working lives. Estela Velázquez Ramírez and
Silvia Herrera Luna remained married to their macho husbands, and
each bore nine or ten children. Some interviewees bore no children
or just one child. Although some stopped working for a few months
after giving birth, most sorters gave birth and immediately went back
to work. All the women interviewed here worked at least ten to thirty years before the mechanization of the plants, except for Socorro
Gómez Reyes, whose mother had sufficient funds to send her to beau-
tician school. Other than Gómez, none of them had more than a primary education, and at least six were functionally illiterate. Like most
obreras, they lived on the margins of provincial society. Frequently
they used survival strategies to lessen domestic workloads, control
their bodies, heal strained gender relations, and confront economic
hardships. Yet they were more than willing to share, with frankness
but also with great pain, their life stories with a U.S. researcher.

From the most advantaged to the least advantaged sorter, their everyday experiences were framed within a context of suffering and
struggle. Economic survival was always uppermost in their minds,
for their wages never kept up with cost-of-living increases, particularly in the forties and the fifties. From childhood on, they endured
unusually heavy workloads.

> Well, she [my mother] put us in school but . . . only for the first
> years, for since she sold food [on the street] we had to help her
> grind the chili; she made champurrados in the style of the region
> she came from, tamales, and everything else during the night, so
> we only slept two hours a night, two hours we slept, because she
> had to make the chocolate drink according to an old recipe from
> the region she came from with cinnamon, cacao, and chocolate.
> . . . We went to sleep at midnight and already at one we were up,
> and I was only a child.[9]

They usually lived in small rented rooms around a patio de vecindad, where they had to perform all the tasks of meal preparation and child care before they left for work. Very often their workdays were eighteen or twenty hours long.

> When . . . I was with my husband, . . . I had to get up at five o'clock in the morning . . . leave the food all prepared for breakfast. . . . If one can really call it breakfast! Something rapid. . . . Take my daily bath, do the daily cleaning . . . bathe the girl . . . or bathe her when I came home from work. At this time . . . we were then a family of three, but in a tiny room, let's say four by four [meters]. In this humble little room, [we lived] very poor, having almost nothing.[10]

These women had few ways to exercise control over their bodies. Teenage pregnancies were common, and multiple pregnancies were a fact of life. The moral and religious dilemma of whether or not to undergo an abortion always haunted them. Should they violate Church teachings to limit the number of children they had to feed? In Estela's case, she recognized her inability to limit her pregnancies; so, although she was a devout Catholic, she resorted to abortion as her only option.

> It was a baby factory . . . one after the other. . . . Under these circumstances . . . there were three abortions. . . . With the fourth child, a doctor was there and it was born. A second son this time. The abortions and the births were not done with great care, never with a doctor in attendance. So the doctor this time remarked, "You are like animals. I will take care of you for this birth . . . because . . . who knows whether later you will have cancer. . . ." Thank God this never happened to me![11]

Herbal remedies and certain "pills" were available to induce an abortion, but their use sometimes had fatal consequences. Brígida remembered how an attempt to end a late-term unwanted pregnancy ended in the death of one teenager. It was common to resort to more dangerous alternatives; an abortionist inserted a rubber tube into the vagina to stimulate contractions.[12] Needless to say, the fear of causing a hemorrhage and the threat of cancer deterred many women from taking these risks.

As more children were born, mothers had to confront the problem of organizing their time, most importantly how to find child care during the workday. You couldn't stop working, or you would lose your job. Most of them could not rely on their partners very much for domestic tasks. Most frequently, members of the extended family came to their assistance. Grandmothers frequently assumed child care responsibilities and early schooling. Or the oldest child was left in charge of the younger children. Eufrosina's fourth child, Salomón, remembered having to learn how to cook and iron and take care of his younger siblings when his mother was working. She also let her grandparents take care of her children during the school year, since she was far too busy with her work and union activities to have much time for child raising.[13] Their neighbors quite naturally looked down on them for working outside the home and not being good mothers.

> When a neighbor told me . . . that my daughter . . . was out in the street, [she gave] two or three spanks to the child and [told me] my place was here at home. Now the other baby girl had been born and when there was no señora to take care of her, I said to the girl: "Look, you give your little sister the milk, here it is." And she said to me, "Cold like this?" "Yes, you give it to her cold, and you give her bread." "Do I warm it up?" "No!" Because I feared that she would burn herself.[14]

Strained gender relations between sorters and their partners were common. Teenage relationships didn't last long, for they were built on passing fancies, sexual experimentation, or adolescent whims to move out of the home. Men came and went quite regularly, and they performed little or no domestic work or child care. Although Estela's husband came home from work before her and would warm up the meal, she recalled clearly, looking back, that she always worked considerably more than her husband.

> If one thinks about it carefully, we worked more than a man. . . .
> Triple what a man worked! A man dedicates himself to work
> eight hours; he comes home and rests because he has finished
> his eight hours. If he is retired, he leaves [and] collects his pension, but he is being paid for not working. We, the housewives,
> what happens? If you work outside of the house, you finish your
> eight hour day, you return home, and in the house you are the
> long-suffering (*abnegada*) housewife [and] mother of the family. You are the maid, you are the laundress, you are the cook, you
> are the lover and the wife. What salary are you paid? Nothing![15]

A double standard existed regarding gender norms in domestic relations. For the most part, the sorters did not challenge the domestic
abuse and philandering of their partners or even consider taking them
to court.[16] Very often they were blamed when a relationship turned
sour or the man took off. When Maria del Carmen Ríos Zavala was
abandoned at the altar, her brother blamed her for not being able to
keep a man and threw her out of the house.

> The day that I was going to marry was December 24, [and] my
> intended fiancé went off to carouse and did not arrive [for the
> ceremony] . . . and so I did not get married. Therefore, when my
> brother arrived, he chased me out [of the house], and I left, and
> since then I have lived in the street. I left [my family], found myself a room, and I went to live all alone by myself, crying . . . because of my disgrace, right? . . . Later on I met the father of my
> son . . . but I did not marry him, but rather we lived together, but
> it was a dog's life.[17]

Even the relationships that endured were fraught with problems. Estela's husband was a jealous macho who often abused her and continued to have extramarital relationships throughout their marriage.
However, she remained faithful and stoic to the end, because the sur-

vival of the family was uppermost in her mind: "The improprieties of the husband do not matter to a woman, for what we are interested in is our children."[18]

In assuming traditional gender roles of mother, wife, and housewife, sorters remained in charge of family affairs in some areas of domestic life. Housewives continued to control the purse strings for household expenses, just as their mothers had done. Daughters who lived at home always turned their wages over to their mothers to help pay for basic necessities. They might leave a few centavos aside for snacks, but that was all.[19] If they became the head of the household, they took over control of all family income. More importantly, they developed economic survival strategies to earn extra money after the regular workday ended or during the summer months, when the beneficios were not in operation. They washed clothes, cleaned houses, waited tables, served as midwives, picked coffee, and worked on neighboring farms. For those less fortunate, bartending and prostitution were other options to make ends meet. A number of different types of brothels dotted the San Miguel neighborhood of Córdoba.[20]

One of the most ambitious and astute sorters, Estela, was determined to do everything she could to improve her socioeconomic status. After the birth of her second child, she and her husband, who worked for the Mexican Telephone Company, decided to build their own house. So she set to work earning money on the side, selling food and clothing within the plant with the idea of saving money for the future.[21] She was also a street vendor on weekends. They bought a plot outside the city limits and built their first house with used lumber. Later, they moved back into town and bought another house lot and built a two-story house with a convenience store on the ground floor and their living quarters upstairs. This is where she still lives today. At the other extreme is Isabel Romero Serrano, who continues to live in the house her parents patched together with secondhand wood many years ago down by the railroad tracks. It has no doors, but a chain fence runs around the outside of the property to keep the dogs inside. Furniture is so sparse that we sat on stools in a cramped kitchen that did not even have a table.

Unlike the majority of Mexican obreras, who usually lived in working-class neighborhoods close to their employment, the residential patterns of the escogedoras were heavily influenced by the seasonal nature of their work. A four-hundred-sorter sampling drawn from the SOECC 1944 membership list reveals no significant residential pattern in Córdoba. They lived in dwellings throughout the downtown. A number of sorters often lived at the same address, which suggests that they rented rooms off patios de vecindad; but many more did not. As for the temporary workers, they frequently lived in the outlying communities and walked or took buses to come into work.[22] Some leaders, in particular Castro and Moya, eventually found houses next to the plants. By the time I interviewed the former sorters, many had finally acquired their own houses or rented single-family dwellings. They were now long-term urban residents. The same scattered residential pattern was found in Coatepec. Some sorters lived in the central district of the town in patios de vecindad, some of which were owned by the coffee producer Dr. Rafael Sánchez. Others, who were often coffee pickers, resided on the outskirts of the town.[23] Thus, the sorters who had obtained the status of permanent workers had become fixtures in Córdoba's and Coatepec's downtown by the 1940s, while the ebb and flow of the lower-rung temporary workers changed according to the availability of seasonal work.

Religion played a much less significant role in the lives of the sorters than in those of their Spanish employers. They simply had no free time when they were raising children and trying to make ends meet. Estela had far too many children to go to mass regularly: "Sunday we went out; with the children on one side and myself on the other side of the basket to sell slices of cake in the patios de vecindad. . . . Instead of enjoying ourselves, we went to the river to wash [clothes]. . . . In the night, it was time to iron all the children's clothes, so one went to bed very late."[24]

On the other hand, Estela was a believer who upheld Catholic values. She insisted on getting married after their second child was born so her two children could be seen as "legitimate." She also prayed regularly to seek help in finding ways to put her children through school. "I am very religious; I entrusted myself to God and told him, 'If you are going to help me, help me to get enough money for my daughter to finish school. But if you believe that I will not be able to do it, put an impediment in my way so my daughter cannot achieve this goal.'"[25] Other sorters likewise admitted that, while they were working, there was no free time to go to mass because of their triple workload. Now that they were no longer working, they had more time to attend mass. December 12 was always a special occasion, for they would participate in the pilgrimages and attend mass to worship the Virgin of Guadalupe, Mexico's patron saint. Although the sorters did not find time to attend mass every week, they baptized their children and chose their compañeras to be their children's godmothers.[26] In this way, working women's social networks were intertwined within the workplace. The sorter community had become their extended family.

Finally, some sorters sought to plan for their children's future. Most importantly, they wanted to give them the opportunity to have the education that they themselves had been denied. Estela was the most successful in achieving her goal, providing some form of professional training for all nine of her children. This is what she had struggled for, achieved, and talked about incessantly. How did she accomplish this? After she lost her position as a sorter, she operated a beauty salon, knitted clothing to sell to her friends, and opened a small store, which she still runs in her late seventies. She contrasted her work ethic with that of other sorters who were no better off than they were forty years ago: "They did not know how to seize opportunities. . . . They did not know how to prepare themselves for today's world. . . . My mind was working for tomorrow, for tomorrow."[27]

While these working women had little time for leisure activities, they came and went from their small, cramped dwellings with much greater frequency than middle-class housewives, who were shut inside their homes most of the day. Adolescent sorters, who had the most free time and some pocket change to spend, often loitered outside the tenement housing without much supervision from their overworked mothers. They had a reputation for putting on makeup and dressing up colorfully when they went out to the bars or dances.[28] Thus, sorters were now moving into new public spaces during their leisure time.

Working Women's Culture, Heterosexuality, and Dances

Leisure for working-class men and women outside the home during the early stages of industrialization was generally gender-specific and occurred in gender-segregated spaces. Men's leisure activities reinforced feelings of male community, male privilege, and manliness and more generally represented a bulwark against economic exploitation. More specifically, trade unionism sought to strengthen bonds of militancy, solidarity, loyalty, and honor in its language and practices. Whether we are speaking of Kathy Peiss's New York men workers, Robert Alegre's Mexican railroad workers, or Thomas Klubock's Chilean miners, working-class men would spend a good part of their leisure time and their extra money in bars, lodges, gymnasia, and union halls. In this all-male environment, they sparred with each other in one-upmanship activities and developed a strong sense of camaraderie. As Kathy Peiss has observed, within this "homosocial world, rituals of aggression and competition became important mechanisms of male bonding."[29]

In contrast, working women's leisure was much more restricted in terms of its location, variety, and duration; it was very closely tied to the work rhythms of the home, where social activities among women family members predominated. Since societal pressures dictated that working women had to perform their domestic duties when they returned from work, little time remained except for family celebrations and religious activities. As a consequence, no clear differentiation existed between work and leisure for women in the nineteenth century and early twentieth century whether we are speaking about the United States or Mexico. Usually, "women had to fit their leisure into their work, rather than around it." The few leisure activities for women took place between women within the family or within the working-class neighborhoods. They were primarily based on reciprocal relations to provide mutual aid, and they promoted sociability among female kinfolk.[30] The onset of urbanization and industrialization changed the nature of leisure activities for working women and for working men. The streets, dance halls, bars, and union halls gradually became new venues where women found a temporary escape from their father's or partner's control, and this created a subtle shift in the balance of power in gender relations.[31]

The roots of Mexico City working women's and working men's cultures outside the home seem to lie in nineteenth-century mutual-aid societies, which were originally organized according to trade, workshop, or gender. While mixed and gender-segregated mutual-aid societies were created primarily to raise funds to assist coworkers in the event of sickness, death, and catastrophe, they also supported child care facilities, educational programs, shorter workdays, and safety for paycheck collection. These societies held dances, dinners, street fairs (*kermesses*), patron saint festivals, and charitable events, all of which provided women workers in particular new opportunities to socialize with nonfamily members outside the home. There is evidence to suggest that women workers collaborated with their compañeras in staging circuses and benefit dances to raise money. These mutualist traditions were passed on to nascent trade unions organized by women garment workers, cigarette workers, and coffee workers at the turn of the twentieth century. Working women also began to imitate their male coworkers in the consumption of alcohol in public places. They would drop by bars and pulque dispensaries (*pulquerías*) on their way home from work.[32]

Dance halls became another important leisure venue for working women and working men in New York City, Buenos Aires, Mexico City, and Veracruz during the first decades of the twentieth century. It was here that the open expression of heterosocial and heterosexual working-class culture blossomed. The latest dancing styles, steps, and body positions allowed dancers to express themselves in entirely different ways. This generated a new sense of personal and sexual independence. While the tango was sweeping Buenos Aires dance halls, the *danzón* was the new craze in Mexico City and Veracruz.[33]

From the time the danzón arrived in the port of Veracruz at the end of the 1870s from Cuba, it exhibited a truly lower-class flavor. Its African rhythm was immediately embraced by the Afro-Veracruzanos (*jarochos*), who were already familiar with the Afro-Caribbean heritage songs—the *mandingo*, *son*, and *huapango*. The danzón became an integral part of everyday life in working-class communities, where it was performed in the streets, parks, bars, and patios and for carnival. The wind-instrument orchestras (*danzoneras*) were developed to meet the big rage. Federico Gamboa mentions that the danzón was being danced at the turn of the century in Mexico City's nightclubs.[34]

The danzón had a direct impact on gender relations and female sexuality. Robert Buffington contends that the danzón became one of the mediums through which obrera culture developed. María Novaro's 1991 film, *Danzón* reminds us that "working-class women have always been central to the cultural practice of danzón." Although its choreography tends to reinforce male control over women, it allows a "relational 'dialogue' between partners that challenges men's 'right' to dominate women."[35]

Dance halls were venues where middle-class gender norms could very often be temporarily ignored or put aside. Lewd language, bawdy behavior, drunkenness, tough dancing, smoking, boisterous laughter, and smoking by either gender were tolerated.[36] However, heterosexual relations in these halls were still bounded by class and gender restraints. Managers of dance halls had to reign in fights, violence, and drunkenness to keep their commercial enterprises open and to make a profit. Moreover, some forms of self-policing or monitoring by fellow workers kept the lid on offensive sexual behavior. Although male dominance continued to prevail in heterosocial relations, women could negotiate with their partners for greater social and sexual freedom. In these nightspots, working women were faced with ambiguous signals about the sanctity of virginity. Lessons about chastity they had learned from their parents, church, and in school conflicted with their everyday experiences on the street. In the United States it was a balancing act between social responsibility, female desire, and male pressures, contends Kathy Peiss. "The pleasure and freedom young women craved could be found in the social world of dance halls, but these always carried a mixed message, permitting expressive female sexuality within a context of dependence and vulnerability."[37] It was not so entirely different in Mexico.

When Mexico City and Monterrey industrialists began organizing dances in their factories, their primary objective was to maintain and reinforce paternalism, in much the same way as hacendados had done on their estates. They sought to create a disciplined, contented labor force and to uphold female virtue on the workshop floor, while simultaneously winning worker loyalty. Sponsoring dances in the factories to celebrate the opening of a business or a religious holiday legitimized their personal authority and highlighted their paternalism toward their workers.[38] Córdoba beneficiadores followed the same practice. They were reinforcing family and religious values when they organized a mass and a dance on December 12 in celebration of the Virgin of Guadalupe. This was also a means for the owners to oblige the sorters to come to work on a national holiday, when the coffee harvest was at its height. They probably were also intent on instilling in their obreras the moral values associated with the Virgin. These religious festivities led to the social intermingling of women workers, men workers, white-collar workers, and even the owners themselves outside the confines of their homes. The night before the holiday, men and women workers would decorate the beneficios' statues of the Virgin in Córdoba with garlands of paper flowers. The sorters remembered participating in a pilgrimage carrying their statues of the Virgin around the town and then attending mass before going to work. They would work until midday, when the priest would conduct a service within the beneficio. After mass, the owner would serve a dinner and provide a marimba band to play for several hours. Under the watchful eye of the owner, different forms of heterosexual intimacy played out on the dance floor. As Delia recalled, "We danced with the loaders, the machinists, [and] the owners. The prettiest girls danced with the owner, no?"[39] Since a majority of the workers were women, they more often than not danced with each other. Female conviviality and comradeship (*compañerismo*) grew out of these shared experiences.

Sorter unions might not have been nearly as cohesive as other unions because of the seasonal nature of the work and the abundance of temporary workers, but the SOECC's headquarters became for many their home away from home to participate in a large variety of social activities. The weekly dances held throughout the entire harvest season were festive occasions for women normally overburdened with domestic responsibilities. They could meet eligible bachelors and enjoy some leisure time with their compañeras. The executive committee organized these Saturday-night events primarily to raise funds to cover union expenses. They were not unlike similar events sponsored by men's unions. The Córdoba and Coatepec sorter-sponsored dances were well-established traditions by the late 1930s and continued well into the 1960s. The SOECC used these revenues to build its union hall, buy uniforms and instruments for their military band, and cover their band's travel expenses. They could raise as much as one thousand pesos from the two or three dances held monthly.[40] These dances generally took place in the CROM's regional headquarters, just like the dances of other unions; but their size dwarfed all the others. The union supplied alcoholic beverages, food, and a band and charged men a two-peso admission fee. In certain respects, these weekly dances were not entirely leisure activities for the obreras. Each week, the executive committee assigned sorters to dance committees to serve the paying customers. If they did not fulfill their responsibilities, they were publically reprimanded the following week in their assembly meeting or lost a week of work. On the other hand, single women would show up anyway, even if they had not been assigned to a committee, just to be able to socialize with the worker community. Some married sorters complained they had to attend almost every Saturday, which took them away from their families during the weekend. Thus, sorter attitudes toward these union functions were quite complex and ambiguous, depending on their marital status.[41]

In Córdoba several hundred working men and working women attended these dances during the preparation season, so they were large, boisterous gatherings that the provincial gente decente recalled were rather rowdy events. Two or three hundred sorters would mingle in the streets around the federation hall. Women would bring along their partners if they also worked in the beneficios; but if they didn't, they usually stayed home. They were often jealous and very reluctant to let them go unaccompanied with their compañeras to the dances, but sorters would insist that they were just following their union obligations and promised not to dance.[42]

Dances began around nine o'clock, and they continued until one or two in the morning. Isabel remembered how Sofía Castro would set off three rounds of firecrackers at fifteen-minute intervals to alert the neighborhood that the festivities were about to begin. As they walked hand in hand with their compañeras to the festivities, they bantered with each other and told off-color jokes, like adolescent girls responding to feelings of liberation upon leaving their homes. Sofía would be standing at the entrance door when they arrived, toting her pistol, and collecting entrance fees. Sorter committees were in charge of selling beer for two pesos, keeping the bathrooms clean, tending to the coats, and maintaining order to prevent fights from breaking out. At the end of the dance, the ticket committee turned in the cash to the leadership, and then the women assigned to the dance cleaned and closed the hall.[43]

Danzonera and marimba bands were definitely the favorites at the escogedora dances in the 1950s. In Córdoba they first used their own band or hired the Santa Rosa band, which came down from Orizaba to play. Other times they hired the market vendors' all-male band or a marimba group. The real celebrities were Chumo, the son of Eufrosina, and Charno Ascona. In Coatepec they would hire a danzonera group to play danzóns, boleros, and pasos dobles.[44]

These dances facilitated greater heterosocial and heterosexual interaction in provincial cities, which had been unheard of before the 1930s. Sorters fondly recalled these social occasions, for they could temporarily forget their domestic chores and overbearing parents to enjoy a few hours of pleasure. This psychological and physical emancipation from everyday drudgery provided an opportunity to engage in small talk with their work buddies and to meet and interact with young men who might become future boyfriends or husbands. Brígida met her husband, who worked in the local rice mill, at one of these dances.[45] These everyday experiences of sociability set these working women apart from nonworking housewives; and in so doing, they were building an alternative working women's culture.

Robert Buffington contends that many Mexican ethnographers, including Oscar Lewis, Larissa Lomnitz, Elena Poniatowska, and Ruth Behar, neglected or minimized working-class women's culture because they adhered to the trickle-down theory of love and wrote about strong confident women who had difficulty entering into intimate relationships.[46] Therefore, these authors were not interested in working women's passion for dancing. Yet dance represents structured and expressive movements that articulate and convey cultural information and assists its participants in developing a new sense of personal and sexual identity.[47] "Dancing was for them an essential act of self-definition, a 'bodily activity' that both reflected and constituted their social and personal identities."[48] This observation seems applicable to sorters' experiences at their dances.

Although the sorters were not dramatically transformed on and off the dance floor, these convivial gatherings undoubtedly provided spaces for them to socially interact in a less inhibited manner with men. They danced, flirted, told risqué jokes, and behaved in ways that were not considered respectable by the gente decente. At a time when morally upright provincial women were forbidden to walk unaccompanied down the street during the daytime, these obreras were contesting middle-class gender norms and practices, while at the same time fashioning new acceptable forms of working women's behavior.

The obreras presented these union dances as one of the highlights of their everyday experiences. They even adopted their own schemes to trick their families so they could attend. They resorted to what Michel de Certeau has called "tactics," or calculated actions, to play on and with a terrain that opposed their freedom of movement.[49] Single women and mothers admitted that they relished the opportunity to attend these Saturday-night events because they just loved to dance and have some fun away from their usual life of drudgery. Whether this love of dancing had more to do with a desire to move and express one's own individuality or sexuality on the dance floor or a yearning to enter into a more intimate relationship with a young man is not entirely clear. In part, they simply yearned to go out with the girls and have a good time. Isabel told with relish how she and her two future comadres and four other close friends would arrive long before the first firecracker was set off to be sure not to miss any opportunity to be with her friends. She would even lie to her family and say that she had been assigned to a committee in order to go to the dance: "Although I was not assigned to a committee, I wanted to go. I would say that I had been, even though it was not true. I went because I wanted to dance. I had to dance, nothing more than dance."[50] If you were put on a committee, you wanted to make sure it was not the ticket committee because then you could not dance until the very end of the evening. "When it was my turn to serve [on a committee], I would make sure that it came soon because I really liked to dance. . . . I did not like to have to do the tickets, because there no one could take off until the end of the dance. I liked to be given the cantina. To take care of the cantina or to take care of the bathrooms meant I could fling myself onto the dance floor."[51]

The emergence of dance-hall cultures was closely associated in the minds of middle-class observers with subversive and inappropriate heterosexual behaviors, including drinking, violence, prostitution, and gambling.[52] This bourgeois perspective tended to obscure the emancipatory qualities of these sociocultural events for the young working poor. It also fails to take into consideration that municipal authorities, union leaders, and the compañeras themselves monitored dance-hall behaviors. Dance committees were charged with preventing what the sorters gingerly referred to as "problems" that arose at the door or on the dance floor. Brawls did, on occasion, break out among intoxicated dancers. Isabel remembered how María Elena Serna had to defend herself when a man attacked her with a knife. On Saturday nights, the municipal police were especially vigilant in patrolling the streets, stopping and questioning any young sorter dilly-dallying with her boyfriend or walking home alone to be sure that their virginity was not being compromised.[53] Thus, escogedora dances were social events that challenged provincial gender norms while simultaneously providing a public venue where working women could individually and collectively construct their own culture.

Bands and Parades as Working Womens' Performance

Obrera band performances were a form of popular culture that served a number of functions at the individual and collective level. Performing at public events empowered individual workers by putting their talents on display outside the home. It also fortified companionship and collective pride among working women through shared experiences. These performances had another gendered dimension. They represented an alternative to men's performances in municipal and union military bands. Finally, they reinforced as well as contested hierarchical relations between the union and the national labor confederation and official party by serving as a means for working women to gain public recognition, respectability, and political inclusion in public ceremonies. Thus, it offered them an opportunity to be integrated into the Mexican body politic.

Municipal brass bands have often been associated with the emergence of popular culture in indigenous villages of the Sierra Norte de Puebla, Michoacán, and Oaxaca. In his pioneering study of brass bands, Guy Thomson suggests that the proliferation of these bands beginning in the Porfiriato served to "dignify and dramatize civic and patriotic ceremonies"; and in so doing, they strengthened village life and legitimized political leadership. He carefully details the intricate relationship of band formation and emerging political leadership with modernity.[54] In much the same manner, when male-dominated labor unions began organizing military brass bands (*bandas de guerras*), they sought to present themselves as respectable, civic organizations outside the factory walls. These musical groups represented workers not as disruptive elements of society, as the elite would have it, but rather as productive members of worker communities who could provide entertainment at union and civic functions. Thus, brass bands became permanent fixtures of twentieth-century working men's cultures.

Textile-worker communities have a long tradition of organized musical celebrations, speeches, and banquets to commemorate days of patron saints, national holidays, and the Constitution of 1857, dating back to the nineteenth century. The celebrations of the San Angel textile-worker community were well-known during the Porfiriato.[55] Workers organized their own brass bands before the Revolution of 1910 with the financial support of mutual-aid societies, industrialists, and the state. During the revolutionary years, one group of Santa Rosa textile workers even petitioned the state authorities for financial assistance to organize a band to raise their profile in the midst of an interunion dispute. Throughout the 1920s and 1930s the Orizaba textile and beer brewery workers organized bands, although they were referred to as musical or instrumental bands. The chamber of labor also organized a mixed, eighty-member orchestra as a way to strengthen union solidarity and culture.[56] The first reference to an obrera musical group came from a U.S. visitor who attended a musical performance put on by Mexico City seamstresses during the early 1920s.[57]

Many of my interviewees had participated in the SOECC's banda de guerra beginning in the late 1940s. In their collective memory this experience was critical in their representation of themselves as women workers and as union loyalists. The band granted Córdoba sorters a unique opportunity to participate in public ceremonies, which they had never previously enjoyed. Their participation in weekly practices, civic and union celebrations, and local parades spawned very strong friendships, social networks, and a remarkable esprit de corps. In short, from their accomplishments, they developed a sense of collective identity and personal pride not found among the other sorters. At the same time, they were assisting in the consolidation of Mexican postrevolutionary political culture.

In November 1946 the secretary general, Castro, decided to raise the profile of the SOECC in the eyes of the public by forming a military band to perform at civic and union functions. At this particular historical juncture, the SOECC had just bolted from the CROM with Eucario León and his Santa Rosa textile workers. Faced with a lack of political and financial support from a well-funded national labor confederation, Sofía must have recognized the need to raise the public image of the union within the local community. She purchased instruments in Mexico City and then returned to recruit teenagers, in particular daughters of sorters, to play in the band. Sixteen- and seventeen-year-olds had considerably more free time on their hands than their overburdened mothers to attend weekly practices. As an incentive to join the band, Sofía promised them permanent positions on the third list after they had played for two years. Their jobs were guaranteed as long as they learned to play well and performed at all required events.[58] For over thirty years, Castro led the band, assisted by Inés Reyes. The band continued to play even after the workers were replaced by machines in 1965. Band members claim that their all-woman marching banda de guerra was the only one in the state and possibly in the nation.

The band was composed of roughly twenty-three members, plus a five-member honor guard (escolta) with two flag bearers (see photograph 9). There was also a 150-member military auxiliary (Grupo Militarizado). Each group practiced every Thursday afternoon after work. Members learned to play the trumpet (clarín), bugle (corneta), or drums (tambores or cajas) under the direction of the Santa Rosa bandleader, Raúl Rojas. Since none of them could read music or had any musical training, he first had them march around the union hall while he played a piece. Once they had memorized the tune, such as

9. Military band of the SOECC, 1946. Photograph by California. Courtesy of Brígida Siriaco García.

one of the nine "Dianas," they would work either in groups or singly under his supervision to master the piece. If an important holiday or event were approaching, they would have to practice every day. While the band practiced upstairs in the union hall, the honor guard and military auxiliary conducted their marching drills downstairs for the May 1, September 16, and November 20 parades.[59]

Like other union bands, the SOECC band served a legitimizing function for the labor movement. Its leaders sought to use its performances to foster union loyalty and solidarity and to present to the community at large a socially respectable and disciplined organization playing in public venues. The band's primary purpose was to provide entertainment at SOECC-sponsored biannual dinners and dances. Each June and December, it played for the installation of the new executive committee. Since the union had been a founding member of the CSOCO, the band performed at almost all its celebrations. The installation of a new Santa Rosa executive committee of the textile union or León's birthday celebrations always found the SOECC band performing. When the SOECC joined the Confederación Regional de

Obreros y Campesinos (CROC, Regional Confederation of Workers and Peasants), its band became a fixture at CROC celebrations throughout the state. It even played in Poza Rica for the oil workers' union, after it affiliated with the CROC. The petroleum workers had earlier organized a mixed-gender band for a few years, but it later returned to an all-male one.[60]

The SOECC band served an overtly political function as well, when it performed on national holidays for municipal and state authorities of the renamed official party, the Partido Revolucionario Institucional (PRI, Institutionalized Revolutionary Party). Since the Porfiriato, municipal bands had become permanent fixtures at patriotic festivals, and now union bands joined them in the postrevolutionary era. In agreeing to participate in official commemorations of the Mexican Revolution, the SOECC band, like other union bands, was inserting itself into the body politic.

Córdoba's PRI-controlled municipal government regularly invited the SOECC band to participate along with the municipal band in the parades for February 24 (Flag Day), March 21 (Benito Juárez's birthday), May 1 (Labor Day), September 15 and 16 (Independence Day), and November 20 (Revolution Day). The banda de guerra was aiding the official party by instilling Mexican nationalist values. Their participation in the May 1 celebrations had another important objective and an interesting gendered dimension. "There is no public act that better dramatizes the power of caciques, nor any ritual that better reaffirms union hierarchy, than the May 1st (Labour Day) celebrations."[61] In these marches, the SOECC and its band always went in front of all the other regional unions. The male street-vendor and the sugarcane-worker bands with their unions followed them. The regional federation most probably decided to give the SOECC greater prominence because it was the largest union, but some interviewees claimed it was because they were women. The sight of the band, honor guard, military auxiliary, and its 1,500 members filling several downtown city blocks on May 1 or November 20 could not but have impressed the townspeople and brought pride to the participants

10. Military band of the SIOECC, November 20, 1961. Sofía Castro (center right), followed by Estela Velázquez. Photograph by Santana. Courtesy of the APIRO.

themselves (see photograph 10). In addition to marching in holiday parades, the band had to play for the raising and lowering of the flag at six o'clock in the morning and in the evening. They also received numerous invitations to play at national ceremonies across the state and in Mexico City during the 1950s and 1960s.[62]

The band likewise performed at the lavish local municipal celebrations on May 21 and August 24, commemorating the founding of the city of Córdoba and the anniversary of the Treaties of Córdoba, when Mexican independence was recognized by Spain. The band was also called on to perform at religious ceremonies; various parishes asked them to play on December 11 and 12 for pilgrimages and fiestas. They also lent their services to civic organizations, including the coronation of the city's queen. These never-ending obligations came at a heavy price for working mothers. Estela recalled the enormous personal sacrifice she had to make to be away for so many hours from her large family.[63]

These everyday experiences contributed to the individual's feeling of autonomy and liberation; and at the same time, they helped to build a cohesive obrera community and culture. The women expressed a sense of liberation from household duties when they practiced each Thursday after work from six until seven. Estela considered this hour the only part of the day when she could have some time and space for herself: "This was the time of rest after a whole day of work."[64] In their interviews, the sorters identified individually and collectively with other band members. They became lifelong friends and chose them as godmothers for their children's baptisms, communions, and marriages. As their union lives became increasingly intertwined, they gradually built a social network, which they fondly recalled forty years later.

The shared experiences of practicing, performing, and traveling long hours together were strongly etched in their collective memory. For "collective memory maintains the lived experience of individuals within groups, according to [Maurice] Halbwach because that individual experience is never remembered without reference to a shared context."[65] The band provided them with opportunities to travel to Mexico City and Oaxaca to visit new places and meet other working women and working men. Their shiny brass instruments and uniforms served as props for claiming ties to the respected military-band tradition. They often expressed enormous pride in having the opportunity to wear three elaborately decorated, military-style uniforms and to perform in front of huge crowds.[66] Never in their wildest dreams did these women imagine that their band would win such widespread public acceptance and respect.

Band performances also provided these socially marginalized women with an opening to insert themselves into the discourse on national citizenship. Mary Kay Vaughan has shown that rural women's participation in fine arts presentations and domestic economy exhibitions during patriot festivals contributed to their inclusion in political citizenship and the democratization process in the 1930s and 1940s.[67] Band performances played the same function for sorters. Although Mexican women had still not won the right to vote, obrera participation in patriotic festivals meant that they were entering into

11. Military band of the SOECC, 1947, Oaxaca. Courtesy of the APIRO.

the political fabric of society, albeit in support of the political establishment. Although the public performances were organized and orchestrated from above by the official party and trade unions, they were empowering these women workers as social and cultural agents. The women themselves were beginning to redefine their own role in civil society and claim their own form of citizenship.

The SOECC band's participation in the annual September 16 parade was a case in point. It did not simply reaffirm the obreras' national identity; it also exhibited a xenophobic tendency that had deep roots in worker culture.[68] As they passed by the shuttered Spanish commercial establishments on First Avenue, they yelled anti-Spanish slogans. Let us not forget that their Spanish bosses owned some of the largest beneficios in the nation. Well-to-do residents have ingrained in their collective memory an image of Eufrosina striding down the street, brandishing the union banner, and yelling derogatory antiga-chupin (anti-Spanish) slogans as she went. The Spaniards could not have been amused by these outbursts or by the rocks hurled at their storefronts.[69] On this particular day, sorters could unite with other Mexicans across the republic in claiming the right of citizenship by attacking the surrogates of colonial oppression.

Everyday Experiences and Obrera Culture 225

In spite of the emancipatory feelings elicited by these public performances, prevailing patriarchal norms upheld by their families, union leaders, the labor confederations, and the PRI circumscribed the workers' autonomy. Their partners were quite jealous when they went out at night alone to perform, particularly if it was an all-male event, such as the installation of the regional committee of the local federation.[70] Most probably they were extensively questioned when they returned home. The leadership made a point of severely reprimanding any worker who did not fulfill her obligations to attend all band practices and performances. Brígida and Estela were often castigated for missing practices. When band members did not march in the parades, Sofía very often had to cajole or force them to participate or face the consequences.[71]

There were a number of other drawbacks to the band's grueling performance schedule. The cost of maintaining the band was extremely burdensome on union resources. Transporting the band back and forth to Mexico City for the May 1 celebrations cost over six thousand pesos, while buying three sets of new uniforms obliged Castro to constantly ask for permission to dip into union funds. At one point the assembly had to approve an allocation of ten thousand pesos to pay for new uniforms. In 1955 they even appealed to the city's mayor and President Adolfo Ruiz Cortines for financial assistance.[72] What is more, their leaders took the sorters away from their families for days at a time without paying them. They were not fed properly on their trips. They were handed a drink and a torta or two and told not to participate in the formal ceremonies. At times, they felt exploited by their leaders and the PRI as clients of the political machine. Although they stoically fulfilled their multiple obligations, some even expressed resentment about their treatment by their leaders.[73]

Obrera Theatrical Performance

Much of what Mexican elites found morally reprehensible in worker communities, which they perceived as the Other, was linked to the behavior of the obrera. She was threatening the stability of the family by going out to work and by putting herself sexually at risk by entering male-dominated public spaces. "Thus, within public discourse virtue became central to female worker identity."[74] As working women began entering the streets and factories, the gente decente increasingly conflated working women and sexual depravity. Factory work became synonymous with prostitution. Working women, who entered daily into these heterosocial spaces, represented threats to the cult of motherhood, female honor, and family respectability. Both working men and working women appropriated some of these gender norms themselves by questioning, at times, women's very presence in the workplace.[75] However, the working poor could not always abide by these norms because economic necessity forced women out of the home to work. What can the union's theatrical performances reveal about their gender norms? Did they always represent themselves as the long-suffering woman (*mujer abnegada*)? How did these productions contribute to an alternative working women's culture?

Córdoba and Coatepec sorters regularly organized theatrical productions to celebrate the installation of the newly elected executive committees, the birthdays of their leaders, and the anniversaries of their unions. The scripts of their plays and their performance often reflected their moral and gender values. These *comedias, cuadros,* and *variedades* were essentially productions, written with the assistance of their fellow trade unionists. Union cacicas once again took the lead in organizing these events, exhibiting their intellectual and artistic talents and heightening their visibility as leaders. They were usually the writers, directors, and principal actors of these productions, assisted by family members. These performances played a legitimizing function for the cacicas. For their subject matter, they drew on Mexican official history, morality, popular culture, and everyday experiences with which working women could easily identify. The dignity and respectability of the working woman, nationalism, and at times defiance of bourgeois morality crept into their skits. These productions were representations of an alternative sorter culture and new forms of popular resistance.

Eager to instill moral respectability and middle-class gender norms among the rank and file, the cacicas produced a number of morality plays. Lino Gómez Reyes described how his mother, Inés, and the baker José Solís put on a play about the perennial problem of alcoholism. The plot revolved around the relationship between an alcoholic father and a mujer abnegada. Inés played the role of the father, while her son, Lino, impersonated his son. At the climax of the play, the father fatally shoots his own son while in a drunken stupor. Another morality play directed by Eufrosina tells the tragic life of a cabaret singer whose life has obviously gone astray. Needless to say, the fallen woman must pay for her sins. Her violent death at the hands of her jealous lover provided the proper moral message. Inés played the role of the tragic heroine, and she used her beautiful voice to add a musical dimension to the performance.[76] In sum, the cacicas were intent on highlighting the ills of drinking and sexual promiscuity while instilling the qualities of the good and virtuous partner and mother. They never seemed to promote the institution of marriage, for it was so infrequent among the working poor.[77] These skits were often accompanied by the recitation of poetry, which was another common form of obrera entertainment. Eufrosina was renowned for her verses, some of which had a moral lesson.[78]

SOECC productions also celebrated national heroes and famous events, which at times challenged the view of warfare as an exclusively masculine sphere. Sofía produced and directed a long play that chronicled the life of the great liberator Miguel Hidalgo y Costilla. The play did not concentrate on his struggle for social justice but rather on his military exploits against the Spaniards. The banda de guerra represented Hidalgo's army. In this case, the obreras took on the masculine role of soldiering, wearing uniforms, marching into battle, and playing martial tunes.[79] Thus, working women were portraying soldiers as well as Mexican liberators.

Both the SOECC and the SODCC presented theatrical productions of *Santa*, which was based on Federico Gamboa's turn-of-the-century novel about a San Angel peasant girl forced into prostitution after a Mexico City police officer takes advantage of her. When her mother and brothers discover that she has had an illicit relationship, she is thrown out of the house and disowned by her family. She has no other alternative but to work in a high-class Mexico City bordello run by a Spanish madam in order to support herself. She eventually succeeds in becoming a well-known courtesan courted by clients, both young and old, who are philandering members of the Porfirian aristocracy. Gamboa first paints Santa as a metaphor for the virgin, pristine countryside, until she falls victim to her first suitor. She then is transformed into a sexual object, a commodity, a piece of flesh, to be enjoyed by profligate urban males. To punish herself for her own moral disgrace, Gamboa has her carry out a form of religious penance, by resolving to remain in this disgraceful profession. As she descends into a life of alcoholism, disease, and impoverishment, she continues to break prevailing norms of proper female behavior. In the end, she perishes from ovarian cancer, which was associated in the public's mind with sexual promiscuity.[80]

As a naturalist writer, Gamboa graphically describes how society heavily influences human behavior, in particular sexual depravity, attacking commodification of urban brothels, schools, and factories in his search for the aesthetic.[81] However, the film versions, which began appearing in 1918, removed much of the sexual, sensual, and religious content to make them more appealing for general audiences. In the 1931 screen adaptation, which was Mexico's first "talkie," Agustín Lara even agreed to compose the music and write the lyrics.[82]

As John Chasteen has observed, the nonprint versions of the novel were wonderful projections of Mexican popular culture. As the first major female protagonist in a Mexican film, the character of Santa inspired numerous songs, dramatic skits, burlesques, and parodies.[83] In certain respects, Santa comes to represent the "everywoman" in midcentury lower-class society. She fits into the genre of the long-suffering female who must pay for her transgressions. At the same time, she comes to represent the spiritual uplifting of women yearning to enjoy the fruits of postrevolutionary modern society. Lara's famous song, "Santa," which he wrote for the blind piano player, epitomizes this theme. He sings about how her beauty, goodness, and honesty lift his spirit out of the depths of despair.[84]

In their interviews, Córdoba and Coatepec sorters took great pride in saying that their unions had presented this play.[85] Unfortunately, the SOECC's script and the movie made of its production have not been recovered, but the 1931 movie provides many hints to why the sorters embraced her story and integrated it into their union culture.

The movie concentrates on Santa's struggle with society's fixation on the virgin/prostitute dichotomy and how two very sympathetic male figures, the blind musician and the Spanish bullfighter, try to save her from her fate. Were the Córdoba and Coatepec sorter unions simply intent on presenting another morality play to persuade working women to internalize appropriate gender norms? This might be partially true; however, there seem to be multiple layers of meaning here.

Coffee sorters could easily identify with the character of Santa because they were almost always associated with prostitution in the eyes of the gente decente. They were regularly lumped together as "street women." They too lived on the fringes of society, where slipping into and out of casual prostitution to make ends meet was a common survival strategy. The film gives considerable agency to the heroine in her relationship with men. At times, she is a strong woman who challenges gender roles, just as the sorters did. For example, she attempts to resist enslavement by refusing to give her heart and even sometimes her body to the libertines, even including the bullfighter and the blind musician. In the end, though, she submits to her fate. The happiest moments of her life are actually spent with her all-women bordello community, whose camaraderie buoys her spirits, and with her kindred spirit, the piano player, who is another social outcast. With them she can share brief moments of emotional and spiritual companionship, away from the demands placed on sex workers.

The nationality of Santa's handlers and bullfighter lover might have been symbolically important for the coffee sorters, who worked under Spanish bosses. However, the overbearing Spanish madam and the ambiance of the bordello filled with flamenco music found in the film accurately portrayed Porfirian upper-class reality, as well as Gamboa's own personal inclinations and bon vivant lifestyle.[86] Moreover, the movie replaces the novel's arrogant gachupin with a handsome, dashing, protective lover, who takes her out of the bordello to help her start a new life.

Santa is a fine symbol for the exploited Veracruz coffee sorter, who had been consigned to the lowest echelons of provincial society. Moreover, the beneficio owners were white Spanish immigrants, who at times displayed the same insular arrogance and racism toward their mestizo workers and a singular lack of understanding of Mexican customs. Thus, a theatrical presentation of Santa, with a prostitute representing the soul of the Mexican obreras, might be interpreted as the ultimate triumph of the obrera spirit. In the words of James Scott, subordinates always have their own "hidden transcript," often times played offstage and composed of "rumors, gossip, folktales, songs, gestures, jokes, and theater of the powerless through which they critique power, while hiding behind innocuous understandings of their conduct."[87] The popularized versions of Gamboa's novel, which transformed Santa into a martyred saint, had widespread appeal from the 1930s through the 1960s among the working women's community.

Another union skit concerning the controversial new dance, the mambo, challenged the moral righteousness of the Spanish entrepreneurs. As a type of music and as a dance form, the mambo has been characterized as "aggressive," "uninhibited," and "seductive."[88] When the well-known Cuban bandleader Damásio Pérez Prado began to popularize the mambo in the early 1950s, Córdoba's gente decente must have found this dance very sexually provocative. The sorters had an entirely different view of this popular dance, and Eufrosina set out to produce a short play to emphasize the disparities in their views. The play opens with the Spanish coffee exporters Ezequiel González, Ricardo Regules, Lázaro Penagos, and Tirso Sainz Pardo sitting around a table discussing their disapproval of the dance. No sorter played these parts quite possibly because they did not want to lose their work, so boys were dressed up in oversized clothing to play the beneficiadores. The owners try to figure out what the economic costs of waging a campaign against the mambo might be. After this exchange of views, Pérez Prado himself enters, and the beneficio owners ask him if he is in agreement with them. As Delia recounted it, the Spaniards explain that they "are against the mambo because the servants in our houses, our wives, and all the world are dancing the mambo. Where and what are we going to have for dinner? For no one takes care of us because they are all out dancing the mambo." The implication here is that this dance was luring respectable women away from their domestic and familial responsibilities and threatening men's patriarchal authority. Pérez Prado then speaks up and says that he is in favor of the mambo. After this declaration, all the actors on the stage break into a mambo, and the audience soon joins in.[89] In this theatrical performance, sorters were defying provincial gender norms by demonstrating a willingness to engage in controversial dance forms that were sexually explicit. In short, this play represents an example of the "world turned upside-down."[90]

In conclusion, small vignettes retrieved from life histories about union dances, bands, and skits can be pasted together into a patchwork that makes up an alternative obrera culture. Although these SOECC activities were not always leisure activities, obrera participation in union-sponsored events provided a unique opportunity to perform in public spaces that had hitherto been beyond the limits of their domestic everyday experiences. Entrance into new spaces and engagement in a variety of forms of heterosocial relations spawned greater physical, social, and sexual expression and intimacy with nonfamily members. These cultural activities bridged the private and the public. They danced with unknown men, played brass and percussion instruments, marched in military-style parades, performed on the public stage, and traveled throughout the republic to put on performances in front of mixed audiences.

Veracruz coffee sorters took enormous pride in these collective activities, for the acts provided these women with a clear sense of community solidarity. This form of union activism strengthened compañerismo among fellow workers, and they could claim for themselves a legitimate role in trade unionism and civic culture. Through their dances, bands, and theater, they were sociocultural agents who were challenging the traditional conception of working women, defying their bosses, and claiming full membership in the national polity. Their collective memory helped them to legitimize their everyday experiences as respected mothers, diligent workers, loyal unionists, and honorable citizens. In so doing, they were not only creating but also strengthening their obrera union culture.

6

Coffee Entrepreneurs, Workers, and the State Confront the Challenges of Modernization

The full mechanization of Veracruz's coffee plants and the replacement of its thousands of coffee sorters with electronic sorters were inevitable by the 1950s, but the ways in which labor, the agro-export industry, and the state responded to this process of modernization needs exploration. The relationship of these three actors during the period that is often referred to as the "Mexican Miracle" shifts as the state increasingly supports industrialization and modernization. The vagaries of the Atlantic market and competition at home and abroad during and after World War II forced the preparers and exporters to make significant readjustments in their commercialization strategies and in their relations with their labor force and the state. To keep up with the rising cost of living, coffee-sorter unions had to negotiate with the agroindustry and the state to win higher wages and more extensive worker benefits to gain greater economic security during the forties and fifties. At the same time, the maturation of the SOECC was directly tied to its increasing dependence on a hierarchically structured labor movement and the consolidation of a women's collective cacicazgo. When modernization of the plants finally did occur in Central Veracruz in the fifties and sixties, it was a long, wrenching legal and financial process for all three parties. The final wage settlement (*liquidación*) had complex political and sociocultural dimensions for all of Central Veracruz. Finally, the sorters' loss of work was a shared experience that in their collective memory became the most traumatic event in their working and personal lives.

Coffee Merchants Confront the Challenges of the Coffee Cycles, 1940s to 1960s

Mexican scholars have tended to study postwar Mexican coffee elites within the framework of internal colonialism. They argued that exporters in alliance with large producers exploited the small and medium coffee producers while collaborating with a prodevelopmentalist state. Margarita Nolasco's seminal study demonstrates how coffee-export firms in Mexico City, Córdoba, Xalapa, Tapachula, and Comitán came to dominate the periphery through multiple levels of intermediary networks from the exporter down to local store owners and producers. The beneficio owners, she argued, occupied a dominant position in the internal coffee chain. Anne Beaumond takes the same position in her fine study of the Xalapa immigrant families and the financial strategies that they used to construct vertical dominance over the coffee agroindustry from the field to the ships.[1] Although both studies correctly emphasize the nodal networks between producer, merchant, and the state, they pay less attention to the creative strategies the regional exporters took to confront the serious fluctuations of the Atlantic coffee market. As one Mexican exporter phrased it, the business of the regional exporter was to make a profit, so they had to explore new strategies in a constantly changing global market.[2] These two studies of coffee elites also place little emphasis on the relationship between the elites and their workforce. It is this subject that I want to address here for Central Veracruz.

Second World War hostilities created two unusual shifts in the demand for coffee: the closing of the European market, whose consumers had purchased 40 percent of world imports before the war, and an increased demand in the U.S. market. The shutting off of the European market by the Allied naval blockade to stymy German expansion led to fierce competition among Latin American coffee-producing countries to gain a larger share of the U.S. market. To prevent further German intrusion into the Atlantic coffee economy, the U.S. initiated talks with fourteen Latin American countries in 1940 to control the supply chain. These negotiations resulted in the signing of the Inter-American Coffee Agreement, which established export quotas for each nation with the world's largest consumer. Before the signing of this agreement, there had been minimal cooperation between Latin American countries and the United States. The Pan-American Coffee Bureau, originally established in 1936 to stimulate increased U.S. consumption and to serve as a fact-finding agency, now took on a much more interventionist role in the regulation of the Atlantic markets, while the New York Coffee Board of Trade was given the authority to supervise the international agreement. Since Mexico was one of the six principal Latin American countries exporting coffee to the United States, its government now became heavily involved in the promotion of its coffee exports. In Brazil, Colombia, and Costa Rica, in particular, the state had played an active role in stimulating coffee exports for many years.[3]

During the war years, President Manuel Avila Camacho's representative on the Pan-American Coffee Bureau was able to obtain a high coffee quota for Mexico. This played into the hands of the Cordobeses and the Xalapa group because their businesses were far larger and more developed than those in Chiapas and Oaxaca. After Mexico declared war on Germany in May 1942, the state seized all the properties of German, Italian, and Japanese citizens. This included the prosperous German plantations and preparation plants in Chiapas, Veracruz, and Oaxaca. These properties were immediately placed into receivership under the Bank of Mexico, but they were operated by the Junta de Administración y Vigilancia de la Propiedad Extranjera (Administrative Board of Foreign Properties) under the Compañía Exportadora e Importadora Mexicana (CEIMSA, Mexican Export and Import Company) in the Department of Foreign Trade.[4] Despite the state's valiant efforts to stimulate coffee exports during the war years, producers were reluctant to start planting more trees because they had bad memories of the depression years. Coffee production continued to hover around the 1929 level, 52,000 metric tons, through 1944, after which it finally began to rise.[5]

At the onset of the war, Veracruzano coffee exporters adopted new strategies to make up for the loss of the European market and lower domestic demand. One strategy practiced by Orizaba beneficiadores was simply to cut back on labor costs in coffee preparation, utilizing their dry beneficios only four months of the year. As a consequence, two hundred sorters were laid off. Owners also began to export coffee that had not been properly cleaned to save money.[6] More drastic strategies to retrench included the dissolution of their companies, business mergers, diversification into other commercial activities, and cooperation with German exporters and CEIMSA to sell Chiapas coffee.

The firms of the Sainz Pardo, Regules Baranda, González López, Sánchez Escobio, and Galván y López families continued to operate one wet and four large dry beneficios in Córdoba throughout the war years. After the Sainz Pardo brothers bought out the Zardains' shares of the Beneficiadora in 1940, they started bringing over the second generation of their family from Spain to help run the family business. Ceferino and Tirso never married and had no children, so they invited their nephews and in-laws, including Luis Sainz López Negrete and Pedro Pardo Zorrilla, to become minor shareholders. They also continued to diversify their family holdings by creating an auto dealership and insurance company with another Spanish family, the Ros Lopis, investing 280,000 pesos in capital. The brothers also opened a sesame seed oil business, El Faro, in 1944.[7]

Ricardo Regules and Ezequiel González experienced greater economic challenges. Regules decided to dissolve his five-year partnership with Manuel Albo in 1941, just a year after he had doubled the firm's capital to 200,000 pesos. He lamented that the company had been passing through an "economically difficult period." He began following the Sainz Pardo strategy, which entailed investing in alternative business ventures that had more stable markets than coffee. In

1945 he joined the coffee exporters Davíd González Rosas, Baltazar Sánchez, and Albo in founding a soap company.[8] Ezequiel González's firm had also fallen on hard times. Although he had opened a roasting company and was marketing coffee under his own label, Café Córdoba, he was unable to manage his spiraling debts. By the end of 1944 he was forced to take on David González, Regules, and the Sainz Pardos as business partners. Eventually, he was obliged to sell the Garza to Regules and the Sainz Pardos.[9] Meanwhile, José Zardain, who had moved his family and his company to Mexico City, was still quite active as a moneylender in the region; and on more than one occasion, he took legal action against delinquent borrowers.[10]

Córdoba, Xalapa, and Huatusco coffee exporters profited handsomely from the state's seizure of German properties. They collaborated actively with their German counterparts, transporting coffee from their holdings in Chiapas and Guatemala to Veracruz plants for preparation and export to the United States. Even though it was more costly, they switched to railroad transportation because the open seas had become too dangerous. Once CEIMSA had taken over the German properties, the agency realized that it lacked administrative expertise to prepare and trade the café verde. So it brought in the experienced Cordobeses to serve as their coffee brokers. Since the Sainz Pardos operated one of the largest dry beneficios in the country, the state frequently contracted them to bring parchment coffee out of Chiapas by rail in unmarked bags, complete its final preparation, and ship it to the U.S. border. They could buy the coffee cheaply at three hundred pesos a quintal in Chiapas and sell it in New York at four hundred pesos.[11] By 1945 Veracruz beneficiadores were preparing almost two-thirds, or 19.4 million pesos, of the nation's 30.9 million pesos' worth of unprepared coffee. The Chiapanecans were a distant second with 8.9 million pesos' worth. However, the latter were gaining ground by investing in more efficient machinery and keeping labor costs low.[12]

The government's intervention in seventy-seven German properties in Chiapas, three in Oaxaca, and three in Veracruz benefited the

Cordobeses in other ways. Three former Boesch beneficios in Oriz-aba, Ixtaczoquitlán, and Fortín came under the jurisdiction of the Administrative Board of Foreign Properties, which rented them out to the local entrepreneur José Revuelta. The sudden disappearance of their German Orizaba, Chiapas, and Oaxaca competitors bode well for the Cordobeses. When CEIMSA and the Banco Nacional de Comercio Exterior (National Bank of Foreign Trade) created the Ben-eficios Mexicanos del Café (BENEMEX, Mexican State Coffee Agen-cy) out of Cafés Tapachula (Tapachula Coffees) in 1943 with a 1 mil-lion-peso capitalization, it decided to move its headquarters from Tapachula to Córdoba, where it operated out of the former Arbuck-le Brothers plant. The Cordobeses seem to have played a significant role in BENEMEX's operations before it moved its headquarters to Mexico City. They were also well positioned to penetrate the Ger-mans' former markets and credit networks in Chiapas. These new opportunities brought considerable windfall profits to the Zardains and the Sainz Pardos, who remained Mexico's major exporters. The Xalapa group was not to be outdone, for Justo Félix Fernández was likewise expanding his commercial operations into Chiapas.[13]

Some Cordobeses faced another challenge, because they were strong supporters of Francisco Franco's pro-Nazi regime. In 1939 the Mexican government withdrew its ambassador to Spain. For the next five years, the two countries did not have formal diplomatic relations. To prevent any form of property seizure, the Sainz Pardo brothers temporarily transferred 66 percent of the stock of Beneficiadora to their Mexican nephews, Luis Sainz López Negrete and Pedro Pardo Zorrilla. When Spanish residents finally were allowed to own prop-erty, if they had resided in Mexico for twenty years, the Sainz Pardo brothers reduced their nephews' holdings to minority positions. José Zardain followed the same strategy, temporarily transferring the ma-jority of his shares to his Mexican-born children.[14]

Mexican coffee producers and exporters were far slower to orga-nize themselves into an association than their Latin American coun-terparts, primarily because they had less interest in creating a political interest group.[15] Moreover, geography played a key role in hindering cooperation among dispersed regional coffee elites in Veracruz, Oaxaca, and Chiapas, despite the state's attempt to organize this sector in 1937. For many years, the state seems to have allowed the industry to regulate itself. In the 1940s the Xalapa group was even deciding whom to issue export licenses to throughout the region. They would propose a firm, and the Trade Ministry would simply ratify its decision. The state left to these politically influential Veracruz exporters the management and policing of the coffee sector up until the 1958 crisis.[16] Thus, the state was primarily acting as a regulator among the rival regional coffee elites. More precisely, it served as a buffer to curtail the negative effects of fluctuating international prices on domestic producers and exporters and to curb exploitative practices of coffee intermediaries in their dealings with small and medium producers.

After the war, the Xalapa group rather than the Córdoba group played an increasingly important role in organizing producers and exporters at the national level. After Justo Félix Fernández married Puebla governor Maximino Avila Camacho's daughter, he gained direct access to the national political elite. He soon began to serve as the principal spokesperson of the Xalapa exporters because of his close ties to Veracruz presidents Miguel Alemán Valdés and Adolfo Ruiz Cortines. Thus it is not surprising that the Xalapa group spearheaded the formation of the first national organization of cafetaleros, the Unión Nacional Agrícola de Cafetaleros (UNAC, National Agricultural Union of Coffee Producers and Exporters), in 1949. It brought together the regional associations of Coatepec, Xalapa, Córdoba-Orizaba-Huatusco, Soconusco, and Oaxaca. Since the Xalapa group controlled the first two associations, it was able to dominate the UNAC's executive council for many years. Fernández served as its first president. While its membership included small, medium, and large producers and preparers, the largest firms dominated its leadership. The exporters used the UNAC to strengthen their financial networks in coffee marketing and trading and to influence state policies.

It also represented the coffee elite on the recently created state agency, the Comisión Nacional del Café (National Coffee Committee). While the Xalapa group had several representatives on the agency's executive board, José Zardain was the only original Córdoba exporter to serve as one of its members. The UNAC used the Comisión as a tool to implement its special interests.[17]

The postwar years have been called the golden age of coffee, for the bean became the single most valuable agricultural commodity in world trade. Between 1947 and 1949 and between 1955 and 1957, world exports rose only by some 15 percent, but prices in U.S. dollars doubled. This was due to a 60 percent increase in U.S. imports over pre-war levels, to tight coffee supplies, to exhaustion of Brazilian stocks that had been held off the market, and to the removal of price controls in the Pan-American Agreement of 1953.[18] Mexico's coffee exports more than doubled between 1946 and 1957, reaching a new high of 88,823 metric tons with a value of 1,233,400,000 pesos.[19] However, this coffee boom brought higher profits for Mexican exporters than for producers. While profits doubled for producers, they tripled for exporters. Exporters took advantage not only of the disparities in the foreign exchange rate, but also of their control over credit. They advanced more loans to local producers with greater alacrity than local banks and at considerably higher interest rates. They likewise had easy access to New York prices by telephone, so they could lower purchase prices at any moment in order to reap higher profits. These factors contributed to the rise of a new postwar generation of Spanish exporters, who included José Zardain's son, Enrique, and Hernán Figueroa, who began to buy up large tracks of virgin land in Chiapas and Oaxaca. In contrast to the Cordobeses, they linked their regional production, preparation, and commercialization operations.[20]

The Zardain, Regules, and Sainz Pardo families continued to expand their coffee operations in the late 1940s and 1950s, not only in Veracruz but also in Oaxaca and Chiapas. While José Zardain concentrated his operations in Chiapas, Oaxaca, and Puebla, his Ventura brother chose to leave the coffee business almost altogether to follow other business pursuits. At least four of José's seven children became involved in coffee in some way or other. Modesto, who lived in the DF, took over the plant in Ixcatepec and purchased from CEIMSA the two former Boesch plants La Matriz and La Concordia between 1945 and 1946 in Orizaba. José's sister María, and her Spanish husband, José Alvarez Fernández, who had been a Zardain employee in the DF, took over operations of these two plants. In the 1970s they changed its name to the Alvarez-Zardain (ALZA) firm and relocated to Córdoba.[21] Another son, Antonio, was sent to administer the beneficio in Oaxaca, while Enrique ran the family's plant in Tuxtla Gutierrez. José's nephew, Aurelio Lombardía Zardain, operated another plant in the Sierra Norte of Puebla. In the Sierra Mazateca, the Zardains operated Cafés Mazatecos, which purchased coffee from Indian producers through several levels of merchants operating out of Tehuacán and Teotitlán. Mexican anthropologist Fernando Benítez once labeled the Casa Zardain firm as the "monarch who reigns" over the prices.[22] The Zardains owned another plant in Tapachula, administered by Jesús Zardain, another relative. As the Zardains expanded into other states, they also acquired cattle haciendas and transport companies, such as Transportes Grijalva (Grijalva Transports). Women family members were also brought into their operations. María Zardain de Alvarez became an important shareholder in the Alvarez-Zardain family business by the 1950s. Her name appears on rental contracts for coffee-producing lands of La Capilla and Buena Vista haciendas and real estate in downtown Córdoba. It is clear that by the 1950s and 1960s the Zardains had become the major coffee-export firm in Mexico.[23]

The Sainz Pardos also prospered throughout the 1950s, albeit on a smaller scale. Their operations remained principally in the Córdoba and Huatusco regions. The coffee boom generated enough profits for Tirso and Ceferino to increase their capital investment in the Beneficiadora from 500,000 pesos to 5 million pesos in 1954. They brought in another nephew Miguel Angel Sainz, the illegitimate son of Manuel, and two nonfamily members as minor partners. Although they continued to acquire small ranchos when their clients went bankrupt, they tended to divest themselves of these rural properties soon thereafter. At times, the Sainz Pardos found themselves competing with their former business partners, the Zardains, who were now operating two beneficios in Orizaba. To further diversify their holdings, the Sainz Pardos founded with Regules and his wife, Candelaria, in 1955 another business, Inmuebles Córdoba, which operated out of the former Garza beneficio.[24]

Ricardo Regules was the exporter who experienced the most dramatic change of fortune during the golden age of coffee. He drew on the financial support of the local manager of the Banco Nacional de México and the financial collaboration and expert knowledge of his good friend and longtime exporter Davíd González Rosas. He also brought over from Spain his brother Alejandro, who helped him run the family business, and his nephew Rafael Regules, who ran his operations in Chiapas. Another close relative, Manuel Vallejo Regules, also worked for him. In 1947 he divided his firm into two companies, a local dry goods store, Los Leones, and a regional preparation and export firm. Reincorporating Casa Regules as a family business, he brought in his brother Alejandro, his cousin Evaristo, three of his children, and his son-in-law, Baltazar Sanchez, who had married his daughter María del Carmen. In the same year, he founded another company, Proveedora, to buy, prepare, and sell coffee with his partners—Manuel Albo Crespo, David González, and two of his children—with a total capitalization of 300,000 pesos.[25] Although Regules had become a naturalized Mexican in 1939 and could now purchase property in his own name, he chose to acquire a lot at Twenty-First Street and Fifth Avenue under his wife's name in 1951. He then constructed, in partnership with Mario Fernández, Córdoba's first new beneficio in twenty years. During the Korean War, Regules's business was earning such high profits that he invested an additional 3 million pesos in his company. He also began to purchase urban real estate in his children's names.[26] Ricardo's two sons, Ricardo Jr. and Humberto, gradually took over management of the business from their father in the 1950s. In the 1960s Humberto introduced his own label—Café Palacios, named after a hotel he had purchased.[27] By the early 1950s Regules had emerged as Cordoba's other leading exporter.

Several Cordobeses branched out into coffee roasting and trading in the internal market in the 1940s after the federal government mandated that exporters had to sell domestically to retain their export licenses. The firms of Baltazar Sánchez and Enrique Galván y López created their own coffee brands: Café Balza, Café Córdoba, and Cafés Mexicanos. As members of the second tier of exporters, they also found it necessary, along with Ezequiel González, to diversify their business strategies, forming new business relationships with Regules and Sainz Pardo.[28]

The Regules and Sainz Pardo firms had become so profitable by the early 1960s that they were able to invest 10 million pesos in their respective companies. The decision to increase their capitalization at this juncture was more than likely linked to the future purchase of imported electronic sorting machinery. Tirso now controlled one-half of Beneficiadora's shares, while Ceferino held one-fifth; and their nephews Eugenio and José Luis Gómez Sainz, sons of their sister, held a good portion of the remaining 250 shares. Meanwhile, they continued to diversify their businesses employing their profits from coffee.[29] That year, Regules followed the same strategy, increasing the capitalization of Proveedora and bringing his immediate family into his company. He allotted equal shares to his wife and his five children. He also branched out into the hotel industry, establishing the Hotel Regules Company under their names also.[30] By the 1960s, on the eve of the mechanization of the plants, the patriarchs of the two remaining family firms had taken pains to concentrate their wealth in the hands of their immediate families. Ricardo had also included his wife in most of his transactions as a passive partner. The inclusion of wives in joint-stock companies, the strategy practiced by Ricardo Regules and José Zardain, was a far cry from what the exporters had pursued in the 1920s and 1930s. For many reasons, coffee workers enjoyed few of the economic benefits generated by the postwar coffee boom. The increasing institutionalization and bureaucratization of the national labor organizations and their affiliated unions made it even more difficult for them to challenge their employers.

Coffee Workers Negotiating with the Beneficiadores

Chapters 3 and 4 have shown the continuity of the Veracruz escogedoras' struggle for their worker rights from the 1910s through the 1930s. They were able to gain more ground after the implementation of the 1931 Labor Code. Despite all their efforts, they still achieved limited success in obtaining a living wage, but still the majority of all Mexican workers were earning less than the sorters. In the face of further centralization of the Mexican political system and the co-optation of major labor organizations during the forties and fifties, their militancy began to wane. Although some have argued that a working-class rather than a gendered consciousness motivated obreras to challenge their employers during the Economic Miracle,[31] it would be more accurate to say that the two were intertwined. While SOECC activists won sizable wage increases, these gains were not sufficient during these inflationary years to obtain a living wage. On the other hand, their acquisition of extensive fringe benefits, including maternal benefits, was highly unusual for seasonal workers.

The forties were not good years for Mexican wage earners, including coffee workers. While the Mexican government tried to meet U.S. wartime needs, domestic demand outpaced supply of food products and sparked severe inflation. This resulted in a 45 percent decline in real wages between 1938 and 1945 in the Federal District. The 1943 3-peso minimum wage was less than half the 6.90-peso estimated daily wage needed to support a family of three in the DF. Like other Mexican workers, sorters had to confront the decline in the value of their salaries, the closure of their plants, and the reduction of workdays during the war years. Presidents Manuel Avila Camacho's and Miguel Alemán's proindustry and antiunion policies only made economic survival more difficult.[32]

The war years were particularly challenging for Veracruz coffee sorters, as beneficio owners cut back on their workforce and closed their plants when demand was very low. In a letter to the beneficiadores in 1942, the SOECC leaders asked for a 50 percent wage increase, citing their extremely difficult economic circumstances. They complained that their wages had not increased in two years while prices had risen 80 percent. In spite of these wage issues, 1,642 women were still working in Córdoba's four dry beneficios in 1944.[33] The employment situation was even more serious in Orizaba, where the Boesch plant was seized by the state and temporarily closed, throwing two hundred sorters out of work. The Córdoba labor federation immediately came to the support of their Orizaba compañeras, entreating Avila Camacho for his personal intervention to save their jobs. The federation argued that the majority of the women were heads of households and the sole source of family income and therefore desperately needed the work.[34] Most probably they were rehired when CEIMSA reopened the plant, but this case illustrates how insecure their employment was.

Meanwhile, the CSOCO began encroaching more and more on the SOECC's political autonomy, which the union had fought so hard to gain in the 1920s and 1930s. Eucario León's hegemony over the union tightened even further when he broke with the CROM, taking his Veracruzano loyalists with him. In 1944 he created the Confederación Nacional de Trabajadores (CNT, National Confederation of Workers), which solidified his control over the Orizaba and Córdoba sorter unions. His close personal ties with Reyes led him to appoint her national treasurer, so she left her family for several years to work for him in Mexico City. To further strengthen his control over the SOECC, León instructed his henchmen—Samuel Vargas, Francisco T. Olivares, and Porfirio Camacho—to oversee Córdoba's labor federation, which included supervision of SOECC meetings and elections.[35]

The coffee boom of the 1950s did not significantly improve the economic conditions of Mexican workers. To begin with, the Mexican state was promoting rapid economic growth in the private sector and neutralizing worker demands by controlling labor negotiation.[36] By

1962 wages were only 66.4 percent of 1938 levels. Not until 1971 did real wages return to the base year. In April 1954 Ruiz Cortines carried out the second devaluation in six years, and the value of the peso dropped from 8.65 to 12.50 per dollar, or a decline of 44.5 percent. It led to the immediate increase in consumer prices. The cost-of-living index that used 1954 as the base year rose from 72.5 in 1950 to 113.6 in 1955.[37] Responding to the workers outcries, the president raised all government workers' salaries by 10 percent and urged the private sector to follow suit in order to prevent greater inflationary pressures. These minor wage adjustments did not alleviate the economic plight of working people and led to serious labor unrest. Over the course of the following months fifty thousand unions went out on strike for higher wages.[38] To make matters worse, the SOECC came thoroughly under the control of León's labor cacicazgo.

When the CNT entered into decline, León merged his supporters in 1952 with those of the newly created CROC. León rapidly rose within its leadership to become its general secretary by the mid-1950s. Meanwhile his henchman, Camacho, was specifically charged with bringing the SOECC and other Córdoba unions into the CROC. In February 1953 under the watchful eye of Camacho and Reyes, the sorters obediently voted to adopt a new name, the Sindicato Industrial de Obreras Escogedoras del Café del Distrito de Córdoba (SIOECC, Industrial Union of Coffee Sorters of Córdoba); approved new statutes; and voted to affiliate with the CROC. Its motto was changed to invoke proletarian emancipation to reflect the CROC's more revolutionary stance in order to challenge the CTM, which had become the predominant organization in the PRI's labor sector. When the CROC held its first national meeting at the end of the year, three sorter leaders—Reyes, Moya, and Francisca Rodríguez Sánchez—were in attendance.[39]

By the 1950s, the union appeared to be in a much stronger financial condition. The minutes of its bimonthly meetings offer an excellent window into the inner workings of its leadership. In 1950 the treasury secretary reported that the SIOECC treasury had nineteen thousand pesos in its coffers and an additional fourteen thousand pesos in its social fund. However, three years later the treasury had been seriously depleted, showing a balance of only 8,354 pesos, while the social fund had ballooned to 99,467 pesos.[40] The septupling of the social fund in just over three years might be explained by new contractual arrangements that required employers and union members to set aside a larger percentage of wages each week for fringe benefits.

Contract negotiations held every other year between the SIOECC and the beneficiadores took place in an atmosphere of economic tension but not outright confrontation during the 1950s. The union's leadership no longer resorted to the strike or plant occupation as it had done before 1940. Although the SIOECC and the CTM-affiliated men's union often threatened to go out on strike if their demands were not met, they never carried out their threats. It was more about political posturing than labor militancy now. The union chose its toughest veteran negotiators—Castro, Reyes, Moya, and Romero— to serve on the contract committee. To keep up with high inflation, they continued to concentrate their demands on higher salaries and job security, but they also sought worker benefits that were guaranteed under the law. What is quite remarkable is that the union won just as many concessions as most full-time workers. Among the remaining four major firms, BENEMEX, which had one of the largest workshops, seems to have been the most sensitive to the economic plight of its escogedoras (see photograph 12). It donated one thousand pesos to pay for the expenses of the band and five hundred pesos to help needy widows in the early 1950s.[41]

The primary concern of the SIOECC's leadership was securing and retaining as many permanent positions as possible. The executive committee continued to control labor recruitment through a three-tiered system based on seniority and union loyalty. It placed on the first list those who were loyal union members and had complied with all union requirements and removed those who had not followed union regulations or did not report for work regularly. Those on the

12. Sorter workshop in Beneficios Mexicanos, 1961. Courtesy of the APIRO.

first list were given the permanent positions. Needless to say, certain leaders abused their authority in the recruitment process. Reyes and Castro clearly manipulated the lists and furnished work for loyal rank-and-file members and, in doing so, reinforced the sorters' layered community. In this manner, they strengthened their own clientele. Union membership remained quite stable at around 1,500 members throughout these two decades.[42]

Obtaining a living wage for coffee sorters was the second key concern in contract negotiations. In the 1940s, Córdoba sorters were earning a piece-rate of twenty-five centavos per kilo of waste.[43] By 1950 they were receiving seventy centavos per kilo, but it was not sufficient to cover family living expenses because of the higher cost of living. To keep up with steady inflation two years later, they asked for an increase in the piece-rate to one peso plus twenty centavos for the social fund for medical expenses and a ten-peso wage for the shop steward. In their bimonthly assemblies, Romero and Castro employed strident language, threatening to go out on strike if the owners did not agree to their conditions. An agreement was finally hammered out, averting a strike. The union actually won more than it had originally asked: a piece-rate of 1.15 pesos per kilo of waste, which meant eighty-four centavos of take-home pay, after fifteen centavos had been deducted for the social fund and an additional sixteen to cover Sunday pay.[44] If a very good sorter, such as Brígida, could remove five to six kilos of waste each day, she could earn 4.20 to 5 pesos of take-home pay every day, or 25 to 30 pesos a week.

Coffee-worker union response to the 1954 devaluation was not unlike other Mexican unions. Although they entered into tense negotiations with the beneficiadores, the results were disappointing. Reyes proudly announced that the SIOECC had won another twenty centavos per kilo of waste increase, or a 1.35-peso piece-rate, which represented only a 10 percent increase for permanent workers. Eighteen centavos would be deducted for the federation to pay for work-related illnesses, a maternity stipend, a death benefit, a fifteen-peso retiree stipend, and paid holidays. The owners were, however, now guaranteeing the permanent workers eighteen weeks of work. The maternity leave stipend ranged from one hundred to four hundred pesos depending on the worker's seniority.[45] The men's organization, the CTM-affiliated Sindicato de Trabajadores del Beneficios de Café, Tabaco, y Cargaduría de la Región de Córdoba (Union of Coffee, Tobacco, and Cargo Workers of the Beneficios of the Córdoba Region) eventually agreed to a 10 to 12 percent increase after protracted negotiations.[46] These two contract settlements were essentially in line with Ruiz Cortines's original recommendation but were far too little to make up the 44 percent decrease in the value of the peso. On the other hand, the willingness of the exporters to abide by the law and extend fringe benefits to both women and men workers was highly unusual for seasonal workers in Mexico, or for that matter in the Latin American developing nations. In a country where only 9 percent of workers were unionized in 1950, their wage package was even more remarkable.

Until 1960 the SIOECC paid the medical bills of sick workers and funeral costs on a case-by-case basis from monies taken out of its social fund. It covered professional illnesses, including ovarian hemorrhages and abortions. Upon the approval of the general assembly, rank-and-file members would receive ten to seventy-five pesos for medicine and for doctor's appointments or to cover 50 percent of the cost of an operation performed in Mexico City. Workers were given medical vouchers that they gave to one of the two local doctors, Horacio Guadarrama or Roberto Balmori. The social fund also gave sorter families one hundred to two hundred pesos to defray the funeral costs of union members. The union continued to pay the medical costs of its workers out of its social fund until it was entirely depleted by mid-1954. At that time, the leadership was forced to suspend the voucher system.[47]

As early as 1953, the leadership had launched a major orientation campaign to educate the union's members about the social security system. The CSOCO assisted the secretary general, Francisca Rodríguez, along with Moya and Reyes, in the arrangements to read the law to the assembly and to invite local federation leaders to speak in favor of entering into the social security system. The union decided to postpone enrolling in the program at this time because it was far too costly for even the permanent workers. Union members would finally enroll in 1960.[48]

Although the SIOECC won new concessions in their 1960 and 1962 contracts, clouds were beginning to appear on the horizon concerning future employment. Full mechanization had already commenced in other Central Veracruz towns. To gain a stronger bargaining position, the union decided to reaffiliate with the CROM a year after León died in a car crash in 1957. The 1962 contract that was signed with the remaining three firms—Beneficiadora, Proveedora, and BENEMEX—included additional work security for permanent workers. The two private firms agreed to furnish at least twenty-two weeks of work. They also promised to provide 355 permanent positions in the three beneficios every year. The piece-rate wage was extended to both the amount of waste removed as well as the amount of coffee cleaned. This meant that if the coffees were unusually dirty or unusually clean, the worker would not suffer a pay loss. The piece-rate they agreed on rose to approximately 1.85 pesos per arroba for all classes of café verde and for one kilo of waste.[49] This meant that sorters who could clean ten arrobas could earn 18.50 pesos before deductions. In 1963 the daily wages of our interviewees ranged from 9.63 pesos for Romero Serrano to 27.36 for Castro, but most earned between 10 and 20 pesos.[50] At the rate of 12.50 pesos to the U.S. dollar, this meant a daily wage between $.80 and $1.60.

The companies also agreed to pay fifty-four centavos for each arroba of coffee cleaned for fringe benefits. They assumed responsibility for work-related accidents for up to ninety days, even for temporary workers, although coverage was slightly lower during the days the plants were not in operation. All workers would receive full pay for seven national holidays, which included March 21 (Benito Juarez's birthday) and May 10 (Mother's Day). Temporary workers would now receive vacation days based on the number of days they had worked. Working mothers would be entitled to eight days' paid maternity leave before the birth of their child and one month of postpartum leave. A special place was designated within the workshop for nursing mothers. Attention was also given to working conditions. The contract called for the owners to provide proper ventilation, water fountains, and toilets and to keep the dust level low with regular sweeping. The beneficiadores also agreed to donate five thousand pesos to the union's band with each contract revision. In spite of all these concessions, the company was able to force the union to agree to abide by Clause 27, which stipulated that when plant modernization began, the union would cooperate with the owners in drawing up plans for the reduction of workforce and the payment of compensation.[51]

Consolidation of an Escogedora Cacicazgo

The collective cacicazgo of the SOIECC took on new dimensions in the late forties and fifties, as Reyes and Castro concentrated more and more power into their own hands. They created a sort of dual cacicazgo, where two leaders took "responsibility for separate functional spheres."[52] This period corresponded to Panster's second phase in the construction of a cacicazgo, where "stabilization, reproduction, and deepening of the cacicazgo" occurred.[53] In the post-1940 period of stabilized development, unions and bureaucratic organizations, just like parties, became platforms for the emergence of labor caciques who adapted themselves to new conditions by fusing institutional and personalist principles of organization.[54] There were only minor differences in the construction of women-dominated and men-dominated cacicazgos.

The SIOECC's most dynamic leaders continued to hold the respect of rank-and-file members based on merit. Members recognized their combativeness and effectiveness during contract negotiations; for even though their paycheck did not increase that much, the fringe benefits were unusually generous. The cacicas were diligent in attending to the individual needs of their clientele. They also sought to raise the level of sorter literacy in hopes of improving the obreras' social status. Castro, who was barely literate herself, organized weekly literacy classes. When workers did not attend their classes regularly, she was so exasperated that she urged the assembly to dock them two weeks of work. The leaders also worked to improve hygienic conditions within the beneficios. Reyes suggested that the union raise the money to bring drinking water into the plants by deducting one peso from all paychecks for three weeks, and the union approved this decision. The leadership also sent their activists, in particular Eufrosina, to help other escogedora unions in Coatepec, Huatusco, and Orizaba.[55] They extended medical vouchers to those that were ill. Their dances, band, and theatrical performances gave even greater legitimacy to the cacicas' authority.

Castro developed into the most formidable cacica of the forties and fifties, rotating in and out of the secretary generalship almost every six months. She would serve as secretary of internal affairs or external affairs one term and secretary general the other term. She often was selected to administer the social fund, although she only had three years of schooling. Her strength lay in handling the union's internal affairs, which included keeping the rank and file content and well disciplined. She was also repeatedly elected union shop steward, just as Inés was, in one of the beneficios. Córdoba residents remembered how she ruled with an iron hand. On one occasion, she forced union members to wait an entire day in the blazing sun just to greet the governor.[56]

Reyes was more agile at handling external relations with other local unions and the csoco. Since the 1930s she had played a key role in managing the union's finances. Although Reyes did not regularly hold the secretary generalship until the sixties, she was a member of almost every executive committee, usually serving as treasurer. She also served on all of the contract negotiation teams.[57] Nepotism now began to raise its ugly head, as these cacicas recruited a second generation of union loyalists. Reyes tapped her sister-in-law, Guadalupe López Osorio de Acevedo, who entered the executive committee and often oversaw the union's treasury or social fund; meanwhile, Castro brought in her niece, Sara Torres Castro, as her protégée and eventually promoted her to leadership positions.[58]

Castro and Reyes expanded their political authority into other local unions, which is a quite common occurrence in caciquismo. When leaders are elected to leadership positions in other organizations, they demonstrate an ability to assume different identities, dominate multiple domains, and enhance their capacity for intermediation.[59] They both owned stalls in the local market where they sold goods to supplement their incomes during the slow summer months. As members of the market vendors' union (the Sindicato de Detallistas Ambulantes y Establecidos en el Mercado de la Revolución), Reyes and Castro served numerous times as secretary general in the 1950s and 1960s. In addition, they trained future leaders, including Sergio López Rosado, who went on to become a very prominent Cromista leader.[60] Castro with her sister operated a cantina, Tres Hermanos, directly across the street from La Beneficiadora, which had a rather dubious reputation.

The third leader, Moya, whom we might characterize as the free spirit, served as secretary general only once during the 1950s, but she often was elected secretary of external affairs. As a skilled orator and accomplished negotiator, she was chosen many times as director of debates, where she frequently shaped the tenor of the union discussions. This charismatic mulatto militant frequently traveled to conventions outside the state as the SIOECC's representative. Most importantly, she strongly supported the economic needs of the rank and file,[61] and for this reason they adored her.

Reyes and Castro kept in constant contact with the CSOCO's cacique, Eucario León. He advised the SIOECC on every major issue, including the introduction of social security and contract negotiations. At union meetings, Eucario's recent political activities were reported on and carefully recorded in the minutes. Union leaders would return from national congresses and praise his "brilliant" speeches, and they would report on all his meetings with high administration officials. For his birthday celebration on December 7, the SIOECC would have to buy an expensive present, send its most gifted orators, and instruct its bands de guerra to play for the festivities in Santa Rosa. As one of the most powerful and corrupt labor caciques in Veracruz, with a reputation for using hired gunmen to carry out his commands, León kept firmly under his tutelage the SOIECC, along with many other unions, until his death. He also exercised control over Orizaba's municipal council through his brother.[62]

The union's increasing dependency on León and the CSOCO had disastrous financial consequences. León and his henchmen must have siphoned off money from its social fund. When it had reached 100,000 pesos in 1953, the executive committee decided or was urged to deposit 50,000 in a Santa Rosa bank account. The money mysteriously disappeared. Moya publically denounced its disappearance and made futile efforts to go to Santa Rosa to track it down. The fund subsequently ran out of money, as expenses for band uniforms, medical costs, and other expenses soared. By early 1954, treasury funds had also plummeted to 1,700 pesos.[63]

León recruited Reyes, Castro, and Moya for positions in the state's union bureaucracy. Reyes was appointed to the executive committee of the Confederación de Sindicatos de Obreros y Campesinos del Estado de Veracruz (Confederation of Workers and Peasants of the State of Veracruz), affiliated with the CROC. All three were chosen at one time or another to represent the city's labor sector on the Junta Municipal de Conciliación. When León brought together all women and men coffee workers in the Federación Nacional de Trabajadores de la Industria del Café (FNTIC, National Federation of Coffee-Industry Workers) in January 1955, he tapped Castro and Moya to serve on its executive committee, although an Orizaba sorter was chosen as its secretary general.[64]

SIOECC cacicas also became active suffragettes, civic reformers, and political leaders; and in so doing, they began to exercise their rights of citizenship. They joined other militants engaged in the struggle to gain women's right to vote in federal elections. Since President Cárdenas had reneged on his pledge to grant women the right to vote in federal elections in the late 1930s, it would take more than a decade before President Ruiz Cortines reintroduced a suffrage bill.[65] However, incremental changes were already beginning to occur at the state and local level. In 1946 women were given the right to vote in state elections. The following year, Veracruz amended Article 111 of its constitution to read that women should not only play a role in society as housewives and as workers but also in the shaping of the destiny of their country. In 1949 a Veracruzana became the nation's first woman to be elected municipal president in President Alemán's home town. These reforms spurred the formation of numerous women's suffrage organizations, including the PRI's local Comité de Acción Femenil Cordobés (Committee of Cordoban Women's Action). Reyes, Castro, Moya, Romero, and Vázquez regularly reported on the suffrage bill's progress through congress to local and state coffee-worker conventions in an effort to encourage obreras to exercise their political rights. Unlike most suffragettes, who were members of the middle class, these working women felt that the rights of full citizenship should also be extended to them. The federal congress finally approved women's suffrage at the national level in 1953. Its passage spurred Reyes, Castro, and Moya to attend two congresses of women citizens (*mujeres ciudadanas*) in Puebla and Mexico City on November 18 and 19, 1953. These were certainly heady days for these labor activists. Reyes would go on to serve as the PRI's regional director of the Asociación Nacional Femenil Revolucionario (ANFER, Women's National Revolutionary Association).[66] It is entirely possible that it was easier for a woman worker to enter municipal politics in an agro-industrial center than an industrial center where male-dominated unions prevailed.

Even before the national suffrage bill was approved, SIOECC leaders had entered municipal politics. They were selected by the PRI's labor sector to serve on the municipal council. For nine out of the seventeen years between 1950 and 1967, they represented Córdoba's unions. Castro was the first sorter leader elected councilwoman during Agustin Sosa's administration (1950–53). Her foremost accomplishment was to obtain a 150-peso monthly subsidy from the municipal government for the union. The union had become such an integral part of the local economy and PRI politics that the official party agreed to subsidize it. Reyes would follow in Castro's footsteps, entering the town council in 1956. Governor Fernando López Arias tapped Moya to serve in 1964, but Reyes and Castro blocked their political rival from occupying the seat and proposed their protégée, Guadalupe Guareña. These women's continual presence in positions of power suggests that they wielded considerable influence within the local federation and the PRI bureaucracy. Town dignitaries even invited Moya and Reyes to serve on the Junta de Mejoramiento Moral, Cívica, y Material (Moral, Civic, and Economic Improvement Board).[67] Notwithstanding their relatively low educational level and socioeconomic status, their leadership skills and talents had won them the respect and confidence of the political and social establishment.

The trio began to travel more frequently out of state to participate in women-sponsored events and to enhance the status of unionized women workers. Moya took the initiative to propose to the CROC's national convention that each district should create a women's department—the Secretaría de Acción Femenil. In her proposal she argued that since there was a general "lack of honest, capable fellow union leaders," she saw a need for reform. Indirectly she was implying that women were more honest leaders than men. She recommended that only women workers should financially support and run these new departments of women's affairs. Although the CROC created women's sections, in later years Moya recognized the failure of this initiative.[68]

Leadership continuity came with its costs for the union's internal affairs. It contributed to the gradual consolidation of the collective cacicazgo into a dual cacicazgo. Leaders constantly manipulated elections by presenting only one slate of candidates to the assembly so that the same persons remained on the executive committee.[69] Those who opposed these strategies were marginalized and eventually expelled from the union. Moya was not the first leader to be denied positions of power, but she was certainly one of the most important. As Moya's daughter put it, the underdogs ("los de abajo") might have been able to become director of debates or secretary of agreements and have a voice in the general debates, but in fact one secretary general dominated as a cacica.[70] Moya was very generous and creative but also volatile and controversial. In 1953 she brazenly accused Porfirio Camacho of controlling the union's elections and turning them into a farce. Moya asked "the assembly if it was right for the secretary general of the local federation to name the compañeras who should lead in the next term."[71] She also spoke up in defense of younger rank-and-file members who had made derogatory remarks about the veteran secretary general Romero. She publically condemned the secretary general's decision to levy heavy fines on these teenagers. She likewise challenged Reyes when she wanted to divide the first list in two to manipulate the selection of permanent positions.[72] By the early 1960s the SIOECC leadership had marginalized Moya because of her outspokenness and her increasingly volatile behavior. Her children claimed that she had become seriously depressed after the death of her talented son Chumo and had taken to the bottle.[73] But rank-and-file sorters had more difficulty explaining precisely why she had become more and more erratic and confrontational. Some attributed it to a drinking problem, while others believed that the leadership had conspired against her. "They gave her something to drink, which made her go crazy. But the truth is no one really knew, . . . the truth, no one really knew what had changed her."[74] Her confrontational be-havior began to seriously affect her ability to control her temper. One day, she offended officials in the local social security office, and they threatened to file formal charges against her for the use of abusive language. The executive committee immediately recommended that the Comisión de Honor y Justicia severely discipline her. In 1961 it voted to deny her permanent employment for the third and last time.[75]

Moya was not the only person to be excluded by the cacicas. Ro-dríguez was likewise singled out and accused of carrying on "a policy of disorientation among workers with the object of taking them over to the rival CROM." Moreover, they attacked her for being disrespect-ful of León. The Comisión de Honor y Justicia, which functioned as an instrument of cacical authority, accused her of high treason, forced her to resign as labor representative on the Municipal Conciliation Board, and cast her out of the union.[76] Rodríguez's exclusion by the cacicas would come back to haunt them later.

Mechanization: Negotiating with the Owners and the State

The coffee boom of the 1950s could not be sustained for long. Coffee prices had risen dramatically from thirty-two dollars per sixty-pound bag in 1949 to seventy dollars in 1951 and to one hundred dollars in 1955. However, steadily expanding African and Latin American pro-duction and lagging demand in U.S. and European markets led to a dramatic downturn in the commodity's price. By 1956 the price had dropped to seventy-eight dollars a bag.[77] Attempts to reimpose ex-port quotas in the Latin America Coffee Agreement of 1958 to stabilize prices did not significantly improve the market. Although the 1963 International Coffee Agreement pushed prices higher for a while, they slipped back down again to forty dollars. Mexican exports peaked in 1957 at 88,823 tons, but then they dropped more than 10 percent in the following year. Beneficios began to close their doors in Central Veracruz, particularly in the Coatepec region.[78] What strategies could Veracruz coffee entrepreneurs adopt to reduce their costs and remain competitive in an increasingly uncertain market? They decided that they had to complete the mechanization of their plants.

Ruiz Cortines had already taken the initiative in 1955 when prices were high to spur industrialization by lifting the ban on imported machinery. Xalapa and Coatepec beneficiadores took advantage of this policy and were the first to experiment with imported electronic sorting machines, which could identify and separate discolored and broken beans from the green ones. The Xalapa coffee exporter Carlos Pineiro became an agent for the English firm Sortex, which manufactured one of the earliest sorting machines. Mechanization, however, took place in a piecemeal fashion, for beneficiadores did not have complete confidence in these small electronic sorters, which could sort faster but less efficiently than manual laborers.[79]

Mechanization started in Coatepec when a group of disgruntled small and medium coffee producers formed the Compania Agricola de Productores y Exportadores de Café SA (CAPECSA, Coatepec Agricultural Company of Coffee Producers and Exporters) in 1953 with the objective of lowering coffee preparation costs in order to circumvent the local monopolistic preparers. At first, the company sent its parchment coffee to a Mexico City dry beneficio to reduce overall costs, and then the company decided to install new electronic sorters in its own beneficio. Both of these decisions adversely affected its beneficio workers. The CROC-affiliated SODCC and the men's organization, the Sindicato Industrial de Obreros de Beneficios en las Plazas de Xalapa, Coatepec, y Teocelo (Industrial Union of Coffee Workers of Xalapa, Coatepec, and Teocelo), decided to resist these decisions. Mechanization had another unfortunate consequence; it widened the split between union leadership and the rank and file. In Cecilia Sheridan's words, "there developed a strong competition between the obreras, who wanted the largest compensation for themselves, and the leaders, who wanted to guarantee for themselves large profits created by the chaos of the disappearance of the only source of employment for the escogedoras."[80] The leaders began by appealing to the Municipal Conciliation Board to seek redress for the loss of work. When this strategy failed, the two unions boycotted the plant, stationing members at the doorways of the beneficio and blocking the roads so that the coffee could not leave the premises. Meanwhile, secretary general Adelina Téxon sent letters to President Ruiz Cortines and Governor Marco Antonio Muñoz Tumbull asking for their assistance. The strike dragged on for six months, during which time the sorters' union continued to occupy the building and insist on the signing of a new collective contract in order to retain their jobs. Executive committee members were jailed and charged with disruptive behavior. In light of the worsening situation that affected five hundred sorters—the president, the governor, the JCCA, and the CROC intervened to prevent unsorted coffee from leaving the region and to mediate negotiations between labor and the company for a resolution of this crisis.[81] The SODCC's executive committee with its CROC advisors traveled to Mexico City to meet with President Ruiz Cortines to see if he would intervene to save their jobs. The CROC representative recalled that he envisaged mechanization as part of the modernization process: "If the United States is so progressive why cannot Mexico be so too . . ." The president assured Téxon that he would come to Coatepec and settle everything, but she understood implicitly that he would do nothing. When she reported to the union, she told them that the president had reiterated Mexico had to progress and that he had promised to create a dress-making cooperative for them.[82] A preliminary settlement was finally hammered out with CAPECSA in March 1956 that favored industry over labor. The plant would be fully mechanized, and only sixteen senior sorters would be guaranteed work and future benefits.[83]

After CAPECSA's laying off of 195 Coatepec workers, the CROC called a meeting of the six small unions of Xalapa and the SODCC to ask for just compensation for these workers. They argued that this case placed in jeopardy the jobs of approximately three thousand escogedoras who worked in the region. The conflict was compounded when some women agreed to accept the owners' terms and others did not. In 1961 only two firms remained in Coatepec—BENEMEX, which was now called INMECAFE, and the Martínez firm. The owners proposed a two-track solution. Half of their 180 permanent workers—that is, 45 from each beneficio—would continue to have work, while the remaining 90 would be terminated along with the 60 occasional workers. Through manipulation of the lists, leaders had abandoned ninety workers to save ninety positions. When the dismissed workers attempted to air their grievances with Juan Martínez Ruiz, their leaders and CROC advisors counseled them to be prudent and not to demand too much. As a consequence, the terminated workers received only 4,500 to 6,000 pesos in severance pay, and they had to relinquish their union rights, which meant that they could never work in the beneficios again. No criteria were ever given for the disparities in their wage settlements.[84] The occasional workers were given a bonus (*gratificación*) of five hundred pesos and told to their faces that the owners did not legally need to give them any compensation. They were so incensed by this ridiculously low sum that some said "it was better to leave without one centavo and be uncorrupted and proud," and this is what a goodly number did. The last group of sorters were compensated in August 1964. During all this time, they continued to hold meetings in their union hall. However, bitter divisions between the two groups still persisted in the 1980s. Enriqueta Salazar remembered forty year later that the permanent workers only received three hundred to six hundred pesos of compensation based on their seniority, but these figures seem too low. In any case, she insisted, the executive committee members and CROC leaders managed to get more for themselves.[85]

As soon as it became clear that Xalapa exporters were likewise plan-

13. Enriqueta Salazar Báez with her husband, 2003. Photograph by author.

ning to mechanize their beneficios, the CROC decided to protect its workers by launching a major campaign to block their efforts. Numerous affiliated unions around the country were instructed to send appeals to the president to prevent the laying off of hundreds of sorters, claiming it would leave them in total misery. To strengthen the bargaining position of the sorters, Eucario León, who was head of the

CROC at this time, organized women and men coffee workers into the FNTIC to present a united front.[86] All these efforts proved fruitless because local unions were far too fractured to obstruct the mechanization process. By the fall of 1956, Xalapa union leaders realized the jobs of their members were in immediate jeopardy, and they persuaded the new CROC secretary general to come to Xalapa to negotiate a fair settlement with Governor Muñoz. To preempt a threatened strike, the beneficiadores decided not to initiate operations at the start of the harvest season. The situation became so tense that the *Diario de Xalapa* raised the specter that seven thousand sorters might go on a statewide strike. The governor immediately established a tripartite committee in early November presided over by the undersecretary of internal affairs to find quickly a solution. As the *Diario* warned, Veracruzanos should be acutely aware that the "final resolution which the committee will take will have repercussions throughout the country owing to the fact that Veracruz has more coffee workers and produces more coffee than any other state."[87] Within six weeks, separate agreements were hammered out with all but one of Xalapa's six unions. Each of these agreements was slightly different. The sorters were only able to win a few concessions, which simply delayed total mechanization. Beneficiadores were still uncertain whether these early electronic sorters could actually perform the cleaning process well, so they agreed to continue to employ a limited number of sorters for the near future. This gave the escogedoras a short breathing space. In the Martínez labor settlement, the union agreed to accept sixty thousand pesos to compensate all but forty permanent workers for the loss of wages in the following year in accordance with the existing contract. The agreement also required the owners to increase fringe-benefit contributions by 50 percent for these remaining workers. Rosa Aurora Fernández initially agreed to a sixty thousand–peso severance pay package for twenty of her forty workers. Then she reduced her worker compensation to twenty thousand pesos. An additional twenty thousand pesos was set aside for union expenses. A laid-off worker, therefore, received one thousand pesos in severance pay.[88] The men workers, both skilled and unskilled, were still needed to run the machines and load the coffee, so their positions remained untouched.

Disputes over the implementation of the agreements between the escogedoras and Exportadores de Café de Xalapa (EXCAXA, Xalapa Coffee Exporters) dragged on for more than six years. During this protracted process, some unions returned to their class-based discourse of the 1920s, labeling their bosses "exploiters" of the proletariat. At one point the Mexican Communist Party decided to take up the sorters' cause. It sent operatives to Xalapa to collaborate with local Communist activist Isaac Fernández to help organize the women against the exporters, who they argued illegally fired two hundred sorters. To resolve this festering conflict, Governor Antonio Modesto Quirasco finally had to take matters into his own hands and force the companies to back down and temporarily rehire some of their sorters. Protracted labor conflicts in Xalapa and Coatepec stretched well into the sixties. Fidel Velazquez, secretary general of the CTM, entered into the fray in 1962, appealing to the president to intervene on behalf of the sorters to force the owners to comply with their agreement and pay fringe benefits. Conflicts between the union leadership and the rank and file also erupted. The obreras accused their leaders of corruption for not distributing the compensation according to the labor settlement.[89]

The Córdoba exporters delayed mechanization until 1964, quite probably because their bigger plants required considerably more machinery to handle the volume of coffee they prepared. In late February the Sainz Pardo and Regules firms sent letters to the SIOECC, notifying the union of their decision to install electronic sorters and asking its leadership to draw up a plan for worker reduction and the criteria to be employed for compensation. Their decision to mechanize, they argued, was based on their precarious economic condition. Their profit margins had declined dramatically over the past years, and it was economically necessary to cut costs. The Sainz Pardos showed a profit of over a million pesos during the 1961–62 season, but their balance sheets revealed that their profits had plummeted to

255,000 pesos in the following year. While they listed the Beneficiadora's net worth at 5 million pesos, they claimed that it was no longer operating profitably. Ricardo and Humberto Regules Huesca stated that Proveedora, whose net worth they placed at 10 million pesos, had seen profits of only 330,000 pesos during the 1962–63 season. They argued it was now considerably cheaper to prepare coffee with machines than with manual labor. In Huatusco, Xalapa, and Coatepec, where mechanization had already taken place, operation costs had dropped by twenty-one pesos per sixty-kilo bag. The Cordobeses argued that they were at a competitive disadvantage unless they installed the same SORTEX G-21 machines that were in Xalapa. They were abiding by Clause 27 of the 1962 labor contract when they asked the union to draft the labor reduction and compensation plans. However, in light of the union's refusal to uphold the contract, the beneficiadores petitioned the JCCA to apply Articles 128, 581, and 570 of the Labor Code. These articles gave a company the right to temporarily reduce its labor force if it was resolving an economic conflict due to new work conditions, as long as it compensated the workers with three months' pay and an additional twenty days' pay for each year of service.[90] How did the sorters' union respond to this challenge?

Reyes, who was once again secretary general, immediately appealed to Governor López Arias, employing feminine discourse to play on his sympathies in order to persuade him to address the plight of the poor working women. "Permit us to distract you from your multiple tasks and inform you about a grave problem that confronts our organization." She then proceeded to accuse the three firms of violating Article 56 of the labor law with regard to the revision of the collective contract. In the name of eight hundred workers, "we have decided to bring to your attention in order to entreat you in the most respectful and polite manner to give us your invaluable help and to intervene. . . . Their desire to carry out the modernization of the plants, and NOT TO REVISE THE COLLECTIVE CONTRACT is unquestionable. . . . We have decided to trouble you and beg you in a very polite and respectful way to intervene and lend us your valuable help."[91]

In her letter to the president of the JCCA, Reyes, assisted by her CROC advisors, adopted more legal terminology to argue the union's case. The companies were in direct violation of the law, she argued, because they had not responded to the SOIECC's February contract proposal. Since the union had an uninterrupted history of collective contracts with these firms dating back to 1927, they were now acting in an illegal manner. A new contract had not been signed since 1960, and salaries had not been raised since then. "We are enduring an economic situation due to the high cost of living, which is no longer possible to endure." The union proceeded to issue a call for a strike on April 30, the day their two-year contract expired.[92] In short, Reyes was following a two-track strategy in her correspondence, opting for a discourse of weakness and supplication with the governor and one of economic necessity with the state's industrial-labor relations board. What is noteworthy is that feminine discourse was now being employed more frequently than in the 1910s and 1920s by women leaders and their advisors, as revolutionary rhetoric and militant labor activism was becoming more and more muted.

The response of the two private firms to the threat of a strike was not long in coming. They argued that they had no intention of revising or renewing their collective contracts because the modernization of the plants would effectively eliminate all need for them to hire what they referred to as "temporary and occasional laborers." They rejected the argument that their companies had signed contracts with the escogedoras since 1927. They also disputed the allegation that the contracts of 1960 and 1962 had not raised the sorters' pay. Furthermore, they argued, the SIOECC had to fulfill its obligations set forth in Clause 27 to devise a compensation plan for all sorters. When the union threatened to carry out a strike, the exporters reluctantly signed a new contract on May 1 for the purpose of postponing the strike until negotiations on mechanization could be finished.[93] They needed to bide their time until the JCCA had ruled on their right to mechanize in accordance with the law.

Unlike the earlier Xalapa case, where the governor had directly intervened to resolve the labor conflict, this time he left the resolution of Córdoba's dispute in the hands of the JCCA, which suggests that the CROM was now in a considerably weaker position than the CROC had been in, in Xalapa. The board's deliberations took four months. In the meantime, the strike was postponed week after week to give more time for a final resolution. At the union's July 23 meeting, the state's representative on the JCCA, the head of the Departamento del Trabajo y Previsión Social (Department of Labor and Social Programs), announced the JCCA's decision, which supported the entrepreneurs by agreeing to the "necessity of modernizing the machinery" in the beneficios. He recognized that this would lead to the replacement of the workers, and he made clear that the obreras would be fully compensated according to the law. The final resolution called for the termination of the collective contract at the end of the 1963–64 season. Beneficiadora and Proveedora agreed to pay a total of 2.8 million pesos to the union to be distributed on a prorated basis to every worker who was a member of the union. The union was now charged with developing a plan for the final financial settlement, which would list the exact amount that each worker would receive. Once this was finalized, the two private firms agreed to hand this sum over to the executive committee, which was charged with the distribution of the workers' compensation. This decision actually violated the law, for the owners were supposed to pay the workers machine by machine. The vague language in the agreement gave union leaders' considerable latitude in the distribution of funds. Each owner also agreed to pay three thousand pesos for prestrike costs. The union was held responsible for paying its own legal fees. Until their warehouses were completely empty, the two firms agreed to continue to employ two hundred workers. The agreement also left open the possibility for future work.[94] BENEMEX's compensation settlement was more complex because it involved three regional plants, so it would take the JCCA an additional four months to resolve.

Within a month Beneficiadora and Proveedora each handed checks for 1,387,869 pesos to Castro and Reyes, the newly elected secretary general and treasurer, to distribute to 272 permanent and 315 temporary workers. However, SIOECC distribution lists reveal that the money was not dispersed equally to all workers. The two cacicas, with their lieutenants, used seniority and personal loyalty as the key criteria for the distribution of the compensation. They devised a three-tiered arrangement. Seventy permanent workers with supposedly forty years of seniority, including all the prominent leaders, were awarded twelve thousand pesos apiece. Rank-and-file workers—such as Brígida Siriaco, Cecilia Hernández, and Silvia Herrera Luna—who had worked fourteen to eighteen years received between 4,200 and 4,800 pesos, while all temporary workers received 1,971 pesos.[95] In the BENEMEX November settlement, the firm gave union leaders 854,411 pesos for its two hundred Córdoba workers. The leadership pledged to use some of these funds to retrain sorters for other types of work, in particular in the clothing industry.[96]

At least three groups of sorters almost immediately lodged protests because of irregularities in the distribution process: permanent workers who claimed they had received nothing because they had been supporters of the marginalized leaders, Moya and Rodríguez; temporary workers; and veteran workers who had left or been ejected from the union before 1964. The discontented workers rallied around Francisca Rodríguez, since Moya was by this time plagued with serious mental problems. The dissidents launched a campaign to regain the funds that they felt they had been denied. In the name of more than five hundred sorters and claiming to represent the official SIOECC, Rodríguez and other plaintiffs wrote to López Arias in the spring of 1965, accusing Castro, Reyes, and Guadalupe López of breach of trust (*abuso de confianza*) and fraud with regard to the disappearance of 1 million pesos. They asked for copies of the original July 23 settlement and the original worker compensation lists to show that the cacicas had not properly compensated those on the list and had not distributed at least a million pesos of the severance pay.[97] The state's Labor Department soon announced that the executive committee had in fact used irregular procedures in distributing the compensation. Rather than calling a meeting, as the law stipulated, in which all beneficiaries signed a collective agreement accepting the settlement, the cacicas had summoned the women in small groups and forced each individual sorter to accept her compensation. The dissident workers also tried to seek redress during the SIOECC's regular meetings. The head of the Labor Department came to Córdoba once more to mediate the dispute in an open assembly meeting. But Castro and Reyes exercised such complete control over the rank and file that they refused to accept Rodríguez's complaint or to give to the temporary workers three months' pay. In desperation, the rebels turned to the CROM authorities in Orizaba to win their support.[98]

The state tried to remain above the fray in this internal dispute and simply asked the CROM to resolve the conflict within its affiliated union. It contacted the CSOCO to investigate the possibility of embezzlement of funds by the SIOECC leadership. Orizaba sent forthwith a delegation to Córdoba to investigate. After consulting with both the leadership and what it termed the "discontented group," the CROM issued its own report supporting the Cromista cacicas. Minor errors had been committed but not on the scale that the media had reported. The leaders had not personally profited from the financial settlement, the report argued, but rather they had had to pay their lawyers 500,000 pesos to work on three rather than one complex legal case. With respect to the supposed missing million pesos, the remaining 400,000 pesos had been located in a Mexico City bank account. These monies were not stolen funds, for the rank and file had approved setting them aside to explore alternative employment opportunities. The report also confirmed that Castro had indeed agreed to pay 5 percent of the settlement to thirty-five disgruntled temporary workers. However, she baulked at giving even a peso to Rodríguez and her 197 supporters, who had not been union members at the time of the settlement. To illustrate how resolutely the CROM supported its entrenched cacicas, the report criticized the discontents for having caused serious damage to the organization through its frequent appeals to the local and national press.[99] This dispute reveals clearly that women union leaders were just as likely to embezzle funds as men leaders, and their national labor organization felt no compunction toward condoning their actions. Meanwhile, the rebels, who had been expelled from the union, refused to accept the CSOCO-brokered compromise, and they decided to continue their challenge of the cacicas in the courts.

This lengthy legal process dragged on for years. In December 1966 a federal judge ruled that Castro, Reyes, Guereña, and López were all guilty of breach of trust and the diversion of funds into two accounts in the Banco de Londres y México (Bank of London and Mexico). He called for their arrest, although he never implemented the order.[100] This formal challenge to a corrupt cacicazgo did not end here. Rodríguez wrote to President Luis Echeverría Alvarez, expressing her displeasure with the governor and the JCCA, who she believed were still supporting Castro and her associates. Once again Rodríguez resorted to the discourse of the poor, female victim, citing the ways in which the cacicas had "treat[ed] persons of the feminine sex of humble condition whose lives have been spent sorting coffee for the agro-export industry. . . . As a defender of the lower class we ask for your intervention."[101] In her rhetoric, there was no difference between a corrupt cacique or cacica.

Rodríguez and approximately four hundred sorters continued to fight through the courts into the mid-1970s for recovery of 583,000 pesos supposedly set aside for retraining workers. They even demanded that an embargo be placed on one of the two bank accounts.[102] Meanwhile, the JCCA tried to bring closure through its local conciliation board. In October 1974 Córdoba's board ruled that the leadership had done nothing wrong. The plaintiffs, they argued, had left the union before the settlement had taken place, and therefore they had renounced their right to sue the union. To mollify the discontented sorters, Castro presented each of them with a five hundred–peso gift or bonus. Among those receiving this payment was Brígida Siriaco, who had been one of the original plaintiffs in the suit.[103] In short, certain sorters who felt that they had been betrayed demonstrated that they were quite capable of defending their rights, and in no way were they passive objects in claiming their severance pay. The state's labor boards had upheld the right of the owners to mechanize and terminate all their women workers and the right of the labor caci-cas to distribute severance pay in an illegal fashion. The sale of the SIOECC's building in 1980 represents the final disbursement of union property. Its prime location on Third Avenue meant that the property sold for 1 million pesos. Each of the 193 remaining loyalists received 5,584 pesos.[104]

Job Loss and Collective Memory

Walter Benjamin suggests that "an experienced event is finite—at any rate, confined to one sphere of experience; [while] a remembered event is infinite, because it is only a key to everything that happened before and after it."[105] Alessandro Portelli frames this issue in another way when he reminds us that the memory "manipulates factual events and chronological sequences in order to serve three major functions": to give them symbolic meaning, to heal a feeling of humiliation and loss of self-esteem, and to give them a formal structure often rearranging or blurring several occurrences to explain or give coherence to the individual or the collectivity.[106] This is precisely what Cecilia Sheridan and I discovered when the sorters recounted their stories about their replacement by machines and the controversial severance packages in Coatepec and Córdoba. Undoubtedly, the elimination of their steady, secure work was personally traumatic for every sorter as well as for the obrera community as a whole. Their way of life as workers and as union members slowly unraveled. For all of them, it split their lives in two: the relativly satisfying formal wage-earning years before mechanization and the difficult informal wage earning years after mechanization. As Daniel James suggests, "The 'collective memory' thus formulated is constructed on the basis of various devices: public myths, founding stories, cultural transforming events, evil and good characters, and the division of the past into the time before and after a 'golden age.'"[107]

When Sheridan interviewed Coatepec sorters, union leaders, and their CROC advisors in 1980, their memories of the labor settlement process were sharper than those of the Córdoba workers in 1999. They had etched in their memories the words of Ruiz Cortines and their leaders with a kind of fatalism. Most workers realized that there did not exist any real possibility of questioning the owners' rationale that they had to modernize their beneficios to survive.[108] The leaders of the SODCC believed the reason for the disappearance of employment was the entrepreneurs' decision to modernize, while for the rank and file it was simply their preference for new machinery. Another group of workers thought it had to do with the introduction of social security, for which the owners did not want to pay.[109] Nevertheless, the SODCC continued to exist, and it survived in part because it was "sustained by the pillars constructed by memories."[110]

In Córdoba the sorters' individual recollections shared much in common. Few blamed the beneficiadores for their loss of work, for they recognized the inevitability of their replacement by machines. They were definitely not the main culprits.[111] A life dominated by a lack of economic security meant that they retained a paternalist vision of their employers, who had always been their source of employment. They already knew that mechanization had occurred in Huatusco, Coatepec, and Xalapa. They did not display any real sense of class consciousness or female victimization forty years after the event, for they had in many respects internalized a fatalistic view of their worker and gender identity.

Their memories were primarily shaped by individual personal experiences arising out of their particular clientelist relationship with one of the cacicas. For the personal is the political, and the political is personal, where power relations are shaped by interactions between individuals and groups. If they had been a member of either the Castro or the Reyes clientele, they had come out ahead. They recalled that the real source of conflict was the plant owners' refusal to sign another collective contract. In their minds, the owners had violated the law. "No one was in agreement with this [owner's behavior]." Since they could not really comprehend the true implications of the mechanization process, they shifted the blame to something they were more familiar with in their everyday experiences—the beneficiadores. They were relatively pleased with their settlement package. Cecilia and her mother, as well as Silvia, who had all worked thirty years, received ten thousand pesos. They considered this fair. Other pro-Castro supporters preferred not to talk about the settlement or did not reveal what they had received so as to cover up the irregularities in the distribution process.[112] The question of compensation for temporary workers was more difficult for pro-Castro and pro-Reyes supporters to rationalize. They blamed the owners for the unequal compensation. In their minds, Castro had actually valiantly supported the temporary workers and had even paid them a small sum.[113] These sorters had essentially internalized the arguments of their cacicas.

The union members belonging to the Moya and Rodríguez factions blamed the two cacicas for their leaders' expulsion from the organization and their loss of employment. Their feelings of injustice and humiliation led them to label these leaders "betrayers." They had to find the perpetrators within their everyday worlds to make this experience meaningful to them. Castro and Reyes "treated us very badly." These leaders had made the fatal mistake of demanding higher wages during early contract negotiations. "They paid us 2.50 [per kilo of waste and per arroba of green coffee] . . . and they wanted to increase it to 3.00. And they wanted, I don't know, other things . . . and the owners became angry. Then, they closed the plants. They laid off the women." While the owners planned to distribute the money "machine by machine," so each worker would be paid the same amount, the leaders wanted to divide it up themselves. As a consequence some temporary workers received more than some permanent workers. Brígida said that she had only received a paltry sum because she had been a supporter of Moya. On the other hand, Castro, Reyes, and López, and their friends, like Estela Velázquez, got more. To prove that the cacicas had embezzled funds, Brígida pointed to the fact that the children of Reyes, López, and Velázquez had attended professional schools and were now very well-off.[114] She broke down in tears, as she told her own personal story. The leaders had distributed the severance pay to the sorters in small groups. When Reyes handed Brígida her envelope, she tore it open and took most of the money out, leaving her only 250 pesos. She complained to Castro about the way she had been treated, but the secretary general simply said that she had no power to do anything and told her go back to speak with Inés. When she did so, Reyes said, "I do not know you."[115]

Moya's children believed their mother had been a victim of a conspiracy. As an increasingly marginalized figure by 1964, Eufrosina enjoyed less and less influence in the decision-making process. Nevertheless, when the mechanization was announced, she had suggested young sorters assist financially strapped older escogedoras by giving up some of their pay. Needless to say, this was not a very popular position. When the negotiations between the union and the exporters entered their critical phase, the cacicas sent Moya on a commission to Monterrey to remove her from the scene. When she returned, the JCCA agreement had already been issued. According to her children, she never received any severance pay, because she was no longer a permanent worker.[116] Thus, the memories of the victors were quite different from those of the losers.

In conclusion, the war and the postwar coffee boom altered the relationship between labor, capital, and the state in Córdoba's coffee economy. The increasing volatility of the world market made coffee's production and preparation for export more and more precarious. By the 1940s only two of the five Spanish immigrant families, the Sainz Pardos and the Reguleses, were still actively engaged in the coffee agribusiness in Veracruz, while the Zardains had relocated their company to Mexico City and extended their operations into at least four other states. To confront the new challenges, they had adopted new strategies to survive. They increasingly relied on second-generation family members as full or passive financial partners in their companies. Expansion of their operations into Chiapas and Oaxaca gave them greater control over the production side of the agro-export industry. By the 1950s they were actively participating in private sector organizations to lobby weak state agencies. Their relations with coffee producers became increasingly exploitative, while those with organized labor continued to remain conflictive. By the early 1960s, the owners carried out full mechanization of their plants, laying off their women workers, while retaining a good portion of their men workers. Full mechanization definitely had a gendered dimension, for women manual workers were the first to lose their jobs.

The state's role in the coffee agro-export industry increased during World War II with its seizure of German properties, but it tended to function more as a regulator or facilitator rather than a major player in the national coffee economy. Undoubtedly, postrevolutionary labor law and its enforcement by the state empowered women and men seasonal coffee workers to negotiate collective contracts that were similar to those in traditional industries and agro-export industries, guaranteeing the workers a minimum wage and ample fringe benefits. The post-1940 state became gradually more supportive of the agro-industry as it recognized the contribution of coffee exports to its export economy. When beneficio owners finally decided to fully mechanize their plants in Veracruz, the governor intervened to oversee the gradual and peaceful transition to full mechanization. The state played a much less active role in Córdoba's labor's settlement than in the Xalapa-Coatepec one, which gave owners and labor cacicas more latitude to manipulate the severance pay package for their own special interests.

The struggle of Central Veracruz sorters, in particular those in Córdoba, to maintain their jobs and to obtain a living wage became increasingly difficult during the Economic Miracle. While their unions and their leadership played a critical role in negotiating with the owners for the retention of permanent positions, wage increases, and the extension of fringe benefits, the contracts never provided a wage sufficient to sustain a family. The SIOECC's leadership benefited from the fact that the agrocommercial center of Córdoba, unlike Orizaba, had no large, male-dominated textile unions to contend with. Union cacicas and their clienteles gained access to public spaces and public offices never considered possible for poor women workers before this. These opportunities allowed them to demonstrate that they were respectable and honorable citizens. Unfortunately, the union's decades-long cacicazgo had its downside. Cacicas proved just as keen to acquire, maintain, and exercise power as their male counterparts.

The gendered nature of the modernization process in the Central Veracruz coffee beneficios was similar to that of traditional industries in developing countries. Women manual workers were replaced by machines, while men skilled workers were retained. In their collective memory their replacement by machines was a traumatic event. It ended a way of life, which had provided them with some semblance of economic sustainability and cultural community. At the same time, the sorters' individual experiences were influenced by their ties to rival patronage systems that shaped their recollections of the compensation controversy.

Conclusions

This regional history from below sought to tease out the interrelationships between entrepreneurs, workers, labor movements, gender relations, and culture on the one hand and social revolution, immigration, modernization, and the Atlantic coffee market on the other. Their interaction helped to shape the evolution of Mexico's coffee agroindustry. At the same time, its cross-disciplinary, comparative perspective sought to single out the similarities and differences between Córdoba's coffee economy and other Spanish American coffee-exporting regions. It has focused specifically on women workers to demonstrate how a subaltern group in revolutionary times can become active in the construction of trade unions, worker culture, and cacicazgos in the pursuit of worker rights.

Córdoba's coffee economy was, in certain respects, distinct from the other coffee economies of Central Veracruz, Chiapas, Oaxaca, and Central America. It seems to have borne more resemblance to the Medellín region, where large-scale preparers and exporters emerged from the urban commercial sector at the turn of the twentieth century. Córdoba's preparation plants became concentrated in an urban setting as these entrepreneurs wrested financial control of production and preparation away from the finqueros. This was due in large part to Córdoba's place or location as well as its fragmented land tenure system. As a result, Córdoba emerged as the linchpin for Mexican coffee trade, preparation, and export to the Atlantic community in the first half of the twentieth century. Located in the center of one of Mexico's most productive coffee-growing regions, Córdoba profited from its easy access to railroad transport and to a thriving port that abutted the Atlantic. These favorable conditions attracted European and U.S. entrepreneurs and export-import companies, who invested heavily in large urban preparation plants during the cusp of the first Atlantic coffee boom. The size of their beneficios meant that they hired hundreds of women workers to manually clean the green coffee for export.

Transatlantic migration was intimately related to the development of Córdoba's coffee economy. In this case, it was the selective immigration of a handful of impoverished European small farmers and herders who shaped the evolution of the region's coffee economy. In contrast to most of Spanish America, they concentrated their attention on the financing, purchasing, preparation, and export of coffee rather than on its production. Five Spanish families in particular built their family firms around financial networks embedded in their immigrant community. They shared more in common with the Medellín merchants and exporters at the turn of the century than other Latin American coffee elites. As first-generation immigrants, they were able to dominate the coffee-export sector by the thirties, long before the emergence of the Xalapa-Coatepec group or the German planters of Chiapas. Their closely knit family businesses, which rested on binational and bicultural immigration traditions, helped them to build strong patriarchal institutions based on gender, age, and generation hierarchies. These forms of clan-like business ventures were similar to those created by French, Lebanese, and Spanish immigrants in Mexico's urban commercial and industrial centers.

The extraordinary financial success of the Spanish commercial entrepreneurs translated into a continued Spanish presence in Córdoba and the construction of a strong sense of Hispanic identity. When the Casino Español of Córdoba, Veracruz, proudly proclaimed on its ninetieth anniversary in 1998 that "Córdoba has always been a Spanish city,"[1] it was not only articulating a strongly held belief that Spanish immigrants had transformed this provincial city into a prosperous agroindustrial center but also that transatlantic migration had no borders. The second and third generation of this Spanish coffee elite continued to uphold the tradition of the self-made Spaniard, who became successful through the cohesiveness and entrepreneurialism of the immigrant community.[2]

The Spaniards' large beneficios, in contrast to those in the Xalapa-Coatepec region, opened up new economic spaces for peasant women, street vendors, and domestic servants to find more secure employment, guaranteed wage work, and better working conditions than ever before. Their sheer numbers and their strong trade-union tradition meant that the sorters became integrated members of the Mexican labor force and export capitalism. Sorting coffee provided a new form of women's employment outside the home with relatively good working conditions and reliable wages that were equivalent to those existing in the textile, garment, and tortilla industries. Like other agro-export workers, such as strawberry or tomato workers, who prepare food products for export to international mark ets, their labor was essential for the preparation of an export-grade commodity. As a consequence beneficiadores and the state very often had to concede to the demands of these seasonal workers to ensure the fulfillment of their international agreements. This gave their unions an unusual amount of leverage to demand wages and benefits during the harvesting season comparable to full-time permanent workers. Although they received only the minimum wage, their economic status was not much different from today's agro-export and assembly plant workers in other developing countries.[3]

The presence of hundreds of coffee sorters in Veracruz's beneficios at the outbreak of the Revolution of 1910 had unintended consequences for Mexico's labor movement and the coffee agroindustry. In the midst of revolutionary ferment, anarchosyndicalists and labor reformists made little distinction between the gender of the workers that they sought to mobilize in the beneficios. Women workers had much the same economic demands as men workers, although their demands were more often couched in terms of family survival and the high price of primary necessities. Because of the political and military fluidity of Central Veracruz in 1915, revolutionary military commanders and foreign coffee exporters were forced to accede to their demands. As a consequence, seasonal women workers benefited as much if not more than men workers from revolutionary labor mobilization, if one takes into account that they entered the workforce at a much lower economic level.

The prolabor ideology of the revolution that supported the implementation of labor laws, the creation of tripartite industrial-labor boards, and the mobilization of women workers furthered the objectives of these seasonal women workers. The national labor movement targeted beneficio women workers before men workers in the 1920s because their numbers were so much larger. Just as in other cities throughout Mexico, women workers were claiming revolutionary justice regardless of their gender, class, or ethnicity. In the 1920s and 1930s, coffee-sorter unions demanded and won their place at the negotiating table with beneficio owners at the proceedings of the industrial-labor boards. These women were, in short, not passive bystanders in the labor movement but union activists. The winning of collective contracts from the beneficio owners signified that direct action, regardless of the gender of the workers, could force owners to make major concessions to its workforce when their work was critical for an agro-export industry. In sum, the revolutionary state created structured spaces within an emerging labor movement and new tripartite industrial-labor relations boards for seasonal women workers to demand and win the right to work, protest, petition, organize, and strike.

The campaign to reorganize the escogedora unions in Central Veracruz's coffee beneficios in the midtwenties came primarily from the outside after the workers themselves had failed to achieve it on their own. The Sindicato de Inquilinos, the Veracruz Peasant League, and the CROM all dispatched men activists to Xalapa, Córdoba, and Coatepec to organize sorters into unions, despite the efforts of exporters to organize rival white unions. Regional factors influenced the nature of their union structure. While anarchosyndicalist militants organized Xalapa sorters into small workshop unions, Cromistas preferred to organize citywide unions in Córdoba and Coatepec, which allowed them to become much more powerful organizations. At first the anarchosyndicalist activists saw no reason to object to the sorters' decision to elect their own women leaders and adopt feminist mottos. Not until the final years of the 1920s did the now fully entrenched, male-dominated CROM, which was headquartered in Orizaba, begin to force the coffee-sorter unions to abandon their feminist mottos, women's leadership, and control over their finances. In the case of Córdoba, these external efforts to control the internal affairs were met with resistance. In their struggle to defend their union's autonomy, the leadership consciously employed a discourse framed by gender oppression.

The postrevolutionary state and its clientelist labor organizations—in particular the CROM, the CTM, and the CROC—also contributed to the empowerment of both women and men cacicazgos. The 1931 Labor Code itself was ambiguous enough to allow aspiring leaders to employ its provisions concerning a closed shop, or the exclusion of nonunion members from employment, and the running of internal elections to their advantage. What is more, ambitious leaders exploited ferocious intraunion struggles of the 1930s to advance their careers. In the case of Córdoba, the rivalry between the Peasant League, the CROM, and the CTM to dominate the coffee-worker unions demonstrates that women's unions suffered the same kinds of trade-union internal conflicts as men unions. The women and men leaders of the coffee workers could demonstrate their ability to confront external threats and, in so doing, legitimize their own authority. Due to the very large membership of Córdoba's union, a collective female leadership emerged that gradually evolved over the course of the thirties, forties, and fifties into a dual cacicazgo. This did not occur in the men's coffee-worker unions, in part because of their extremely fractured nature. The cacicas relied heavily on their negotiating skills to confront the coffee exporters and to gain worker rights guaranteed under Article 123 and the 1931 labor law. They acted as articulate, obstreperous power brokers between a largely illiterate rank and file and the coffee merchants, Orizaba labor confederation, and the state. These cacicas used similar strategies to men's caciques in building their cacicazgos that were not necessarily linked to masculinity. They constructed personal patron-client relationships with individual members of the rank and file, controlled the unions' funds, monopolized hiring and firing practices, and rotated power among themselves. They also employed the mechanisms of intermediation and exclusion to legitimize their authority. Women union bosses resorted to less physical threats and violence than the men, preferring to use persuasion and economic violence, or the threat of job loss. As brokers or intermediaries, they maintained the same exclusive access as other labor caciques to Orizaba's nationally recognized cacique.

The everyday experiences of coffee sorters reveal how subalterns become agents of change, appropriating and challenging hegemonic structures and struggling to alter their socioeconomic status. As members of the working poor, they were situated somewhere between the disorganized poor and the permanent wage worker in the urban-wage work hierarchy, and this informed their politics. The interrelationship between the workplace and the community was just as strong as between the workplace and the family. Their working experiences loosened the bonds of the patriarchal household, as they became primary wage earners and as they interacted with nonfamily members on and off the workshop floor. Their lives clearly demonstrate how the private and the public are integral parts of worker culture and how the personal is the political. At the same time, they found a voice as gendered subjects, as workers, mothers, union activists, and as citizens. They created their own alternative workshop culture that shared certain common characteristics with working men's culture, but they engendered it in distinctive ways. It was not through the official transcripts of labor unions, municipal authorities, or plant owners that their sense of a dual identity as mothers and principal wage earners becomes evident but through their oral interviews. They represented themselves as hard workers and honorable wives and mothers. Reconciling their sense of being a self-respected worker and member of a working women's community with the provincial norms that every self-respecting woman should be a housewife was no easy task. Needless to say, there was always an underlying tension between these contradictory meanings of what it meant to be a working woman. Their interviews reveal also a strong desire to refute the gente decente's representation of them as nothing more than women of the streets. Their resistance to these stereotypes is evidenced particularly in the life histories of permanent workers, who enjoyed all the union privileges. They were more positive in their construction of their own identities as productive workers than occasional workers, who saw themselves simply as exploited objects. Thus, a three-layered hierarchy existed within the sorter community: leaders, permanent workers, and occasional workers.

Coffee sorters forged an alternative working women's culture through the efforts of their leaders to organize union-sponsored events and to perform at public events. Their participation in band and theatrical performances as well as on dance committees transformed them into active, responsible citizens. While their agency was bounded by bourgeois gender and moral norms and the lack of material resources, sorters confronted and, at times, transgressed these norms to create their own gender-specific working women's culture. At the same time that union cacicas organized these activities to improve union solidarity and demonstrate to the public that these women were responsible and disciplined citizens, they were also legitimizing their own authority among the rank and file. Individual experiences in the band, on the stage, on the dance floor, on trips forged a collective memory of a vibrant working women's culture. It was constructed outside the bounds of their immediate family. They recalled their performances in public spaces as forms of psychological and social liberation from household drudgery.

In their campaigns to promote literacy, introduce social security, and gain the right to vote in the 1950s, these cacicas were showing their merit to the rank and file. They also had a very active public presence, serving on municipal conciliation boards; local, state, and national labor-confederation executive committees; and Córdoba's municipal council. This activism raised the political visibility of women workers in general, and it presaged a more prominent role for women in municipal politics during the 1990s.[4] Needless to say, caciquismo also bred leadership continuity, arbitrary manipulation of hiring policies, exclusion of recalcitrant members and leaders, and corruption, all of which reared their ugly heads within the coffee sorters' unions.

The state had an ambivalent relationship with both commercial entrepreneurs and their workers over this seventy-year span. Since coffee never was Mexico's most important export commodity, the state did not actively intervene to promote the nation's international coffee trade until the onset of the Second World War. This hands-off approach was in sharp contrast with other Latin American coffee-producing economies. Since the state's regulatory coffee agency never controlled more than 10 percent of the internal coffee market, its ability to control the coffee market was quite limited. State support of the installation of modern electronic sorters in the 1950s and 1960s came at the obreras' expense.

The agency exercised by these coffee sorters should not be seen as unique to obrera culture, for women-dominated workshops existed and continue to exist in Mexico's textile, garment, tortilla, hat-making, match-making, munitions, food industry, and cigarette workshops. Many of these workplaces have not been fully explored. In the United States, Vicki Ruiz's Monterey cannery workers and Nancy Hewitt's Tampa tobacco workers built the same kinds of women's communities around their workplace. As export agroindustries and maquiladora industries become increasingly feminized, women's unions, communities, and cultures are becoming more and more prevalent in Mexico and other developing nations. In many respects, the coffee-sorter culture can be seen as one of the precursors of contemporary agro-export working women's culture.

Unfortunately, the surviving coffee sorters have not experienced any significant socioeconomic mobility over the past fifty years. As grandmothers and great-grandmothers, they are still strong matriarchal figures surrounded by family members. In most cases, they are still working as street vendors, waitresses, owners of small stores, and food preparers. Those who were privileged enough to send their children to school embraced bourgeois gender norms. The sons obtained professional degrees in teaching, law, and medicine, while the daughters and nieces more often than not became hairdressers, public employees, waitresses, owners of small shops, and union leaders. In spite of all the adversities, in their collective memory their working women's community still lives on, shaped by their difficult everyday working experiences, their convivial compañera community, strong authoritarian leaders, and a vibrant union culture.

NOTES

Introduction

1. *Diario de Xalapa*, November 10, 1955. "La resolución final que tome la comisión repercutirá entre todo el país, debido a que Veracruz ocupa más personal y mejor producción en la industria cafetalera."
2. Topik and Wells, introduction to *Second Conquest of Latin America*, 20–22.
3. Topik, "Coffee," 40–41; and Samper Kutschbach, "Historical Construction of Quality and Competitiveness," 120–24.
4. Bergquist, *Coffee and Conflict*, 7.
5. Games, "Atlantic History," 747; Elliot, "Atlantic History," 239.
6. Moore, *Forty Miles from the Sea*, 3.
7. See Bergquist, *Coffee and Conflict*; Palacios, *Coffee in Colombia, 1850–1970*; Carolyn Hall, *El café y el desarrollo histórico-geográfico de Costa Rica*; Pérez-Brignoli and Samper, *Tierra, café y sociedad*, 495–565; Roseberry, *Coffee and Capitalism in the Venezuelan Andes*; Font, *Coffee, Contention, and Change in the Making of Modern Brazil*; Roseberry, Gudmundson, and Samper Kutschbach, *Coffee, Society, and Power*; Topik, *Political Economy of the Brazilian State, 1889–1930*; and Cambranes, *Sobre los empresarios agrarios y el estado en Guatemala*.
8. The best studies on coffee exporters include Paige, *Coffee and Power*; Beaumond, "Élite et changement social"; Peters, "Empresarios e historia del café en Costa Rica, 1930–50"; and Peters, "La formación territorial de las fincas grandes de café en la meseta central."

9. Palacios, *Coffee in Colombia, 1850–1970*, 25; Roseberry, *Coffee and Capitalism in the Venezuelan Andes*; Topik and Wells, *Second Conquest of Latin America*, 82–83; and Samper Kutschbach, "Historical Construction of Quality and Competitiveness," 153.

10. Roseberry, introduction to *Coffee, Society, and Power*, 21, 7–8.

11. Samper Kutschbach describes coffee commodity chains as "agroindustrial chains" that are linkages between cultivation, harvesting, local transportation, processing, overseas transportation, and distribution abroad ("Historical Construction of Quality and Competitiveness," 124).

12. Lida, *Una inmigración privilegiada*, 13–18; Herrero, *Los empresarios mexicanos del origen vasco y el desarrollo del capitalismo en México 1850–1950*, 9–12; and Gamboa Ojeda, *Empresarios de ayer*, 121–28, 159–67.

13. Moya, *Cousins and Strangers*, 4. See also Kenny, "Emigración, inmigración, remigración," 36–37.

14. For studies on Middle Eastern and French immigrants who developed a binational culture, see Luis Alfonso Ramírez, *Secretos de familia*, 240–58; Gamboa Ojeda, "Barcelonnettes en México," 34–36; and Paredes Cruz, "Los Barcelonnettes."

15. Sheridan Prieto, *Mujer obrera y organización sindical*; Dominguez Pérez, "Historia de una lucha"; and Carrillo Padilla, "Sufridas hijas del pueblo."

16. Meyer, *La Revolución Mexicana*, 220–22. Also cited in Rodríguez Centeno, "Paisaje agrario y sociedad rural," 243–49.

17. See Topik, *Political Economy of the Brazilian State, 1889–1930*; Font, *Coffee, Contention, and Change in the Making of Modern Brazil*; Palacios, *Coffee in Colombia, 1850–1970*; and Williams, *States and Social Evolution*.

18. María del Carmen Collado Herrera presents a much more nuanced assessment of the increasing collaboration between business and the Obregónista state, in *Empresarios y políticos entre la Restauración y la Revolución, 1920–1924* (17–20).

19. Lear, *Workers, Neighbors, and Citizens*, 119–23, 252; and Womack, "Historiography of Mexican Labor," 745.

20. Hart, *Anarchism and the Mexican Working Class, 1860–1931*; Huitrón,

Orígenes e historia del movimiento obrero en México; and Womack, "Historiography of Mexican Labor," 749.

21. Ruiz, *Labor and Ambivalent Revolutionaries;* Carr, *El movimiento obrero y la política en México;* and Middlebrook, *Paradox of Revolution.*

22. Lear, *Workers, Neighbors, and Citizens,* 301–39; and Bortz, *Revolution within the Revolution,* 2.

23. Lear, *Workers, Neighbors, and Citizens,* 301–39, 149; Wood, *Revolution in the Street,* 75–80; and Porter, *Working Women in Mexico City,* 96–109.

24. Lear, *Workers, Neighbors, and Citizens,* 149. On Guadalupe Zuno, see Fernández-Aceves, "Struggle between the *Metate* and the *Molino de Nixtamal* in Guadalajara, 1920–1940," 148–49. On Felipe Carrillo Puerto, see Joseph, *Revolution from Without,* 216–19. On Francisco Múgica and Lázaro Cárdenas, see Boyer, *Becoming Campesinos,* 220–21, 235; and Olcott, *Revolutionary Women in Postrevolutionary Mexico,* 64–90.

25. Olcott, "Miracle Workers," 46, 58.

26. Vaughan, "Rural Women's Literacy and Education during the Mexican Revolution," 118–24; and Vaughan, "Modernizing Patriarchy," 194–214.

27. Porter, *Working Women in Mexico City,* 109–18; Fernández-Aceves, "Struggle between the *Metate* and the *Molino de Nixtamal* in Guadalajara, 1920–1940," 154–60; and Goldsmith Connelly, "Política, trabajo y género," 232–34.

28. Pellicer de Brody and Reyna, *El afianzamiento de la estabilidad política,* 73–106, 157–214.

29. Dawn Keremitsis argued capitalism marginalizes women workers as industries mechanize in order to maximize profit, in "Latin American Women Workers in Transition". Jocelyn Olcott and María Teresa Fernández-Aceves show that the constraints of the patriarchal society led the Mexican state and trade unions to marginalize women workers in order to secure work for men workers in mixed workshops (Olcott, "Miracle Workers"; and Fernández-Aceves, "Once We Were Corn Grinders").

30. Joseph and Nugent, "Popular Culture and State Formation in Revolutionary Mexico," 17.

31. Stuart Hall, "Notes on Deconstructing 'The Popular,'" 228–31; and Mallon, "Promise and Dilemma of Subaltern Studies."

32. Canning, "Difficult Dichotomies," 107.

33. Eley, forward to *History of Everyday Life*, viii.

34. Eley, forward to *History of Everyday Life*, vii; and Lüdtke, "What Is the History of Everyday Life and Who Are Its Practitioners?" 1, 4, 7.

35. Canning, "Difficult Dichotomies," 103–4; E. P. Thompson, *Making of the English Working Class*, 9–12; and Montgomery, *Fall of the House of Labor*, 1–4.

36. Canning, "Feminist History after the Linguistic Turn," 75. Canning relies heavily on William Sewell's essay, "How Classes Are Made: Critical Reflections on E. P. Thompson's Theory of Working-Class Formation," in *E. P. Thompson: Critical Perspectives*, ed. Harvey J. Kaye and Keith McClelland (Philadelphia: Temple University Press, 1990): 55–56, 64. In this essay, Canning was challenging Joan Scott's definition of experience as a "linguistic event" in the original version of Scott's essay "Evidence of Experience," *Critical Theory* 17, no. 3 (1991), 773–97.

37. Canning, "Difficult Dichotomies," 120.

38. French and James, "Squaring the Circle," 11–21; Klubock, "Morality and Good Habits"; Vecchia, "'My Duty as a Woman,'"; Bachelor, "Toiling for the 'New Invaders,'" 291–94; James, *Doña María's Story*, 231–34; Alegre, "Las Rieleras"; Lear, *Workers, Neighbors, and Citizens*, 92–105; Trujillo Bolio, *Operarios fabriles en el Valle de México, 1864–1884*, 279–320; William E. French, *Peaceful and Working People*, 110–39; and Camarena Ocampo, *Jornaleros, tejedores y obreros*, 138–42.

39. Porter, *Working Women in Mexico City*, 122.

40. Joan W. Scott, "Gender," 42.

41. Ramos Escandón, "Mujeres trabajadoras en el México porfiriano," 32–33; William E. French, "Prostitutes and Guardian Angels"; William E. French, *Peaceful and Working People*, 87–90, 97–106; Garza, *Imagined Underworld*, 3–4, 42–43; and Weinstein, "Unskilled Worker, Skilled Housewife," 93–95.

42. French and James, "Squaring the Circle," 11, 20.

43. Porter, *Working Women in Mexico City*, 74–86; and CEHSMO, *La mujer y el movimiento obrero mexicano en el siglo XIX*.

44. Porter, *Working Women in Mexico City*, xviii–xix.
45. Fernández-Aceves, "Struggle between the *Metate* and the *Molino de Nixtamal* in Guadalajara, 1920–1940," 149–50; and Fernández-Aceves, *Cambio social, politica, y género*.
46. James C. Scott, *Domination and the Arts of Resistance*, xii.
47. Paul Thompson, *Voice of the Past*, 5.
48. See the contributions of Barbara Weinstein, Mirta Zaida Lobato, Theresa Vecchia, and Ann Farnsworth-Alvear in *Gendered Worlds of Latin American Women Workers*, edited by John French and Daniel James; James, *Doña María's Story*; and Snodgrass, "Birth and Consequences of Industrial Paternalism."
49. Leñero Franco, *El huso y el sexo*; Wilson, *De la casa al taller*; and Sheridan Prieto, *Mujer obrera y organización sindical*.
50. Snodgrass, "Birth and Consequences of Industrial Paternalism"; Camarena Ocampo, *Jornaleros, tejedores, y obreros*, 71–76; Levenson-Estrada, "Loneliness of Working-Class Feminism," 224–25; James, "'Tales Told out on the Borderlands,'" 47.
51. Stacey, "Can There Be a Feminist Ethnography?" 112.
52. Mallon, "Editor's Introduction," 1; Stephen, *Hear My Testimony*; and Behar, *Translated Women*, 269–73.
53. James, *Doña María's Story*, 214. See his discussion of the tension between the perspectives of oral testimony as empirical knowledge and as a joint production of the interviewer and the interviewed (122–25).
54. See Sheridan Prieto, *Mujer obrera y organización sindical*.

I treated the interviewees' opinions and views with dignity and respect in order to build a high level of trust. I conveyed the idea that we shared a common purpose of uncovering the daily life of working women and their struggle for survival. It was quite difficult to tape-record many interviews because these women were still working. Some interviews were held on park benches, in kitchens, or in bedrooms where the noise of children, traffic, and the TV or the presence of relatives and friends inhibited the interviewee's ability to express her thoughts freely. See Florencia Mallon on building trust, in her "Editor's Introduction."

I began with a semistructured format based on the obrera's life cycle and her working experiences inside the workplace. This approach helped me to build up a certain level of trust between the interviewee and myself. Then I proceeded on to the topics of the meaning of work and family, religion, work experience, trade-union experience, and participation in the sorter community.

55. Crane. "Writing the Individual Back into Collective Memory," 1382.
56. Portelli, *Death of Luigi Trastulli and Other Stories*, 26; and James, *Doña María's Story*, 123.

1. Emergence of a Coffee Commercial Elite

1. Moore applied this term to Xalapa (*Forty Miles from the Sea*, 1).
2. Games, "Atlantic History," 747.
3. Mariano Arango, Marco Palacios, and Mario Samper Kutschbach trace similar evolutionary stages of coffee commercialization in Colombia and Costa Rica, respectively, in *Café e industria, 1850–1930*, 198; *Coffee in Colombia, 1850–1970*, 1–145; and "Historical Construction of Quality and Competitiveness," 125.
4. A similar process occurred in Colombia during this same period. See Arango, *Café e industria, 1850–1930*, 178; and Palacios, *Coffee in Colombia, 1850–1970*, 38–42.
5. Roseberry, introduction to *Coffee, Society, and Power*, 7–8.
6. Luis Alfonso Ramírez, *Secretos de familia*, 323–25.
7. Moya, "Continent of Immigrants," 3.
8. "Mexico! Mexico! Time to grow coffee!" This is the title of a section in Rafael Herrera's *El estudio sobre la producción del café*, 120.
9. Naveda Chávez-Hita, *Esclavos negros en las haciendas azucareras de Córdoba, Veracruz, 1630–1830*, 67–69, 118; Herrera Moreno, *El cantón de Córdoba*, 136; and Deans-Smith, *Bureaucrats, Planters, and Workers*, 106–11, 135–39.
10. Romero, "Córdoba," 554; and Ukers, *All about Coffee*, 9.
    Coffee plantations were first reported in Acayucan, Xalapa, and La Antigua, Veracruz in 1809 (Rojas, *El café*, 13). General Mariano Michelena first brought coffee to Michoacán in 1828 to the district of Ario (Herrera, *El estudio sobre la producción del café*, 47; Sánchez Diaz, *El café de Uruapan*, 22; and Romero, "Michoacán," 467–72). One source says coffee was flourishing before the 1830s in Oaxaca (Chassen-López, *From Liberal to Revolutionary Oaxaca*, 137–38). Coffee

came to Chiapas from Guatemala around the 1850s (Spenser, "Soconusco," 129).

11. Ward, *Mexico in 1827*, 339, 455; Romero, "Córdoba," 554; "Homenaje a Don Juan Antonio Gómez de Guevara"; Mario Ramírez, "Estadística del Partido de Córdoba, formado en 1840," 73, 77; Herrera, *El estudio sobre la producción del café*, 48; Rodríguez Centeno, "Caficultura y modernidad," 65; and Rodríguez Centeno, "Paisaje agrario y sociedad rural," 122–24. For the collapse of the sugarcane plantation after the abolition of slavery, see Naveda Chávez-Hita, *Esclavos negros en las haciendas azucareras de Córdoba, Veracruz, 1630–1830*, 154–59.

12. Sartorius, *Mexico about 1850*, 158–62; Sartorius, "Memoria sobre el estado de la agricultura en el partido de Huatusco," 164, 162–65; and Von Mentz, *Los pioneros del imperialismo*, 255–56.

13. Herrera, "El café de Córdoba," 64–65. For the dry preparation process, see "El cultivo del café por un aficionado," April 17, 1880, 218–21, and April 23, 1880, 237; and Ukers, *All about Coffee*, 251.

14. Ukers, *All about Coffee*, 522.

15. See Warren Dean for the role of railroads in the development of the Brazilian coffee economy (*Rio Claro*, 41–43, 45).

16. Studies have shown that Córdoba, Orizaba, and Huatusco profited handsomely from the construction of the Mexican Railroad line in terms of their coffee shipments to the exterior and sugarcane shipments to the interior of the republic. Calderón, *La vida económica*, 694; Blázquez Domínguez, *Breve historia de Veracruz*, 134; Sánchez Vargas, "Remembranzas de Córdoba," 4, 83–85; and Coatsworth, *Growth against Development*, 124–25. Export rates from Córdoba to Veracruz were lower than domestic rates (Schmidt, *Social and Economic Effect of the Railroad in Puebla and Veracruz, Mexico, 1867–1911*, 51–52, 77, 218, 225).

17. Calderón, "Los ferrocarriles," 532, 588–90; Blázquez Domínguez, *Breve historia de Veracruz*, 177; Chassen-López, *From Liberal to Revolutionary Oaxaca*, 70–71; and Rojas, *El café*, 87.

18. Southworth, *El Estado de Veracruz-Llave*, 73–80; and Sánchez Vargas, "Remembranzas de Córdoba," 4.

19. González y González, *La vida social*, 74.

20. González Navarro, *La vida social*, 124; and Dirección General de Es-

tadística, *Tercer censo de población de los Estados Unidos Mexicanos verificado el 27 de octubre de 1910,* 1:23.

21. Romero, "Coffee Culture on the Southern Coast of Chiapas," 283, 345.

22. Romero, "Córdoba," 560.

23. See his frank assessments of the other major coffee regions in Romero, "Huatusco"; Romero, "Jalacingo"; and Romero, "Orizaba." Von Mentz confirms that Sartorius and his son did not start expanding coffee production at El Mirador, Huatusco, until around the time of his death in 1872 (*Los pioneros del imperialismo,* 256). On Colima, Michoacán, and Oaxaca, see Romero's articles in BSAM. The Ministry of Development used the *Boletín de la Sociedad Agrícola Mexicana* as one of its principal outlets for publishing numerous articles on all forms of commercial agriculture in the 1880s and 1890s.

24. Romero, "Córdoba," 555. Romero visited seven haciendas and five ranchos around Córdoba, and his figures suggest that they had over 1.9 million coffee trees, not including the thousands being grown on minifundios and in family orchards (*huertas*) in town. They were producing approximately sixty thousand quintals of coffee in 1879. Ten of these twelve properties were large fincas with sixty thousand trees, approximately sixty hectares in size with one thousand trees per hectare. Mario Samper Kutschbach categorizes a large coffee farm as one with over sixty thousand trees ("In Difficult Times," 153). The largest plantings of 300,000 to 400,000 trees were on the Trinidad Grande, Tapia, and Las Animas haciendas. Romero relied heavily on information passed on to him by U.S.-farmer and botanist Hugo Finck and Swiss Juan Tonel, who owned the Hacienda Trinidad Chica on the outskirts of Córdoba. They had planted 150,000 trees. Former U.S. minister to Mexico General John Foster also reported to Romero about his installation of the latest steam machinery on his Hacienda de la Luz in Fortín. See Romero, "Córdoba," 555–59.

25. Gómez, *Cultivo y beneficio del café,* 153–54.

26. Cossío Silva, "Agricultura," 98–99; and Rosenzweig, "El comerico exterior," 662–63.

27. "Memoria presentada a la H. Legislatura del Estado Libre y Soberano de Veracruz-Llave, el 18 de septiembre de 1890 por el gobernador

constitucional, Juan Enriquez, comprende el período corrido del 1 de julio de 1888 a 30 de junio de 1890," 7:3675–712, 8:4099–100. Hugo Finck estimated that the canton actually produced 7 to 8 million kilos in good years, which is considerably more than the governor's estimates. Finck was not bothered by Córdoba's extremely low yields due to its exhausted soils and the long-established practice of planting trees too close together (Herrera, *El estudio sobre la producción del café*, 114–15). Colegio de México, *Estadísticas económicas del porfiriato*, 1:340.

28. Herrera, "El café de Córdoba," 66. By bargaining with importers in Liverpool, Hamburg, and other European cities, the major coffee producers—Rafael Gomez Vargas, Ramón Garay, and a Mr. Quinas—could get over twenty-six or twenty-seven pesos a quintal for export-grade green coffee. The practice of selling the harvest in advance supposedly brought a higher price (65–66).

29. Colegio de México, *Estadísticas económicas del porfiriato*, 1:340; and Rodríguez Centeno, "Paisaje agrario y sociedad rural," 80–83.

30. Herrera, *El estudio sobre la producción del café*, 18, 30–35, 45, 120. Herrera, Romero, and Gabriel Gómez all wrote glowing reports for the Ministry of Development about the future of coffee. Government bureaucrats, including Antonio Peñafiel, were even beginning to invest in coffee lands (Cossío Silva, "Agricultura," 98, 101; and Rodríguez Centeno, "Paisaje agrario y sociedad rural," 81–83).

31. Herrera, *El estudio sobre la producción del café*, 75–78.

32. Ukers, *All about Coffee*, 184; García Morales, *Coatepec*, 119, 122; Córdova Santamaría, *Café y sociedad en Huatusco, Veracruz*, 186–95; and Southworth, *El Estado de Veracruz-Llave*, 41–43, 77.

33. Herrera, *El estudio sobre la producción del café*, 118.

34. Arriaga, "El café de Córdoba," 64.

35. Kuntz Ficker, *Las exportaciones mexicanas durante la primera globalización (1870–1929)*, 291–92.

36. Topik, *Political Economy of the Brazilian State, 1889–1930*, 61.

37. Roseberry, introduction to *Coffee, Society, and Power*, 12.

38. Topik, *Political Economy of the Brazilian State, 1889–1930*, 62, 82.

39. Romero describes the process in Chiapas, in "Coffee Culture on the Southern Coast of Chiapas," 345–49.

40. Gómez, *Cultivo y beneficio del café*, 117–41. He also describes the dry method (137).

41. Gómez, *Cultivo y beneficio del café*, 117–30; Secretaría de la Economía Nacional, *El café*, 111–15.

42. Gómez, *Cultivo y beneficio del café*, 130–38; and Secretaría de la Economía Nacional, *El café*, 116–17. For descriptions of the preparation process in the late 1930s, see Flandrau, *Viva Mexico*, 82–87; and Springett, "Curing of 'Washed' Coffees." Sheridan Prieto describes the process in Coatepec in the 1980s (*Mujer obrera y organización syndical*, 147–50).

43. Herrera, *El estudio sobre la producción del café*, 114, 99–100; and Gómez, *Cultivo y beneficio del café*, 117–38. Ukers focuses on the types of imported machinery needed to prepare the green coffee for market (*All about Coffee*, 245–51).

    Finck and Vivanco described in detail the multiple stages of preparation of export-grade coffee by larger coffee finqueros in Córdoba. The English-made Gordon and Lidgewood depulpers were the favorites. The latest steam- or water-powered models could handle five hundred to six hundred *canastas* (arroba baskets) in one day at the cost of three to four pesos (Herrera, *El estudio sobre la producción del café*, 113–14).

44. Arango, *Café e industria, 1850–1930*, 198; Samper Kutschbach, "Historical Construction of Quality and Competitiveness," 125; and Topik and Wells, introduction to *Second Conquest of Latin America*, 5.

45. Rodríguez Centeno argues that domination of the countryside was based on control over the land, preparation, and trade. She contends quite rightly that banks were at the top of the pyramid ("Paisaje agrario y sociedad rural," 181–82). For more on Colombia, see Palacios, *El café en Colombia, 1850–1970*, 186–87.

46. Although the capital assets claimed at the time of the incorporation and dissolution of companies do not accurately reflect all active and passive assets of a company, the *Registro Público de la Propiedad Privada y Comercio de la Ciudad de Córdoba* (RPPPCC) still remains the best primary source when private family archives are not available.

47. AGEV/NCI, box 30, no. 84, agreement, August 7 1882; and AGEV/NCI, box 28, no. 154, mortgage, June 21, 1893.

48. AGEV/NCI, box 28, no. 126, dissolution of Menéndez and Co., May 22, 1895. Menéndez had also amassed 198,000 pesos in outstanding debt, which demonstrated the highly speculative nature of his commodity trading. For his loans to coffee growers, see AGEV/NCI, box 28, no. 139, no. 152, no. 154, mortgages, June 8, 20, 21, 1895.

    The contract reveals the financial networks emerging among this burgeoning commercial bourgeoisie. Menéndez planned to raise most of his contribution from future rents, mortgages, and interest. Krap contributed no cash, but he was to receive 10 percent of the profits (RPPPCC, business, no. 73, re-creation of Menéndez and Co., June 24, 1895).

49. AGEV/NCI, box 28, no. 178, separation of Krap, November 28, 1898; and RPPPCC, sales, no. 248, dissolution of Menéndez, October 9, 1906. In the 1904 dissolution, Tomblin paid Menéndez 50 percent of what he owed in cash and another 30 percent over the next year at 8 percent interest. He retained 20 percent of the capital of the company, which comprised the active and passive accounts, and various small properties in Amatlán and Cuichapa. He also acquired a house at 415 Ocampo, which had been built by the company in 1895.

50. RPPPCC, business, no. 195, re-creation of Menéndez and Co., February 18, 1905; RPPPCC, business, no. 280, re-creation of Menéndez and Co., September 4, 1908; AGEV/NCI, box 26, no. 42, mortgage, March 27, 1900; AGEV/NCI, box 26, no. 132, cancelation of mortgage, November 8, 1900; and AGEV/NCI, box 28, no. 236, sales, November 9, 1909. AMC, box 300 (1906), file 5, "Aguas," Antonio G. Menéndez to Ayuntamiento, September 11, 1906; and RPPPCC, sales, no. 226, acquisition of coffee machinery, August 27, 1910.

51. RPPPCC, business, no. 47, creation of Sociedad sobre bienes rústicos, August 11, 1891; AGEV/NCI, box 30, no. 30, sale, May 12, 1891; AGEV/NCI, box 26, no. 47, sales, August 12, 1891; and AGEV/NCI, box 26, no. 82, loan cancelation, May 24, 1893.

52. RPPPCC, business, no. 67, creation of Sociedad agrícola, Tomblin y Díaz Ferán, July 8, 1895; AGEV/NCI, box 30, no. 88, mortgage, May 9, 1895; AGEV/NCI, box 28, no. 212, mortgage in Soyaltepec, September 20, 1895; and AGEV/NCI, box 30, no. 178, reversion sale, September 18, 1896.

53. AGEV/NCI, box 30, no. 47, mortgage of Sainz Gutiérrez, May 15, 1902; RPPPCC, business, no. 161, poder general, October 3, 1902; and RPPPCC, business, no. 196, March 1, 1905. Tomblin lent seventeen thousand pesos to Sainz Gutiérrez in 1902, who had been forced to mortgage his lands and storage facilities in Peñuela after the 1897 slump.

54. RPPPCC, business, no. 111, creation of Krap and Co., March 16, 1899; and RPPPCC, business, no. 209, withdrawal of contract, November 25, 1905. Southworth, *El Estado de Veracruz-Llave*, 135; Sánchez Vargas, "Remembranzas de Córdoba," 28; and Veracruz, *Enciclopedia municipal veracruzana: Córdoba*, 206.

55. RPPPCC, business, no. 282, creation of El Emporio SA, November 26, 1908; RPPPCC, business, no. 327, increase in capital, December 30, 1911; and RPPPCC, business, no. 453, substitution of president, October 16, 1916.

56. Sainz Gutiérrez extended short-term loans of one hundred to one thousand pesos on trees; farmers would mortgage their lands or their trees until they could repay their loans after the harvest. The slump in coffee prices during the 1896–97 season forced many growers to default on their loans. He continued extending larger and larger loans of up to forty thousand pesos to cash-strapped landowners in the late 1890s. AGEV/NCI, box 27, no. 52, mortgage, January 12, 1890; AGEV/NCI, box 27, no. 109, sale, May 6, 1895; AGEV/NCI, box 28, no. 127, mortgage, May 18, 1896; AGEV/NCI, box 28, no. 134, sale, May 23, 1896; and AGEV/NCI, box 27, no. 154, reversion sale, July 3, 1896.

57. RPPPCC, mortgages, no. 27, mortgage, April 13, 1905; IRPPPCC, sales, no. 190, sale, November 21, 1897; RPPPCC, sales, no. 55, sale, March 11, 1898; RPPPCC, sales, no. 84, transfer of rights, November 12, 1897; AGEV/NCI, box 28, no. 126, mortgage, August 10, 1900; and AGEV/NCI, box 30, no. 47, mortgage, May 15, 1902.

58. AGEV/NCI, box 28, no. 167, mortgage, July 16, 1893; AGEV/NCI, box 28, no. 140, June 11, 1895; AGEV/NCI, box 26, no. 181, mortgage, November 25, 1896; AGEV/NCI, box 26, no. 29, March 11, 1898; IRPPPCC, mortgages, no. 47, mortgage, August 14, 1897; IRPPPCC, mortgages, no. 15, mortgage, October 21, 1897; IRPPPCC, mortgages, no. 45, mortgage, April 11, 1898; and IRPPPCC, mortgages, no. 18, cancelation of mortgage, May 12, 1904.

59. IRPPPCC, sales, no. 184, sale, June 23, 1880; AGEV/NCI, box 28, no. 201, sale, October 28, 1893; AGEV/NCI, box 28, no. 218, sale, September 4, 1893; AGEV/NCI, box 28, no. 2, sale, January 13, 1896; AGEV/NCI, box 28, no. 19, sale, February 1, 1896; AGEV/NCI, box 30, no. 189, sale, October 12, 1896; and AGEV/NCI, box 30, no. 119, sale, July 3, 1897.

    For Candaudap's land speculation deals and commodity exports see AGEV/NCI, box 28, no. 146, division of Hacienda San José de Enmedio, June 15, 1895; AGEV/NCI, box 28, no. 90, sale of thirty thousand trees, April 11, 1896; AGEV/NCI, box 30, no. 47, sale of hacienda, May 15, 1902; IRPPPCC, sales, no. 133, house purchase, May 20, 1898; and IRPPPCC, mortgages, no. 80, mortgage of part of hacienda, November 15, 1904.

60. His loans to wealthy farmers in Córdoba and the relatively undeveloped regions of Zongolica and Tuxtepec, which were important coffee and tobacco producing regions, continued unabated through the 1900s. His other financial interest was urban real estate, which he placed under his wife's name. AGEV/NCI, box 26, no. 136, mortgage, December 14, 1899; AGEV/NCI, box 26, no. 63, mortgage cancelation (Tuxtepec), May 4, 1908; AGEV/NCI, box 26, no. 210, sale (Zongolica), October 11, 1911; AGEV/NCI, box 26, no. 281, mortgage cancelation (Huatusco), October 14, 1913; and AMC, box 310 (1908), file "Estadísticas." When Candaudap died in 1910, his estate was valued at 471,304 pesos (AGEV/NCI, box 26, no. 223, cessation of rights, October 15, 1909; and AGEV/NCI, box 27, no. 146, protocol, October 20, 1910).

61. The *Banco Nacional de México* opened its office in the port in 1882, and the *Banco de Londres y México* followed in 1887 (Southworth, *El Estado de Veracruz-Llave*, 97, 136–38). USBI/NCI, no. 115, bank creation, June, 11 1906; AGEV/NCI, box 26, no. 92, sale, April 2, 1909; AGEV/NCI, box 26, no. 129, sale, July 29, 1909.

62. Palacios, *El café en Colombia, 1850–1970*, 186–87.

63. Cárdenas, "Inflación y establilización monetaria en México," 450–51; and Hart, *Revolutionary Mexico*, 170–71. Mabel Rodríguez Centeno shows how Díaz's fiscal policies aided coffee production in "Fiscalidad y café mexicano."

64. The Milwaukee Mexican Coffee Company was given a tax exemption to open a roasting plant in Xalapa (Decree no. 14, June 3, 1903, in Veracruz, *Leyes, decretos y circulares del Estado de Veracruz, 1903*, 92).

65. Southworth, *El Estado de Veracruz-Llave*, 42–43.

66. Ukers, *All about Coffee*, 484, 522; and Topik, "Integration of the World Coffee Market," 42, 48.

67. NARA/RG76, entry 125, case files of U.S. claimants, 1924–36, agency 937, box 163, no. 1, affidavits of the Arbuckles, February 14 and December 22, 1925, pp. 7–8. Cited also in Hart, *Empire and Revolution*, 185.

68. Hart, *Empire and Revolution*, 186.

69. NARA/RG76, entry 125, agency 937, box 164, affidavit of Louis Hewlett, January 25, 1927; and NARA/RG76, entry 125, agency 937, box 164, affidavit of Casimiro C. Muñoz, June 10, 1925.

70. NARA/RG76, entry 125, box 165, balance of Xalapa books of Arbuckle Bros. as of September 30, 1916. In Coatepec the hacendados Guillermo Pasquel and Sanchez Rebolledo were the Arbuckles' primary debtors, while in Huatusco, Luis Croda was their most important client. In 1910 they advanced Menéndez 56,000 pesos to provide ten thousand quintals of parchment coffee (RPPPCC, mortgages, no. 8, mortgage, January 26, 1910).

71. Dominguez Pérez, "Historia de una lucha," 6. The Córdoba plant, which is still standing, had four trains for preparation with three Engelberg hullers, classifiers for hulled coffee, an electric motor, a Gordon dryer, and a twenty-horsepower steam engine. It listed forty-seven small tables for sorting, twenty-six benches, and an additional twelve sorting tables. NARA/RG76, entry 125, agency 927, box 165, affidavit of Arbuckles, "Inventario de los muebles y ensures pertenientes a la negociación de los Sres. Arbuckles, Sucursal Córdoba, November 13, 1913." RPPPCC, sales, no. 165, land sale, June 28, 1909.

72. NARA/RG76, entry 125, agency 927, boxes 163–64, Arbuckles claim, February 14 and December 22, 1925; NARA/RG76, entry 125, agency 927, boxes 163–64, affidavit of Louis Hewlett, January 25, 1927. Hart, *Empire and Revolution*, 186.

73. NARA/RG76, entry 125, agency 927, boxes 163–64, affidavit of Louis Hewlett, January 25, 1927; Domenech, *Guía general descriptive de la República Mexicana*, 700; IRPPPCC, sales, nos. 360–61, sale, April 8, 1913; and AGEV/NCI, box 32, no. 191, special authority to trade in Oaxaca, September 7, 1920. Ukers, *All about Coffee*, 480–86; Kraeger, *Ag-*

ricultura y colonización en México, 78; and Southworth, *El Estado de Veracruz-Llave*, 141.

74. For example, the Córdoba Coffee and Sugar Company purchased half of the Hacienda Toliguilla from former state deputy Licenciado Hesquio Marañon in 1898 (IRPPPCC, sales, no. 161, sale, July 1, 1898; and IRPPPCC, mortgages, no. 87, mortgage, July 6, 1898). The Cafetera y Frutas de Tlacotengo, the Chicago and Mexico Coffee and Fruit Company, and the Veracruz Coffee Company were three other U.S. firms investing heavily in the canton prior to the revolution (AGEV/NCI, box 26, no. 75, poder general, March 12, 1909; and AGEV/NCI, box 26, no. 50, mortgage, March 21, 1910).

75. Topik, *Political Economy of the Brazilian State, 1889–1930*, 67–72, 82. Thirteen importing firms in New York, London, Hamburg, and Le Havre signed a contract with Brazil to buy 2 million sacks of coffee for 20 million dollars or 80 percent of its value ("El mercado de café," 778).

76. Katz, *Life and Times of Pancho Villa*, 48–50; Hart, *Empire and Revolution*, 163; and González Sierra, *Monopolio del humo*, 81. Coffee exports dropped from 22,203 tons in 1901–2 to 14,160 tons in the 1906–7 season (INEGI, *Estadísticas históricas de México* [1990], 2:706).

77. AGEV/NCI, box 26, no. 23, partial sale of Hacienda Ojo de Agua Grande, January 19, 1909; AGEV/NCI, box 26, no. 115, partial sale of Hacienda Tapia, May 4, 1909; AGEV/NCI, box 26, no. 35, partial sale of La Defensa, Paso del Macho, March 23, 1898; AGEV/NCI, box 26, no. 148, partial rental of La Defensa with option to buy, December 13, 1900; and AGEV/NCI, box 26, no. 322, mortgage cancelation, La Defensa, November 28, 1913. Rodríguez Centeno, "Paisaje agrario y sociedad rural," 165–66; Southworth, *Official Directory of Mines and Estates of Mexico*, 243; and Fowler-Salamini, "Gender, Work, and Coffee," 57–58.

78. AGEV/NCI, box 26, no. 57, complaint for failure to pay, September 14, 1908; AGEV/NCI, box 26, no. 220, October 13, 1909; AGEV/NCI, box 26, nos. 208–9, failure to pay, July 25, 1912; AGEV/NCI, box 26, no. 226, failure to pay, August 13, 1912; AGEV/NCI, box 26, no. 129, mortgage cancelation for Augusto H. McLean, June 13, 1914; AGEV/NCI, box 27, no. 114, complaint for failure to pay, October 21, 1911; and RPPPCC, mortgages, no. 8, mortgage, January 26, 1910.

79. AGEV/NCI, box 30, no. 47, mortgage to Tomblin, May 15, 1902; RPPPCC, mortgages, no. 27, mortgage, April 13, 1905; and RPPPCC, sales, no. 52, sale, March 14, 1909.

80. Tomblin drowned without a will, leaving an estate of 748,625 pesos. AGEV/NCI, box 26, no. 7, complaint for failure to pay, February 28, 1910; AGEV/NCI, box 26, no. 82, intestacy, March 28, 1912; AGEV/NCI, box 26, no. 96, April 5, 1912; RPPPCC, business, no. 430, power of attorney granted by Banco de Londres, January 7, 1916; and Calatayud, interview.

81. Steven C. Topik points to the positive and negative aspects of the coffee boom in "Coffee Anyone?" 249–50. See also Topic and Wells, *Second Conquest of Latin America*, 219.

82. For the impact of sugarcane, see Womack, *Zapata and the Mexican Revolution*, chaps. 1 and 2. For henequen, see Wells and Joseph, *Summer of Discontent, Seasons of Upheaval*, chap. 5.

83. Kuntz Ficker, "El café," 329–33; Sánchez Díaz, "Las ciudades michoacanas"; Camas Reyes, "El desarrollo económico del Soconusco." Córdova Santamaría shows how coffee transformed Huatusco society (*Café y sociedad en Huatusco, Veracruz*, 223–95).

84. "Informe del jefe politico del cantón del Córdoba (Regino Zenteno), noviembre 9 de 1897," 158–60.

85. Wages in Córdoba were considerably higher than in other parts of the republic. The average rural daily wage hovered around sixty-two centavos in 1895, but it was predicted to rise to seventy-five centavos because of the scarcity of labor. In Oaxaca it was fifty centavos or less (Arriaga, "El café de Córdoba," 64; Rodríguez Centeno, "Paisaje agrario y sociedad rural," 89–91; and Kraeger, *Agricultura y colonización en México*, 88).

86. AMC, box 174 (1872), file "Fomento, Geografía y Estadísticas," *Censo Municipal de 1872*; Dirección General de Estadística, *División territorial de los Estados Unidos Mexicanos, correspondiente al censo de 1910*, 1:24. Rodríguez Centeno, "Paisaje agrario y sociedad rural," 169–72. For Huatusco, see Córdova Santamaría, *Café y sociedad en Huatusco, Veracruz*, 166–96. For Coatepec, see García Morales, *Coatepec*, 150–52.

87. Panabiere, *Itinerarios de una disidencia*, 33.

88. Panabiere, *Itinerarios de una disidencia*, 45.

89. De la Fuente, "Relaciones sociales en una ciudad de provincia," 94.
90. Herrera Moreno, *El cantón de Córdoba*, 266; Trens, *La historia de Ve-racruz*, 328; AMC, box 244 (1896), file "Aguas"; AMC, box 250 (1897), file "Aguas"; AMC, box 283 (1902); AMC, box 283 (1902), file "Memoria de Adalberto Porte-Petit al jefe politico, 1902"; Decree no. 4, *Periódico Oficial* 16, no. 15 (February 4, 1897): 1–4; "Informe del jefe político del cantón del Córdoba (Regino Zenteno), noviembre 9 de 1897," 200–201.
91. AMC, box 294 (1904), file "Hacienda Municipal"; AMC, box 300 (1906), file "Aguas"; Decree no. 6, June 11, 1904, and "Contrato celebrado entre los señores don Adalberto Porte-Petit y don Francisco P. Pardo y el ciudadano gobernador del Estado . . . los senores ingenieros Paul S. Lietz e Ignacio Muñoz en nombre de la Companía Mexicana de Construcción y Obra de Ingeneria SA," in Veracruz, *Leyes, decretos, y circulares, 1904–7*, 30–56. Sánchez Vargas discusses the importance of introducing water and a drainage system for Tomblin's beneficio La Garza ("Remembranzas de Córdoba," 59).
92. AGEV/NCI, box 30, no. 153, Luz Eléctrica rental, September 6, 1895; AGEV/NCI, box 27, no. 65, contract renewal, April 14, 1910; AGEV/NCI, box 27, no. 99, business re-creation, August 16, 1912; and AMC, box 283 (1902), "Memoria de Porte-Petit." Sánchez Vargas, "Remembranzas de Córdoba," 28, 91; González Sierra, *Córdoba*, 54–55.
93. AMC, box 258 (1898), file "Fomento, Geográfica, y Estadística." I would like to thank Mabel Rodríguez Centeno for sharing this data with me. Candaudap had a direct line to his own holdings, San José de Enmedio and San José de Abajo, while Tomblin installed lines to ten coffee fincas: Ojo de Agua Chico, Ojo de Agua Grande, Potrero, Paraje Nuevo, Piedra de la Peñuela, Omealca, Las Animas, Tienda Nueva, San Francisco, and San Miguelito. He also installed telephone service to San Lorenzo and Amatlán, where he probably owned several warehouses.
94. RPPPCC, business, no. 328, creation of the Casa del Casino Cordobés, January 4, 1912. Southworth, *El Estado de Veracruz-Llave*, 131; Casino Español de Córdoba, *Casino Español de Córdoba, AC, 1908–1998*, 217. Sánchez Vargas, "Remembranzas de Córdoba," 91.
95. The towns of Coatepec and Huatusco also underwent major mod-

ernization as a direct consequence of the profits generated from the coffee boom. The *coatepecanos* erected a magnificent neoclassical town hall, which was not finished until 1910, and vastly improved the potable water system (García Morales, *Coatepec*, 150–52). In Huatusco a foreign hydroelectric power company installed the public lighting system by 1897, while its telephone system had fifty-eight phones by 1903. Córdova Santamaría shows that Huatusco's telephone system was still organized around the coffee haciendas for the specific purpose of staying in direct contact with European and U.S. coffee buyers. This pattern suggests that Huatusco's larger coffee producers vertically controlled coffee cultivation, production, preparation, and commercialization from their haciendas, in contrast to Córdoba (Córdova Santamaría, *Café y sociedad en Huatusco, Veracruz*, 230–31, 252–53, 274, 282–83n90).

96. Rodríguez Centeno, "Paisaje agrario y sociedad rural," 182–83; and Sánchez Vargas, "Remembranzas de Córdoba," 91. The church courtyard plaques bear the names of the Zevallos Segura, Vivanco, Gómez Vargas, Marure, Abascal, and Braniff families, as well as Orizaba industrialists.

97. AMC, box 247 (1896), file "Teatro"; and AMC, box 292 (1904), file "Expropriation." Veracruz, *Enciclopedia municipal veracruzana: Córdoba*, 83.

98. Gavira, *Su actuación político-militar revolucionaria*, 10; González Sierra, *Córdoba*, 55–56; Turner, *Barbarous Mexico*, 62, 69, 111; and Chassen-López, *From Liberal to Revolutionary Oaxaca*, 160.

99. AMC, box 283 (1902), file *"Memoria de Porte-Petit"*; and AMC, box 244 (1896), file "Mujeres Públicas." González Sierra, *Córdoba*, 55–56.

100. Palacios, *Coffee in Colombia, 1850–1970*, 153.

101. Arango, *Café e industria, 1850–1930*, 214–20; and Palacios, *El café en Colombia, 1850–1970*, 171–91.

102. Arango, *Café e industria, 1850–1930*, 173–78, 216–20; Palacios, *Coffee in Colombia, 1850–1970*, 17–18, 25; Samper Kutschbach, "Historical Construction of Quality and Competitiveness," 148; and Roseberry, introduction to *Coffee, Society, and Power*, 6.

103. Palacios, *Coffee in Colombia, 1850–1970*, 5, 9, 26–30, 38–42, 47–48, 83.

104. INEGI, *Estadísticas históricas de México* (1990), 1:376–77, 706 (the year 1917 is unavailable).

105. Meyer, *La Revolución Mexicana*, 220–22. Also cited in Rodríguez Centeno, "Paisaje agrario y sociedad rural," 236.

106. Fowler-Salamini, "Revuelta popular y regionalismo en Veracruz, 1906–1913"; and Corzo Ramírez, González Sierra, and Skerritt Gardner, *... nunca un desleal*, 19–83. See also Karl B. Koth for a contrasting view on the Maderista revolution, in *Waking the Dictator*, 98–113.

107. Rosas Juárez, "La revolución en el ex-cantón de Córdoba," 27–49; and Corzo Ramírez, González Sierra, and Skerritt, *... nunca un desleal*, 38–49, 72–74.

108. Juarez Rivera, *Las capitales del Estado de Veracruz*, 67–69. John Womack Jr., e-mail correspondence with author, June 13, 2010. For Aguilar's rise to power, see Corzo Ramírez, González Sierra, and Skerritt, *... nunca un desleal*, 175, 200; and Rosas Juárez, "La revolución en el ex-cantón de Córdoba," 111, 118–19.

109. Corzo Ramírez, González Sierra, and Skerritt, *... nunca un desleal*, 224–26; and Rosas Juárez, "La revolución en el ex-cantón de Córdoba," 136.

110. Knight, *Mexican Revolution*, 2:236–51; Joseph, *Revolution from Without*, 93–149; and Fowler-Salamini, "Revolutionary Caudillos in the 1920s," 173.

111. NARA/RG76, entry 125, agency 927, box 163, no. 1, affidavits of Arbuckles, February 14 and December 22, 1925. Rodríguez Centeno, "Paisaje agrario y sociedad rural," 239–40; Kuntz, "El café," 298, 309.

112. NARA/RG76, entry 125, agency 927, box 163, no. 1, affidavits of Arbuckles, February 14 and December 22, 1925.

113. AMC, box 342 (1914), file "Camara Agrícola." Corzo Ramírez, González Sierra, and Skerritt, *... nunca un desleal*, 107; Rodríguez Centeno, "Paisaje agrario y sociedad rural," 240; and León Fuentes, "Conformación de un capital en torno a la cafeticultura," 54–55.

114. León Fuentes, "Conformación de un capital en torno a la cafeticultura," (78), 60–61; Juárez Martínez, "Especulación y crisis en el centro de Veracruz, 1915."

115. Justo Fernández continued selling his coffee to the Westfield Brothers in New Orleans. When ships sank off Havana, he lost nothing because he was fully insured. León Fuentes, "Conformación de un capital en torno a la cafeticultura," 55, 63–64, 68–75, table 5; and Beaumond, "Élite et changement social," 137–46.

116. According to Thomas Benjamin, the authorities in Chiapas did not attempt to regulate the production or marketing of coffee, for "coffee was too valuable to both the planters and the government to let a revolution disrupt production." However, German exporters were definitely hurt by the outbreak of the world war because their markets dried up. Prices dropped, and German investment came to a halt (Benjamin, *Rich Land*, 131; Spenser, "Soconusco y la revolución," 117–20; and Kuntz, "El café," 298, 321).

117. The Xalapa-Coatepec families moved to Puebla and Mexico City (León Fuentes, "Conformación de un capital en torno a la cafeticultura," 63–64). Antimaderistas did assault a few Spanish and German Veracruz coffee rancheros in 1912, overrunning their properties and assassinating one Spanish administrator (AMC, box 333 (1912); Rodríguez Centeno, "Paisaje agrario y sociedad rural," 203; and Illades, *Presencia española en la Revolución Mexicana, 1900–1915*, 79–85).

118. Rodríguez Centeno, "Paisaje agrario y sociedad rural," 243–49.

119. INEGI, *Estadísticas históricas de México* (1990), 2:706. Topik, *Political Economy of the Brazilian State, 1889–1930*, 73–74, 82. For a thorough study of the impact of World War I on the Colombian agroindustry, see Arango, *Café e industria, 1850–1930*, 179–232.

120. AMC, box 344 (1915), file "Diversos." Sánchez Vargas, "Remembranzas de Córdoba," 6, 51. In 1917 George Bergman, the Arbuckle Veracruz manager, sent his agents out to collect on their debts in Xalapa and Misantla because relative peace had returned to the countryside (NARA/RG76, entry 125, agency 927, box 144, affidavit of George G. Bergman, March 28, 1926).

121. AGEV/NCI, box 25, no. 97, complaint, June 1917.

122. Cárdenas, "Inflación y estabilización monetaria en México," 451.

123. Sánchez Vargas, "Remembranzas de Córdoba," 54.

124. NARA/RG76, entry 125, agency 927, box 164, affidavit of Casamiro Muñoz, June 10, 1925. In 1916 the Arbuckles extended a 350,000-peso loan to Miguel Palacios, owner of the Hacienda San Lorenzo, to cultivate both coffee and sugarcane (Rodríguez Centeno, "Paisaje agrario y sociedad rural," 246). For more on their activities in Huatusco, see Córdova Santamaría, *Café y sociedad en Huatusco, Veracruz*, 217n124.

125. NARA/RG84/290/865.1, "Monthly Exports from Veracruz to New Orleans and New York, 1918."

126. NARA/RG76, entry 125, agency 927, box 165, "Balance of Xalapa Books of the Arbuckle Bros., September 30, 1916."

127. NARA/RG76, entry 125, agency 927, box 165, "Balance of Xalapa Books of the Arbuckle Bros., September 30, 1916"; AGEV/NCI, box 27, no. 33, mortgage, March 9, 1910; and RPPPCC, mortgages, no. 84, mortgage cancelation, July 9, 1914. Panabiere, *Itinerarios de una disidencia*, 45.

128. *Blue Book of Mexico*, 104–5. AMC, box 350 (1917), file "Aguas," September, 17, 1917; and AMC, box 395 (1929), file "Sanidad," Davíd González to Junta de Administración Civil, October 23, 1928.

129. NARA/RG84/290/861.3, C. H. Burke to Francis Stewart, December 3, 1918; and NARA/RG84/290/861.3, W. Stacpoole to Francis Stewart, December 2, 1918.

130. NARA/RG59/463.72112/9150 and NARA/RG59/611.126/76, William A. Jamison to Dept. of State, September 9, 1918.

131. The Arbuckle Brothers complained that their water rates had increased from twenty-five to sixty pesos a month. Felipe Marure de Ochoa, owner of the Hacienda Buena Vista, who likewise tapped into the municipal water supply to run his pulpers, also complained to the municipal government to no avail (AMC, box 350, file "Aguas," Aurelio Valdovino and Enrique Galván y López (Arbuckle Bros.) to Ayuntamiento, September 17, 24, 1917). Cárdenas, "Inflación y establilización monetaria en México," 462.

132. NARA/RG84/290/850, "Economic Conditions in the Veracruz Consular District since the Beginning of the European War," June 19, 1918.

133. Zardain de Alvarez, interview; and Eduardo Alvarez Amieva, e-mail correspondence with author, July 17, 2007. AMC, box 360 (1919), petitions by Manuel Zardain and David Gonzalez to Junta de Sanidad; and AGEV/NCI, box 27, no. 42, creation of Mercantil Colectivo, Manuel, Ventura, and José Zardain Monteserín, August 8, 1919. In 1919 the Arbuckle Brothers and Hard and Rand were both licensed as "acopiadores de fruta" (AMC, box 361 (1919), town hall meetings).

134. Topik, *Political Economy of the Brazilian State, 1889–1930*, 74–77, 82. Prices increased to 888 pesos per metric ton by 1920 and reached a

height of 1,114 pesos in 1928 (INEGI, *Estadísticas históricas de México* [1999], 2:728–29).

135. Topik, *Political Economy of the Brazilian State, 1889–1930*, 82.

136. NARA/RG84/307/350, Paul Foster, "American Capital Invested in Veracruz Consular District," May 20, 1920; and NARA/RG84/322/861.3, "Agricultural Conditions," December 6, 1921.

137. NARA/RG84/368/861.33, "Periodic Report on Coffee," January 15, 1928.

138. NARA/RG84/359/850.31, "Information on Foreign Investments in Mexico," August 10, 1927; and NARA/RG84/368/861.33, Wood to Hamberge-Pelhemus Co., April 18, 1928. Among Hard and Rand's debtors were the Marure and Roig families. At the height of the coffee boom, the company advanced 15,000 pesos to both families based on the future sale of six hundred quintals of coffee. Ambrosio Marure served as one of their agents. Hard and Rand also purchased coffees in Huatusco, Coatepec, Xalapa, Isthmus, Oaxaca, and Puebla (AGEV/NCI, box 32, no. 182, sale of coffee, October 10, 1927; AGEV/NCI, box 32, no. 183, commission, November 11, 1927; AGEV/NCI, box 32, no. 184, sale of coffee, December 12, 1927; AGEV/NCI, box 32, no. 185, loan, September 27, 1927; and NARA/RG84/352/861.3, Frank Meehan to Wood, October 28, 1926).

139. NARA/RG84/329/861.3; AGEV/NCI, box 27, no. 4, protocol, January 29, 1920; AGEV/NCI, box 27, no. 25, sale, February 1, 1920; and AGEV/NCI, box 32, no. 42, sale, February 24, 1921.

140. NARA/RG59/812.512/3131, George T. Summerlin to DS, February 28, 1924; NARA/RG59/812.512/3167, Wood to DS, May 17, 1924; NARA/RG59/812.512/3167, Arthur Schoenfeld to G. Bergman, August 13, 1925; and NARA/RG59/812.512/3282, DS to Mexican Embassy, May 20, 1924.

141. NARA/RG84/344/861.33, Frank Meehan to Wood, June 19, 1925, November 5, 1925, November 19, 1925. NARA/RG76, entry 125, agency 927, box 163, affidavits of Arbuckles, February 14 and December 22, 1925. "Informe del gobernador (Abel S. Rodríguez) del Estado, septiembre 1927 a septiembre 1928," 11:6028.

142. AMC, box 375 (1921), file "Negociaciones, industriales y mercantiles." See Rodrígues Centeno, "La tierra y la gente," 83.

143. AGN/G/DM, Twentieth Century Spaniards, box 218, files 110–11; Sainz López Negrete, interview, March 23, 1999.

144. Ezequiel González López left for Mexico in 1910 to dodge the draft and avoid fighting in the interminable Moroccan wars (AGN/G/DM, Twentieth Century Spaniards, box 110, file 180; Domínguez Sánchez, interview).

145. Izquierdo de Regules, interview, December 1, 1998.

146. AMC, box 395 (1929), file "Sanidad."

147. AMC, box 395 (1929), file "Sanidad," Davíd González to Junta de Administración Civil, October 22, 1928; AMC, box 395 (1929), file "Sanidad," Manuel Domínguez to Presidente de la Junta de Administración Civil, October 23, 1928; AMC, box 395 (1929), file "Sanidad," Presidente de la Junta to Davíd González, November 9, 1929. In Huatusco, townspeople were much more adamant about keeping the beneficios out of the town. When a beneficiador tried to install a new plant in 1900, the citizens objected to the noise created by the gas motors as well as the machinery. A city ordinance banned their construction in the center (Córdova Santamaría, *Café y sociedad en Huatusco, Veracruz*, 218–19).

148. Sánchez, "Remembranzas," 48–49.

149. Two of the four Spanish immigrants in the Xalapa group came from *déclassé* aristocratic backgrounds (Beaumond, "Élite et changement social," 35–36).

150. Moya, "Continent of Immigrants," 3.

151. Paredes Cruz, "Los Barcelonnettes," 472–73.

152. Secretaría de la Economía Nacional, *El café*, 118.

153. Secretaría de la Economía Nacional, *El café*, 133–34.

154. Secretaría de la Economía Nacional, *El café*, 119, 135–37.

155. Veracruz had 236 machines with a total of 2,795 horsepower, while Chiapas had 165 machines with 2,680 horsepower. Veracruz's industry primarily relied on steam power, while Chiapas relied more heavily on hydraulic power (Secretaría de la Economía Nacional, *El café*, 143).

156. Dirección General de Estadística, *Primer censo industrial de 1930, Estado de Veracruz*, 1023; Olvera, "La estructura económica y social de Veracruz hacia 1930," 53. Córdoba sold primarily to consigners in the Federal District (DF), Santa Cruz, Pachuca, Santa Cruz, Puebla,

Manzanillo, Guadalajara, and Piedras Negras, while the Xalapa coffee exporters shipped their coffee only to the Federal District (Secretaría de la Economía Nacional, *El café*, 162–64).

157. Dirección General de Estadística, *Primer censo industrial de 1930, Estado de Veracruz*, 994, 1003.

158. Secretaría de la Economía Nacional, *El café*, 163.

159. Secretaría de la Economía Nacional, *El café*, 120–24, 128–29, 131. Córdoba and Tapachula prepared more coffee than any other municipalities in the nation. When their plant efficiency was measured, the latter came out ahead. Tapachula's nine plants, which prepared 5,614,148 kilos, had a utilization capacity of 19.4 percent, while Córdoba's twenty-two plants produced 6,855,675 kilos and used only 16.27 percent of their capacity. One can assume that Tapachula's plants were newer, for the state had a higher level of capital investment. On the other hand, two of the three largest plants in the republic, which could prepare between 20,001 and 25,000 kilos, were the Arbuckle and the Hard and Rand plants in Córdoba (Secretaría de la Economía Nacional, *El café*, 123, 131, 136–37).

The Secretaría de la Economía Nacional measured Córdoba's yields from the preparation process. One hundred kilos of coffee cherries yielded 23.96 percent of its weight in parchment coffee in the first stage of preparation. In both stages of preparation, 235 kilos of coffee cherries were reduced to one quintal (46 kilos) of cleaned coffee (*café pulido, café verde*, or *café de oro*). This is to say, the preparation process reduced the coffee to approximately one-fifth of its original weight (Secretaría de la Economía Nacional, *El café*, 141).

160. Secretaría de la Economía Nacional, *El café*, 131.

161. Secretaría de la Economía Nacional, *El café*, 142. Coffee workers' daily wages were approximately 2 pesos in Córdoba, Orizaba, and Xalapa, while those of Chiapas were between .96 and 1.80 pesos. However, this appears to be for the male salaried workers. In Huiztla, Chiapas, sorters received .8 to 2.5 centavos to clean one kilo (Secretaría de la Economía Nacional, *El café*, 144).

162. Veracruz produced 15.9 million kilos of the total 39.1 million kilos. Chiapas produced 12.7 million kilos (Secretaría de la Economía Nacional, *El café*, 95).

163. NARA/RG84/374/861.33, *Journal of Commerce*, October 30, 1929. Topik, *Political Economy of the Brazilian State, 1889–1930*, 82; and Samper Kutschbach, "In Difficult Times," 160.

164. Meyer, *El conflicto social y los gobiernos del maximato*, 3. Despite Mexico's increase in coffee production, its percentage of world production actually dropped from 2.2 percent in the years 1924–29 to 1.7 percent during the years 1929–34 (Wickizer, *World Coffee Economy*, 242).

165. Samper Kutschbach, "In Difficult Times," 160–64; Palacios, *Coffee in Colombia, 1850–1970*, 214.

166. INEGI, *Estadísticas históricas de México* (1990) 1:386; and INEGI, *Estadísticas históricas de México* (1999), 2:728–29.

167. INEGI, *Estadísticas históricas de México* (1994), 2:1006; and NARA/RG84/397/361.33, Leonard Dawson, "Periodic Report on Coffee, December 5, 1931." Rodríguez Centeno, "Paisaje agrario y sociedad rural," 292–93.

168. AGEV/ACG, boxes 1–3 (1933), file 51.4, "Salidas de café." I would like to thank Rubi Minerva Garcia Andrade and Davíd Ruiz Ramón for data collection and Gina Meeks for entering and formatting the data.

169. INEGI, *Estadísticas históricas de México* (1999), 2:728–29.

170. By 1934 and 1935, preparers were receiving even more out-of-state coffee. The Zardains were preparing coffee beans from San Antonio, San Geronimo, and Matías Romero (Oaxaca), while the Sainz Pardos received it from San Marcos (Puebla) and Mario Fernández from Esperanza (Puebla). Davíd González was preparing coffee from San Marcos, Esperanza, and La Ventosa with Banco de Córdoba loans (AMC, boxes 420 [1934] and 425 [1935], files "Informes sobre el Ganado, Fruta, y Café").

171. Central Veracruz's socioeconomic structure more closely resembled Antioquia and Viejo Caldas in northwestern Colombia than other coffee economies. They shared a multicrop economy and a two-step coffee preparation process, with the wet preparation performed in the countryside and the dry preparation in provincial towns (Samper Kutschbach, "In Difficult Times," 157–59, 166–69).

172. Secretaría de la Economía Nacional, *El café*, 106–8.

173. Secretaría de la Economía Nacional, *El café*, 107–8.

174. RPPPCC, business, no. 44, creation of Sociedad Mercantil Sainz Par-

do Hermanos, April 20, 1933; and Sainz López Negrete, interviews, March 23, 1999, and July 19, 1999.

175. RPPPCC, business, no. 54, dissolution of Sociedad Zardain Hermanos, September 1, 1933; RPPPCC, business, no. 56, re-creation of Sociedad Zardain Hermanos, September 14, 1933; and AMC, box 415 (1933), file "Extranjeros."

176. RPPPCC, business, no. 104, creation of Beneficiadora y Exportadora SA, October 15, 1934. Sainz López Negrete, interviews, March 23, 1999, and July 19, 1999.

177. IRPPPCH, business, no. 1, commercial agreement, December 1, 1942; and AMC, box 430 (1935), file 1, "Café." Sainz López Negrete, interview, July 19, 1999.

178. RPPPCC, business, no. 103 (1934), contract with Ezequiel González, February 10, 1934; RPPPCC, business, no. 118, first meeting of Beneficiadora, December 16, 1934; RPPPCC, business, no. 299, stockholder meeting of Beneficiadora, January 5, 1940; and RPPPCC, business, no. 99, sale of Zardain theater and the Pedro Díaz theater for 100,000 pesos, March 10, 1940. According to Beaumond, Mario Fernández operated a business in Coatepec from 1935 to 1943, after he discovered the competition with the Xalapa group too intense ("Élite et changement social," 169).

179. Sánchez Vargas, "Remembranzas de Córdoba," 55–57, 74–75.

180. Izquierdo de Regules, interview, March 16, 1999. RPPPCC, business, no. 531, creation of Sociedad Regules y Soler, October 10, 1921; RPPPCC, business, no. 559, dissolution of Regules y Soler, June 13, 1923; RPPPCC, rentals, no. 83, machinery rental, Virginia Alducin to Regules y Ros, November 4, 1932; and IRPPPCC, rentals, no. 20, machinery rental, Tobias García to Ricardo Regules, November 24, 1933.

181. AMC, box 421 (1934), file 1, "Informes sobre Salidas de café."

182. RPPPCC, business, no. 179, creation of Sociedad Regules y Cia, January 5, 1937; RPPPCC, business, no. 304, extension of Sociedad Regules, November 18, 1940; RPPPCC, business, no. 405, dissolution of Regules, September 12, 1941; IRPPPCH, rentals, no. 19, beneficio rental, José Sanfilippo to Regules, November 18, 1937; AGEV/ACG, box 397, file 524-74, meeting of Junta Municipal Permanente de Conciliación, September 11, 1937.

183. Archivo Ramón Fernández y Fernández, Colegio de Michoacán (AFYF), box 29, no. 80, Enrique López y Galván, "Sugerencias generales sobre el café que presenta al Primero Congreso Nacional de Exportación, October 1938."

184. "Informe que rinde el C. Ing. Adalberto Tejeda, Gobernador Constitucional del Estado, ante la trigésimacuarta Legislatura (del período de 1928–1932)," 11:6117. Rodrigúez Centeno, "Paisaje agrario y sociedad rural," 285–86.

185. NARA/RG84/397/361.33, Leonardo Dawson, "Periodic Reports on Coffee, April 7, December 5, 1931"; AGN/ALR, 533.1/2, Hard and Rand, Arbuckle Brothers, Zardain Brothers, Ezequiel González, Ceferino Sainz Pardo, Davíd González to President (telegraph), February 24, 1932; and AGN/ALR, 533.1/2, Ignacio de la Torre (Secretario de Hacienda) to Javier Gaxiola, October 21, 1932.

186. "Mexican News," *Spice Mill* 59, no. 6 (June 1936): 410; "Mexican Coffee News," *Spice Mill* 61, no. 1 (January 1938): 25; "Mexican Notes," *Spice Mill* 61, no. 9 (September 1938): 410; and "Mexican Exporters Protest Taxes," *Spice Mill* 62, no. 9 (September 1939): 78.

187. AMC, box 430 (1935), file "Café," Decree no. 243, December 22, 1932; *Gaceta Oficial*, January 16, 1925; *Gaceta Oficial*, July 19, 1932; *Gaceta Oficial*, December 22, 1932 (Decree no. 243); *Gaceta Oficial*, January 25, 1936; *Gaceta Oficial*, January 22, 1936; *Gaceta Oficial*, March 24, 1936; "Mexican Coffee News," *Spice Mill* 59, no. 3 (March 1936): 163, 213; and "Mexican Coffee News," *Spice Mill* 60, no. 1 (January 1938): 25. Rodríguez Centeno, "Paisaje agrario y sociedad rural," 308–10.

188. Fernández y Fernández, *El café de Veracruz*, 142–44.

189. Fernández y Fernández, *El café de Veracruz*, 62. "Brazil News," *Spice Mill* 61, no. 4 (April 1938): 213.

190. Colegio de México, *Estadísticas económicas, del Porfiriato* (1990), 1:386–87; Colegio de México, *Estadísticas económicas, del Porfiriato*, (1999), 2:728–29; and "Mexican News Notes," *Spice Mill* 61, no. 12 (December 1938): 44.

191. The Banco de México did initiate a project to stimulate coffee sales abroad by extending long-term loans at low interest to exporters. It even considered the creation of a special bank to assist with unusual foreign exchange problems and currency restrictions to regain access

to German markets. See "Mexican Coffee News," *Spice Mill* 60, no. 4 (April 1937): 236; "Mexican Coffee News," *Spice Mill* 60, no. 1 (January 1938): 59; "Mexican Coffee News," *Spice Mill* 61, no. 3 (March 1938): 154.

192. Fernández y Fernández, *El café de Veracruz*, 71, 74, 137–42. He enumerated four types of intermediaries: the *acopiador, beneficiador, exportador*, and *comprador extranjero*, who were often one in the same (137).

193. Fernández y Fernández, *El café de Veracruz*, 108–11, 140–41.

194. Beneficiadores would advance 70 to 75 percent of the loan based on the present price of coffee before the season started and then wait until the prices dropped before giving out the remaining portion. They would sometimes lower their purchase price when the coffee was not of the highest quality. Fernández y Fernández bemoaned the loss of the agroindustrial cooperation between producer and preparer of bygones days, and he suggested that the small- and medium-sized producers, whose cause he was championing, must find new ways to organize. To achieve this objective, he recommended that the state intervene through the BNCA to establish an export center, which would become the principal intermediary between the producer cooperatives and the market (Fernández y Fernández, *El café de Veracruz*, 148–49).

2. Work, Gender, and Workshop Culture

1. Keremitsis, "Del metate al Molino," 301–2; Keremitsis, "Latin American Women Workers in Transition," 491–504; Ramos Escandón, "Mujeres trabajadoras en el México porfiriano," 27–44; and Arizpe and Aranda, "'Comparative Advantages' of Women's Disadvantages," 453–73.

2. Radkau, *"La Fama" y la vida*, 97–98; Ramos Escandón, "Gender, Labor, and Class Consciousness in the Mexican Textile Industry, 1880–1910," 87–89; Porter, *Working Women in Mexico City*, 119–32; Fernández-Aceves, "Struggle between the *Metate* and the *Molino de Nixtamal* in Guadalajara, 1920–1940," 147–58; Lear, *Workers, Neighbors, and Citizens*, 307–12, 339; Olcott, *Revolutionary Women in Postrevolutionary Mexico*, 123–58.

3. See Sheridan Prieto, *"Mujer obrera y organización sindical"*; and Dominguez Pérez, "Historia de una lucha."

4. Bortz, *Revolution within the Revolution*, 50–82.

5. Canning, *Languages of Labor and Gender*, 220.

6. Crane, "Writing the Individual Back into Collective Memory," 1375; and Canning, "Difficult Dichotomies," 113.

7. Luisa Passerini argued that the subjective dimensions of oral sources are not simply direct reconstructions of the past, for they link the past and present in a combination that is laden with symbolic significance: "Personal memory combines with the collective memory, and individual mythology turns into a tradition shared by the family, circles of friends or a political party" or group (*Fascism in Popular Memory*, 17, 19).

8. This is discussed in greater detail in Fowler-Salamini, "Gender, Work, and Coffee," 51–73.

9. Southworth, *El Estado de Veracruz-Llave*, 41–42.

10. Tomás Pineiro, an Orizaba merchant, employed 5 men workers and 200 escogedoras in his dry beneficio (Southworth, *El Estado de Veracruz-Llave*, 132; and Cordova Santamaría, *Café y sociedad en Huatusco, Veracruz*, 101). The other Orizaba mill, Cafetera, employed 140 women and 10 men (AMO, 1907, loose, file 6). By 1911 in Coatepec, Carlos Polanco, Guillermo Boesch, Justo Fernández, and the Arbuckles had installed or acquired large beneficios that employed at least 200 sorters (Domínguez Pérez, "Historia de una lucha," 6).

11. AGEV/DTPS, box 21, file 111, Luz Vera (secretary general) to Governor Abel Rodriguez, October 19, 1927; AGEV/DTPS, box 58, file "Sindicato de la Peñuela," Adalberto Tejeda to Samuel Montiel (CROM) (telegram), August 25, 1930; AGEV/JCCA/S, 1932, loose, file 16, "Coatepec," 1934 union membership list; and AGN/ALR, 561.8/61, Antonio Hidalgo to Governor, February 17, 1933.

12. Dirección General de Estadística, *Quinto Censo de Población, 1930*, table 20, 233.

13. Keremitsis, "Latin American Women Workers in Transition," 497; Fernández-Aceves, "Once We Were Corn Grinders," 87–88; González Sierra, *Monopolio del humo*, 221–24; and Porter, *Working Women in Mexico City*, 115–18.

14. See photo of Brazilian conveyor belts for sorting (*Spice Mill* 54 (1936): 592). Antonio García estimated that there were approximately 2,412 sorters in the Department of Caldas in the late 1930s, 60 percent of whom were working in semimechanized trilladoras equipped with conveyor belts (*Geografía económica de Caldas*, 313). See also Bergquist, *Labor in Latin America*, 351–52; and *Tea and Coffee Trade Journal* 74 (March 1938): 11.

15. Chassen-López, "'Cheaper Than Machines,'" 27–50.

16. Lino Alejandro Gómez Reyes, interview, July 19, 1999; Serna, interview; López Osorio, interview; Téxon, interview; and Sheridan Prieto, *Mujer obrera y organización sindical*, 13–14.

17. Bernardo García Díaz and Leticia Gamboa Ojeda found similar two-stage migratory patterns among textile workers (*Textiles del Valle de Orizaba*, 13–64; and *La urdimbre y la trama*, 67–101). González, interview, March 12, 1999.

18. Susan Tiano shows clearly that export assembly workers in Mexicali in the 1980s did not fit this stereotype either (*Patriarchy on the Line*, 98–105).

19. In December 1932 there were 679 members in one of Córdoba's two unions, which represented approximately one half of the total number of sorters. They fell primarily into three age groups: the thirty- to thirty-nine-year group made up 39.9 percent, the twenty- to twenty-nine-year group made up 36.5 percent, and the forty- to forty-nine-year group made up 12.5 percent of membership (AGEV/JCCA/S, 1933, loose file, "Membership list of the Grupo Mayoritario del Sindicato de Escogedoras del Café y Tabaco de la Ciudad y la Región de Córdoba, Veracruz").

20. The low level of marriages and high level of free unions among textile workers are treated by Gamboa Ojeda in *La urdimbre y la trama*, 171–72; by Gómez-Galvarriato Freer in "Impact of Revolution," 202; and by Bortz in *Revolution within the Revolution*, 69.

21. Canning, *Languages of Labor and Gender*, 219.

22. Sartorius, *Mexico about 1850*, 175; and Fowler-Salamini, "Gender, Work, and Coffee," 54–55.

23. This description is based on visits to Córdoba's La Garza and Arbuckle plants and on the 1927 blueprint of Carlos Polanco's mixed beneficio in Coatepec located in the AHA.

24. Most recent studies of coffee preparation do not mention the sorting stage. For example, see William Roseberry's short description of the wet process in his introduction to *Coffee, Society, and Power,* 13.

25. Ana María Hernández, interview by Olivia Domínguez Pérez, May 1982, in Domínguez Pérez, "Historia de una lucha," 12.

26. For a pictorial history of the evolution of coffee sorting, see Fowler-Salamini, "Fotografía y mujeres."

27. Aldegunda Montaño, undated interview by Olivia Domínguez Peréz, in Domínguez Peréz, "Historia de una lucha," 13.

28. It was more difficult for twelve-year-olds to run the machines. "Well, I couldn't do it because . . . I was still very small, so my feet did not reach the pedal. And the belt moved forward and brought the coffee towards me, and I [had to] bend over so the coffee arrived, for me to clean. It was a real problem" (Romero Serrano, interview).

29. In 1898 Córdoba's daily rural wage was twenty-five centavos for women and fifty to seventy-five centavos for men (AMC, box 258 [1898], file "Datos referentes a los salarios o jornales"). Over the next decade, it did not increase significantly (AMC, box 310 [1908], file "Fomento, Geografía e Estadística"; AMC, box 325 [1911], file "Fomento, Geografía e Estadística"); see also Fowler-Salamini, "Gender, Work, and Coffee," 57.

30. AGEV/FL, box 83, file 262, Rafael Alcalde (Labor Inspector) to Cándido Aguilar, March 31, 1915.

31. Sheridan Prieto, *Mujer obrera y organización sindical,* 29. In Xalapa the owners paid between ten and forty-five centavos per kilo of waste (AGEV/DTPS, box 7, file "Apolinar Espino (Labor Inspector)," collective contract, April 29, 1924.

32. AGEV/JCCA/D, 1934, box 121, file 78, "Xalapa." Sheridan Prieto, *Mujer obrera y organización sindical,* 48.

33. AGEV/JCCA/S, 1930, box 58, file 2, "Reglamento Interior de las obreras escogedoras de la Casa Zardain Hnos.," October 1, 1930; AGEV/JCCA/S, 1933, file 9, "Reglamento Interior (según el contrato) Casa de Sainz Pardo Hnos.," May 29, 1933; and AMC, box 417 (1933), file 44-51, "Salario Mínimo."

34. AGEV/DTPS, box 3, file 524-7, Huatusco contract, December 27, 1932, revision, April 3, 1935; and AGEV/JCCA/S, 1936, box 81, file "Huatusco," contract, November 12, 1935.

35. Tiano, *Patriarchy on the Line*, 49, 148–50; and Lim, "Women's Work in Export Factories," 108–9.

36. AGEV/JCCA/S, 1936, box 81, file "Huatusco, Contratos y Reglamentos" collective contract with seven coffee firms, November 19, 1935.

37. AGEV/JCCA/S, 1931, loose, file 118, Union Sindical Contract, November 25, 1931; and AGEV/JCCA/S, 1938, loose, file 6, "Porte Petit."

38. Sorters were earning twenty to twenty-five centavos per kilo of waste in Xalapa and Coatepec (AGEV/JCCA/S, 1936, box 82, file 29, "Coatepec," contract, January 10, 1936; and AGEV/ACG, 1938, box 537, file 524-93, Xalapa Contract (CTM), August 5, 1938.

39. AGEV/JCCA/S, 1938, box 535, file 524-44, "Estudio relacionado con el desmanche," April 4, 1938. The labor inspector supervised an elaborate exercise over a three-day period in Huatusco where dozens of sorters cleaned coffee to ascertain what the daily average output of an escogedora was in order to establish what the average price of a bucket of cleaned coffee and its equivalent, a kilo of waste, should be. He wanted to peg both piece-rate wages to the minimum rural wage. After taking into account the time lost while the sorter had her coffee revised by the receiver, he calculated that the average sorter could clean on average eight fourteen-kilo buckets a day. To obtain the equivalent of the rural minimum wage, sorters would have to receive a minimum of thirty-five centavos and a maximum of thirty-six centavos per bucket of cleaned coffee and the same for a kilo of mancha to earn 17.28 pesos a week. This piece-rate wage would include her Sunday pay and her paid holidays. AGEV/ACG, 1938, box 539, file 524, "Junta Municipal de Conciliación, Córdoba," meeting, July 21, 1938.

40. After the passage of the 1931 Federal Labor Code, the federal government sent a small number of labor inspectors to factories employing full-time workers. The interviewees could not recall many visits by labor inspectors to their plants. Besides, they said, the beneficio owners always persuaded them to write favorable reports.

41. Maria del Carmen Ríos Zavala, interview.

42. Maria del Carmen Ríos Zavala, interview. The files of the Department of Labor in the AGN and the AGEV have not been organized after the 1920s, so it is very difficult to locate labor inspector reports on working conditions. A few 1946 industrial reports were located for

Xalapa in the AGN, but they only contain statistical data and have no information on labor conditions.

43. López Osorio, interview; AGEV/JCCA/D, 1921, loose, file 34, "Coatepec," Desmanchadoras vs. Arbuckle Brothers; and Sheridan Prieto, *Mujer obrera y organización sindical*, 30, 35.

44. A Córdoba shirtwaist worker was paid by the piece-rate and earned forty to sixty pesos a month, or approximately the same amount as a sorter (AGEV/ACG, 1938, box 531 file 524-10, "Sindicato de Sastres y Costureras").

45. Passerini, *Fascism in Popular Memory*, 50; Vecchia, "'My Duty as a Woman,'" 105–8; and Porter, *Working Women in Mexico City*, 122–28.

46. Levenson-Estrada, "Loneliness of Working-Class Feminism," 224. Susan Gauss also argues that working-class masculinity revolves around profamily and prounion behavior patterns where militancy, violence, solidarity, loyalty, and responsibility are primordial for the primary breadwinner ("Working-Class Masculinity and Rationalized Sex," 182–86).

47. Porter, *Working Women in Mexico City*, 132.

48. Sainz López Negrete, interview, June 5, 2000.

49. Silvia Herrera Luna, interview. Silvia's husband was so jealous that he would not let her go out of the house alone, although her two unmarried sisters could. Sheridan Prieto, *Mujer obrera y organización sindical*, 22–23; and Radkau, "La Fama" y la vida, 50.

50. Canning found that German textile workers had to shape their identity based on "the rhythms of their [work] . . . careers, the pride they expressed in their work, the bonds that formed and fractured among coworkers, employers, families, and communities, and the needs and desires that propelled women workers into strikes and informal protests" (*Languages of Labor and Gender*, 220). Vecchia details how material reality generated tensions in the gendered dynamics of everyday working-class life ("'My Duty as a Woman,'" 101).

51. Sheridan Prieto, *Mujer obrera y organización sindical*, 22–23. In her study of rural women who entered the Michoacán textile and garment sweatshops in the 1980s, Wilson takes a similar position. She contends, as does Joan Scott, that the women workers bring the unequal class and gender relations—that is, the "domestic model"—di-

rectly into the workshop (*De la casa al taller*, 147–66). For Brazil, see Vecchia, "'My Duty as a Woman,'" 103–8.

52. Siriaco García, interview, June 6, 2000.

53. Their explanations varied little from those of the textile worker Doña Justa, who entered a Tlalpan textile mill in 1916: "They went to work only because it was necessary. It was not because they felt like it" (Radkau, *"La Fama" y la vida*, 79). See also Lobato, "Women Workers in the Cathedrals of Corned Beef," 58–61.

54. Lino Alejandro Gómez Reyes, interview, July 19, 1999; Serna, interview; López Osorio, interview; Eufrosina Moya (Sarmiento) married a musician from a well-to-do family, who was unable to support his family alone (Salomón and Delia Ortiz Sarmiento, interview, March 23, 1999). The Herrera Luna sisters started working with their mother as sorters at eight years old (Magdalena Herrera Luna, interview).

55. Sheridan Prieto, *Mujer obrera y organización sindical*, 14–15. María Elena Serna, Inés Reyes Osorio, and Isabel Romero Serrano came from three-generation sorter families. For more on textile-worker three-generation families, see Estrada Urroz, *Del telar a la cadena de montaje*, 74–75; and Bortz, *Revolution within the Revolution*, 72–73.

56. Farnsworth-Alvear, *Dulcinea in the Factory*, 70.

57. Baltazar, interview. Sheridan Prieto, *Mujer obrera y organización sindical*, 14.

58. James, *Doña María's Story*, 164; Radkau, *"La Fama" y la vida*, 96; and Wilson, *De la casa al taller*, 176–77.

59. Hernández de Huerta, interview; and Romero Serrano, interview.

60. Velázquez Ramírez, interview, May 13, 1999.

61. Siriaco García, interview, July 3, 2001.

62. Salazar Báez, interview, June 12, 2002.

63. Limón, interview; Maria del Carmen Ríos Zavala, interview; Siriaco García, interview, July 3, 2001. Alessandro Portelli discusses the use of personal and impersonal pronouns in terms of personal and institutional meaning in *Battle of Valle Giulia*, 27–32.

64. Magdalena Herrera Luna, interview; and Velázquez Ramírez, interview, March 3, 1999.

65. Bortz, *Revolution within the Revolution*, 72–73.

66. Porter describes the women cigarette workers' "cohesive work cul-

ture" of the nineteenth century, which, like that of the coffee sorters, was in part "based upon the sheer numbers and the percentage of these workers who were women" ("In the Shadow of Industrialization," 44). See also Vicki Ruiz's discussion of "cannery culture" as "an intermingling of gender roles and assembly line conditions, family and peer socialization, and at times collective resistance and change" (*Cannery Women, Cannery Lives*, 82).

67. Anderson, *Outcasts in Their Own Land*, 75–78; Lear, *Workers, Neighbors, and Citizens*, 92–95; Bortz, *Revolution within the Revolution*, 26; Camarena Ocampo, *Jornaleros, tejedores, y obreros*, 71–76; and Porter, *Working Women in Mexico City*, 128–29.

68. Snodgrass, "Birth and Consequences of Industrial Paternalism," 122–24; and Snodgrass, *Deference and Defiance in Monterrey*, 55–57. See also Camarena Ocampo, *Jornaleros, tejedores, y obreros*, 75–76.

69. Snodgrass, *Deference and Defiance in Monterrey*, 62.

70. Snodgrass, *Deference and Defiance in Monterrey*, 73.

71. Kessler-Harris, "Reconfiguring the Private in the Context of the Public," 171–74; Fernández-Aceves, "Struggle between the *Metate* and the *Molino de Nixtamal* in Guadalajara, 1920–1940," 151–52; Lobato, "Women Workers in the Cathedrals of Corned Beef," 61–64; and Vecchia, "'My Duty as a Woman,'" 109–10.

72. Bortz, *Revolution within the Revolution*, 61–62; Snodgrass, *Deference and Defiance in Monterrey*, 63–64; Olcott, "Miracle Workers," 46–58; and Gauss, "Working-Class Masculinity and Rationalized Sex," 181–83.

73. AGEV/JCCA/S, 1939, box 524, file 14, "Huatusco," collective contract between José Vallejo and the Sindicato de Trabajadores en General de la Industria del Café en el Estado de Veracruz (Huatusco), November 5, 1939; AGEV/JCCA/S, 1939, box 524, file 136, "Xalapa," individual contract between Juana García and Mario Fernández, November 29, 1939; AGEV/JCCA/S, 1938, loose, file 6, "Porte Petit," collective contract of Sindicato de Trabajadores en General de la Industria del Café and Arbuckles, August 4, 1938; and AGEV/ACG, 1940, box 62, file 524-94, contract proposal, March 1940. Siriaco García, interview, July 3, 2001; and Díaz Sanauria, interview, July 4, 2004.

74. Siriaco García, interview, July 3, 2001. In Colombia, teenage sorters

were at the mercy of male supervisors who monitored their output (Bergquist, *Labor in Latin America*, 352).

75. Snodgrass, *Deference and Defiance in Monterrey*, 55. Camarena Ocampo suggests that paternalism began to fade at the end of the nineteenth century as Mexico City workers organized mutual aid societies and unions (*Jornaleros, tejedores, y obreros*, 95–97). For the same practice in the United States, see Kessler-Harris ("Reconfiguring the Private in the Context of the Public," 160).

76. Romero Serrano, interview; Baltazar, interview; and Siriaco García, interview.

77. Téxon, interview; and Limón, interview.

78. Lino Alejandro Gómez Reyes, interview, July 19, 1999. He was told by his grandmother about Tirso Sainz Pardo's first employment as a laborer in his brother's beneficio.

79. Siriaco García, interview, July 3, 2001.

80. Lino Alejandro Gómez Reyes, interview, May 13, 1999.

81. Farnsworth-Alvear, *Dulcinea in the Factory*, 116.

82. Siriaco García, interview, June 6, 2000.

83. Díaz Sanauria, interview, July 10, 2001.

84. Leticia Gamboa Ojeda, e-mail correspondence with author, June 13, 2002. Leñero Franco found no sense of community among Tlaxcalan women textile workers, who were a distinct minority in the workplace. In her interviews, they talked about discrimination on the shop floor based on gender hierarchies and paternalism. This kept women workers isolated, without friendships outside the factory, and in continual conflict with other women over who was the better mother or who could capture a man more easily (*El huso y el sexo*, 46–52).

85. Sheridan Prieto, *Mujer obrera y organización sindical*, 42–43.

86. Siriaco García, interview, July 3, 2001; Velázquez Ramírez, interview, May 13, 1999; and Romero Serrano, interview.

87. Peiss, *Cheap Amusements*, 6.

88. Velázquez Ramírez, interview, May 13, 1999; Siriaco García, interview, July 3, 2001; Maria del Carmen Ríos Zavala, interview; Limón, interview; and Salazar Báez, interview, June 12, 2002. Porter describes how Mexico City men and women workers ate lunch together on the street (*Working Women in Mexico City*, 16).

89. Porter, *Working Women in Mexico City*, 16; and Velázquez Ramírez, interview, March, 3, 1999; and Díaz Sanauria, interviews, July 10, 2001, and July 4, 2004.

90. Siriaco García, interview, June 7, 2000; Salomón and Delia Ortiz Sarmiento, interview, March 23, 1999; and Delia Ortiz Sarmiento, interview, May 11, 1999; and Salazar Báez, interview, June 12, 2002. Bortz emphasizes close family ties among textile workers who returned home at midday to eat, even if it was for ten minutes (*Revolution within the Revolution*, 69).

91. Lino Alejandro Gómez Reyes, interview, July 19, 1999; Velázquez Ramírez, interview, March 3, 1999; Serna, interview; Maria del Carmen Ríos Zavala, interview; and Hernández de Huerta, interview.

92. Porter, *Working Women in Mexico City*, 132. See also James and French, who argue that for the Latin American public the workplace is a hostile and sexualized place where a woman's honor is tested ("Squaring the Circle," 9).

93. To this day, upright Veracruzanos conflate the escogedora with the prostitute. They still represent undesirable, marginal women on the fringes of provincial urban society.

94. Sheridan Prieto, *Mujer obrera y organización sindical*, 30; and Limón, interview.

95. Maria del Carmen Ríos Zavala, interview.

96. Maria del Carmen Ríos Zavala, interview. "No eramos mujeres de la calle!" Baltazar, interview.

97. Crane, "Writing the Individual Back into Collective Memory," 1383.

3. Negotiations with Exporters and State

1. French and Pedersen Cluff, "Women and Working-Class Mobilization in Postwar São Paulo, 1945–1948," 177. This phenomenon occurred in Mexico also. See Lear, *Workers, Neighbors, and Citizens*, 222–28; Porter, *Working Women in Mexico City*, 99–102; and Wood, *Revolution in the Street*, 75–80.

2. Lear, *Workers, Neighbors, and Citizens*, 309; and Kaplan, "Female Consciousness and Collective Action."

3. Joseph and Nugent, "Popular Culture and State Formation in Revolutionary Mexico," 12.

4. Lear, *Workers, Neighbors, and Citizens*, 349–54; and Porter, *Working Women in Mexico City*, 110–17.

5. Anderson, *Outcasts in Their Own Land*, 99–171, 223–97; Gutiérrez Álvarez, *Experiencias contrastadas*, 191–239; Knight, "Working Class and the Mexican Revolution," 51; and Lear, *Workers, Neighbors, and Citizens*, 5.

6. Womack, *Posición estratégica y fuerza obrera*, 15; Anderson, *Outcasts in Their Own Land*, 279, 282–85, 288, 292.

7. Ruiz, *Labor and Ambivalent Revolutionaries*, 49–51; Ulloa, *Veracruz, capital de la nación*, 47–56; Hart, *Anarchism and the Mexican Working Class, 1860–1931*, 132–35; Carr, *El movimiento obrero y la política en México*, 1:83–90; and Carr, "Casa del Obrero Mundial."

8. Martínez Assad was the first to use the term "laboratorio de la revolución" extensively for Tabasco in *El laboratorio de la revolución*. Gilbert Joseph applied the term "social laboratory for the Revolution" to characterize Salvador Alvarado's pace-setting regime in Yucatan, which began in March 1915 (*Revolution from Without*, 102). See also Smith, *Gender and the Mexican Revolution*, 14–18; and Carr, *El movimiento obrero y la política en México, 1910–1929*, 1:81.

9. Corzo Ramírez, González Sierra, and Skerritt Gardner characterize his agrarian reform programs as following the nineteenth-century liberal tradition. They call his labor law an instrument to block the spread of Magonismo and anarchosyndicalism. The interventionist role of the state was critical to achieve these objectives (*. . . nunca un desleal*, 52–61). Williman, *La iglesia y el estado en Veracruz, 1840–1940*, 33.

10. Decree 11, "Ley del Trabajo, 19 de octubre de 1914," Soledad de Doblado, *Gaceta Oficial* 1 (October 29, 1914); and Agetro, *Las luchas proletarias en Veracruz*, 167–71. Corzo Ramírez, González Sierra, and Skerritt Gardner, *. . . nunca un desleal*, 58–61.

11. Smith, *Gender and the Mexican Revolution*, 69; and Suárez-Potts, "Mexican Supreme Court and the Juntas de Conciliación y Arbitraje, 1917–1924," 739.

12. Ulloa, *Veracruz, capital de la nación*, 152–53; Hart, *Anarchism and the Mexican Working Class, 1860–1931*, 135; García Díaz, *Textiles del Valle de Orizaba*, 69–71; and Carr, "Casa del Obrero Mundial," 616.

13. AMC, box 346 (1915), file "Leyes y Decretos," Oficina Central de Propaganda Revolucionaria program. Hart, *Anarchism and the Mexican Working Class, 1860–1931*, 135; Ulloa, *Veracruz, capital de la nación*, 57.

14. AGEV/FL, box 83, file 476, "Jalapa," flyer of Mateo Rodríguez, Perote, Veracruz, August 14, 1915.

15. AMC, box 347 (1916), file 1, "Leyes y decretos," Decree no. 19, Orizaba, Veracruz, February 19, 1916.

16. For the anarchist and anarchosyndicalist mobilization of women workers in the nineteenth century, see CEHSMO, *La mujer y el movimiento obrero mexicano en el siglo XIX*; Hernández, *La mujer mexicana en la industria textil*, 35–38; Lear, *Workers, Neighbors, and Citizens*, 174–75; Ramos Escandón, "Mujeres trabajadores en el México porfiriano," 38–39; Trujillo Bolio, *Operarios fabriles en el Valle de México, 1864–1884*, 269–70; Hart, *Anarchism and the Mexican Working Class, 1860–1931*, 54–55; Porter, *Working Women in Mexico City*, 74–95; and John Hart, e-mail correspondence with author, January 29, 2000.

17. Hart, *Anarchism and the Mexican Working Class, 1860–1931*, 112–18; and Huitrón, *Orígenes e historia del movimiento obrero en México*, 213–27. The Mexican Liberal Party's views on gender are outlined in McGee Deutsch, "Gender and Sociopolitical Change in the Twentieth Century Latin America," 262–63.

18. Medel y Alvarado, *Historia de San Andrés Tuxtla*, 403–4; and González Sierra, *Monopolio del humo*, 97–99.

19. Hernández, *La mujer mexicana en la industria textil*, 31; Huitrón, *Orígenes e historia del movimiento obrero en México*, 115–16; Anderson, *Outcasts in Their Own Land*, 157; García Díaz, *Un pueblo fabril del porfiriato*, 133, 141, 154; and Ramos Escandón, "Gender, Labor, and Class-Consciousness in the Mexican Textile Industry, 1880–1910," 88.

20. Huitrón, *Orígenes e historia del movimiento obrero en México*, 215; Wood, *Revolution in the Street*, 26–31; and Fowler, "Orígenes laborales de la organización campesina en Veracruz," 243–44.

21. AGEV/FL, 1915, box 83, file 262, "Coatepec," Rafael Alcalde to Governor and Military Commander Cándido Aguilar, March 31, 1915.

22. AMC, box 344 (1915), file 25, founding act of the Sindicato de Escogedoras de Café y Obreras Tabaqueras, January 26, 1915; AMC, box 344 (1915), file 25, Ana R. Herrera (president) and María Mendoza (sec-

retary) to Junta de Administración Civil, January 27, 1915; and Ulloa, *Veracruz, capital de la nación*, 153–54.

23. AGEV/F/AL, 1915, box 95, file 314, "Córdoba," session of the Cámara del Trabajo of the CSORM, March, 1, 1915. The Coffee Sorters Union became the second section as soon as male unions were organized.

24. AMC, box 344 (1915), file 25, "Sindicato de Cargadores," Ana Herrera and María Mendoza (Sindicato de Escogedoras de Café y Obreras Tabaqueras) to Junta de Administración Civil, February 6, 1915.

25. AMC, box 344 (1915), file 25, "Sindicato de Cargadores," circular of the Sindicato de Cargadores y Enfardeladores del Comercio de Café y Tabaco, February 8, 1915. The collective agreement signed between the urban transit workers union and the Companía de Ferrocarriles Urbanos, February 9, 1915, is much less specific. It raised wages to sixty pesos a month for the conductors.

26. Lino Gómez Reyes's grandmother, who was a sorter activist in the 1920s, worked in both the tobacco and coffee plants (Lino Alejandro Gómez Reyes, interview, July 19, 1999).

27. Lear, *Workers, Neighbors, and Citizens*, 307–12; and Tilly, "Paths of Proletarianization," 416–17.

28. AMC, box 344, file 25, "Convenio entre los dueños y las desmanchadoras, obreras tabaquereras, y Agustín Arrazola (CSORM), 10 de febrero de 1915." Its provisions are summarized in Ulloa, *Veracruz, capital de la nación*, 154–55. Veracruz's most important newspaper, *El Dictamen*, did not report this strike.

29. AMC, box 344, file 25, Aguilar to President of the Junta de Administración Civil (telegram), February 10, 1915.

30. AMC, box 344, file 25, Matías Rueda (secretario general de gobierno) to Junta de Administración Civil (telegram), February 8, 1915.

31. Limones Ceniceros, "Las costureras anarcosindicalistas de Orizaba, 1915," 238; Huitrón, *Orígenes e historia del movimiento obrero en México*, 222–31; García Díaz, *Textiles del Valle de Orizaba*, 72–77; and Salazar and Escobedo, *Las pugnas de la gleba, 1906–1922*, 116–17. For the organization of tobacco women and men workers see González Sierra, *Monopolio del humo*, 145–68. See also Fowler-Salamini, "La movilización obrera veracruzana y la cuestión de género (1915 a 1919)."

Limones Ceniceros shows how the Orizaba seamstresses organized by the Carrancistas framed their demands in terms of consumption but also in terms of class and national identity: "The struggle for life is getting more and more difficult each day, for the articles of primary necessity, clothes, shoes, etc., are getting more expensive to the degree that the market prices are exorbitant. . . . Although we belong to the Unión de Resistencia we ask for [a wage increase] not only for ourselves and our compañeras, but also in general for all factory workers, for we are all in the same difficult circumstances, we are all Mexicans, brothers, and we all have the same needs" (Limones Ceniceros, "Las costureras anarcosindicalistas de Orizaba, 1915," 238).

32. Rosas Juárez, "La revolución en el ex-cantón de Córdoba," 112. AGEV/FL, 1915, box 95, file 314, "Córdoba," Sucursal no. 2 (Córdoba), CSORM, to Cándido Aguilar, March 1, 1915; AGEV/FL, 1915, box 95, file 314, "Córdoba," Provisional Municipal President to Secretario General de Gobierno, March, 17, 1915; and AGEV/FL, 1915, box 95, file 314, "Córdoba," meeting at exchurch San Sebastián, December 2, 1915. Ulloa, *Veracruz, capital de la nación*, 153.

33. AMC, box 347 (1916), file 6, "Leyes y Decretos," Ana R. Herrera (secretary general) and Inez Olasy (secretary of internal affairs) to President of the Junta de Administración Civil, March 27, 1916. On the serious inflation, see Ulloa, *Veracruz, capital de la nación*, 93–96; and Juárez Martínez, "Especulación y crisis en el centro de Veracruz, 1915."

34. Rural day workers sometimes wrote their petitions in terms of consumption issues. They asked for the one-peso daily rural wage, which was stipulated in the labor law, because basic food prices were too high (AGEV/F/AL, 1915, box 83, file 476.1, Juan Hernández to Governor, April 14, 1915).

35. Lear, *Workers, Neighbors, and Citizens*, 225, 307–9, 331–39.

36. In 1916 the Sindicato de Cortadores y Escogedoras de Café of Huatusco, with the assistance of Agustín G. Arrazola, secretary general of the CSORM, presented a queja for eight workers who had been suspended from their work without proper notification. They asked for compensation of four pesos, or the equivalent of the piece-rate for harvesting forty kilos of coffee in one day. (Córdova Santamaría, *Café y sociedad en Huatusco, Veracruz*, 347–48).

37. AMC, box 347 (1916), file 6, Ana Herrera and Inez Olasy to Ayuntamiento de Córdoba, November 18, 1916.

38. AGEV/F/AL, box 83, file 476, "Jalapa," Faustina Portilla (secretary general) to Mateo Rodríguez, November 2, 1915; and AGEV/F/AL, box 83, file 476, "Jalapa," Faustina Portilla (secretary general) to José Pineiro (treasurer-manager), November 2, 1915.

39. AGEV/F/AL, box 83, file 476, "Jalapa."

40. AGEV/F/AL, box 83, file 476, "Jalapa," Juan Barcena (cashier), Pan Mexican Coffee Company (Importers and Exporters of Coffee, Buyers of Coffee and Beef) to Sindicato de Escogedoras de Café, November 3, 1915.

41. AGEV/F/AL, box 83, file 476, "Jalapa," Cándido Aguilar (Veracruz) to General Adalberto Palacios (Jalapa), November 17, 1915; AGEV/F/AL, box 83, file 476, "Jalapa," Provisional Minister of Government to Mateo Rodríguez, November 24, 1915; and AGEV/F/AL, box 83, file 476, "Jalapa," Provisional Minister of Government to Mateo Rodríguez, November 25, 1915.

42. AGEV/F/AL, box 83, file 476, "Jalapa," José Pineiro to General Agustin Millán (provisional governor and military commander of Veracruz), November 19, 1915.

43. AGEV/F/AL, box 83, file 476, "Jalapa," agreement signed in the offices of the labor inspector, Mateo Rodríguez, between José Pineiro, Miguel Mondragón (representative of A. Salvitano), Angel Contreras (representative of M. and F. Vignola), and six union leaders, December 14, 1915.

44. Smith, *Gender and the Mexican Revolution*, 178.

45. Delgado Rannauro, "El Sindicato de Santa Rosa," 24–41; García Díaz, *Textiles del Valle de Orizaba*, 65–202; and Gómez-Galvarriato Freer, "Impact of the Revolution," 264–80.

46. Ulloa, *Veracruz, capital de la nación*, 157.

47. Veracruz, *Ley del Trabajo*; Bortz, *Revolution within the Revolution*, 42–46; Clark, *Organized Labor in Mexico*, 52; and Corzo Ramírez, González Sierra, and Skerritt Gardner, . . . *nunca un desleal*, 214, 222.

48. John Womack Jr., e-mail correspondence with author, September 10, 2001.

49. AGEV/JCCA/S, 1918, box 3, file 50, Federación Sindicalista de Orizaba

to Municipal President, March 19, 1918. Article 72 refers to the patrons' financial and social responsibilities toward their domestic laborers. Article 99 lists the reasons why an employee could refuse to work (Veracruz, *Ley del Trabajo*, 815, 823).

50. AGEV/JCCA/S, 1918, box 3, file 50, contract between Lemaistre Bros. and Sindicato de Obreras del Desmanche de Café, May, 27, 1918.

51. AGEV/JCCA/S, 1918, box 3, file 50, Trinidad Hernández (secretary general of the Coffee Sorters Union) to Municipal President, July 8, 1918.

52. AGEV/JCCA/S, 1918, box 3, file 50, meeting of Junta Municipal de Conciliación, August 29, 1918. See Article 33, paragraph 7 of Veracruz, *Ley del Trabajo*, 807.

53. AGEV/JCCA/S, 1918, box 3, file 50, Ernesto de la Fuente to JCCA, September 10, 1918.

54. AGEV/JCCA/S, 1918, box 3, file 50, M. Emy to JCCA, September 16, 1918.

55. AGEV/JCCA/S, 1918, box 3, file 50, resolution of the JCCA, September 30, 1918. See Article 33, paragraph 4 of Veracruz, *Ley del Trabajo*, 807.

56. In 1919 the women corn mill workers (*molineras*) unions in various Central Veracruz cities filed a large number of grievances with the JCCA. See Fowler-Salamini, "La movilización obrera veracruzana y la cuestión de género (1915 a 1919)."

57. Article 33 was never fully implemented due to the industrialists' adamant opposition to it. During the 1920s, companies challenged its constitutionality in the courts and won.

58. Delgado Rannauro, "El Sindicato de Santa Rosa," 41–43; Domínguez Pérez, *Política y movimientos sociales en el tejedismo*, 19–20; and Falcón and García Morales, *La semilla en el surco*, 135, 234, 237.

59. Bortz is the most insistent in emphasizing worker agency: "In the absence of a central government, the workers defeated the owners, imposed unions, a new labor regime, and ultimately union control over the workplace. It was a social revolution from below" (*Revolution within the Revolution*, 3). See also García Díaz, "Sindicalismo textil orizabeño," 174, 178; Gómez-Galvarriato Freer, "Impact of the Revolution," 305–6; and Behrens, *Ein Laboratorium der Revolution*, 115–21.

60. Falcón and García Morales, *La semilla en el surco*, 234.

61. Falcón and García Morales, *La semilla en el surco*, 238; and Norvell, "Los ciudadanos sindicalistas," 97.

62. Agetro [Rafael García] called 1923 the most agitated and tragically misguided period in the port's labor history (*Las luchas proletarias en Veracruz*, 184–85). See also Norvell, "Los ciudadanos sindicalistas."

63. Fowler, "Orígenes laborales de la organización campesina en Veracruz," 254–55; and Wood, *Revolution in the Street*, 119–31, 175.

64. Delgado Rannauro, "El Sindicato de Santa Rosa," 42–44; Domínguez Pérez, "Historia de una lucha," 20–56; Falcón and García Morales, *La semilla en el surco*, 135–37; Agetro, *Las luchas proletarias en Veracruz*, 184–85; and Norvell, "Syndicalism and Citizenship."

65. "Informe que rinde el Ejecutivo libre y soberano de Veracruz-Llave ante la H. Legislatura del mismo por el período comprendido del 16 de octubre de 1920 al 5 de mayo de 1921 (Adalberto Tejeda)," 105439.

66. For Garrido Canabal, see Martínez Assad, *El laboratorio de la revolución*, 178–86. For Mújica and Cárdenas, see Embriz Osorio, *La Liga de Comunidades y Sindicatos Agraristas del Estado de Michoacán*, 119–24; and Olcott, *Revolutionary Women in Postrevolutionary Mexico*, 72–73. For Carrillo Puerto, see Joseph, *Revolution from Without*, 217–19; Macías, *Against All Odds*, 90–91, 95–100; and Smith, *Gender and the Mexican Revolution*, 47–51, 176–77. For Zuno, see Fernández-Aceves, "Struggle between the *Metate* and the *Molino de Nixtamal* in Guadalajara, 1920–1940," 148–51.

67. AGEV/JCCA/D, 1919, box 3, file 34, "Laudo en favor de la Cía contra la huelga de Molineras, September 17, 1919"; and Bolio Trejo, *Rebelión de mujeres*.

68. Wood, "'Proletarian Women Will Make the Social Revolution,'" 151–64; and Norvell, "Los ciudadanos sindicalistas," 67, 72–73.

69. Wood, *Revolution in the Street*, 115–24.

70. When oil workers went out on strike in the Huasteca in 1925, the governor supported the workers in direct opposition to the secretary general of the CROM and the minister of industry, commerce, and labor, Luis Morones. The ensuing strikes and work stoppages throughout the state led to federal intervention to mediate the dispute, the ascendency of the CROM, and the eventual overthrow of Governor Jara. The hegemony of the CROM in the Valley of Orizaba was never

seriously challenged again (Domínguez Pérez, *Política y movimientos sociales en el tejedismo*, 72–73; Carr, *El movimiento obrero y la política en México*, 2:23–24, 81–82; Delgado Rannauro, "El Sindicato de Santa Rosa," 135–43; and García Díaz, "El sindicalismo textil orizabeño," 181). Miguel Angel Velasco Muñoz recognized that the PCM had made a bad mistake by withdrawing its support of Governor Jara because it was following Soviet directives (Velasco Muñoz, interview).

71. AGEV/F/AL, 1923, box 43, file 520, "Sindicato de Inquilinos," Governor Tejeda to Attorney General, March 20, 1923; AGEV/F/AL, 1923, box 43, file 590, "Sindicato de Inquilinos," Governor Tejeda to Attorney General, April 17, 1923; Calvo Cruz, "Historia social de Córdoba, Veracruz," 65–70, 79–83, 94–95; Wood, *Revolution in the Street*, 94–95; and Hernández Rojas, interview.

72. AMC, box 376 (1923), file 1, "Sindicatos."

73. AGEV/JCCA/S, 1932, box 546, file 18, "Acta de Fundación, 6 de febrero, 1925"; AMC, box 380 (1925), file "Junta de Conciliación de Arbitraje"; Calvo Cruz, "Historia social de Córdoba, Veracruz," 90; and Hernández Rojas, interview. When the Veracruz tortilla makers joined the CGT in 1923, they embraced the feminist motto in their banners, "Por los derechos de la mujer" (Norvell, "Syndicalism and Citizenship," 114).

74. The Sindicato de "Unión y Progreso" de Obreros Escogedoras de Café in Xalapa was organized in 1922 and obtained a collective contract in 1924 (AGEV/JCCA/S, 1923, box 33, file 3; and AGEV/DTPS, 1924, box 7, file "Inspector Apolinar Espino"). Tanus formed a white union in 1923 to block it ("Informe de las Escogedoras de café al Presidente de la República, 17 de febrero, 1923," in *Boletin del Archivo General de la Nación* 3, no. 9 [July–September 1979]: 17–19, taken from AGN/DT, information, 1923).

75. AGN/DT, 1925, box 389, file 1, "Conflictos," Desmanchadoras Libres to Minister of Industry, Commerce, and Labor, August 27, 1925; and AGEV/DTPS, 1926, box 13, file "Inspector Jesús Trejo," Jesús Trejo to Department of Labor, November 8, 1926.

76. AGEV/NCI, file 32, notary public no. 2 (León Sánchez Arévalo), collective contract with the Arbuckles and with Hard and Rand, November 25, 1926.

77. AGEV/DTPS, 1927, box 21, file 111, Jesús Trejo to Department of Labor,

January 24, 1927; AGEV/DTPS, 1927, box 21, file 111, Luz Vera (secretary general) to Governor Abel Rodríguez, October 19, 1927; AGEV/DTPS, 1927, box 21, file 111, Luz Vera (secretary general) to Governor Abel Rodríguez, November 8, 1927; AGEV/DTPS, 1927, box 21, file 111, Municipal President to Governor, November 14, 1927; AGN/G, 12-A, file 4,2.331.4 (26), flyer of FSOCC, December 30, 1926; AGN/G, 12-A, file 4,2.331.4 (26), Virginia Sanchez (secretary general) to Tejeda (minister of internal affairs), January 22, 1927; and AGN/DT, 1927, box 1160, file 12. The Arbuckle Brothers contract is mentioned in AGEV/NCI, box 38, notary no. 3 (Heriberto Román), collective contract between beneficiadores and escogedoras, October 11, 1927.

78. AGEV/JCCA/S, 1931, box 796, file 4, "Sindicato Industrial"; AGEV/JCCA/S, 1931, box 796, file 4, meeting of the Unión Sindical de Trabajadores y Similares en General de las Casas Beneficiadores de Café y Tabaco de la Región de Córdoba, October 25, 1931; and AGEV/JCCA/S, 1931, box 796, file 4, collective contract, November 1931.

79. Sheridan Prieto, *Mujer obrera y organización sindical*, 23–31, 44–45.

80. "Feminismo," *Pro-Paria*, June 19, 1921, and July 18, 1922.

81. Porter, *Working Women in Mexico City*, 109; AGEV/JCCA/S, 1922, box 25, file 9, statutes of the Sindicato de Campesinos, Hacienda de Tuzamapan (CROM).

82. AMC, box 395 (1929), file "Sindicatos."

83. Delgado Rannauro, "El Sindicato de Santa Rosa," 144.

84. AGEV/DPTS, 1930, box 29, meeting of the Sindicato de Desmanchadores de Córdoba, March 1, 1930; and AGEV/DPTS, 1930, box 29, file "Sindicato de Desmanchadores de Córdoba," María Pura Herrera to Governor Tejeda, March 6, 1930.

85. AGEV/DPTS, 1930, box 29, file "Sindicato de Desmanchadores de Córdoba," José Oropeza to Department of Labor, March 8, 1930. The social fund was taking in at least five thousand pesos a year. If each of the seven hundred permanent workers was removing approximately seven kilos of waste each day and contributing one centavo per kilo, this meant that forty-nine pesos a day were sent to the social fund. If sorters worked twenty-seven days a month over four months, this added up to approximately five thousand pesos.

86. AGEV/DPTS, 1930, box 29, file "Sindicato de Desmanchadores de Cór-

doba," Alfonso Torres Silva (secretary general FROC) to Tejeda, March 12, 1930; and AGEV/DPTS, 1930, box 29, file "Sindicato de Desmanchadores de Córdoba," Secretary of Internal Affairs (FROC) to Secretary General of SDC, March 10, 1930.

87. AGEV/DPTS, 1930, box 29, file "Sindicato de Desmanchadores de Córdoba," executive committee's draft of modification of external relations between the union and the federation, March 14, 1930.

88. Porter, *Working Women in Mexico City*, xviii.

89. The Veracruz branch of the PCM emerged out of the Antorcha Libertaria group in the port in 1919. It was led by Úrsulo Galván, Manuel Almanza, Herón Proal, and Manuel Díaz Ramírez. After the decline of the Syndicate of Tenants, Galván and Almanza turned to organizing the peasantry and concentrated their attention on the formation of the Peasant League. The PCM had a strong influence over the Peasant League in its early years (Fowler-Salamini, *Agrarian Radicalism in Veracruz*, 29–33, 49–50).

90. *El Dictamen*, January 21, 1925, and March 2, 1925. Heather Fowler, "Orígenes laborales de la organización campesina en Veracruz," 235–64. Hernández Rojas, interview.

91. AGEV/F/AL, 1927, box 95, file "Sindicatos," report on Veracruz unions; and Fowler-Salamini, *Agrarian Radicalism in Veracruz*, 60.

92. AGEV/DTPS, 1930, box 30, file "La Peñuela," Ramona Martínez (secretary general of the SDC and the Peñuela union) to Tejeda, September 25, 1930; AGEV/DTPS, 1930, box 30, file "La Peñuela," Ramona Martínez to Tejeda, October 2, 1930; and AGEV/DTPS, 1930, box 30, file "La Peñuela," Ramona Martínez to Tejeda, October 17, 1930.

4. Caciquismo, Organized Labor, and Gender

1. For studies on Native American women's cacicazgos during the preconquest and colonial periods, see Silverblatt, *Moon, Sun, and Witches*; and Kellogg, *Weaving the Past*.

2. Knight, "*Caciquismo* in Twentieth-Century Mexico," 13.

3. Friedrich, "Mexican Cacicazgo," 192–94; Friedrich, *Agrarian Revolt in a Mexican Village*, 78–89; Guillermo de la Peña, "Poder local, poder regional," 39; Salmerón Castro, "Caciquismo"; and Joseph, "Caciquismo and the Revolution," 209.

4. Knight, "*Caciquismo* in Twentieth-Century Mexico," 18; Guillermo de la Peña, "Poder local, poder regional," 32; Joseph, "Caciquismo and the Revolution," 198; and Falcón, *Revolución y caciquismo*, 175–222. All these authors analyze male caciquismo. For the purposes of this discussion, I have used the pronoun "they" to refer to caciques in general.

5. See in particular the essay collection edited by Knight and Pansters, *Caciquismo in Twentieth-Century Mexico*. Buve, "Caciquismo, un principio de ejercicio de poder a lo largo de varios siglos," 36–37.

6. Buve, "Caciquismo, un principio de ejercicio de poder a lo largo de varios siglos," 39. For a discussion of a cacique who failed to adapt, see Fowler-Salamini, "Caciquismo and the Mexican Revolution."

7. Pansters, "Building a *Cacicazgo*," 299. See also Hernández Rodríguez, "Challenging *Caciquismo*." Enrique Guerra Manzo points out the limits of traditional caciquismo and suggests that a distinction should be made between the informal brokering of prerevolutionary caciquismo and formal brokering of the postrevolutionary period, in *Caciquismo y orden público en Michoacán, 1920–1940*, 245–81.

8. Pansters, "Building a *Cacicazgo*," 299.

9. Hernández Rodríguez, "Challenging *Caciquismo*," 251–54; and Pansters, "Goodbye to the Caciques?" 354.

10. I would like to thank Wil Pansters for his suggestion to link caciquismo and gender in this way.

11. Rubin, *Decentering the Regime*, 261. Cited also by Pansters, "Goodbye to the Caciques?" 363–64.

12. Fernández-Aceves, "En-gendering *Caciquismo*," 205; James, *Doña María's Story*, 220; Levenson-Estrada, "Loneliness of Working-Class Feminism"; Alegre, "Las Rieleras," 166–67.

13. Chassen-López, "Patron of Progress."

14. Womack, *Zapata and the Mexican Revolution*, 170; Rocha, *El album de la mujer*, 82–83; Reséndez Fuentes, "Battleground Women"; and Cano, "When Gender Can't Be Seen."

15. Fernández-Aceves, "En-gendering *Caciquismo*," 202.

16. Fernández-Aceves, "En-gendering *Caciquismo*," 202, 208–14, 224. See also Fernández-Aceves, "Advocate, or *Cacica*?"

17. Pansters, "Building a *Cacicazgo*," 302–3.

18. The population of the municipality of Córdoba was approximately thirty thousand in 1930 and 1940. Dirección General de Estadística, *Sexto Censo de Población, 1940, Veracruz*, 80.

19. Samuel Vargas Reyes, the Santa Rosa textile leader, served simultaneously as secretary of interior of the CSOCO and secretary general of the Sindicato "Emancipación" in 1932 (Delgado Rannauro, "El Sindicato de Santa Rosa," 257). In 1938–39 Miguel Gutiérrez and Tomás Torreblanca were the secretary generals of the Orizaba sorter union. AGEV/JCCA/S, 1938, box 540, file 524; and AGN/LCR 4323/54.

20. Sheridan Prieto, *Mujer obrera y organización sindical*, 47.

21. Knight, "*Caciquismo* in Twentieth-Century Mexico," 37. Joseph discusses dual or troika cocacicazgos, where leaders have "different functional spheres" ("Caciquismo and the Revolution," 198).

22. Maldonado Aranda, "Between Law and Arbitrariness," 227.

23. Maldonado Aranda, "Between Law and Arbitrariness," 230.

24. Crider, "Material Struggles," 150–55; and Fernández-Aceves, "En-gendering *Caciquismo*," 215–21.

25. AGEV/JCCA/S, 1931, box 546, file 18, meetings, June 15, 1937, December 14, 1937, June 21, 1938, December 13, 1938, and January 7, 1942.

26. Siriaco García, interview, July 3, 2001.

27. AGEV/JCCA/S, 1931, box 546, file 18, meetings, June 21, 1938, December 13, 1938, June 20, 1939, and July 2, 1940; and Romero Serrano, interview.

28. For the struggle between Calles and Morones, see Córdova, *En una época de crisis*, 14–43.

29. The CTM was supporting the radical candidate Manlio Fabio Altamirano in 1936, when women were given the right to vote in primary elections for the first time (AGEV/JCCA/D, 1936, box 524, file 103, "Sindicato de Obreras Desmanchadoras del Café, (Coatepec).")

30. AGEV/JCCA/S, 1931, box 546, file 18, meeting, December 13, 1938; and Siriaco García, interview, June 3, 2007.

31. Siriaco García, interviews, June 6, 2000, and June 3, 2007.

32. Guillermo de la Peña, "Poder local, poder regional," 35; and Fernández-Aceves, "En-gendering *Caciquismo*," 200–202.

33. Crider, "Material Struggles," 153–55; Fernández-Aceves, "En-gendering *Caciquismo*," 214–21; and Gauss, "Working-Class Masculinity and Rationalized Sex," 186–87.

34. López Osorio, interview; and Hernández, interview.

35. Gabriela Cano has suggested that women can masculinize themselves in a form of strategic transvestitism as "a pragmatic desire to enjoy the social advantages of men." For instance, Amelia/Amelio Robles wanted to challenge the female identity assigned to her at birth and to become masculine in every aspect of life (Cano, "When Gender Can't Be Seen," 37).

36. Inés Reyes Ochoa's life history is based on interviews by the author with her daughter, Socorro Gómez Reyes, and her son, Lino Alejandro Gómez Reyes.

37. Hernández, interview. "No tenía pelos en la lengua para comunicar."

38. For the patron-client system developed by the Atlixco caciques, see Crider, "Material Struggles," 8, 51–106.

39. AGN/ALR 561.8/13, Sindicato de las Obreras Escogedoras de Café to Abelardo Rodriguez, March 6 1933, printed in *Boletín del Archivo General de la Nación, México* 3, no. 9 (July–September 1979): 19–23; and AGEV/JCCA/S, 1931, box 546, file 18, meetings, June 15, 1937, and December 13, 1937.

40. Lino Alejandro Gómez Reyes, interviews, May 13, 1999, and July 19, 1999; and APIRO, purchase, lot no. 34, Colonia Miguel Hidalgo, 1936.

41. Siriaco García, interview, June 7, 2000.

42. In the APIRO there are many photographs of SOECC celebrations honoring Eucario León. León often recruited Córdoba sorters to go to Orizaba and Oaxaca to participate in pro-CROM rallies (Siriaco García, interview, June 3, 2007).

43. Maldonado Aranda, "Between Law and Arbitrariness," 231. Kevin Middlebrook argues that Articles 43, 49, and 111, which guaranteed to the officially recognized unions the right to negotiate a contract and to use the closed shop, became a form of "legal subsidy" granted by the state. Union leaders employed these provisions to their advantage to consolidate their control over their members (Middlebrook, *Paradox of Revolution*, 95–97).

44. Pansters, "Building a *Cacicazgo*," 304.

45. Levenson-Estrada shows how Guatemalan women's militancy was not simply an extension of their gender identity as mothers, wives, and daughters or of politics based on their femaleness. Class-conscious

trade unionism, usually associated with masculinity, could generate gender specific grievances (Levenson-Estrada, "Loneliness of Working-Class Feminism," 216–17).

46. Gutmann, *Meanings of Macho*, 257; and Levenson-Estrada, "Loneliness of Working-Class Feminism," 221–22. Nancy Hewitt uses the term "virile unionism" to distinguish between manliness and masculinity. In the case of the Tampa women tobacco workers, "virile unionism" embraced broad-based community support, nonviolent militancy, and decentralized leadership (Hewitt, "'Voice of Virile Labor,'" 151).

47. Women workers have a long tradition of militant activism. Cigarette workers in 1887 and seamstresses in 1912 walked off their jobs, stationed workers at plant doors, and resorted to violent tactics to improve their salaries (Porter, *Working Women in Mexico City*, 106–9; and Porter, "In the Shadow of Industrialization," 189–99).

48. AMC, box 408 (1932), file 1d, circular of José García (secretary general of the Peasant League) to all municipal presidents, June 21, 1932; and AMC, box 408 (1932), file 1, Mauro L. Colina (delegate of the Regional League) to Eduardo Valverde, December 14, 1932.

49. Sheridan Prieto, *Mujer obrera y organización syndical*, 100–102.

50. AGEV/JCCA/S, 1931, box 546, file 18, meeting, January 24, 1932.

51. Articles 49 and 234 of the 1931 Labor Code call the exclusion clause legal but not obligatory, but unions insisted on its inclusion in all collective contracts in Veracruz and Tamaulipas from the 1920s (Middlebrook, *Paradox of Revolution*, 96–97; and Córdova, *En una época de crisis*, 114).

52. *El Dictamen*, February 2, 4, and 7, 1932; AMC, box 411 (1932), file "Sindicatos y Uniones," Tejeda to Valverde, February 4, 1932 (telegram); and AGEV/JCCA/S, 1933, box 773, unnumbered file, report of the Labor Department to Provisional Governor Francisco Salcedo Casas, February 6, 1933.

53. "En Córdoba las escogedoras de café libraron ruda pelea," *El Dictamen*, February 13 and 14, 1932; and AMC, box 411 (1932), file "Sindicatos y Uniones," Subsecretary of Internal Affairs to Municipal President, February 16, 1932.

54. AGEV/JCCA/S, 1933, unnumbered file, provisional governor's report

sent to Abelardo Rodriguez, February 6, 1933; and *El Dictamen*, February 24, 1932.

55. AMC, box 408 (1932), file 1, circular of José García to all municipal presidents, July 21, 1932; AMC, box 408 (1932), file 1, José García to Eduardo Valverde, November 23, 1932; AMC, box 410 (1932), file "Ayuntamiento y Junta Municipal de Conciliación," letterhead of regional delegation of the League of Agrarian Communities and the Úrsulo Galván Social Center, November 2, 1932; AMC, box 411 (1932), file "Sindicatos y Uniones," Rosendo Pérez to Valverde, February 17, 1932.

56. Fowler-Salamini, *Agrarian Radicalism in Veracruz*, 108–25; and Falcón and García Morales, *La semilla en el surco*, 318–37.

57. AGEV/JCCA, 1933, box 773, unnumbered file, Carmen Hernández (president of Majority Group) to Salcedo Casas, December 26, 1932.

58. AGN/ALR, 561.8/13, Luz Vera (secretary general) to President, December 28, 1932; and AGN/ALR, 561.8/13, Salcedo Casas to President, February 6, 1933. See also "Condiciones laborales y de la vida de las mujeres trabajadoras," 19–21.

59. AGEV/JCCA/S, 1933, box 773, unnumbered file, Carmen Hernández, letter to the editor, *El Globo* (Veracruz), January 26, 1933; AGEV/JCCA/S, 1933, box 101, file 66, Eduardo Valverde and Odilón Zorrilla to JCCA (telegram), February 3, 1933; *El Dictamen*, February 3, 1933; and AGN/ALR, 5611.8/13, CROM and Secretary General of Sorters Union to President, February 3, 1933.

60. AGEV/JCCA/S, 1933, box 101, file 66, Córdoba Chamber of Commerce to JCCA (telegram), February 3, 1933.

61. AGEV/JCCA/S, 1933, box 773, unnumbered file, report of Santiago Mota Barrientos to Provisional Governor, February 8, 1933; AGEV/JCCA/S, box 101, file 66, Ramona Martínez to Enrique César Jr. (municipal president) (telegram), February 4, 1933; and AGEV/JCCA/S, box 101, file 66, Isauro González to JCCA (telegram), February 4, 1933.

62. AGEV/JCCA/S, 1933, box 773, unnumbered file, report of Santiago Mota Barrientos, February 8, 1933; AGEV/JCCA/S, 1933, box 101, file 66, Gonzálo Vázquez Vela to JCCA, agreement, March 6, 1933; and AGN/ALR, 561.8/13, Salcedo Casas to President, February 8, 1933.

63. AMC, box 419 (1934), file 2, "Agrupaciones Obreras," CROM circular, December 5, 1933.

64. Elias, "Theoretical Essay on Established and Outsider Relations," xviii.

65. AGEV/JCCA/S, 1931, box 546, file 18, results of the SOECC election, July 15, 1933. Although the Tejedistas never won control of the SOECC, they continued to control some sorter unions in Xalapa, Córdoba, Peñuela, and Huatusco until 1938 through the Confederación Regional de Obreros y Campesinos, "Úrsulo Galván" (AGEV/JCCA/S, 1938, box 102, file 2).

66. Tinsman, Politics of Gender, Sexuality, and Labor in the Chilean Agrarian Reform, 272.

67. Jocelyn Olcott maintains that these kinds of actions by women militants were forms of "revolutionary citizenship" (Revolutionary Women in Postrevolutionary Mexico, 6–7).

68. Torres was a member of the executive committee of the FSOCC as early as 1927 (AGEV/DTPS, 1927, box 19, file 83; and AGEV/JCCA/S, 1931, box 796, file 4, "Sindicato Industrial de Trabajadores, Córdoba").

69. AGEV/JCCA/S, 1931, box 796, file 4, "Sindicato Industrial de Trabajadores, Córdoba"; AMC, box 415 (1933), file 49.2-3, "Organizaciones Obreras Locales"; AGEV/GyJ, 1934, box 1145, file "Union Sindical," Luz Vera to Governor, January 18, 1934.

70. AGEV/JCCA/S, 1934, box 65, file 81, "Contratos."

71. AGEV/JCCA/S, 1934, box 65, file 81, "Contratos"; AMC, box 419 (1934), file 2, "Agrupaciones Obreras"; AGEV/GyJ, 1935, box 1179, file 1, "Paros. Cargadores de Café, Córdoba"; and AMC, box 430 (1935), file 1, "Conciliación."

72. AGEV/ACG, 1936, box 236, file 524-46, Sofía Castro to Cafés Mexicanos, December 7, 1936; AGEV/ACG, 1937, box 397, file 524-74; and AGEV/JCCA/S, 1931, box 790, file "Sindicato Industrial."

73. AGEV/ACG, 1936, box 240, file 524-45, contract, November 23, 1936. For a discussion of Lombardista organizing campaigns, see Arturo Anguiano, El estado y la política obrera del cardenismo, 58–65.

74. El Dictamen, June 30, 1938; AGEV/ACG, 1938, box 661, file "Huatusco," "Estatutos del Sindicato de Trabajadores en General de la Industria del Café en el Estado de Veracruz (CTM)" (Xalapa-Enríquez, 1938); and AGEV/JCCA, 1931, box 796, file 4, "Sindicato Industrial de Trabajadores, Córdoba," CROM membership list, November 1938.

75. AGN/LCR, 432.3/54, file "Beneficiadores de Café," Provisional Governor Fernando Casas Alemán to Godofredo E. Beltrán, January 21, 1938; AGN/LCR, 432.3/54, file "Beneficiadores de Café," Córdoba Chamber of Commerce to President, January 13, 1939; AGN/LCR, 432.3/54, file "Beneficiadores de Café," Luz Vera to President, September 9, 1939; and *El Dictamen*, January 18, 1938, and January 12, 1939.

76. Sheridan Prieto, *Mujer obrera y organización syndical*, 103–11.

77. Clark, *Organized Labor in Mexico*, 231; and Córdova, *En una época de crisis*, 96–110.

78. Middlebrook, *Paradox of Revolution*, 56.

79. Clark, *Organized Labor in Mexico*, 242–59; and Middlebrook, *Paradox of Revolution*, 56–58.

80. Jorge Frankenburger lowered the piece-rate wage from thirty to twenty-five centavos per kilo of mancha in his 1935 contract with the Tejedista union (AGEV/DTPS, 1932–35, box 3, file 524-7, contracts, December 27, 1932, and April 13, 1935).

81. "Informe del Lic. Miguel Alemán a la XXXVI Legislatura de Veracruz, septiembre 16 de 1937," 126625.

82. Ashby, *Organized Labor and the Mexican Revolution*, 98–99; León and Marván, *En el cardenismo*, 199–237.

83. See Article 26 of Secretaría de Industria, Comercio y Trabajo, *Ley Federal del Trabajo*, 7–8.

84. The dispute was still continuing two years later in the same workshop. Sorter-leader Belem Carmona articulated well the mentality of the sorters toward the exporters: "Este dinero es el sudor de los trabajadores que en el taller y como elementos de producción hagotamos nuestra energía física y en la conclución del concurso de la vida quedamos conbertidos en vagazos humanos mientras la burocracia confuvulada con el Capital se dan modica presiada la vida en Casinos y Manciones arrobatadas a la miseria de los Trabajadores que como antes desinos quedamos convertidos en impotentos espectros humanos" (AGEV/JCCA/D, 1934, box 128, file 175; and AGEV/JCCA/D, 1936, box 172, file 48, Belem Carmona to JCCA, November 26, 1936; spelling consistent with the original).

85. Article 35 stipulates that a change of ownership does not affect the existence of the contract. Article 36 stipulates that in cases of bankrupt-

cy, liquidations, embargos, or changing ownership, the owner is obligated to pay the workers who are still employed within one month of transaction.

86. AGEV/ACG, 1937, box 397, file 524-74, Eufrosina Moya et al. to Miguel Alemán and Eduardo Sánchez (chief of the Labor Department), January 28, 1937; AGEV/ACG, 1937, box 397, file 524-74, Eufrosina Moya et al. to Miguel Alemán and Eduardo Sánchez (chief of the Labor Department), April 5, 1937; AGEV/ACG, 1940, box 762, file 524-94, Sorters Union to Fernando Casas Alemán, March 10, 1940; and AGEV/ACG, 1940, box 762, file 524-94, Joaquin Gómez (secretary general of the FSOCC) to Governor, March 14, 1940.

87. Article 57 stipulates that when judicial liquidation occurs, workers are entitled to one month's salary. In the case of the closure of a firm, the company is obligated to pay three months' salary compensation.

88. AGEV/JCCA/D, 1933, box 19, file 8, "Córdoba," Abundio Torres, Procurador del Trabajo del Estado, to JCCA, February 13, 1933. The men's complaint, which is similar, is found in the same file.

89. AGEV/ACG, 1935, box 53, file 524-166, Apolinar Espino (Dept. of Economy) to Ernesto Sierra (subsecretary of interior), August 26, 1935; and AGEV/ACG, 1935, box 53, file 524-166, meeting in Beneficiadora (signed by Inés Reyes), November 6, 1935.

90. AGEV/ACG, 1938, box 539, file 524-119, meeting of Junta Municipal de Conciliación de Córdoba, August 6, 1938. For the men's complaint of the same practice, see AGEV/ACG, 1939, box 663, file 524-47.

Ricardo Regules would hire nonunion or white union workers and pay them lower salaries in Huatusco. The coffee sorter union, the Sindicato Pro-Ursulo Galván (Pro-Úrsulo Galván Union) protested against this labor policy, but Regules did not desist. In Xalapa, Rosaura de Fernández, owner of the hacienda Las Animas, followed a similar strategy. Since the sorter unions were organized workshop by workshop, they could put up little resistance. To add insult to injury, the Fernández collective contracts permitted the shipping of unsorted coffee out of the region (AGEV/JCCA/S, 1934, box 64, file 19, "Sindicato de Cortadoras"; AGN/LCR, 432.3/246, Ricardo Regules to President, May 11, 1937; and AGEV/ACG, 1936, box 236, file 524-65, "Sindicato Unico [Xalapa]").

91. AGEV/ACG, 1938, box 539, file 524-112, meetings of Junta Municipal de Conciliación de Córdoba, July 21, 1938, and August 5, 1938.

92. AGEV/ACG, 1940, box 762, file 524-94, "Sindicato de Obreras Escogedoras."

93. A Xalapa 1924 contract had a different type of pay scale to avoid unfair wages. It called for ten centavos for every 100–159 grams of waste removed and forty-five centavos for 1,800 to 3,000 grams of cleaned coffee (AGEV/DTPS, 1924, box 7, file "Apolinar Espino," agreement, April 29, 1924).

94. While the SOECC did not file any complaints for sickness compensation during the 1930s, Belem Carmona and Juana Suchil did in Coatepec in 1939. The law required medical exams for all permanent workers before they entered the factory after the 1938–39 harvest. When Carmona asked for medical compensation for pulmonary problems, Julia E. de Donde, coffee producer and exporter, accused her of having unprotected sex and venereal disease in order to deny her benefits (AGEV/ACG, 1940, box 762, file 524-90, "Coatepec").

95. AGEV/ACG, 1940, box 762, file 524-94, "Sindicato de Obreras Escogedoras, Córdoba."

96. AGEV/ACG, 1940, box 762, file 524-94, "Sindicato de Obreras Escogedoras, Córdoba," SOECC to Beneficiadores, April 20, 1940; and AGEV/ACG, 1940, box 762, file 524-94, "Sindicato de Obreras Escogedoras, Córdoba," Concepción Rodríguez to Bernardo Miranda, May 20, 1940.

97. RPPPCC, sales, no. 183, Carlos Nuñez to Sorters Union, July 11, 1939; AGEV/JCCA, 1931, box 547, file 18, "Notario León Sánchez Arévalo," sale of June 12, 1939; and Siriaco García, interview, June 28, 2005.

98. Colombian Communists and union activists mobilized sorters to carry out work stoppages to demand better salaries in the late 1930s; however, the sorters never were able to win collective contracts (Bergquist, *Labor in Latin America*, 351–54).

5. Everyday Experiences and Obrera Culture

1. De la Fuente, "Relaciones sociales en una ciudad de provincia," 96. The other groups mentioned were lower level railroad workers, loaders, factory and beneficio workers, garment workers, hat-makers, and paper-makers.

2. Lüdtke, "What Is the History of Everyday Life and Who Are Its Practitioners?" 1, 4.

3. Elias, "Apuntes sobre el concepto de lo cotidiano," 340.

4. Elias, "Apuntes sobre el concepto de lo cotidiano," 341–42.

5. Lüdtke, "What Is the History of Everyday Life and Who Are Its Practitioners?" 15–16.

6. Barbieri, *Mujeres y vida cotidiana*, 11.

7. Crane, "Writing the Individual Back into Collective Memory," 1381; and Beezley, *Mexican National Identity*, ix.

8. I located the workers primarily through word of mouth, because so few of them were still alive. The workers themselves were the best source for other potential interviewees. This suggests that they still remained in contact with each other in Córdoba and Coatepec. Local residents also helped me locate sorters in Coatepec and Orizaba.

9. Maria del Carmen Ríos Zavala, interview.

10. Velázquez Ramírez, interview, March 3, 1999.

11. Velázquez Ramírez, interview, March 3, 1999.

12. Siriaco García, interview, July 3, 2001.

13. Siriaco García, interview, July 3, 2001; Delia Ortiz Sarmiento, interviews, March 22, 1999 and May 11, 1999; Salomón and Delia Ortiz Sarmiento, interview, March 23, 1999.

14. Velázquez Ramírez, interview, March 3, 1999.

15. Velázquez Ramírez, interview, May 13, 1999.

16. Gregory Swedberg argues that the state's legalization of divorce and the Civil Code of 1928 opened legal spaces for women to challenge their husband's authority in Orizaba. Since most sorters were not married, they seldom, if ever, took advantage of these legal options (Swedberg, "Divorce and Marital Equality in Orizaba, Mexico, 1915–1940," 132).

17. Maria del Carmen Ríos Zavala, interview.

18. Velázquez Ramírez, interview, March 3, 1999.

19. Delia Ortiz Sarmiento, interview, May 11, 1999; Siriaco García, interview, July 3, 2001; and Velázquez Ramírez, interview, May 13, 1999.

20. Siriaco García, interview, July 3, 2001.

21. Velázquez Ramírez, interview, March 3, 1999.

22. I would like to thank Gilberto Cházaro García for plotting these addresses.

23. Fernández Álvarez, interview.

24. Velázquez Ramírez, interview, March 3, 1999.

25. Velázquez Ramírez, interview, March 3, 1999.

26. Siriaco García, interview, July 3, 2001; and Romero Serrano, interview.

27. Velázquez Ramírez, interview, May 13, 1999; and Maria del Carmen Ríos Zavala, interview.

28. Fernández Alvarez, interview.

29. Peiss, *Cheap Amusements*, 21, 16–21. See also Alegre, "Las Rieleras," 164, 170–71; and Klubock, "Morality and Good Habits," 233, 238.

30. Peiss, *Cheap Amusements*, 23, 26, 32; and Stansell, *City of Women*, 55–56.

31. Enstad, *Ladies of Labor, Girls of Adventure*, 6–7.

32. Porter, *Working Women in Mexico City*, 74–77, 82, 85; and Radkau, *"La Fama" y la vida*, 79.

33. Peiss, *Cheap Amusements*, 89–99; Bergero, *Intersecting Tango*; and Buffington, "La 'Dancing' Mexicana," 87, 89.

34. Flores y Escalante, *Salón México*, 39, 54–55; Wood, *Revolution in the Street*, 5, 9; and Gamboa, *Santa*, 75, 78–79.

35. Buffington, "La 'Dancing' Mexicana," 88. Celeste Fraser Delgado and José Esteban Muñoz also characterize the film *Danzón* as an articulation of the sexuality of a working-class woman in *Everynight Life*, 29–30.

36. Peiss, *Cheap Amusements*, 99.

37. Peiss, *Cheap Amusements*, 110, 112.

38. Porter, *Working Women in Mexico City*, 188; La Fama in Tlalpan put on dances for their mixed-gender workforce in the 1950s (Radkau, *"La Fama" y la vida*, 80); and Snodgrass, "Birth and Consequences of Industrial Paternalism," 124. See Farnsworth-Alvear for other types of paternalistic activities sponsored by the Medellín owners of textile mills ("Talking, Fighting, Flirting," 147).

39. Delia Ortiz Sarmiento, interview, May 11, 1999; and Siriaco García, interview, July 3, 2001.

40. Delia Ortiz Sarmiento, interview, May 11, 1999; APIRO, Libro de Actas del Sindicato Industrial de Obreras Escogedoras de Café y Similares de Córdoba, 1950–55 (henceforth appearing as APIRO/Actas), meet-

ings, February 7, 1950, February 21, 1950, March 28, 1950, April 25, 1950, and September 22, 1953. Coatepec's cacica Amparo Ortiz required all sorters to attend dances in Coatepec in the late 1930s, which was deeply resented. The dances were used to raise money for the CROC building. Afterward, it became a financial business for the leadership (Sheridan Prieto, *Mujer obrera y organización sindical*, 79).

41. Siriaco García, interviews, June 7, 2000, July 3, 2001, and June 28, 2005; Romero Serrano, interview; Limón, interview; and Salazar Báez, interview, July 5, 2003.

42. Siriaco García, interview, July 3, 2001; Velázquez Ramírez, interview, July 19, 1999; Salazar Báez, interview, July 5, 2003; and Limón, interview. In Coatepec, La Puente textile workers and Mahuixtlán coffee and sugar mill workers would ride into town for these Saturday night dances.

43. Romero Serrano, interview; Delia Ortiz Sarmiento, interview, May 11, 1999; and Siriaco García, interviews, June 7, 2000, and June 29, 2005.

44. Siriaco García, interviews, July 3, 2001, and June 29, 2005; and Limón, interview.

45. Siriaco García, interviews, July 3, 2001, and June 29, 2005; and Romero Serrano interview. For Coatepec, AL, July 10, 2001, ESB, July 5, 2003. Robert Alegre found that railway women cared more about the Fiesta de San Matías dances than railway men because it offered them spaces to socialize outside the home ("Las rieleras," 171).

46. Buffington, "La 'Dancing' Mexicana," 91.

47. Peiss, *Cheap Amusements*, 89.

48. Buffington, "La 'Dancing' Mexicana," 95.

49. De Certeau, *Practice of Everyday Life*, xix, 36–37. Cited also by Buffington, "La 'Dancing' Mexicana," 100.

50. Romero Serrano, interview; Siriaco García, interview, June 29, 2005; and Silvia Herrera Luna, interview.

51. Delia Ortiz Sarmiento, interview, May 11, 1999.

52. Peiss, *Cheap Amusements*, 99.

53. Romero Serrano, interview; and Siriaco García, interviews, June 7, 2000, and June 28, 2005.

54. Thomson, "Ceremonial and Political Roles of Village Bands," 319, 325–36.

55. Camarena Ocampo, *Jornaleros, tejedores y obreros*, 143–44.
56. Governor Cándido Aguilar approved a municipal subsidy for the Santa Rosa Sindicato de Obreros Progresistas band. More than likely, this decision was politically motivated to challenge the dominant anarchosyndicalist-controlled union. AGEV/F, 1917, box, 251, file "Banda de Música, Santa Rosa"; and AGEV/DTPS, box 17, report of labor inspector Apolinar Espino to Labor Department, May 16, 1923–September 16, 1923. See also photos in García Díaz, *Los trabajadores del Valle de Orizaba y la Revolución Mexicana*, 102–10.
57. Porter, *Working Women in Mexico City*, 183.
58. Brígida Siriaco, Celia Hernández, and Inés Reyes entered with the first group to gain coveted permanent positions. A second generation entered in 1950, including Estela Velázquez, Isabel Romero, and Elena Serna. During the late 1950s when the amount of work declined, the union leadership moved the band members from the third list to the second list to guarantee them steady work (Siriaco García, interview, June 6, 2000; and Velázquez Ramírez, interview, March 3, 1999).
59. APIRO/Actas, Reglamento de la Banda de Guerra y el Grupo Militarizado, meeting, April 11, 1950; Serna, interview; Hernández de Huerta, interview; Romero Serrano, interview; Velázquez Ramírez, interview, March 3, 1999; and Siriaco García, interviews, June 6, 2000, and June 28, 2005.
60. Velázquez Ramírez, interview, March 3, 1999; Romero Serrano, interview; and Siriaco García, interview, June 28, 2005.
61. Maldonado Aranda, "Between the Law and Arbitrariness," 232.
62. APIRO/Actas, meetings, February 21, 1950, February 13, 1951, September 25, 1951, March 4, 1952, and March 25, 1952.
63. APIRO/Actas, meetings, May 8, 1951, July 17, 1951, March 25, 1952, and September 23, 1952; and Velázquez Ramírez, interview, March 3, 1999.
64. Siriaco García, interview, June 6, 2000; and Velázquez Ramírez, interview, March 3, 1999.
65. Crane, "Writing the Individual Back into Collective Memory," 1381. See also Halwachs, *On Collective Memory*.
66. I want to thank Marco Velázquez for pointing out to me the importance of the band uniform in integrating municipal bands into the respected Mexican military tradition.

67. Vaughan, "Construction of Patriotic Festival in Tecamachalco, Puebla, 1900–1946," 234–35.
68. Antigachupin worker demonstrations on national holidays date back to the nineteenth century (Bortz, *Revolution within the Revolution*, 75). For worker protests, see Gamboa Ojeda, "Inserción, hispanidad e hispanismo entre los empresarios españoles de Puebla (1895–1930)," 125. For women tobacco workers, see Granados, *Debates sobre españa*, 84.
69. González, interview, June 24, 2001.
70. Velázquez Ramírez, interview, July 19, 1999.
71. APIRO/Actas, meetings, September 11, 1951, March 25, 1952, and April 21, 1953.
72. APIRO/Actas, meetings, October 13, 1953, November 24, 1953, and July 5, 1955.
73. Siriaco García, interview, July 3, 2001.
74. Porter, *Working Women in Mexico City*, xvi.
75. Porter, *Working Women in Mexico City*, 60–68, 190. For other Latin American countries see James, *Doña María's Story*, 256–57. See also Guy, *Sex and Danger in Buenos Aires*.
76. Lino Alejandro Gómez Reyes, interview, May 13, 1999.
77. French points out that while Porfirian workers upheld "the distinction between women's duties in the home and men's responsibilities in working for a wage, the ideal of the middle-class marriage was not" (William E. French, *Peaceful and Working People*, 123).
78. Delia Ortiz Sarmiento, interview, May 11, 1999. Her daughter could recite one poem about a wayward father: "Papá, porqué no vienes en una Nochebuena como vienen los Reyes, trayendo cosas buenas? Recuerda que José que es el padre de Jesús jamás en sus dolores hizo esa ingratitud."
79. Siriaco García, interviews, July 3, 2001, and June 28, 2005. Sofía Castro's niece, Sara Torres, played Hidalgo.
80. Gamboa, *Santa*.
81. Chasteen, "Why Read *Santa*?" x; Bliss, *Compromised Positions*, 41–42; and Castillo, *Easy Women*, 41–48.
82. Noriega Hope, *Santa*.
83. Chasteen, "Why Read *Santa*?" ix; and Castillo, "Easy Women," 38.

84. Agustín Lara, "Santa (bolero)," lyrics.time, http://www.lyricstime. com/agust-n-lara-santa-bolero-lyrics.html (accessed July 25, 2012).

85. Coatepec sorters also presented this play (Téxon, interview).

86. Daniel Gier has suggested that Gamboa was laying the blame for Mexico's social ills on the gachupines ("El element español en *Santa, de Federico Gamboa*," 134–42). Chasteen discounts this antigachupin interpretation, arguing quite rightly that Gamboa was very pro-Spanish ("Why Read *Santa?*" xi).

87. James C. Scott, *Domination and the Arts of Resistance*, xiii.

88. Pérez Firmat, "I came, I saw, I Conga'd," 246.

89. Delia Ortiz Sarmiento, interview, May 11, 1999.

90. Chartier, "World Turned Upside-Down," 115.

6. Challenges of Modernization

1. Nolasco, *Café y sociedad en Mexico*, 21, 171–72; and Beaumond, "Élite et changement social," 195–246.

2. Figueroa, interview.

3. FAO, *World Coffee Economy*, 2, 6–7, 20; Ukers, *Ten Years of Coffee Progress*, 5–8, 19; and Bulmer-Thomas, *Political Economy of Central America*, 90–91. According to Stephen Niblo, Mexico committed itself to sell all its coffee exports as well as its hard fiber, chicle, lumber, edible oils, and minerals to the United States before offering it to other countries (Niblo, *War, Diplomacy, and Development*, 136).

4. Niblo, *War, Diplomacy, and Development*, 80, 103; and Beaumond, "Élite et changement social," 206. Most Soconusco plants were placed under the control of the Banco Nacional de Comercio Exterior (Nolasco, *Café y sociedad en Mexico*, 177).

5. Coffee production averaged about 52,000 metric tons through 1945 (INEGI, *Estadísticas históricas de México* [1990], 1:386). See other figures in Amorós and Pablo Duque, *Comisión Nacional del Café*, 93, 95–96.

6. AGN/MAC, file 521/25, Córdoba and Orizaba Escogedora Unions to President, June 30, 1942; AGN/MAC, file 432/502, Manuel Pimental and Victor López (CROM) to President, April 27, 1945.

7. AMC, box 480 (1941), file "Comercio e Industria"; RPPPCC, business, no. 299, assembly of Beneficiadora, January 5, 1940; RPPPCC, busi-

ness, no. 461, November 2, 1942; RPPPCC, business, no. 414, creation of Compañia Automovilista; and IRPPPCC, no. 471, creation of Sociedad El Faro, January 29, 1943.

8. RPPPCC, business, no. 179, creation of Ricardo Regules and Co., January 5, 1937; RPPPCC, business, no. 304, 100,000 peso capital increase and Albo's registration of the company in Tapachula, March 2, 1940; RPPPCC, business, no. 404–5, dissolution of Ricardo Regules Co., September 12 and 23, 1941, shareholders divided 200,000 pesos of capital and 50,000-peso debt up equally; and RPPPCC, business, no. 643, creation of Sociedad Jabonera, February 12, 1943.

9. RPPPCC, business, no. 630, re-creation of La Garza under multiple ownership, December 2, 1944; and RPPPCC, sales, no. 529, sale of La Garza warehouse to Regules and Sainz Pardo, October 26, 1945.

10. IRPPPCC, no. 99, sales of Zardain and Pedro Díaz theaters, March 27, 1940; IRPPPCC, no. 267, adjudication of José Zardain against Máximo Fernández, August 15, 1940; and IRPPPCC, no. 415, sale of 116-hectare ranch, August 4, 1945.

11. Sainz López Negrete, interviews, March 23, 1999, May 11, 1999, and June 27, 2002; and Guillaumin, interview. Guillaumin recalls how his father went to Guatemala to transport coffee grown by German producers across the border for Justo Félix Fernández in 1942 and 1943. He was also contracted by the Boesch firm to sell its coffee. Ukers lends credence to Sainz's argument that the Xalapa and Córdoba exporters dominated the Mexican export coffee economy during the World War II. He notes that the chief coffee-market centers were Xalapa, Córdoba, Tapachula, Oaxaca, and Mexico City (Ukers, *Coffee Facts*, 27).

12. Veracruz prepared a little less than one half of Mexico's total coffee crop in 1945. Its value was 19,876,177 pesos of the total 41,269,275-peso national production. Chiapas was second in production. However, Chiapas entrepreneurs were already investing more money in their businesses and reported lower labor costs. Dirección General de Estadística, *Censo industrial de los Estados Unidos Mexicanos, 1945,* chart 6.

Figueroa claims that the Figueroa, Zardain, and Muguira families, in particular, moved into central Chiapas in the 1940s and 1950s and were soon exporting 40 percent of Mexico's coffee (Figueroa, interview).

13. AHA/FAS, box 2041, file 31.822, correspondence of the Junta de Administración y Vigilancia de la Propiedad Extranjera, 1945–48; RPPPCC, business, no. 587, creation of Cafés Tapachula, August 10, 1944; RPPPCC, business, no. 698, meeting of Asemblea, BENEMEX, October 5, 1945; Beaumond, "Élite et changement social," 207; and Nolasco, *Café y sociedad en Mexico*, 177.

14. Pérez Monfort, *Hispanidad y falange*, 157. Sainz López Negrete, interview, March 23, 1999; and RPPPCC, business, no. 461, reforms of Beneficiadora, November 3, 1942.

15. The Unión Cafetera del Soconusco was created during the Porfiriato to influence state policies (Spenser, "Los incios del cultivo de café en Soconusco," 68). Costa Rican producers established the Asociación Nacional de Productores de Café in 1933 (Winson, *Coffee and Democracy in Modern Costa Rica*, 22). The Colombian Federation of Coffee Growers was formed in 1927 (Bergquist, *Coffee and Conflict*, 261–62).

16. Beaumond, "Élite et changement social," 195, 214.

17. For example, Mario Fernández began exporting instant coffee in collaboration with a U.S. company in 1957, which the Xalapa group perceived as a threat to their export businesses. The Xalapa group used the UNAC to pressure the federal government into establishing a special tax on instant coffee to block Fernández's business (Beaumond, "Élite et changement social," 207–14; and Nolasco, *Café y sociedad en Mexico*, 178–81).

18. FAO, *World Coffee Economy*, 1, 7.

19. INEGI, *Estadísticas históricas de México* (1999), 2:729. A 1948 Mexican government report predicted optimistically that Mexico could move from sixth into third position behind Colombia in overall Latin American production because of soaring prices (Amorós and Duque, *Comisión Nacional del Café*, 100–101, 116ff).

20. Benoit Daviron, "Le role de Etat dans l'insertion du Mexique sur le marché du café" (doctoral thesis, École Nacional Supérieure Agronomique de Montepelier, 1988), cited by Beaumond, "Élite et changement social," 202; and Figueroa, interview.

21. AHA/FAS, box 2041, file 31.822; and Figueroa, interview.

22. Alvarez Zardain, interview; Eduardo Alvarez Amieva, e-mail correspondence with author, June 27, 2007; Calatayud, interview; and Benítez, *Los indios de México*, 3:190–91. According to Benítez, they could make a profit of fifty to one hundred pesos per quintal by purchasing coffee through a set of interlocking brokers and by maintaining artificially low coffee prices, which unfairly disadvantaged small producers.

23. IRPPPCC, no. 3, rental of one hundred hectares and beneficio of Hacienda La Capilla, September 13, 1954; IRPPPCC, no. 248, sale of house, March 22, 1956; Figueroa, interview; and Eduardo Alvarez Amieva, e-mail correspondence with author, June 27, 2007.

24. RPPPCC, sales, nos. 468–71, sale of five lots of Rancho Santa Elena by Ceferino Sainz Pardo, June 10–11, 1953; RPPPCC, business, no. 18, increase of capital to 5 million pesos, April 12, 1954; and RPPPCC, business, no. 798, creation of Inmuebles Cordoba, October 17, 1955. The Public Registry has very few examples of coffee beneficiadores extending credit to coffee producers or for that matter taking out loans to cover their expenses, which is in sharp contrast with the highly capitalized large sugar industry. The sugar mill El Potrero was constantly taking out 5 million-peso loans (RPPPCC, business, no. 299, October 2, 1964; and RPPPCC, no. 317, October 14, 1964). It appears that most beneficiadores were now handling their transactions through Mexico City banks. The exporters dealt directly by phone or cable with New York City buyers, who would place orders with them after several days of bargaining over the sale price. Once a price had been agreed on, the U.S. importer would send a bank draft to the exporter's account at the Banco de México or Banco de Comercio in Mexico City. Thus, money no longer changed hands (Sainz López Negrete, interview, May 11, 1999).

While the spread of modern communications vastly accelerated the coffee trade, local transportation continued to lag far behind. Luis Sainz remembered that mule trains brought the coffee down from the sierra, and the muleteers and small finqueros were still paid in cash, sometimes even in silver pesos. On the other hand, coffee transport to the port had modernized considerably by the 1940s, for the truck transport was less expensive and faster than train (Sainz López Negrete, interviews, July 19, 1999, and June 5, 2000).

25. RPPPCC, business, no. 786, creation of Casa Regules, March 12, 1947; RPPPCC, business, no. 788, creation of La Proveedora, March 20, 1947; and Izquierdo de Regules, interview, March 18, 1999.

26. RPPPCC, sales, no. 779, October 11, 1951, Candelaria Huesca's purchase of urban lot at Twenty-First Street, October 11, 1951; RPPPCC, business, no. 1050, Proveedora capital increase to 1 million pesos, November 16, 1950; RPPPCC, business, no. 1158, Proveedora capital increase to 3 million pesos, March 24, 1952; IRPPPCC, no. 129, sale of house to Regules children, February 22, 1951; and AGEV/JCCA/S, 1964, file 526.5-222-43, "Tirzo Sainz Pardo, Beneficiadora y Exportador de Café Cia. Proveedora de Café SA."

27. Izquierdo de Regules, interview, March 18, 1999; and Sánchez Regules, interview, July 1, 2005.

28. Sánchez Regules, interview, July 1, 2005; RPPPCC, business, no. 614, incorporation of Sociedad Fraccionaria y Constructoria by Galván y López and others, October 18, 1944; and RPPPCC, business, no. 630, re-creation of La Garza by Regules, Sainz Pardos brothers, Ezequiel González, and Davíd González, December 2, 1944.

29. RPPPCC, business, no. 324, October 17, 1964; and RPPPCC, business, no. 323, loan of 15 million pesos for El Farol, October 16, 1964.

30. RPPPCC, business, no. 86, increase in capital of Proveedora, March 13, 1964; and RPPPCC, business, no. 364, creation of Hotel Regules, November 17, 1964. His five children were Luz del Carmen, Dolores, Humberto, Clemencia, and Ricardo Jr.

31. Ravelo Blancas and Sánchez, "Las mujeres en los sindicatos en México," 438–39.

32. Medina, *Civilismo y modernización del autoritarismo*, 163–66; Bortz, "Wages and Economic Crisis," 45; Niblo, *Mexico in the 1940s*, 4, 220–21; and Niblo, *War, Diplomacy, and Development*, 146–47.

33. AGEV/JCCA/S, 1931, box 546, file 18, SOECC to Enrique Galván, Patricio Sainz, Ricardo Regules, and Zeferino Sainz Pardo, December 2, 1942; and AGEV/JCCA/S, 1931, box 546, file 18, 1944 membership list of SOECC.

34. AGN/MAC, file 432/502, Manuel Pimental and Victor López (CROM) to President, April 27, 1945.

35. Niblo, *Mexico, Diplomacy, and Development*, 195; and Lino Alejandro Gómez Reyes, interview, May 13, 1999.

36. Pellicer de Brody and Reyna, *El afiancamiento de la estabilidad política*, 2, 29–31, 108.
37. Bortz, "Wages and Economic Crisis," 45; and Reyna, "La negociación controlada con el movimiento obrero," 83, 89.
38. Reyna, "La negociación controlada con el movimiento obrero," 92.
39. Niblo, *Mexico, Diplomacy, and Development*, 240; and APIRO/Actas, meetings of SIOECC, February 24, 1953, and November 10, 1953. The CROC statutes were not finalized and approved until the following year (AGEV/JCCA/S, 1931, box 546, file 18).
40. APIRO/Actas, meetings, January 24, 1950, April 25, 1950, August 4, 1953, and August 11, 1953.
41. APIRO/Actas, meetings, July 21, 1953, August 4, 1953, May 18, 1954, and July 25, 1955.
42. APIRO/Actas, meeting, January 24, 1950. For discussions on contract proposals and getting more permanent jobs, see APIRO/Actas, meetings, March 28, 1950, April 15, 1952, and May 18, 1954. AGEV/G/DT, 1950, file "Padrones y Sindicatos," list of Sindicato de Obreras Escogedoras de Café y Tabaco (CNT). The 1950 membership list contained the names of 1,498 active members working in four beneficios: BENEMEX, Beneficiadora, Proveedora, and La Garza, which was under new ownership. The sorters ranged in age from fifteen to fifty-eight, although the majority of the workers were in their thirties. Approximately two-thirds were illiterate. BENEMEX relied more heavily on temporary workers than Beneficiadora or Proveedora.
   The first list was composed of approximately two hundred of the oldest workers, and they were the first to be hired back when the plants reopened in the fall. The workers on the second list, which included band members, were almost always certain to obtain steady work. These two groups would have work for seven to ten months depending on the size of the harvest. The third list might have intermittent work. The temporary workers were called up on a week-to-week basis. Each Friday, the plant owners would ask the union to supply fifty to four hundred temporary workers for the following Monday (Velázquez Ramírez, interviews, March 3, 1999, and May 13, 1999).
43. Siriaco García, interview, June 6, 2000. The piece-rate was the same in Coatepec (Salazar Báez, interview, June 12, 2002).

44. APIRO/Actas, meetings, March 28, 1950, April 1, 1952, and April 15, 1952. A domestic worker could earn forty-five pesos weekly, and a rural schoolteacher could bring home ninety pesos. As teenagers Brígida and Estela said that they preferred to work as sorters because they could earn almost as much as a domestic worker, and it was steady work with fringe benefits and a better work environment (Siriaco García, interview, June 6, 2000; and Velázquez Ramírez, interview, May 13, 1999).

45. APIRO/Actas, meetings, April 27, 1954, and May 5, 1954.

46. AGEV/JCCA/S, Huelgas, 1953–54, box 632, file 526.1-307, "Sindicato de Trabajadores de Beneficiadores de Café vs. 11 Beneficiadores, Córdoba."

47. APIRO/Actas, meetings, April 11, 1950, April 25, 1950, April 24, 1951, August 14, 1951, December 11, 1951, July 7, 1954, April 19, 1955, and May 17, 1955.

48. APIRO/Actas, meetings, October 5 and 8, 1953.

49. AGEV/JCCA/S, 1964, file 526.5-222-43, contract, May 1, 1962.

50. AGEV/JCCA/S, 1964, file 526.5-222-43, "Relación de Trabajadores eventuales a destajo, que se ocupan en el desmanche manual del café. La Proveedora y La Beneficiadora, 1963." The wage for Velázquez Ramírez was 21.35 pesos per week; for Delia Ortiz Sarmiento, 13.11; and for Hernández de Huerta, 12.80. The 1956 Veracruz daily minimum wage was 7 to 8 pesos for men and 5 pesos for women and for men under twenty-one (*Pro-Paria*, December 17, 1955), or the equivalent of 30 pesos per week for sorters. Thus, in the early 1960s they were earning less than the 1956 women's minimum wage. Sorters seemed to work more slowly in Proveedora than in Beneficiadora, where wages were higher.

51. AGEV/JCCA/S, 1964, file 526.5-222-43, contract, May 1, 1962. The basic 1960 contract was not altered in 1962.

52. Joseph, "Caciquismo and the Revolution," 198.

53. Pansters, "Building a *Cacicazgo*," 303.

54. Pansters, "Building a *Cacicazgo*," 299.

55. APIRO/Actas, meetings, April 25, 1950, June 27, 1950, and November 27, 1951.

56. APIRO/Actas, meetings, April 25, 1950, June 13, 1950, November 28, 1950, June 12, 1951, December 11, 1951, June 17, 1952, December 2, 1952,

February 24, 1953, June 22, 1954, and December 14, 1954; AGEV/
JCCA/S, 1931, box 546, file 18, "Sindicato de Escogedoras," meetings,
December 16, 1959, December 20, 1960, and December 26, 1961; AMC,
box 142 (1960–69), file 4, "Agrupaciones Generales," election results,
June 1962; and Luna López, interview.

57. APIRO/Actas, meetings, March 27, 1951, December 11, 1951, June 3,
1952, December 2, 1952, March 9, 1953, April 27, 1953, May 5, 1953, June
9, 1953, June 22, 1954, and August 2, 1965; AGEV/JCCA/S, 1931, box 546,
file 18, "Sindicato de Escogedoras," meeting, December 6, 1958; and
AMC, box 142 (1960–69), file 4, "Agrupaciones Generales," election
results, June 1962.

58. APIRO/Actas, meeting, March 28, 1950; and AGEV/JCCA/S, 1931, box
546, file 18, meetings, December 20, 1960, and December 26, 1961.

59. Pansters, "Building a *Cacicazgo,*" 304.

60. APIRO/Actas, meeting, December 1, 1954; AMC, box 101 (1960–69),
file "Agrupaciones Obreras, Union de Detallistas," election results,
June 1962 and June 1963; and Lino Alejandro Gómez Reyes, interview, May 13, 1999.

61. APIRO/Actas, meetings, March 27, 1950, March 18, 1953, May 4, 1954,
November 16, 1954, and April 15, 1955.

62. APIRO/Actas, meetings, November 28, 1950, August 4, 1953, January
26, 1954, December 1, 1954, March 1, 1955, and July 25, 1955. Gillingham, "Force and Consent in Mexican Provincial Politics," 210–11.

63. APIRO/Actas, meetings, August 18, 1953, May 4, 1954, and April 19,
1955; and Velázquez Ramírez, interview, March 3, 1999.

64. APIRO/Actas, meetings, December 11, 1951, November 10, 1953, January 4, 1955, February 1, 1955, March 1, 1955, and June 14, 1955.

65. Olcott, *Revolutionary Women in Postrevolutionary Mexico,* 159–200;
Fernández-Aceves, "En-gendering *Caciquismo,*" 210–13.

66. Paul Gillingham, e-mail correspondence with author, July, 10, 2012;
APIRO, Sindicato de Obreras Escogedoras-Córdoba (CROC) to Del-
egados que celebran la XXXI Gran Convención de la Confederación
Sindicalista de Obreros y Campesinos (Córdoba), December 20,
1952; APIRO/Actas, meeting, November 27, 1953; and Lino Alejandro
Gómez Reyes, interview, July 17, 1999.

67. APIRO/Actas, meetings, December 2, 1952, August 4, 1953, and De-

cember 1, 1954; Lino Alejandro Gómez Reyes, interview, July 19, 1999; and Salomón Ortiz Sarmiento and Delia Ortiz Sarmiento, interview, March 23, 1999.

68. APIRO/Actas, meetings, December 15, 1953, and July 25, 1955; and Lino Alejandro Gómez Reyes, interview, July 19, 1999.

69. Delia Ortiz Sarmiento, interview, May 11, 1999.

70. Delia Ortiz Sarmiento, interview, May 11, 1999.

71. APIRO/Actas, meeting, June 9, 1953.

72. APIRO/Actas, meetings, November 6, 1951, November 27, 1951, May 13, 1953, and March 23, 1954.

73. Salomón Ortiz Sarmiento, interview, July 14, 2003.

74. Romero Serrano, interview; and Siriaco García, interview, July 11, 2003.

75. AGEV/JCCA/S, 1931, box 546, file 18, meeting, March 13, 1961. See Fowler-Salamini, "'La Negra Moya.'"

76. AGEV/JCCA/S, 1931, box 546, file 18, report of Comisión de Honor y Justicia, September 23, 1955.

77. FAO, *World Coffee Economy*, 7, 21, 36; and Sheridan Prieto, *Mujer obrera y organización sindical*, 121.

78. FAO, *World Coffee Economy*, 7, 19; INEGI, *Estadísticas históricas de México* (1999), 2:729; Bulmer-Thomas, *Political Economy of Central America*, 153, 187; and Sheridan Prieto, *Mujer obrera y organización sindical*, 122.

79. Sheridan Prieto, *Mujer obrera y organización sindical*, 54, 121; and Puig Hernández, interview.

80. Sheridan Prieto, *Mujer obrera y organización sindical*, 122.

81. AGN/ARC, 432/377, Adelina Téxon to President, telegram, February 10, 1955; AGN/ARC, 432/377, Agricultural Company of Coffee Producers and Exporters to President, February 7, 1956; APAT, Adelina Téxon to President and to Governor, February 10, 1956; and Díaz Sanauria, interview, July 4, 2002.

82. Sheridan Prieto, *Mujer obrera y organización sindical*, 123–25.

83. AGEV/JCCA/S, conventions (1936–56), Coatepec, box 593, file 526.6/149, agreement, April 17, 1956; *Pro-Paria*, March 31, 1956; and Sheridan Prieto, *Mujer obrera y organización sindical*, 51–59. Sheridan Prieto argues that the sorters were in a weak bargaining position be-

cause they were organized at the workshop level in Xalapa, Coatepec, and Teocelo. There was also a conflict between the sorters organized by the CROC and the CTM. Moreover, the men loaders did not continue to collaborate with the sorters in their struggle against the owners (Sheridan Prieto, *Mujer obrera y organización syndical*, 58–59).

84. Sheridan Prieto, *Mujer obrera y organización sindical*, 122, 125–30. The Maxhuitlán, Casa Cortino, Bola de Oro, and Casa Polanco beneficios had already closed.

85. Sheridan Prieto, *Mujer obrera y organización sindical*, 131–40; and Salazar Báez, interview, July 5, 2003.

86. AGN/ARC, 432/377, Labor Federation of Xalapa Region to President, January 22, 1955; and *Pro-Paria*, January 5, 1955.

87. *Diario de Xalapa*, November 8, 1955, November 10 1955, and January 11, 1956.

88. AGEV/JCCA/S, convenios (1952–55), Xalapa, box 615, file 526.6/487, "Sindicato de Desmanchadoras Veinte de Noviembre vs. Juan E. Martinez Ruiz, December 24, 1955"; AGEV/JCCA/S, convenios (1952–55), Xalapa, box 615, file 526.6-488, "Sindicato 'Primero de Mayo' vs. Rosa Autora Fernández de Falcón, December 24, 25, 1955"; AGEV/JCCA/S, convenios (1952–55), Xalapa, box 615, file 526.6-490, "Sindicato 'Carlos Marx' vs. José Pinerio, December 28, 1955"; AGEV/JCCA/S, convenios (1952–55), Xalapa, box 615, file 526.6/491, "Sindicato 'Carlos Marx' vs. Sociedad de Café de Café de Xalapa, December 25, 1955"; and AGEV/JCCA/S, convenios (1952–55), Xalapa, box 615, file 526.6/493, "Sindicato 'Martín Torres,' vs. Manuel Pineiro, December 28, 1955."

89. AGN/ARC, 432/377, unsigned letter to Isaac Fernandez (c. 1956); AGN/ARC, 432/377, November 20 Union to President, November 20, 1957; AGN/ALM, 432/348, Fidel Velázquez to President, March 14, 1962; and Rare Book and Manuscript Collection, Columbia University, Mexican Communist Party Records, 1951–58, reel 3, folder 28, pp. 1618–22. I would like to thank Jocelyn Olcott for alerting me to these documents. Beaumond, "Élite et changement social," 232–33. Huatusco owners began mechanizing in 1957 (Guillaumin, interview).

90. AGEV/JCCA/S, 1964, file 526.5-222-43, "Relaciónes de impuestos pagados por Cia. Beneficiadora y Cia. Proveedora durante el ejercicio de

1963, April 22, 1964"; and AGEV/JCCA/S, 1964, file 526.5-222-43, Tirso Sainz Pardo and Humberto and Ricardo Regules Huesca to JCCA, April 20, 1964.

91. AGEV/JCCA/S, 1964, file 526.4-H-49-43, "SIOECC, Cia Proveedora de Café, SA," Reyes to Governor, April 12, 1964.

92. AGEV/JCCA/S, 1964, file 526.4-H-49-43, Reyes to JCCA, April 20, 1964.

93. AGEV/JCCA/S, 1964, file 526.4-H-49-43, Tirso Sainz Pardo and Ricardo and Humberto Regules Huesca to SIOECC, April 22, 1964; AGEV/JCCA/S, 1964, file 526.4-H-49-43, José Luis Dávila Reyes (BENEMEX) to JCCA, April 22, 1964; and AGEV/JCCA/S, 1964, file 526.4-H-49-43, collective contract, May 1, 1964. The owners agreed to raise the piece-rate to 2.15 pesos per arroba of green coffee or per kilo of waste and to guarantee thirty weeks of work to permanent workers. The coffee receiver would earn a daily wage of 27 pesos.

94. AGEV/JCCA/S, 1964, file 526.4-H-49-43, JCCA meetings, April 24–July 23, 1964; and AGEV/JCCA/S, 1964, file 526.4-H-49-43, resolution of July 23, 1964.

95. AGEV/JCCA/S, 1964, file 526.4-H-29-43, meeting of the Junta Municipal Permanente de Conciliación, August 28, 1964; AGEV/JCCA/S, 1964, file, 526.4-H-29-43, executive committee of the SIOECC, "Listas de Personal de Planta de Beneficiadora y Proveedora," August 28, 1964.

96. AGEV/JCCA/S, 1964, file, 526.4-H-29-43, JCCA meetings, September 22–October 15, 1964; AGEV/JCCA/S, 1964, file, 526.4-H-29-43, BENEMEX resolution, November 24, 1964; AGEV/JCCA/S, 1964, file, 526.4-H-29-43, meeting, March 15, 1965. *El Mundo de Córdoba*, February 1, 1965, and March 19, 1965. The two other affected BENEMEX plants were in Sumidero (Huatusco) and Naranjal.

97. AGEV/JCCA/S, 1964, file 526.4-H-49-43, Francisca Rodríguez Sánchez et al. to Governor, March 16, 1965; and AGEV/JCCA/S, 1964, file 526.4-H-49-43, Francisca Rodríguez Sánchez et al. to Governor, April 21, 1965. The complaint of the temporary workers was based on the fact that they had only been given 5 percent of the compensation.

98. APIRO/Actas, 1965–73, meetings, August 2, 1965, August 10, 1965, and August 26, 1965.

99. AGEV/JCCA/S, 1964, file 526.4-H-49-43, Confederación Sindicalista

de Obreros y Campesinos de Orizaba (CROM), circular, no. 91, January 26, 1966.

100. AGEV/JCCA/S, 1964, file 526.4-H-49-43, Juzgado de Primera Instancia, January 12, 1971; and AMC, box 81 (1960–69), file A-7, "Amparo, Castro, Reyes, Guereña, y López contra actas de esta Autoridad Municipal."

101. AGEV/JCCA/S, 1964, file 526.5-222-43, Rodríguez to Governor, May 21, 1970; and AGEV/JCCA/S, 1964, file 526.4-H-49-43, Rodríguez to President, March 29, 1971.

102. AGEV/JCCA/S, 1972, file 77-EP-972, embargo.

103. AGEV/JCCA/S, 1931, box 547, file 18, meeting of Junta Local Permanente de Conciliación, October 19, 1974.

104. AGEV/JCCA/S, 1931, box 547, file 18, meetings, August 16, 1977, and March 28, 1978; and AGEV/JCCA/S, 1931, box 547, file 18, "Lista Nominal de Compañeras que componen el Sindicato Industrial Obreras Escogedoras y Similares, May 20, 1980." While Celia Hernández, María Elena Serna, Estela Velázquez, and Sylvia Herrera received payments, Brígida Siriaco and Delia Ortiz did not.

105. Quoted in Portelli, "Death of Luigi Trastulli," 1.

106. Portelli, "Death of Luigi Trastulli," 26.

107. James, *Doña María's Story*, 228.

108. Sheridan Prieto, *Mujer obrera y organización sindical*, 122.

109. Sheridan Prieto, *Mujer obrera y organización sindical*, 123.

110. Sheridan Prieto, *Mujer obrera y organización sindical*, 132, 133–44.

111. Siriaco García, interview, June 6, 2000.

112. Baltazar, interview; Hernández de Huerta, interview; Silvia Herrera Luna, interview; and Velázquez Ramírez, interview, October 14, 2008.

113. Baltazar, interview.

114. Siriaco García, interviews, June 6, 2000, and July 3, 2001.

115. Siriaco García, interview, June 28, 2005.

116. Salomón Ortiz Sarmiento and Delia Ortiz Sarmiento, interview, March 23, 1999.

Conclusions

1. Casino Español de Córdoba. *Casino Español de Córdoba, AC, 1908–1998*, 86.

2. Casino Español de Córdoba. *Casino Español de Córdoba,* AC, *1908–1998,* 69–90.
3. Tiano, *Patriarchy on the Line,* 148; and Lim, "Women's Work in Export Factories," 108–9.
4. In 1996 eight middle- and upper-class panista women were elected to fill half of the seats on Córdoba's municipal council. They were following a long tradition within the local PRI, PRD, and PT, which placed women from the popular classes in municipal offices. Córdoba women had a historical record not only of political participation but also of union activism (Rodríguez Rocafuerte, "Mujeres y participación ciudadana en un ayuntamiento panista," 230n8, 237, 247).

GLOSSARY

abnegada	long-suffering
abonos	voucher
abuso de confianza	breach of trust
acaparador	monopolist
amparo	stay of execution
asoleadora	drying terrace
arroba	11.5 kilograms
aviador	financier
banda de guerra	military band
barrio	neighborhood
beneficiador	coffee preparer
beneficiar	to prepare coffee
beneficio	coffee preparation plant
beneficio seco	dry preparation plant
burra	large table
cacica	female local boss
cacicazgo	boss rule
cacique	male local boss
caciquismo	boss politics
café corriente	ordinary coffee
café en cereza	coffee cherry

café en pergamino	parchment coffee
café pulido	polished coffee
cafetalero	coffee producer and exporter
café verde	green or hulled coffee
caficultura	coffee economy
cajas	boxes
cámara del comercio	chamber of commerce
cámara del trabajo	chamber of labor
canasta	basket, approximately 11.5 kilos
caracolillo	peaberry
cargador	loader
casa de exportación	coffee export firm
clarín	trumpet
clasificadora	classifying machine
comadre	godmother
compañerismo	camaraderie
compañero	partner or fellow worker
continuismo	leadership continuity
Cordobeses	Veracruzano term for Córdoba's coffee elite
corneta	bugle
danzoneras	wind-instrument orchestras
de planta	permanent worker
demanda	demand
descascadora	huller
desmanchadora	coffee sorter
desmanche	cleaning or sorting
despulpadora	depulper
ejidatario	communal farmer
empleada de confianza	trustworthy employee
encargada	shop steward
escogedora	coffee sorter
escogida	cleaning or sorting
escolta	honor guard
eventual	seasonal, temporary, or occasional worker

ferrocarril urbano	urban rail line
finca	medium-sized or large coffee farm
finquero	coffee farmer
gachupin	Spaniard
gente decente	respectable or upright people
gerente	administrator
granelero	stirrer
gratificación	bonus
grupo militarizado	military auxiliary
grupo rojo	Communist or anarchosyndicalist group
habilitator	financier
hacendado	hacienda owner
huerta	family orchard
itacate	lunch
jarocho	Afro-Veracruzano
jefe politico	cantonal prefect
kermess	outdoor fair
ley de inquilinato	tenancy law
libre	nonunionized temporary worker
liga femenina	women's league
liquidación	wage settlement package
madrina	godmother or female patron
madrona	strong woman
majadora	huller
mancha	coffee waste
máquina	pedal machine
mesa a metro	short coffee-sorting table
mesa de pedal	pedal machine
minifundio	subsistence farm
morteadora	huller
mujer abnegada	long-suffering, oppressed woman
mujer ciudadana	woman citizen
mujeres de la calle	street women
obrera	woman worker

obrero	man worker
oficio	occupation
operario	industrial worker
padrino	godfather
padrote	father figure
pambaso	sandwich roll
patio de vecindad	tenement housing
patria chica	birthplace
patrón/patrona	owner, patron
planchuela	large flat coffee bean
porteño	from the port of Veracruz
progresar	to make something of oneself
pulidora	polisher
pulquería	pulque dispensary
queja	complaint
quintal	46 kilos or 100 U.S. pounds
rancho	medium-sized farm or ranch
ranchero	owner of a medium-sized farm or ranch
recibidora	coffee receiver
sala	small workshop
salidas de café	coffee shipments
salón	large workshop
secadora	cylindrical coffee dryer
separadora	separator
sindicato blanco	company union
sociedad en comandita	joint-stock partnership
supermujer	superwoman
taller	small workshop
tambor	drum
tiempo de guayaba	offseason
trilladora	Colombian huller or a coffee preparation plant
triple jornada	triple work-day
vocal	committee member

BIBLIOGRAPHY

Archival and Library Collections

AGEV (Archivo General del Estado de Veracruz), Xalapa, Veracruz).
   Archivo Histórico
      Fondo: Secretario General de Gobierno
         ACG (Archivo Clasificado General), 1926–49
         DTPS (Trabajo y Previsión Social), 1922–30
         F (Fomento), 1898–1931
         F/AL (Asuntos Laborales)
         GyJ (Gobernación y Justicia), 1900–35
         G/DT (Dirección de Trabajo)
         JCCA (Junta Central de Conciliación y Arbitraje)
         JCCA/D (Demandas Laborales)
         JCCA/S (Sindicatos)
      Archivos Particulares
         ATO (Adalberto Tejeda Olivares)
         ELL (Eucario León López)
      Biblioteca del Instituto Mexicano del Café
         Spice Mill, 1935–45
         Tea and Coffee Trade Journal, 1936–45
      Hermeroteca
         El Dictamen
         Diario de Xalapa
         Gaceta Oficial del Estado de Veracruz

NCI (Notarias, Córdoba, Índices), 1880–1967
AGN (Archivo General de la Nación), Mexico City.
   DT (Departamento del Trabajo)
   G (Gobernación)
      G/DM (Departamento de Migración)
   Presidentes
      ACR (Lázaro Cárdenas Ríos)
      ALM (Adolfo López Mateos)
      ALR (Abelardo L. Rodríguez)
      ARC (Adolfo Ruiz Cortines)
      MAC (Manuel Ávila Camacho)
AHA (Archivo Histórico del Aguas), Mexico City.
   FAS (Fondo Aprovechamientos Superficiales)
AMC (Archivo Municipal y Hermeroteca de Córdoba), Córdoba, Veracruz.
AMO (Archivo Municipal de Orizaba y Hermeroteca), Orizaba, Veracruz.
APAT (Archivo Personal de Adelina Téxon), Coatepec, Veracruz. In the possession of Antonio Díaz Sanauria.
APIRO (Archivo Personal de María Jesús Inés Reyes Ochoa), Córdoba, Veracruz. In the possession of her children.
   Libro de Actas del Sindicato Industrial de Obreras Escogedoras de Café y Similares de Córdoba, 1950–55, 1965–73
   Unclassified documents and pictures
Biblioteca Daniel Cosío Villegas, El Colegio de México, Mexico City.
Biblioteca del Instituto de Ciencias Sociales y Humanidades, Benemérita Universidad Autónoma de Puebla, Puebla, Mexico.
Biblioteca del Instituto de Investigaciones Histórico-Sociales, Universidad Veracruzana, Xalapa, Veracruz.
Biblioteca del Instituto Nacional de Estudios Históricos de las Revoluciones de México, Mexico City.
Biblioteca Gonzalo Aguirre Beltrán, Centro de Investigaciones y Estudios Superiores en Antropología Social, Golfo, Xalapa, Veracruz.
Biblioteca Nacional de México, Universidad Nacional Autónoma de México (UNAM), Mexico City.
   Hermeroteca Nacional
   Fondo Comtemporáneo
      El Dictamen

Excelsior

El Universal

Fondo Reservado

BSAM (*Boletín de la Sociedad Agrícola Mexicana*)

BSMGE (*Boletín de la Sociedad de Geografía y Estadística*)

Columbia University, Rare Books and Manuscripts Library, New York.

Mexican Communist Party Collection, 1951–58

Joseph Regenstein Library, University of Chicago, Chicago.

NARA (U.S. National Archives and Records Administration), II. College Park, MD.

RG59 (Record Group 59), State Department Central File. 1910–29. Subject-Numeric File

RG76 (Record Group 76), Records of the U.S. and Mexican Claims Commissions

RG84 (Record Group 84), Records of the Foreign Service Posts of the State Department, 1912–35

Registro Público de la Propiedad Privada, Índice, Xalapa, Veracruz.

IRPPPCC (Córdoba [1898–1951])

IRPPPCH (Huatusco [1921–45])

RPPPCC (Registro Público de la Propiedad Privada de la Ciudad de Córdoba), 1885–1964, Córdoba, Veracruz.

University Library, University of Illinois, Urbana–Champaign.

USBI (Unidad de Servicios Bibliotecarios), Universidad Veracruzana.

Colecciones Especiales

NCI (Notarías, Córdoba, Índice), 1906

Interviews

Álvarez Zardain, Joaquín. Grandson of José Zardain Monteserín. Interviewed by author, June 29, 2002, Córdoba, Veracruz (not taped).

Baltazar, Juana de Jesús. Coffee sorter. Interviewed by author, May 13, 1999, Córdoba, Veracruz (not taped).

Calatayud, Rubén. Córdoba chronicler. Interviewed by author, July 6, 2004, Córdoba, Veracruz (not taped).

Díaz Sanauria, Antonio. Coffee plant manager. Interviewed by author, February 22, 1999, July 10, 2001, July 4, 2004, Coatepec, Veracruz (not taped).

Domínguez Sánchez, Javier. Grandson of Severo Sánchez. Interviewed by author, March 18, 1999, Córdoba, Veracruz (not taped).

Fernández Alvarez, Consuelo [pseud.]. Coatepec resident. Interviewed by author, October 20, 2008, Xalapa, Veracruz (not taped).

Figueroa, Jorge. Oaxacan exporter and executive director of Asociación Mexicana de Exportadores de Café (AMEC). Interviewed by author, November 5, 2008, Mexico City (not taped).

Gómez Reyes, Lino Alejandro. Son of Inés Reyes Ochoa. Interviewed by author, May 13, 1999 (taped), July 19, 1999 (not taped), Córdoba, Veracruz.

Gómez Reyes, Socorro. Daughter of Inés Reyes Ochoa. Interviewed by author February 17, 1999 (not taped), Córdoba, Veracruz.

González, Rosa [pseud.]. Longtime Córdoba resident. Interviewed by author, March 12, 1999, June 24, 2001, Córdoba, Veracruz (not taped).

Guillaumin, Rafael Fentane. Huatusco coffee preparer and exporter. Interviewed by author with Susan Córdova Santamaría, June 8, 2007, Huatusco, Veracruz (taped).

Hernández, José Antonio. Son of Gonzalo Hernández. Interviewed by author, July 1, 2003, Córdoba, Veracruz (not taped).

Hernández de Huerta, Cecilia. Córdoba sorter. Interviewed by author, July 20, 1999, Córdoba, Veracruz (not taped).

Hernández Rojas, Gonzalo. Inquilino leader. Interviewed by author, October 23, 1968, Córdoba, Veracruz (not taped).

Herrera Luna, Magdalena. Coffee sorter. Interviewed by author, June 30, 2005, Córdoba, Veracruz (not taped).

Herrera Luna, Silvia. Córdoba sorter. Interviewed by author with Beatriz Calvo Cruz, June 30, 2005 (not taped).

Izquierdo de Regules, Carmela. Wife of Ricardo Regules Jr. Interviewed by author, December 1, 1998, March 18, 1999, Córdoba, Veracruz (not taped).

Limón, Alicia. Coatepec sorter leader. Interviewed by author with Antonio Díaz Sanauria, July 10, 2001, Coatepec, Veracruz (not taped).

López Osorio, Guadalupe. Córdoba sorter leader. Interviewed by author, February 18, 1999, Córdoba, Veracruz (not taped).

Luna López, Zenon Gabino. Córdoba accountant. Interviewed by author, June 7, 2007, Córdoba, Veracruz (not taped).

Ortiz Sarmiento, Delia. Daughter of Eufrosina Sarmiento (Moya). Interviewed by author, May 11, 1999 (taped), June 6, 2009 (not taped), Córdoba, Veracruz.

Ortiz Sarmiento, Salomón. Son of Eufrosina Sarmiento (Moya). Interviewed by author with Delia Ortiz Sarmiento on March 23, 1999, and alone on July 14, 2003, Córdoba, Veracruz (not taped).

Puig Hernández, Luis. Former Banco Nacional de Crédito Agrícola official. Interviewed by author, November 22, 2008, Córdoba, Veracruz (not taped).

Ríos Zavala, Gloria Aurora. Orizaba sorter. Interviewed by author, July 5, 1999, Orizaba, Veracruz (not taped).

Ríos Zavala, Maria del Carmen. Orizaba sorter. Interviewed by author, May 10, 1999, Orizaba, Veracruz (taped).

Romero Serrano, Isabel. Córdoba sorter. Interviewed by author with Beatriz Calvo Cruz, June 23, 2004, Córdoba, Veracruz (taped).

Sainz López Negrete, Luis. Son of Manuel Sainz Pardo. Interviewed by author, March 23, 1999 (not taped), May 11, 1999 (taped), July 19, 1999 (taped), June 5, 2000 (taped), June 27, 2002 (not taped), Córdoba, Veracruz.

Salazar Báez, Enriqueta. Coatepec sorter. Interviewed by author, June 12, 2002, July 5, 2003, Coatepec, Veracruz (not taped).

Sánchez Regules, Baltazar. Grandson of Ricardo Regules and son of Baltazar Sánchez. Owner of Grupo Basa. Interviewed by author, July 1, 2005, June 3, 2007, October 30, 2008, Córdoba, Veracruz (not taped).

Serna, María Elena. Córdoba sorter. Interviewed by author, February 17, 1999, Córdoba, Veracruz (not taped).

Siriaco García, Brígida, Córdoba sorter. Interviewed by author, June 6, 2000 (not taped), June 7, 2000 (not taped), July 3, 2001 (taped), June 27, 2003 (not taped), July 11, 2003 (not taped), June 28, 2005 (not taped), June 3, 2007 (not taped), Córdoba, Veracruz.

Téxon, Adelina. Coatepec sorter leader. Interviewed by author with Antonio Díaz Sanauria, July 9, 2001, Coatepec, Veracruz (not taped).

Velasco Muñoz, Miguel. Córdoba baker and PCM member. Interviewed by author with Raymond Buve, June 5, 1968, Mexico City (not taped).

Velázquez Ramírez, Estela. Córdoba sorter. Interviewed by author, March 3, 1999 (taped), May 13, 1999 (taped), July 19, 1999 (not taped), October 14, 2008 (not taped), Córdoba, Veracruz.

Zardain de Alvarez, María. Daughter of José Zardain Monteserín. Telephone interview by author, July 20, 1999 (not taped).

Published and Unpublished Sources

Agetro, Leafar [Rafael García Auli]. *Las luchas proletarias en Veracruz: Historia y autocrítica*. Xalapa, Veracruz: Editorial "Barricada," 1942.

Alegre, Robert E. "Las Rieleras: Gender, Politics, and Power in the Mexican Railway Movement, 1958–59." *Journal of Women's History* 23, no. 2 (Summer 2011): 162–86.

Amorós, Roberto, and Juan Pablo Duque. *Comisión Nacional del Café*. Mexico City, 1950.

Anderson, Rodney D. *Outcasts in Their Own Land: Mexican Industrial Workers, 1906–1911*. DeKalb: Northern Illinois University Press, 1976.

Andrade, Antonio. *Córdoba a 350 años de su fundación*. Mexico City, 1968.

Anguiano, Arturo. *El estado y la política obrera del cardenismo*. México City: Ediciones Era, 1999.

Arango, Mariano. *Café e industria, 1850–1930*. Antioquia: Carlos Valencia Editores, 1977.

Arizpe, Lourdes, and Josefina Aranda, "The 'Comparative Advantages' of Women's Disadvantages; Women Workers in the Strawberry Export Agribusiness in Mexico," *Signs* 7, no. 2 (Winter 1981): 453–73.

Arriaga, J. "El café de Córdoba." *Boletín de la Sociedad Agrícola Mexicana* 18, no. 4 (January 12, 1894): 64.

Ashby, Joe C. *Organized Labor and the Mexican Revolution under Lázaro Cárdenas*. Chapel Hill: University of North Carolina Press, 1967.

Bachelor, Steve. "Toiling for the 'New Invaders': Autoworkers, Transnational Corporations, and Working-Class Culture in Mexico City, 1955–1968." In *Fragments of a Golden Age: The Politics of Culture in Mexico since 1940*, edited by Anne Rubenstein, Gilbert Joseph, and Eric Zolov. Durham NC: Duke University Press, 2001, 273–326.

Barbieri, Teresita de. *Mujeres y la vida cotidiana*. Mexico City: SEP/80, 1984.

Beaumond, Anne. "Élite et changement social: L'histoire du groupe de Xalapa et la cafeiculture mexicaine, 1880–1987." PhD diss., Ecole Nationale Superieure Agronomique de Montepellier, 1988.

Beezley, William H. *Mexican National Identity: Memory, Innuendo, and Popular Culture*. Tucson: Arizona University Press, 2008.

Beezley, William H., Cheryl Martin, and William E. French, eds. *Rituals of Rule, Rituals of Resistance: Public Celebrations and Popular Culture.* Wilmington DE: Scholarly Resources, 1994.

Beezley, William H., and David E. Lorey. "The Functions of Patriotic Festival in Mexico." Introduction to Beezley and Lorey, *Viva Mexico! Viva la Independencia!* ix–xviii.

———. *Viva Mexico! Viva la Independencia! Celebrations of September 16.* Wilmington DE: Scholarly Resources, 2001.

Behar, Ruth. *Translated Women: Crossing the Border with Esperanza's Story.* Boston: Beacon Press, 1993.

Behrens, Benedikt. *Ein Laboratorium der Revolution: Stadtische soziale Bewegungen und radicale Reformpolitik im Mexikanishen Bundestaat, Veracruz, 1918–1930.* Frankfurt am Main: Peter Lang, 2002.

BENEMEX. *BENEMEX, su evolución, 1956–70.* México City: BENEMEX, 1970.

Benítez, Fernando. *Los indios de México.* 3 vols. Mexico City: ERA, 1973.

Benjamin, Thomas. "Laboratories of the New State, 1920–29." In *Provinces of the Revolution: Essays on Regional Mexican History, 1910–1929,* edited by Benjamin and Mark Wasserman, 71–90. Albuquerque: University of New Mexico Press, 1990.

———. *A Rich Land, a Poor People: Politics and Society in Modern Chiapas.* Rev. ed. Albuquerque: University of New Mexico Press, 1996.

Bergero, Adriana J. *Intersecting Tango: Cultural Geographies of Buenos Aires, 1900–1930.* Pittsburgh: University of Pittsburgh Press, 2008.

Bergquist, Charles W. *Coffee and Conflict in Colombia, 1886–1910.* Durham NC: Duke University Press, 1978.

———. *Labor in Latin America: Comparative Essays on Chile, Argentina, Venezuela, and Colombia.* Stanford: Stanford University Press, 1986.

Blázquez Domínguez, Carmen. *Breve historia de Veracruz.* México City: El Colegio de México, 2000.

Bliss, Katherine. *Compromised Positions: Prostitution, Public Health, and Gender Politics in Revolutionary Mexico City.* University Park: Pennsylvania State University Press, 2001.

Blue Book of Mexico. Mexico City: Editorial Pan-Americana, 1923.

Bolio Trejo, Arturo. *Rebelión de mujeres: Versión histórica de la revolución inquilinaria de Veracruz.* Veracruz: Editorial "Kada," 1959.

Bortz, Jeffrey. *Revolution within the Revolution: Cotton Textile Workers and the Mexican Labor Regime, 1910–1922*. Stanford: Stanford University Press, 2006.

———. "Wages and Economic Crisis." In *The Mexican Left, Popular Movements, and the Politics of Austerity*, edited by Barry Carr, 33–46. San Diego: Center for U.S.–Mexican Studies, 1986.

Boyer, Christopher R. *Becoming Campesinos: Politics, Identity, and Agrarian Struggle in Postrevolutionary Michoacán, 1920–1935*. Stanford: Stanford University Press, 2003.

Buffington, Robert. "La 'Dancing' Mexicana: Danzón and the Transformation of Intimacy in Post-Revolutionary Mexico City." *Journal of Latin American Cultural Studies* 14, no. 1 (March 2005): 87–105.

Bulmer-Thomas, Victor. *The Political Economy of Central America since 1920*. Cambridge: Cambridge University Press, 1987.

Buve, Raymond. "Caciquismo, un principio de ejercicio de poder a lo largo de varios siglos." *Relaciones* 96 (Autumn 2003): 19–39.

Calderón, Francisco R. "Los ferrocarriles." In *La vida económica: El Porfiriato*, 483–634. Vol.7 of *La historia moderna de México*, edited by Daniel Cosío Villegas. 2nd ed. Mexico City: Editorial Hermes, 1974.

———. *La vida económica: La república restaurada*. Vol. 2 of *La historia moderna de México*, edited by Daniel Cosío Villegas. 2nd ed. Mexico City: Hermes, 1974.

Calvo Cruz, Beatriz. "Historia social de Córdoba, Veracruz, 1915–22." Unpublished manuscript, 1986.

Camarena Ocampo, Mario. *Jornaleros, tejedores y obreros: Historia social de los trabajadores textiles de San Angel (1850–1930)*. Mexico City: Plaza y Valdés, 2001.

Camarena Ocampo, Mario, and Susana A. Fernández Apango. "Culture and Politics: Mexican Textile Workers in the Second Half of the Nineteenth Century." In *Border Crossings: Mexican and Mexican-American Workers*, edited by John Mason Hart, 27–47. Wilmington DE: Scholarly Resources, 1998.

Camas Reyes, Fernando Javier. "El desarrollo económico del Soconusco: crecimiento demográfico y territorial de Tapachula, 1880–1990." In Muro, *Ciudades provincianas de México*, 219–39.

Cambranes (Castellanos), Julio C. *Sobre los empresarios agrarios y el estado en Guatemala*. Guatemala: Centro de Estudios Rurales Centroamericanos, 1988.

Canning, Kathleen. "Difficult Dichotomies: 'Experience' between Narratives and Materiality." In *Gender History in Practice: Historical Perspectives on Bodies, Class, and Citizenship*, 101–20. Ithaca: Cornell University Press, 2006.

———. "Feminist History after the Linguistic Turn: Historicizing Discourse and Experience." In *Gender History in Practice: Historical Perspectives on Bodies, Class, and Citizenship*, 63–100. Ithaca NY: Cornell University Press, 2006.

———. "Gender and the Politics of Class Formation: Rethinking German Labor History." *American Historical Review* 87 (June 1992): 736–68.

———. *Languages of Labor and Gender: Female Factory Work in Germany, 1850–1914*. Ithaca NY: Cornell University Press, 1996.

Cano, Gabriela. "When Gender Can't Be Seen amid the Symbols: Women and the Mexican Revolution." In Olcott, Vaughan, and Cano, *Sex in Revolution*, 35–56.

Cárdenas, Enrique. "Inflación y estabilización monetaria en México durante la Revolución." In *Historia económica de México*, edited by Enrique Cárdenas, 4:447–70. Mexico City: Fondo de Cultura Económica, 1992.

Cárdenas García, Nicolás, and Enrique Guerra Manzo, eds. *Integrados y marginados en el México posrevolucionario: Los juegos de poder local y sus nexos con la política nacional*. Mexico City: Porrua / Universidad Autónoma Metropolitana–Xochimilco, 2009.

Carr, Barry. "The Casa del Obrero Mundial: Constitutionalism, and the Pact of February 1915." In Frost, Meyer, and Vásquez, *El trabajo y los trabajadores en la historia de México*, 603–31.

———. *El movimiento obrero y la política en México, 1910–1929*. 2 vols. Mexico City: SepSetentas, 1976.

Carrillo Padilla, Ana Lorena. "Sufridas hijas del pueblo: La huelga de las escogedoras de café de 1925 en Guatemala." *Mesoamérica* (Antigua) 15, no. 27 (June 1994): 157–73.

Casino Español de Córdoba. *Casino Español de Córdoba, AC, 1908–1998: Una historia . . . nuestra historia*. Córdoba: Talleres Lara, 1999.

Castillo, Debra A. *Easy Women: Sex and Gender in Modern Mexican Fiction*. Minneapolis: University of Minnesota Press, 1998.

CEHSMO (Cento de Estudios Históricos del Movimiento Obrero Mexicano). *La mujer y el movimiento obrero mexicano en el siglo XIX: antología
de la prensa obrera.* Mexico City: CEHSMO, 1975.

Chartier, Roger. "The World Turned Upside-Down." In *Cultural History:
Between Practices and Representations*, translated by Lydia G. Co-
chrane, 115–26. Ithaca NY: Cornell University Press, 1988.

Chassen-López, Francie R. "'Cheaper Than Machines': Women and Agri-
culture in Porfirian Oaxaca, 1880–1911." In *Women of the Mexican
Countryside, 1850–1980: Creating Spaces, Shaping Transitions*, edited by
Heather Fowler-Salamini and Mary Kay Vaughan, 27–50. Tucson:
University of Arizona Press, 1994.

———. *From Liberal to Revolutionary Oaxaca: The View from the South,
Mexico, 1867–1911.* University Park: Pennsylvania State University
Press, 2004.

———. "A Patron of Progress: Juana Catarina Romero, the Nineteenth-
Century Cacica of Tehuantepec." *Hispanic American Historical Review*
88, no. 3 (2008): 393–426.

Chasteen, John. "Why Read *Santa?*" Introduction to Gamboa, *Santa: A
Novel of Mexico City*, Chapel Hill: University of North Carolina, 2010.

Clark, Marjorie. *Organized Labor in Mexico.* 2nd ed. New York: Russell
and Russell, 1934.

Coatsworth, John. *Growth against Development: The Economic Impact of
Railroads in Porfirian Mexico.* DeKalb: Northern Illinois University
Press, 1980.

Colegio de México. *Estadísticas económicas del porfiriato.* 2 vols. 2nd ed.
Mexico City: Colegio de México, 1977.

Collado Herrera, María del Carmen. *Empresarios y políticos entre la Restauración y la Revolución, 1920–1924.* Mexico City: Instituto Nacional
de Estudios Históricos de las Revoluciones Mexicanas, 1996.

"Condiciones laborales y de vida de las mujeres trabajadoras, 1914–1933."
Boletín del Archivo General de la Nación, México 3, no. 9 (July–September 1979): 14–23.

Córdova, Arnaldo. *En una época de crisis (1928–1934).* Vol. 9 of *La clase obrera en la historia de México.* Mexico City: Siglo XXI / Universidad
Nacional Autónoma de México, 1981.

Córdova Santamaría, Susana. *Café y sociedad en Huatusco, Veracruz: For-*

mación de la cultura cafetalera (1870–1930). Chapingo, Mexico: Conaculta, 2005.

Corzo Ramírez, Ricardo, José González Sierra, and David Skerritt Gardner. *. . . nunca un desleal: Cándido Aguilar (1889–1960).* Mexico City: El Colegio de México and Gobierno del Estado de Veracruz, 1986.

Cossío Silva, Luis. "La agricultura." In *La vida económica: El Porfiriato,* 1–133. Vol. 7 of *La historia moderna de Mexico,* edited by Daniel Cosío Villegas. 2nd ed. Mexico City: Editorial Hermes, 1974.

Crane, Susan A. "Writing the Individual Back into Collective Memory." *The American Historical Review* 120, no. 5 (December 1997): 1372–85.

Crider, Gregory S. "Material Struggles: Workers' Strategies during the 'Institutionalization of the Revolution' in Atlixco, Puebla Mexico, 1932–42." PhD diss., Department of History, University of Wisconsin, 1996.

Dean, Warren. *Rio Claro: A Brazilian Plantation System, 1820–1920.* Stanford: Stanford University Press, 1976.

Deans-Smith, Susan. *Bureaucrats, Planters, and Workers: The Making of the Tobacco Monopoly in Bourbon Mexico.* Austin: University of Texas Press, 1992.

De Certeau, Michel. *The Practice of Everyday Life.* Translated by Steven Randall. Berkeley: University of California Press, 1984.

De la Fuente, Julio. "Relaciones sociales en una ciudad de provincia." In *Relaciones Interétnicas,* 1965. 2nd ed., 87-110. Mexico City: Instituto Nacional Indigenismo, 1989.

De la Peña, Guillermo. "Poder local, poder regional: Perspectivas socio-antropológicas." In *Poder local, poder regional,* edited by Jorge Papua and Alain Vanneph, 27–56. Mexico City: El Colegio de México / CEMCA, 1986.

De la Peña, Moises T. *Veracruz económico.* 2 vols. Mexico City: Gobierno del Estado de Veracruz, 1946.

Delgado Rannauro, Ana Laura. "El Sindicato de Santa Rosa y el movimiento obrero de Orizaba, Veracruz." Master's thesis in history, Universidad Veracruzana, 1977.

Departamento de la Estadística Nacional. *Censo general de habitantes: 30 de noviembre de 1921, Estado de Veracruz.* Mexico City: Talleres Gráficos de la Nación, 1928.

Díaz Meléndez, Antonio. "Carranza en Córdoba." In *Andrade, Córdoba a 350 años de su fundación*, 124–26. Mexico City, 1968.

Dirección General de Estadística. *Cuarto censo industrial de los Estados Unidos Mexicanos, 1945.* Mexico City: Secretaría de la Economía, 1953.

————. *División territorial de los Estados Unidos Mexicanos, correspondiente al censo de 1910, Estado de Veracruz.* Mexico City: Secretaría de Fomento, 1918.

————. *Estadisticas sociales del porfiriato, 1877–1910.* Mexico City: Secretaría de la Economía Nacional, 1956.

————. *Primer censo industrial de 1930, Estado de Veracruz.* Mexico City: Secretaría de la Economía Nacional, 1933–34.

————. *Quinto censo de población, 1930, Estado de Veracruz.* Mexico City: Secretaría de la Economía Nacional, 1933–34.

————. *Segundo censo general de la República Mexicana verificado el 28 de octubre de 1900.* Mexico City: Secretaría de Fomento, 1904.

————. *Sexto censo de población, 1940, Estado de Veracruz.* México City: Talleres Gráficos de la Nación, 1943.

————. *Tercer censo de población de los Estados Unidos Mexicanos verificado el 27 de octubre de 1910.* Mexico City: Secretaría de Hacienda, 1918.

Directorio de Exportadores de la Republica Mexicana para el año 1935. Mexico City: Talleres Gráficos de la Nación, 1935.

Domenech, Figueroa. *Guía general descriptiva de la República Mexicana.* Vol. 2. Mexico City: Ramón S. N. Araluce, 1899.

Domínguez Pérez, Olivia. "Historia de una lucha: Obreras desmanchadoras de café en Coatepec." In *Estudios sociales: Revista cuatrimestral del Instituto de Estudios Sociales* (Guadalajara) 1, no. 1 (July–October 1984): 3–28.

————. *Política y movimientos sociales en el tejedismo.* Xalapa: Universidad Veracruzana, 1986.

"El café." *Boletín de la Sociedad Agrícola Mexicana* 20, no. 47 (December 24, 1896): 752.

"El café de México en los Estados Unidos." *Boletín de la Sociedad Agrícola Mexicana* 20, no. 13 (May 8, 1896): 208.

"El cultivo del café por un aficionado." *Boletín de la Sociedad Agrícola Mexicana* 1, nos. 15–16 (April 17, 1880): 218–20; (April 23, 1880): 237–38.

Eley, Geof. Forward to Lüdtke, *The History of Everyday Life*, viii–x.

Elias, Norberto. "Apuntes sobre el concepto de lo cotidiano." In *La civilización de los padres y otros ensayos,* edited and translated by Vera Weiler, 331–47. Bogota: Grupo Editorial Norma, 1998.

———. "A Theoretical Essay on Established and Outsider Relations." Introduction to *The Established and the Outsiders: A Sociological Enquiry into Community Problems,* by Norbert Elias and John Scotson, 1976. 2nd ed. London: Sage, 1994, xv–lii.

Elliot, John. "Atlantic History: A Circumnavigation." Afterward to *The British Atlantic World, 1500–1800,* edited by David Armitage and Michael J. Braddick, 233–49. New York: Palgrave, 2002.

"El mercado de café" *Boletín de la Sociedad Agrícola Mexicana* 30, no. 39 (October 17, 1906): 778.

"El precio de café." *Boletín de la Sociedad Agrícola Mexicana* 19, no. 25 (July 8, 1895): 402–3.

Embriz Osorio, Arnulfo. *La Liga de Comunidades y Sindicatos Agraristas del Estado de Michoacán.* Mexico City: CEHAH, 1984.

Enstad, Nan. *Ladies of Labor, Girls of Adventure: Working Women, Popular Culture, and Labor Politics at the Turn of the Twentieth Century.* New York: Columbia University Press, 1999.

Estrada Urroz, Rosalinda. *Del telar a la cadena de montaje: La condición obrera en Puebla, 1940–1976.* Puebla: Benemérita Universidad Autónoma de Puebla, 1996.

Falcón, Romana. *El radicalismo agrario en Veracruz.* Mexico City: El Colegio de México, 1977.

———. *Revolución y caciquismo, San Luis Potosí (1910–1938).* Mexico City: El Colegio de México, 1984.

Falcón, Romana, and Soledad García Morales. *La semilla en el surco.* Xalapa: El Colegio de México and Gobierno del Estado de Veracruz, 1986.

FAO (Food and Agriculture Organization of the United Nations). *The World Coffee Economy.* Commodity Bulletin Series. Rome: FAO, 1961.

Farnsworth-Alvear, Ann. *Dulcinea in the Factory: Myths, Morals, Men and Women in Colombia's Industrial Experiment, 1906–1960.* Durham NC: Duke University Press, 2000.

———. "Talking, Fighting, Flirting: Workers' Sociability in Medellín Textile Mills." In French and James, *Gendered Worlds of Latin American Women Workers,* 147–75.

Fernández-Aceves, María Teresa. "Advocate, or *Cacica*? Guadalupe Urzúa Flores, Modernizer and Peasant Political Leader in Jalisco." In *Soft Authoritarianism in Mexico, 1940–1968*, edited by Paul Gillingham and Benjamin Smith. Durham NC: Duke University Press, forthcoming.

―――. *Cambio social, politica, y género: Las mujeres en el siglo XX mexicano*. Mexico City: CIESAS, forthcoming.

―――. "En-gendering *Caciquismo*: Guadalupe Martínez, Helio Hernández Loza and the Politics of Organized Labour in Jalisco." In Knight and Pansters, *Caciquismo in Twentieth-Century Mexico*, 201–24.

―――. "Once We Were Corn Grinders: Women and Labor in the Tortilla Industry of Guadalajara, 1920–40." *International Labor and Working-Class History* 63 (Spring 2003): 81–101.

―――. "The Struggle between the *Metate* and the *Molino de Nixtamal* in Guadalajara, 1920–1940." In Olcott, Vaughan, and Cano, *Sex in Revolution*, 147–61.

Fernández-Aceves, María Teresa, Carmen Ramos Escandón, and Susie Porter, eds. *Orden social e identidad de género: México, siglos XIX y XX*. Guadalajara: CIESAS / Universidad de Guadalajara, 2006.

Fernández Tejeda, Isabel, and Carmen Nava Nava. "Images of Independence in the Nineteenth Century: The *Grito de Dolores*, History and Myth." In Beezley and Lorey, *Viva Mexico! Viva la Independencia!* 1–41.

Fernández y Fernández, Ramón. *El café de Veracruz*. Mexico City: Banco Nacional de Crédito Agrícola, 1939.

Flandrau, Charles. *Viva Mexico*. New York: Appleton, 1910.

Flores y Escalante, Jesús. *Salón México: Historia documental y gráfica del danzón en México*. Mexico City: Asociación Mexicana de Estudios Fonográficos, 1993.

Font, Mauricio A. *Coffee, Contention, and Change in the Making of Modern Brazil*. Cambridge MA: Basil Blackwell, 1990.

Fowler, Heather. "Orígenes laborales de la organización campesina en Veracruz." *Historia Mexicana* 78 (October–December 1970): 235–64.

Fowler-Salamini, Heather. *Agrarian Radicalism in Veracruz, 1920–1938*. Lincoln: University of Nebraska Press, 1978.

―――. "Caciquismo and the Mexican Revolution: The Case of Manuel Peláez." In *Los intelectuales y el poder en México*, edited by Roderick A.

Camp, Charles Hale, and Josefina Zoraida Vázquez, 189–209. Mexico City: El Colegio de México; Los Angeles: UCLA Latin American Center, 1991).

———. "Caciquismo, sindicalismo y género en la agroindustria cafetalera de Córdoba, Veracruz." In Cárdenas García and Guerra Manzo, *Integrados y marginados en el México posrevolucionario*, 205–45.

———. "Fotografía y mujeres: Las escogedoras de café." *Memorial: Boletín del Archivo General del Estado de Veracruz* 2, no. 5 (1999): 3–8.

———. "Gender, Work, and Coffee in Córdoba, Veracruz, 1850–1910." In *Women of the Mexican Countryside, 1850–1980: Creating Spaces, Shaping Transitions*, edited by Heather Fowler-Salamini and Mary Kay Vaughan, 51–73. Tucson: University of Arizona Press, 1994.

———. "Gender, Work, and Working-Class Women's Culture in the Veracruz Coffee Export Industry." *International Labor and Working-Class History* 63 (Spring 2003): 102–21.

———. "Gender, Work, Trade-Unionism, and Working-Class Women's Culture in Post-Revolutionary Veracruz." In Olcott, Vaughan, and Cano, *Sex in Revolution*, 162–80.

———. "La movilización obrera veracruzana y la cuestión de género (1915 a 1919)." In *Movimiantos sociales en un ambiente revolucionario*, edited by Coralia Gutiérrez Álvarez. Puebla, Puebla: Benemerita Universidad Autónoma de Puebla, forthcoming.

———. "'La Negra Moya': Alma, leyenda y líder de las desmanchadoras de café de Veracruz en el México posrevolucionario." In *Mujeres en Veracruz: Fragmentos de una historia*, edited by Rosa María Spinoso Arcocha and Fernanda Nuñez Becerra, 2:40–66. Xalapa: Gobierno del Estado, 2010.

———. "Revolutionary Caudillos in the 1920s: Francisco Múgica and Adalberto Tejeda." In *Caudillo and Peasant in the Mexican Revolution*, edited by D. A. Brading, 169–92. Cambridge: Cambridge University Press, 1980.

———. "Revuelta popular y regionalismo en Veracruz, 1906–13." *Eslabones: Revista semestral de estudios regionales*, 5 (January–June 1993): 99–117. Reprinted in *La Revolución Mexicana en Veracruz: Antología*, edited by Bernardo García Díaz and David Skerritt Gardner, 155–207. Xalapa: Gobierno del Estado, 2009.

Fraser Delgado, Celeste, and José Esteban Muñoz, eds. *Everynight Life: Culture and Dance in Latin/o America*. Durham NC: Duke University Press, 1997.

French, John D., and Daniel James, eds. *The Gendered Worlds of Latin American Women Workers: From Household and Factory to the Union Hall and Ballot Box*. Durham NC: Duke University Press, 1997.

——— . "Squaring the Circle: Women's Factory Labor, Gender Ideology, and Necessity." In French and James, *Gendered Worlds of Latin American Women Workers*, 1–21.

French, John D., and Mary Lynn Pedersen Cluff. "Women and Working-Class Mobilization in Postwar São Paulo, 1945–1948." In French and James, *Gendered Worlds of Latin American Women Workers*, 176–207.

French, William E. *A Peaceful and Working People: Manners, Morals, and Class Formation in Northern Mexico*. Austin: University of Texas Press, 1996.

——— . "Prostitutes and Guardian Angels: Women, Work, and Family in Porfirian Mexico." *Hispanic American Historical Review* 72, no. 4 (1992): 529–53.

Friedrich, Paul. *An Agrarian Revolt in a Mexican Village*. Englewood Cliffs NJ: Prentice Hall, 1970.

——— . "A Mexican Cacicazgo," *Ethnography* 4 (April 1965): 190–209.

Frost, Elsa Cecilia, Michael C. Meyer, and Josefina Vásquez, *El trabajo y los trabajadores en la historia de México: Labor and Laborers through Mexican History*. Mexico City: El Colegio de México and University of Arizona Press, 1979.

Gamboa, Federico. *Santa*. Mexico City: Ediciones Leyenda, 2004.

——— . *Santa: A Novel of Mexico City*. Translated by John Charles Chasteen. Chapel Hill: University of North Carolina Press, 2010.

Gamboa Ojeda, Letica. "Inserción, hispanidad e hispanismo entre los empresarios españoles de Puebla (1895–1930)." In *Extraños en tierra ajena: Migración, alteridad e identidad, siglos XIX, XX, y XXI*, edited by Raquel Ofelia Barceló Quintal, 95–139. Mexico City: Plaza y Valdés, 2009.

——— . *La urdimbre y la trama: Historia social de los obreros textiles de Atlixco, 1899–1924*. Mexico City: Fondo de Cultura Económica, 2001.

——— , ed. *Los Barcelonnettes en México: Miradas regionales, siglos XIX y*

XX. Puebla: Benemérita Universidad Autónoma de Puebla / Universidad Juárez del Estado de Durango, 2008.

———. "Los Barcelonnettes en México: Reafirmaciones, correcciones y nuevos aportes e interpretaciones." In Gamboa Ojeda, *Los Barcelonnettes en México*, 7–50.

———. *Los empresarios de ayer: El grupo dominante en la industria textil de Puebla, 1906–1929*. Puebla: Editorial Universidad Autónoma, 1985.

Games, Alison. "Atlantic History: Definitions, Challenges, and Opportunities." *American Historical Review* 111, no. 3 (June 2006): 747–57. http://www.jstor/org/stable/10.1086/ahr.111.3.741.

García, Antonio. *Geografía económica de Caldas*. 2nd ed. Bogotá, Colombia: Banco de la República, 1978.

García Díaz, Bernardo. "El sindicalismo textil orizabeño (1915–25)." In *Actores sociales en un proceso de transformacion: Veracruz en los años veinte*, edited by Manuel Reyna Muñoz, 159–89. Xalapa: Universidad Veracruzana, 1996.

———. *Los trabajadores del Valle de Orizaba y la Revolución Mexicana: Retratos de grupo*. Xalapa, Veracruz: Gobierno del Estado / Universidad Veracruzana / IVEC, 2011.

———. *Textiles del Valle de Orizaba (1880–1925)*. Xalapa: Universidad Veracruzana, 1990.

———. *Un pueblo fabril del porfiriato: Santa Rosa, Veracruz*. 2nd ed. Ciudad Mendoza, Veracruz: FOMECA, 1997.

García Morales, Soledad. *Coatepec: Una vision de su historia, 1450–1911*. Coatepec: Ayuntamiento, 1986.

Garza, James Alex. *The Imagined Underworld: Sex, Crime, and Vice in Porfirian Mexico City*. Lincoln: University of Nebraska Press, 2007.

Gauss, Susan M. "Working-Class Masculinity and the Rationalized Sex: Gender and Industrial Modernization in the Textile Industry in Postrevolutionary Puebla." In Olcott, Vaughan, and Cano, *Sex in Revolution*, 181–96.

Gavira, Gabriel. *Su actuación político-militar revolucionaria*. Mexico City: Tipografía del Bosque, 1933.

Gervase Clarence-Smith, William, and Steven Topik, eds. *The Global Coffee Economy in Africa, Asia, and Latin America, 1500–1989*. Cambridge: Cambridge University Press, 2003.

Gier, Daniel. "El elemento español en *Santa* de Federico Gamboa." *Revista canadiense de estudios hispánicos* 23, no. 1 (Fall 1998): 132–43.

Gillingham, Paul. "Force and Consent in Mexican Provincial Politics: Guerrero and Veracruz, 1945–1953." PhD diss., University of Oxford, 2005.

Goldsmith Connelly, Mary R. "Espacios laborales y sindicalización de las mujeres, en los margenes del poder: Las trabajadoras domésticas en Tampico y Ciudad Madero, 1929–1944." In Cárdenas García and Guerra Manzo, *Integrados y marginados en el México posrevolucionario*, 247–96.

——— . "Política, trabajo y género: La sindicalización de las y los trabajadores domésticos y el estado mexicano." In Fernández-Aceves, Ramos Escandón, and Porter, *Orden social e identidad de género*, 215–44.

Gómez, Gabriel. *Cultivo y beneficio del café.* 2nd ed. Mexico City: Secretaría de Fomento, 1899.

Gómez-Galvarriato Freer, Aurora. "The Impact of the Revolution: Business and Labor in the Mexican Textile Industry, Orizaba, Veracruz, 1900–1930." PhD diss., Department of History, Harvard University, 1999.

González Casanova, Pablo. *En el primero gobierno constitucional (1917–1920).* Vol 6 of *La clase obrera en la historia de México.* 4th ed. Mexico City: Siglo XXI, 1996.

González Navarro, Moisés. *La vida social: El Porfiriato.* Vol. 4 of *Historia moderna de México*, edited by Daniel Cosío Villegas. 2nd ed. Mexico City: Editorial Hermes, 1974.

González Sierra, José. *Córdoba: Imagenes de su historia.* Veracruz: El Naranjo, 2000.

——— . *Monopolio del humo: Elementos para la historia del tabaco en México y algunos conflictos de tabaqueros veracruzanos, 1915–30.* Xalapa: Universidad Veracruzana, 1987.

González y González, Luis. *La vida social: La república restaurada.* Vol. 3 of *Historia moderna de México*, edited by Daniel Cosío Villegas. 2nd ed. Mexico City: Hermes, 1974.

Gortari Rabiela, Hira de. "Hacia una renovación de la historia urbana." In Muro, *Ciudades provincianas de México*, 27–30.

Granados, Aimer. *Debates sobre españa: El hispanoamericanismo en México a fines del siglo XIX.* 2ed. Mexico City: Colegio de México / Universidad Autónoma Mexicana–Cualimalpa, 2010.

Guerra Manzo, Enrique. *Caciquismo y orden público en Michoacán, 1920–1940*. Mexico City: El Colegio de México, 2002.

Gutiérrez Álvarez, Coralia. *Experiencias contrastadas: Industrialización en los textiles del centro-oriente de México, 1884–1917*. Mexico City: El Colegio de México, 2000.

Gutmann, Matthew. *The Meanings of Macho: Being a Man in Mexico City*. Berkeley: University of California Press, 1996.

Guy, Donna. *Sex and Danger in Buenos Aires: Prostitution, Family and Nation in Argentina*. Lincoln: University of Nebraska Press, 1991.

Hall, Carolyn. *El café y el desarrollo histórico-geográfico de Costa Rica*. San José: Editorial Costa Rica, 1991.

Hall, Stuart. "Notes on Deconstructing 'The Popular.'" In *People's History and Socialist Theory*, edited by Rafael Samuel, 227–40. London: Routledge, Kegan, and Paul, 1981.

Halwachs, Maurice. *On Collective Memory*. Edited and translated by Lewis Coser. Chicago: University of Chicago Press, 1992.

Hart, John M. *Anarchism and the Mexican Working Class, 1860–1931*. Austin: University of Texas Press, 1978.

———. *Empire and Revolution: Americans in Mexico since the Civil War*. Berkeley: University of California Press, 2002.

———. *Revolutionary Mexico: The Coming and Process of the Mexican Revolution*. Berkeley: University of California Press, 1987.

Heller, Agnes. *Everyday Life*. Translated by G. L. Campbell. London: Routledge, Kegan, and Paul, 1984.

Hernández, Ana María. *La mujer mexicana en la industria textil*. Mexico City: Tipografía Moderna, 1940.

Hernández Rodríguez, Rogelio. "Challenging *Caciquismo*: An Analysis of the Leadership of Carlos Hank González." In Knight and Pansters, *Caciquismo in Twentieth-Century Mexico*, 249–71.

Herrera, Rafael. "El café de Córdoba." *Boletín de la Sociedad Agrícola Mexicana* 18, no. 4 (January 31, 1889): 64–67.

———. *El estudio sobre la producción del café*. Mexico City: Secretaría de Fomento, 1893.

Herrera Moreno, Enrique. *El cantón de Córdoba: Apuntes de geografía, estadísticas, e historia*. Vol. 1. Mexico City: Editorial Citlaltepetl, 1959.

Herrero, Carlos B. *Los empresarios mexicanos del origen vasco y el desarrollo* del capitalismo en México 1850–1950. Mexico City: Universidad Autónoma Metropolitana–Iztapalapa, 2004.

Hewitt, Nancy A. "'The Voice of Virile Labor': Labor Militancy, Community Solidarity, and Gender Identity among Tampa's Latin Workers, 1880–1921." In Work Engendered: Toward a New History of American Labor, edited by Ava Baron, 142–67. Ithaca NY: Cornell University Press, 1991.

"Homenaje a Don Juan Antonio Gómez de Guevara: Proceder de la agricultura nacional y programa festejos, 1878." Córdoba, ca. 1940.

Huitrón, Jacinto. Orígenes e historia del movimiento obrero en México. 2nd ed. Mexico City: Editores Mexicanos Unidos, 1980.

Illades, Carlos. "Los propietarios españoles y la Revolución Mexicana." In Lida, Una inmigracion privilegiada, 170–89.

———. Presencia española en la Revolución Mexicana, 1900–1915. Mexico City: Universidad Nacional Autónoma de México / Mora, 1991.

INEGI (Instituto Nacional de Estadísticas, Geografía e Información). Estadísticas históricas de México. 2 vols. Aguascalientes, 1990.

———. Estadísticas históricas de México. 2 vols. Aguascalientes, 1994.

———. Estadísticas históricas de México. 2 vols. Aguascalientes, 1999.

"Informe del jefe politico del cantón del Córdoba (Regino Zenteno), noviembre 9 de 1897." In Veracruz, Memorias y informes de jefes políticos y autoridades del regimen porfirista, 4:157–212.

"Informe del gobernador (Abel S. Rodríguez) del Estado, septiembre 1927 a septiembre 1928." In Veracruz, Informes de sus gobernadores, 11:6013–62.

"Informe del Lic. Miguel Alemán a la XXXVI Legislatura de Veracruz, septiembre 16 de 1937." In Veracruz, Informes de sus gobernadores, 12:6617–755.

"Informe que rinde el Ejecutivo libre y soberano de Veracruz-Llave ante la H. Legislatura del mismo por el periodo comprendido del 16 de octubre de 1920 al 5 de mayo de 1921 (Adalberto Tejeda)." In Veracruz, Informes de sus gobernadores, 10:5409–68.

"Informe que rinde el C. Ing. Adalberto Tejeda, Gobernador Constitucional del Estado, ante la tregésimacuarta Legislatura (del período de 1928–1932)." In Veracruz, Informes de sus gobernadores, 11:6065–222.

Instituto Mexicano del Café. México y el III Convenio Internacional del Café. Mexico City, 1976.

James, Daniel. *Doña María's Story: Life History, Memory, and Political Identity*. Durham NC: Duke University Press, 2000.

———. "'Tales Told out on the Borderlands': Doña Maria's Story, Oral History and Issues of Gender." In French and James, *Gendered Worlds of Latin American Women Workers*, 31–52.

Joseph, Gilbert M. "Caciquismo and the Revolution: Carrillo Puerto in Yucatán." In *Caudillo and Peasant in the Mexican Revolution*, edited by D. A. Brading, 193–221. Cambridge: Cambridge University Press, 1980.

———. *Revolution from Without: Yucatán, Mexico, and the United States, 1880–1924*. Cambridge: Cambridge University Press, 1982.

Joseph, Gilbert M., Anne Rubenstein, and Eric Zolov. "Assembling Fragments: Writing a Cultural History of Mexico since 1940." In *Fragments of a Golden Age: The Politics of Culture since 1940*, edited by Gilbert M. Joseph, Anne Rubenstein, and Eric Zolov, 3–22. Durham NC: Duke University Press, 2001.

Joseph, Gilbert M., and Daniel Nugent. "Popular Culture and State Formation in Revolutionary Mexico." In *Everyday Forms of State Formation: Revolution and the Negotiation of Rule in Modern Mexico*, edited by Gilbert M. Joseph and Daniel Nugent, 3–23. Durham NC: Duke University Press, 1994.

Juárez Martínez, Abel. "Especulación y crisis en el centro de Veracruz, 1915." *Anuario 6* (Centro de Investigaciones Históricas, Universidad Veracruzana): 231–61.

Juárez Rivera, Hilda. *Las capitales del Estado de Veracruz*. Xalapa: Universidad Veracruzana, 1987.

Kaplan, Temma. "Female Consciousness and Collective Action: The Case of Barcelona, 1910–1918." *Signs: Journal of Women in Culture and Society* 7, no. 3 (1982): 545–66.

Katz, Friedrich. *The Life and Times of Pancho Villa*. Stanford: Stanford University Press, 1998.

Kellogg, Susan. *Weaving the Past: A History of Latin America's Indigenous Women from the Prehispanic Period to the Present*. Oxford: Oxford University Press, 2005.

Kenny, M. "Emigración, inmigración, remigración: El ciclo migratorio de los españoles en México." In Kenny, et al., *Inmigrantes y refugiados españoles en México (Siglo XX)*, 15–92.

Kenny, M., et al. *Inmigrantes y refugiados españoles en México (Siglo XX)*. Mexico City: Ediciones Casa Chata, 1979.

Keremitsis, Dawn. "Del metate al molino: La mujer mexicana de 1910 a 1940." *Historia Mexicana* 33 (October–December 1983): 285–302.

———. "Latin American Women Workers in Transition: Sexual Division of the Labor Forces in Mexico and Colombia in the Textile Industry." *Americas* 40 (1984): 491–504.

Kessler-Harris, Alice. "Reconfiguring the Private in the Context of the Public." In *Gendering Labor History*, 158–74. Champaign: University of Illinois Press, 2007.

Klubock, Thomas Miller. *Contested Communities: Class, Gender, and Politics in Chile's El Teniente Copper Mine, 1904–1951*. Durham NC: Duke University Press, 1998.

———. "Gender, the Working Class, and the History of the Post-Revolutionary State in Mexico." *International Labor and Working-Class History* 63 (Spring 2003): 37–44.

———. "Morality and Good Habits: The Construction of Gender and Class in the Chilean Copper Mines, 1904–51." In French and James, *Gendered Worlds of Latin American Women Workers*, 232–63.

Knight, Alan. "*Caciquismo* in Twentieth-Century Mexico." Introduction to Knight and Pansters, *Caciquismo in Twentieth-Century Mexico*, 1–48.

———. *The Mexican Revolution*. 2 vols. Cambridge: Cambridge University Press, 1986.

———. "The Working Class and the Mexican Revolution, c. 1900–1920." *Journal of Latin American Studies* 16 (1984): 51–79.

Knight, Alan, and Wil Pansters, eds. *Caciquismo in Twentieth-Century Mexico*. London: Institute for the Study of the Americas, 2005.

Koth, Karl B. *Waking the Dictator: Veracruz, the Struggle for Federation and the Mexican Revolution, 1870–1927*. Calgary: University of Calgary Press, 2002.

Kraeger, Karl. *Agricultura y colonización en México*. Translated by Pedro Lewin and Gudrun Dohrmann. Mexico City: Universidad de Chapingo / CIESAS, 1986.

Kuntz Ficker, Sandra. "El café." In *Las exportaciones mexicanas durante la primera globalización (1870–1929)*, 291–343. Mexico City: El Colegio de México, 2010.

————. *Las exportaciones mexicanas durante la primera globalización (1870–1929)*. Mexico City: El Colegio de México, 2010.

Lau, Ana, and Carmen Ramos, eds. *Mujeres y revolución, 1900–1917*. Mexico City: INERHM, 1993.

Lear, John. *Workers, Neighbors, and Citizens: The Revolution in Mexico City*. Lincoln: University of Nebraska Press, 2001.

Leñero Franco, Estela. *El huso y el sexo: La mujer obrera en dos industrias de Tlaxcala*. Mexico City: Cuadernos de la Casa Chata, 1984.

León, Samuel, and Ignacio Marván. *En el cardenismo (1934–1940)*. Vol. 10 of *La clase obrera en la historia de México*. México: Siglo XXI / Instituto Nacional de Antropología e Historia, 1985.

León Fuentes, Nelly Josefa. "Conformación de un capital en torno a la cafeticultura en la región de Xalapa-Coatepec, 1840–1940." Master's thesis in history, Universidad Veracruzana, 1983.

Levenson-Estrada, Deborah. "Loneliness of Working-Class Feminism: Women in the 'Male World' of Labor Unions, Guatemala City, 1970s." In French and James, *Gendered Worlds of Latin American Women Workers*, 208–31.

Lida, Clara E., ed. *Una inmigracion privilegiada: Comerciantes, empresarios y profesionales españoles en México en los siglos XIX y XX*. Madrid: Editorial Alianza, 1994.

Lim, Linda Y. C. "Women's Work in Export Factories: The Politics of a Cause." In *Persistent Inequalities: Women and World Development*, edited by Irene Tinker, 101–19. New York: Oxford University Press, 1990.

Limones Ceniceros, Georgina. "Las costureras anarcosindicalistas de Orizaba, 1915." In *Trabajo, poder y sexualidad*, edited by Orlandina de Oliveira, 219–40. Mexico City: El Colegio de México, 1989.

Lobato, Mirta Zaida. "Women Workers in the Cathedrals of Corned Beef: Structure and Subjectivity in the Argentina Meatpacking Industry." In French and James, *Gendered Worlds of Latin American Women Workers*, 53–71.

López de Parra, R. "El café." *Boletín de la Sociedad Agrícola Mexicana* 26, no. 41 (November 1, 1902): 807–8.

Lüdtke, Alf, ed. *The History of Everyday Life: Reconstructing Historical Experiences and Ways of Life*. Translated by William Templar. Princeton: Princeton University Press, 1995.

———. "What Is the History of Everyday Life and Who Are Its Practitioners?" Introduction to Lüdtke, *History of Everyday Life*, 1–40.

Macías, Anna. *Against All Odds: The Feminist Movement in Mexico to 1940.* Westport CT: Greenwood Press, 1984.

Maldonado Aranda, Salvador. "Between Law and Arbitrariness: Labour Union Caciques in Mexico." In Knight and Pansters, *Caciquismo in Twentieth-Century Mexico*, 227–48.

Mallon, Florencia E. "The Promise and Dilemma of Subaltern Studies: Perspectives from Latin American History." *American Historical Review* 99, no. 5 (December 1994): 1491–515.

———. "Editor's Introduction." In *When a Flower Is Reborn: The Life and Times of a Mapuche Feminist*, by Rosa Isolde Reuque Paillalef, 1–16. Edited and translated by Florencia E. Mallon. Durham NC: Duke University Press, 2002.

Martínez Assad, Carlos. *El laboratorio de la revolución: El Tabasco garridista.* Mexico City: Siglo XXI, 1979.

McGee Deutsch, Sandra. "Gender and Sociopolitical Change in Twentieth-Century Latin America." *Hispanic American Historical Review* 71, no. 2 (1991): 259–306.

Medel y Alvarado, León. *Historia de San Andrés Tuxtla.* Vol. 1. Mexico City: Editorial Citlaltepetl, 1963.

Medina, Luis. *Civilismo y modernización del autoritarismo.* Vol. 20 of *Historia de la Revolución Mexicana, 1940–1952.* Mexico City: El Colegio de México, 1979.

"Memoria presentada a la H. Legislatura del Estado Libre y Soberano de Veracruz-Llave el 18 de septiembre de 1890 por el gobernador constitucional, Juan Enríquez, comprende el período corrido del 1 de julio de 1888 a 30 de junio de 1890." In Veracruz, *Informes de sus gobernadores*, 7–8:3489–4107.

"Memoria que comprende el período de 1 de julio de 1886 a 30 de junio de 1888 presentada a la H. Legislatura del Estado de Veracruz-Llave por el gobernador constitucional del mismo C. Juan Enríquez, el 17 de septiembre del ultimo de los citados años." In Veracruz, *Informes de sus gobernadores*, 5–6:2715–3408.

"Memoria que rinde el jefe político del cantón de Coatepec (Manuel Martínez de Castro) al gobernador del Estado de Veracruz, 15 de marzo de 1897." In Veracruz, *Memorias y informes de jefes políticos y autoridades del regime porfirista*, 4:157–212.

"Memoria que rinde el jefe político del cantón de Córdoba al gobernador del Estado de Veracruz, 5 de julio de 1890." In Veracruz, *Memorias y informes de jefes políticos y autoridades del régimen porfirista*, 4:131–42.

Meyer, Jean. *La Revolución Mexicana*. Mexico City: Editorial Jus, 1991.

Meyer, Lorenzo. *El conflicto social y los gobiernos del maximato*. Vol. 13 of *Historia de la Revolución Mexicana*. Mexico City: El Colegio de México, 1980.

Middlebrook, Kevin. *The Paradox of Revolution: Labor, the State, and Authoritarianism*. Baltimore MD: Johns Hopkins University Press, 1995.

Montgomery, David. *The Fall of the House of Labor: The Workplace, the State, and American Labor Activism, 1865–1925*. Cambridge: Cambridge University Press, 1987.

Moore, Rachel A. *Forty Miles from the Sea: Xalapa, the Public Sphere, and the Atlantic World in Nineteenth-Century Mexico*. Tucson: University of Arizona Press, 2011.

Moya, José C. "A Continent of Immigrants: Postcolonial Shifts in the Western Hemisphere," *Hispanic American Historical Review* 86, no. 1 (February 2006): 1–28.

———. *Cousins and Strangers: Spanish Immigrants in Buenos Aires, 1850–1930*. Berkeley: University of California Press, 1998.

Muro, Victor Gabriel, ed. *Ciudades provincianas de México: Historia, modernización y cambio cultural*. Zamora: El Colegio de Michoacán, 1998.

Naveda Chávez-Hita, Adriana. *Esclavos negros en las haciendas azucareras de Córdoba, Veracruz, 1630–1830*. Xalapa, Veracruz: Universidad Veracruzana, 1986.

Niblo, Stephen. *Mexico in the 1940s: Modernity, Politics, and Corruption*. Wilmington DE: Scholarly Resources, 1999.

———. *War, Diplomacy, and Development: The United States and Mexico, 1938–1954*. Wilmington DE: Scholarly Resources, 1995.

Nolasco, Margarita. *Café y sociedad en Mexico*. Mexico City: Centro de Ecodesarrollo, 1985.

Noriega Hope, Carlos. *Santa*. Starring Lupita Tovar. Directed by Antonio Moreno. Music by Agustín Lara. Mexico City: Companía Nacional

Productora de Película, 1931. Filmstrip stored at Filmoteca de la Universidad Nacional Autónoma de México, Mexico City.

Norvell, Elizabeth Jean. "Los ciudadanos sindicalistas: La Federación Local de Trabajadores del Puerto de Veracruz, 1919–1923." In *Actores sociales en un proceso de transformación: Veracruz en los años veinte*, edited by Manuel Reyna Muñoz, 55–75. Xalapa: Universidad Veracruzana, 1996.

——. "Syndicalism and Citizenship: Postrevolutionary Worker Mobilization in Veracruz." In *Border Crossings: Mexican and Mexican-American Workers*, edited by John Mason Hart, 93–116. Wilmington DE: Scholarly Resources, 1998.

Olcott, Jocelyn. "Miracle Workers: Gender and State Mediation among Textile Workers in Mexico's Transition to Industrial Development." *International Labor and Working-Class History* 63 (Spring 2002): 45–62.

——. *Revolutionary Women in Postrevolutionary Mexico*. Durham NC: Duke University Press, 2005.

Olcott, Jocelyn, Mary Kay Vaughan, and Gabriela Cano, eds. *Sex in Revolution: Gender, Politics, and Power in Modern Mexico*. Durham NC: Duke University Press, 2006.

Ober, Frederik. *Travels in Mexico and Life among the Mexicans*. Boston: Estes and Larriat, 1887.

Olvera, Alberto. "La estructura económica y social de Veracruz hacia 1930," *Anuario* 3 (ca. 1985): 9–58.

Paige, Jeffrey. *Coffee and Power: Revolution and the Rise of Democracy in Central America*. Cambridge: Harvard University Press, 1997.

Palacios, Marco. *Coffee in Colombia, 1850–1970: An Economic, Social, and Political History*. Cambridge: Cambridge University Press, 1980.

——. *El café en Colombia, 1850–1970: Una historia económica, social y política*. 4ed. Mexico City: El Colegio de México, 2009.

Panabiere, Louis. *Itinerarias de una disidencia: Jorge Cuesta*. Mexico City: Fondo de Cultura Económica, 1983.

Pansters, Wil. "Building a *Cacicazgo* in a Neoliberal University." In Knight and Pansters, *Caciquismo in Twentieth-Century Mexico*, 296–326.

——. "Goodbye to the Caciques? Definition, the State and the Dynamics of *Caciquismo* in Twentieth-century Mexico." In Knight and Pansters, *Caciquismo in Twentieth-Century Mexico*, 349–76.

Paredes Cruz, Armando. "Los Barcelonnettes: Memoria e identidad." In Gamboa Ojeda, *Los Barcelonnettes en México*, 469–91.

Pasquel, Leonardo. *La revolución en el Estado de Veracruz.* 2 Vols. Mexico City: Citlaltepetl, 1971.

Passerini, Luisa. *Fascism in Popular Memory: The Cultural Experience of the Turin Working Class.* Translated by Robert Lumley and Jude Bloomfield. Cambridge: Cambridge University Press; Paris: Editions de la Maison des Sciences de l'Homme, 1987.

Peiss, Kathy. *Cheap Amusements: Working Women and Leisure in Turn-of-the-Century New York.* Philadelphia: Temple University Press, 1986.

Pellicer de Brody, Olga, and José Luis Reyna, eds. *El afianzamiento de la estabilidad política.* Vol 22 of *Historia de la Revolución Mexicana.* Mexico City: Colegio de México, 1978.

Pérez-Brignoli, Hector, and Mario Samper, eds. *Tierra, café y sociedad.* San José: FLASCO, 1994.

Pérez Firmat, Gustavo. "I came, I saw, I Conga'd: Contexts for Cuban-American Culture." In *Everynight Life, Culture and Dance in Latin/o America* edited by Celeste Fraser Delgado and José Esteban Muñoz. Durham: Duke University Press, 1997, 239–54.

Pérez Monfort, Ricardo. *Hispanidad y falange: Los sueños imperiales de la derecha española.* Mexico City: Fondo de Cultura Económica, 1992.

Peters, Gertrud. "Empresarios e historia del café en Costa Rica, 1930–50." In Pérez-Brignoli and Samper, *Tierra, café y sociedad*, 495–565.

———. "La formación territorial de las fincas grandes de café en la meseta central: Estudio de la firma Touron (1877–1955)." *Revista de Historia* (Costa Rica) 9–10 (July–December 1980): 81–151.

Portelli, Alessandro. *The Battle of Valle Giulia: Oral History and the Art of Dialogue.* Madison: University of Wisconsin Press, 1995.

———. *The Death of Luigi Trastulli and Other Stories: Form and Meaning in Oral History.* Albany: State University of New York Press, 1991.

Porter, Susie S. "In the Shadow of Industrialization: The Entrance of Women into the Mexican Industrial Work Force, 1880–1940," PhD diss., Department of History, University of California at San Diego, 1997.

———. *Working Women in Mexico City: Public Discourses and Material Conditions, 1870–1931.* Tucson: University of Arizona Press, 2003.

Radkau, Verena. *"La Fama" y la vida: Una fábrica y sus obreras.* Mexico City: Cuadernos de la Casa Chata: 1984.

Ramírez, Luis Alfonso. *Secretos de familia: Libanéses y elites empresariales en Yucatán.* Mexico City: CONACULTA, 1994.

Ramírez, Mario. "Estadística del Partido de Córdoba, formado en 1840." *Boletín de la Sociedad Mexicana de Geografía y Estadística* 2 (1854): 73–110.

Ramos Escandón, Carmen. "Gender, Labor, and Class-Consciousness in the Mexican Textile Industry, 1880–1910." In *Border Crossings: Mexican and Mexican-American Workers,* edited by John Mason Hart, 71–92. Wilmington DE: Scholarly Resources, 1998.

———. "Mujeres trabajadoras en el México porfiriano: Género e ideología del trabajo femenino 1876–1911." *Revista Europea de Estudios Latinoamericanos y del Caribe* 48 (June 1990): 27–44.

Ravelo Blancas, Patricia, and Sergio Sánchez. "Las mujeres en los sindicatos en México (una aproximación al tema)." In *Voces disidentes,* edited by Sara Elena Pérez and Patricia Ravelo Blancas, 417–42. Mexico City: Centro de Investigaciones y Estudios Superiores en Antropología Social–Porrúa, 2003.

"Reglamentación de la producción del café en Brasil." *Boletín de la Sociedad Agrícola Mexicana* 30, no. 37 (May 17, 1906): 367–68.

Reséndez Fuentes, Andrés. "Battleground Women: *Soldaderas* and Female Soldiers in the Mexican Revolution," *Americas* 51, no. 4 (April 1995): 525–53.

Reyna, José Luis. "La negociación controlada con el movimiento obrero." In Pellicer de Brody and Reyna, *El afianzamiento de la estabilidad política,* 73–106.

Rocha, Marta Eva, ed. *El album de la mujer: Antologia ilustrada de las mexicanas.* Vol. 4. Mexico City: INAH, 1991.

Rodríguez Centeno, Mabel M. "Caficultura y modernidad: Las transformaciones del entorno agrícola, agrario y humano en Córdoba, Veracruz (1870–1930)." *Secuencia* 52 (January–April 2002): 63–97.

———. "Fiscalidad y café mexicano: El porfiriato y sus estratégias de fomento económico para la producción y comercialización del grano (1870–1910)." *Historia Mexicana* 54, no. 1 (July–September 2004): 93–127.

———. "La producción cafetalera mexicana: El caso de Córdoba Veracruz." *Historia Mexicana* 43, no.1 (1993): 81–115.

———. "La tierra y la gente: Un estudio histórico sobe la población rural en Córdoba, Veracruz." *Historia y Sociedad* 11 (1999): 7–89.

———. "Paisaje agrario y sociedad rural: Tenencia de la tierra y caficultura en Córdoba, Veracruz (1870–1940)." PhD diss., Centro de Estudios Históricos, El Colegio de México, 1997.

Rodríguez Rocafuerte, Beatriz. "Mujeres y participación ciudadana en un ayuntamiento panista: Córdoba, Veracruz." In *Mujeres, ciudadanía y poder*, edited by Dalia Barrera Bassols, 227–93. Mexico City: El Colegio de México, 2000.

Rojas, Basilio. *El café: Estudio de su llegada, implantación y desarrollo en el estado de Oaxaca, México*. Mexico City: Editorial Luz, 1964.

Romero, Matías. "Coffee Culture on the Southern Coast of Chiapas." In *Coffee and India-Rubber Culture in Mexico Preceded by Geographical and States Notes on Mexico*, 283–360. New York: Knickerbocker Press, 1898. Translation of Romero, *Cultivo del café en la costa meridional de Chiapas*.

———. *Cultivo del café en la costa meridional de Chiapas*. 3rd ed. Mexico City: Imprenta del Gobierno, 1875.

———. "El cultivo del café en Colima." *Boletín de la Sociedad Agrícola Mexicana* 1, no. 25 (July 4, 1880): 390–91.

———. "El cultivo del café en el cantón de Córdoba." *Boletín de la Sociedad Agrícola Mexicana* 1, no. 33 (August 21, 1880): 553–60.

———. "El cultivo del café en el cantón de Huatusco." *Boletín de la Sociedad Agrícola Mexicana* 1, no. 34 (August 28, 1880): 573–79.

———. "El cultivo del café en el cantón de Jalacingo." *Boletín de la Sociedad Agrícola Mexicana* 2, no. 2 (September 18, 1880): 21–36.

———. "El cultivo del café en el cantón de Orizaba." *Boletín de la Sociedad Agrícola Mexicana* 2, no. 4 (October 2, 1881): 62–73.

———. "El cultivo del café en Michoacán." *Boletín de la Sociedad Agrícola Mexicana* 1, no. 29 (July 24, 1880): 467–72.

———. "El cultivo del café en Oaxaca." *Boletín de la Sociedad Agrícola Mexicana* 1, no. 35 (September 4, 1880): 580–88.

Rosas Juárez, Aquileo. "La revolución en el ex-cantón de Córdoba." Manuscript, 2001. In the possession of the author and Adriana Naveda Chávez-Hita.

Roseberry, William. *Coffee and Capitalism in the Venezuelan Andes*. Austin: University of Texas Press, 1983.

———. Introduction to Roseberry, Gudmundson, and Samper Kutschbach, *Coffee, Society, and Power in Latin America*, 1–37.

Roseberry, William, Lowell Gudmundson, and Mario Samper Kutschbach, eds. *Coffee, Society, and Power in Latin America*. Baltimore MD: Johns Hopkins University Press, 1995.

Rosenzweig, Fernando. "El comercio exterior." In *El porfiriato: La vida economica*. Vol. 7 of *La historia moderna de México*, edited by Daniel Cosío Villegas, 635–729. 2nd ed. Mexico City: Hermes, 1974.

Rubin, Jeffrey W. *Decentering the Regime: Ethnicity, Radicalism, and Democracy in Juchitán, Mexico*. Durham NC: Duke University Press, 1997.

Ruiz, Ramon Eduardo. *Labor and Ambivalent Revolutionaries: Mexico, 1911–23*. Baltimore MD: Johns Hopkins University Press, 1976.

Ruiz, Vicki. *Cannery Women, Cannery Lives: Mexican Women, Unionization, and the California Food Processing Industry, 1930–1950*. Albuquerque: University of New Mexico Press, 1987.

Salazar, Rosendo, and José G. Escobedo. *Las pugnas de la gleba, 1906–1922*. Vol 1. Mexico City: Avante, 1923.

Salmerón Castro, Fernando. "Caciquismo." In *Encyclopedia of Mexico: History, Society, and Culture*, edited by Michael S. Werner, 1:177–79. Chicago: Fitzroy Dearborn, 1997.

Samper Kutschbach, Mario. "In Difficult Times: Colombian and Costa Rican Coffee Growers from Prosperity to Crisis, 1920–1936." In Roseberry, Gudmundson, and Samper Kutschbach, *Coffee, Society, and Power in Latin America*, 151–80.

———. "The Historical Construction of Quality and Competitiveness: A Preliminary Discussion of Coffee Commodity Chains." In Clarence-Smith and Topik, *Global Coffee Economy in Africa, Asia, and Latin America, 1500–1989*, 120–53.

Sánchez Diaz, Gerardo, ed. *El café de Uruapan*. Morelia: Universidad Michoacana de San Nicolás de Hidlago, 1999.

———. Introduction to *El café de Michoacán*, 9–18. Morelia: Universidad Michoacana de San Nicolaás, Instituto de Investigaciones Históricas, 1999.

————. "Las ciudades michoacanas: Continuidad y cambio entre dos siglos (1880–1920)." In Muro, *Ciudades provincianas de México*, 31–42.

Sánchez Vargas, Gustavo Eduardo S. "Remembranzas de Córdoba: Biografía de Don Severo Sánchez, un fundador de la industria del café." Manuscript, 1987. In the possession of the author and Javier Domínguez Sánchez.

Sartorius, Carlos. "Memoria sobre el estado de la agricultura en el partido de Huatusco." *Boletín de la Sociedad Mexicana de Geografía y Estadística* 2, no. 2 (1870): 141–99.

————. *Mexico about 1850*. Stuttgart: F. A. Brockhaus Komm, 1961.

Schmidt, Arthur. *The Social and Economic Effect of the Railroad in Puebla and Veracruz, Mexico, 1867–1911*. New York: Garland, 1987.

Scott, James C. *Domination and the Arts of Resistance*. New Haven CT: Yale University Press, 1990.

————. *Weapons of the Weak: Everyday Forms of Peasant Resistance*. New Haven CT: Yale University Press, 1985.

Scott, Joan Wallach. "Gender: A Useful Category of Historical Analysis." In *Gender and the Politics of History*, 28–50. Rev. ed. New York; Columbia, 1988.

Secretaría de Fomento. *Anuario de la República Mexicana de 1895*. Mexico City: Oficina Tipográfica de la Secretaría de Fomento, 1896.

————. *Anuario de la República Mexicana de 1900*. Mexico City: Oficina Tipográfica de la Secretaría de Fomento, 1901.

————. *Anuario de la República Mexicana de 1907*. Mexico City: Imprenta y Oficina de Tipográfica de la Secretaría de Fomento, 1912.

Secretaría de Industria, Comercio y Trabajo. *Ley Federal del Trabajo*. In *Diario Oficial* 67, no. 51 (August 28, 1931). Mexico City: Talleres Gráficos de la Nación, 1931.

Secretaría de la Economía Nacional. *El café: Aspectos económicos de la producción y distribución en México y el extranjero*. Mexico City: Editorial Cultura, 1933.

Sheridan Prieto, Cecilia. *Mujer obrera y organización sindical: El sindicato de obreras desmanchadoras de café, Coatepec, Veracruz; Un estudio histórico-monográfico*. Mexico City: Casa Chata, 1984.

Smith, Stephanie J. *Gender and the Mexican Revolution: Yucatán Women* and the Realities of Patriarchy. Chapel Hill: University of North Carolina Press, 2009.

Silverblatt, Irene. *Moon, Sun, and Witches: Gender Ideologies and Class in Inca and Colonial Peru*. Princeton: Princeton University Press, 1987.

Snodgrass, Michael David. "The Birth and Consequences of Industrial Paternalism in Monterrey, Mexico, 1890–1930." *International Labor and Working-Class History* 53 (Spring 1998): 115–36.

———. *Deference and Defiance in Monterrey: Workers, Paternalism, and Revolution in Mexico, 1890–1950*. Cambridge: Cambridge University Press, 2003.

Southworth, J[ohn] R[eginald]. *El Estado de Veracruz-Llave: Su historia, agricultura, comercio e industrias*. Veracruz: El Gobierno de Estado, 1900.

———. *The Official Directory of Mines and Estates of Mexico*. Mexico City, 1910.

Spenser, Daniela. "Los inicios del cultivo de café en Soconusco." In Von Mentz, Radkau, Spenser, and Montfort, *Los empresarios alemanes, el Tercer Reich y la oposición de derecha a Cárdenas*, 1:61–88.

———. "Soconusco: The Formation of a Coffee Economy in Chiapas." In *The Other Mexicos: Essays in Regional Mexican History, 1876–1911*, edited by Thomas Benjamin and William McNellie, 123–43. Albuquerque: University of New Mexico Press, 1984.

———. "Soconusco y la revolución." In Von Mentz, Radkau, Spenser, and Montfort, *Los empresarios alemanes, el Tercer Reich y la oposición de derecha a Cárdenas*, 1:106–20.

Springett, Leslie. "Curing of 'Washed' Coffees," *Spice Mill* 58 (January 1935): 6, 10; (February 1935): 88, 90, 94; (March 1935); 156, 168; (April 1935): 228, 234; (May 1935): 302, 306; (June 1935): 368, 380.

Stacey, Judith. "Can There Be a Feminist Ethnography?" *Women's Words: The Feminist Practice of Oral History*, edited by Sherna Berger Gluck and Daphne Patai, 111–17. London: Routledge, Kegan, and Paul, 1991.

Stansell, Christine. *City of Women: Sex and Class in New York, 1789–1850*. New York: Alfred A. Knopf, 1986.

Stephen, Lynn, ed. *Hear My Testimony: María Teresa Tula, Human Rights Activist of El Salvador*. Boston: South End Press, 1994.

Súarez-Potts, William J. "The Mexican Supreme Court and the Juntas de

Conciliación y Arbitraje, 1917–1924: The Judicalisation of Labour after the Revolution." *Journal of Latin American Studies* 41, no. 4 (November 2009): 723–55.

Swedberg, Gregory. "Divorce and Marital Equality in Orizaba, Mexico, 1915–1940." In *Journal of Family History* 34, no. 1 (January 2009): 116–37.

Thomson, Guy. "The Ceremonial and Political Roles of Village Bands, 1846–1974." In Beezley, Martin, and French, *Rituals of Rule, Rituals of Resistance*, 307–42.

Thompson, E. P. *The Making of the English Working Class*. 2nd ed. New York: Vintage, 1966.

Thompson, Paul. *The Voice of the Past: Oral History*. 2nd ed. Oxford: Oxford University Press, 1988.

Tiano, Susan. *Patriarchy on the Line: Labor, Gender, and Ideology in the Mexican Maquila Industry*. Philadelphia: Temple University Press, 1994.

Tilly, Louise. "Paths of Proletarianization: Organization of Production, Sexual Division of Labor, and Women's Collective Action." *Signs* 8, no. 2 (Winter 1981): 400–417.

Tinsman, Heidi. *The Politics of Gender, Sexuality, and Labor in the Chilean Agrarian Reform, 1950–1973*. Durham NC: Duke University Press, 2002.

Topik, Steven C. "Coffee." In Topik and Wells, *Second Conquest of Latin America*, 37–84.

——. "Coffee Anyone? Recent Research on Latin American Coffee Societies." *Hispanic American Historical Review* 80, no. 2 (May 2000): 225–67.

——. "The Integration of the World Coffee Market." In Clarence-Smith and Topik, *Global Coffee Economy in Africa, Asia, and Latin America*, 21–49.

——. *The Political Economy of the Brazilian State, 1880–1933*. Austin: University of Texas Press, 1987.

Topik, Steven C., and Allen Wells. Introduction to Topik and Wells, *Second Conquest of Latin America*, 3–36.

——. *The Second Conquest of Latin America: Coffee, Henequen, and Oil during the Export Boom, 1850–1930*. Austin: University of Texas Press, 1998.

Topik, Steven C., and William Gervase Clarence-Smith, "Coffee and Global Development." Introduction to Clarence-Smith and Topik, *Global Coffee Economy in Africa, Asia, and Latin America, 1500–1989,* 1–20.

Trens, Manuel. *La historia de Veracruz.* Vol. 6. Mexico City: La Impresora, 1950.

Trujillo Bolio, Mario. *Operarios fabriles en el Valle de México, 1864–1884.* Mexico City: CIESAS / El Colegio de México, 1997.

Turner, John Kenneth. *Barbarous Mexico.* Austin: University of Texas Press, 1969.

Ukers, William H. *Coffee Facts.* New York: Tea and Coffee Trade Journal, 1951.

———. *All about Coffee.* New York: Tea and Coffee Trade Company, 1922.

———. *Ten Years of Coffee Progress: The Highlights of Coffee Developments during the Decade, 1935–1944.* New York: Pan-American Coffee Bureau, 1945.

Ulloa, Berta. *Veracruz, capital de la nación.* Mexico City: El Colegio de México, 1986.

Vaughan, Mary Kay. "The Construction of the Patriotic Festival in Tecamachalco, Puebla, 1900–1946." In Beezley, Martin, and French, *Rituals of Rule, Rituals of Resistance,* 213–45.

———. *Cultural Politics in Revolution: Teachers, Peasants, and Schools in Mexico, 1930–1940.* Tucson: University of Arizona Press, 1997.

———. "Modernizing Patriarchy: State Policies, Rural Households, and Women in Mexico." In *Hidden Histories of Gender and the State in Latin America,* edited by Elizabeth Dore and Maxine Moyneux, 194–214. Durham NC: Duke University Press, 2000.

———. "Rural Women's Literacy and Education during the Mexican Revolution: Subverting a Patriarchal Event?" In *Women of Mexican Countryside, 1850–1980: Creating Spaces, Shaping Transitions,* edited by Heather Fowler-Salamini and Mary Kay Vaughan, 106–24. Tucson: University of Arizona Press, 1994.

Vecchia, Teresa R. "'My Duty as a Woman': Gender Ideology, Work, and Working-Class Women's Lives in São Paulo, Brazil, 1900–1950." In French and James, *Gendered Worlds of Latin American Women Workers,* 100–146.

Veracruz. *Colección de leyes y decretos de Veracruz, 1824–1919,* vol. 15. Edited by Carmen Blázquez Domínguez and Ricardo Corzo. Xalapa: Tipografía del Gobierno del Estado, 1985.

———. *Enciclopedia municipal Veracruzana. Córdoba.* Xalapa: Gobierno el Estado, 1998.

———. *Enciclopedia municipal veracruzana: Coatepec.* Xalapa: Gobierno del Estado, 1998.

———. *Informes de sus gobernadores, 1826–1986,* edited by Carmen Blázquez Domínguez. 22 vols. Xalapa: Gobierno del Estado, 1986.

———. *Ley del Trabajo del Estado Libre y Soberano de Veracruz-Llave, 14 enero de 1918.* In Veracruz, *Colección de leyes y decretos de Veracruz, 1824–1919* 15, no. 2:773–842.

———. *Leyes, decretos y circulares del Estado de Veracruz, 1903.* Xalapa-Enríquez: Tipografía del Gobierno del Estado, 1903.

———. *Leyes, decretos, y circulares, 1904-7.* Xalapa: Imprenta Ruiz, 1908.

———. *Memorias y informes de jefes políticos y autoridades del régimen porfirista, 1883–1911,* edited by Soledad García Morales and José Velasco Toro. 6 vols. Xalapa, Veracruz: Gobierno del Estado, 1997.

Von Mentz, Brigida. "Los empresarios alemanes en Mexico (1920–42)." In Von Mentz, Radkau, Spenser, and Montfort, *Los empresarios alemanes, el Tercer Reich, y la oposición de derecha a Cárdenas,* 1:121–230.

———. *Los pioneros del imperialismo.* México: Casa Chata, 1982.

Von Mentz, Brigida, Verena Radkau, Daniela Spenser, and R. Pérez Montfort. *Los empresarios alemanes, el Tercer Reich, y la oposición de derecha a Cárdenas.* Mexico City: Col. Miguel Othón de Mendizabal, 1988.

Ward, H. G. *Mexico in 1827.* London: Henry Colbaum, 1828.

Weinstein, Barbara. "Unskilled Worker, Skilled Housewife: Constructing the Working-Class Women in São Paul, Brazil." In French and James, *Gendered Worlds of Latin American Women Workers,* 72–99.

Wells, Allen, and Gilbert M. Joseph, *Summer of Discontent, Seasons of Upheaval.* Stanford: Stanford University Press, 1996.

Wickizer, V. D. *The World Coffee Economy.* Stanford: Food Research Institute, 1943.

Wilkie, James W. and Edna Monzón de Wilkie, eds. *México visto en el siglo XX: Entrevistas de historia oral.* Mexico City: Instituto Mexicano de Investigaciones Económicas, 1969.

Williams, Robin A. *States and Social Evolution: Coffee and the Rise of National Governments in Central America.* Chapel Hill: University of North Carolina Press, 1994.

Williman, John B. *La iglesia y el estado en Veracruz, 1840–1940.* Mexico City: SepSetentas, 1976.

Wilson, Fiona. *De la casa al taller: Mujeres, trabajo y clase social en la industria textil y del vestido; Santiago Tangamandapop.* Zamora: El Colegio de Michoacán, 1990.

Winson, Anthony. *Coffee and Democracy in Modern Costa Rica.* New York: St. Martin's Press, 1989.

Womack, John, Jr. "The Historiography of Mexican Labor." In Frost, Meyer, and Vásquez, *El trabajo y los trabajadores en la historia de México,* 739–56.

———. *Posición estratégica y fuerza obrera: Hacia una nueva historia de los movimientos obreros.* Mexico City: FCE, 2007.

———. *Zapata and the Mexican Revolution.* New York: Knopf, 1968.

Wood, Andrew Grant. "'Proletarian Women Will Make the Social Revolution': Female Participation in the Veracruz Rent Strike, 1922–1927." In *The Women's Revolution in Mexico, 1910–53,* edited by Stephanie Mitchell and Patience A. Schell, 151–64. Lanham MA: Rowman and Littlefield, 2007.

———. *Revolution in the Street: Women, Workers, and Urban Protest in Veracruz, 1870–1927.* Wilmington DE: Scholarly Resources, 2001.

INDEX

and, 220, 223, 226; union hall acquisition and, 195; wages earned by, 253; women's suffrage and, 257–58

Catholic Church, 134–35, 175, 204

CEIMSA. *See* Compañía de Exportación y Importación Mexicana (CEIMSA)

Ceniceros, Georgina Limones, 328–29n31

Central America, 4, 5, 40, 43, 45, 68, 279

Central Veracruz, 5, 7, 12, 16, 20, 21, 23, 24, 35, 38, 48, 46, 47, 48, 59, 63, 70, 73, 80, 83, 123, 129, 151, 158, 166, 235, 236, 252, 261, 277, 279, 282

CGOCM. *See* Confederación General de Obreros y Campesinos de México (CGOCM)

CGT. *See* Confederación General de Trabajadores (CGT)

Chassen-López, Francie, 164

Chasteen, John, 229

Chiapas, 5, 6, 29, 40, 45, 46, 47, 49, 50, 56, 63–64, 65, 80, 239, 241, 279, 297n39, 308n116, 351n12; government involvement in coffee exports in, 237, 240; Zardain Brothers and, 76, 351n12

citizenship, 225, 257–58, 285

CNT. *See* Confederación Nacional de Trabajadores (CNT)

Coatepec, 4, 5, 12, 15, 27, 28, 38, 52, 53, 65, 66, 67, 73, 76, 201, 208, 241, 298n42; leaders, 166, 167, 188, 190; mechanization, 261–63, 266; men workers, 153, 261; modernization of, 305–6n95; unions of, 111, 118,

123, 149, 153, 171, 172, 185; wages in, 98, 129; workers, 86, 87, 88, 93, 94, 95, 96, 98, 100, 115, 254; worker culture, 200, 214, 215, 227, 274; working conditions, 100, 107. *See also* Xalapa-Coatepec region

coffee agroindustry, 4–5; beneficios, 50–51, 59–64, 65, 73–74, 80, 239–40; credit and finance, 27, 31–35, 52, 72–74, 300n56, 312n159, 353n24; cycles, 1940s to 1960s, 236–46, 260–61; during the Depression, 67–80; early years of organized labor and, 6–9; first boom and first wave of foreign entrepreneurs and, 31–36; foreign investment and economic crisis, 36–40, 81; global market and, 2–3; growth of coffee culture/demand and, 21–22, 40–45; hierarchical networks, 3–4; introduction of coffee to the region and, 20–21; land ownership and, 21, 39–40; layoffs, 1, 238, 264; machinery, 27, 29–31, 245, 252, 260–73; origins in Córdoba, Veracruz, 17–19; paternalism and, 109–10; postwar years, 242–44, 276–77; preparing coffee for export and, 29–31; prices and, 25–26, 28–29, 39, 56, 67–68, 79; production increases in, 25–28, 35–36; prominent promoters of, 6; during the Revolution of 1910, 49–50; second boom of the 1920s, 56–67; study of, 2–6, 15–16; taxes, 78–79; technological advancements and, 43, 353n24, 261; transportation and, 22–25, 280, coffee agroindustry (*continued*) 353n24; working conditions, 100–101, 194–95; during World War I, 50–55, 308n116. *See also* exporters and plant owners; workers, coffee agroindustry

collective memory of workers, 16, 85, 113, 118, 200, 201, 219, 224, 225, 233, 236, 273–78, 285

Colombia, 4, 5, 13, 35, 40, 68, 73, 87, 294n3–4; workers in, 114, 323n74

COM. *See* Casa del Obrero Mundial (COM)

Comisión Nacional de Café, 242

Compania Agricola de Productores y Exportadores de Café SA (CAPECSA), 261, 262–63

Compañía Agrícola Francesa, 69, 70, 72. *See also* Lemaistre Brothers

Compañía de Exportación y Importación Mexicana (CEIMSA), 237–38

Confederación de los Sindicatos Obreros de la República Mexicana (CSORM), 129, 131–32, 133

Confederación de Trabajadores Mexicanos (CTM), 171–72, 184–86

Confederación General de Obreros y Campesinos de México (CGOCM), 183

Confederación General de Trabajadores (CGT), 153

Confederación Nacional de Trabajadores (CNT), 247, 248

Confederación Regional Obrera Mexicana (CROM), 59, 111, 123, 145, 147, 152, 161, 174, 269; cacicazgos and, 171; men cacicazgos and, 183; militant union activism by, 177–

83; SOECC band and, 220–21; tenant movement and, 149–50

Confederación Revolucionaria de Obreros y Campesinos (CROC), bargaining power and, 264–65; worker strikes and, 261–63

Confederación Sindicalista de Obreros y Campesinos de la Región de Orizaba (CSOCO), 146–47, 150, 152–53, 171, 176, 247

Confederación Sindicalista de Obreros y Campesinos del Estado de Veracruz (CSOCEV), 154

Córdoba, 1–2, 5, 52; agricultural advantages of, 19–20; beneficios, 59–64; coffee culture of, 40–45, 210–33; coffee plants of, 57; during the Depression, 68–80; domestic experiences of sorters in, 201; dominance of coffee agroindustry by, 70–72, 279–81, 312n159; early production of coffee in, 26–28; introduction of coffee plants to, 20–21; landowners of, 39–40; men workers and, 87–88; men's unions in, 131, 133, 150, 152, 158, 183; mobilization of workers in, 130–36; modernization of, 42–44; organized labor in, 9, 318n19; origins of coffee agroindustry in, 17–19; Peasant League in, 156–59; population of, 25, 41; preparation costs in, 66–67; state capital, 47; strikes, 131–33; tenant movement in, 149–50; tourism, 23–25; transportation routes and, 22–25; wages in, 98–100; workforce profile, 86–89. *See also* Veracruz

exporters and plant owners (*cont.*) 342n84; union negotiations with, 136–39, 151–59, 246–53, 260–69; World War I and, 50–55; World War II and, 238–40. *See also* beneficiadores, coffee agroindustry

62–63, 81; oral histories of, 13–15; railroads, 22–25, 44–45. *See also* Veracruz; *individual cities*

Mexico City, 22, 122, 124, 128, 146, 182, 192, 211, 212, 213, 258, 353n24

Meyer, Jean, 46

Meyer, Lorenzo, 67

Michoacán, 8, 25, 40, 88, 201, 218, 294n10

Middlebrook, Kevin, 187

militant labor activism, 177–83

Millán, Agustín, 127, 138

Misantla, 38, 72, 86

modernization, 305–6n95; of Córdoba, 42–44; machinery and, 27, 29–31, 245, 252, 260–73; Mexican Miracle and, 235; of patriarchy, 8

Modesto Quirasco, Antonio, 266

Monterrey, 70, 109, 213

Moore, Rachel, 3

Morones, Luis, 145, 147, 153, 332n70

Moya, Eufrosina, 157, 169, 171, 176, 182, 191, 196, 205, 248; consolidation of power by, 256–60; home of, 208; negotiations by, 249; public opinion of, 275–76; women's suffrage and, 257–58

Moya, José C., 5, 63

Múgica, Francisco, 148

municipal conciliation boards, 127–28, 133, 187–88, 193

Muñoz Tumbull, Marco Antonio, 262, 265

New York NY, 27, 38, 51, 58, 66, 70, 115, 210; prices and, 26, 50, 56, 239

New York Coffee Board, 237

New Orleans LA, 27, 38, 52, 58, 66, 70

nonunion workers, 192–93, 343n90

Nugent, Daniel, 122–23

Oaxaca, 5, 6, 20, 22, 40, 46, 47, 50, 56, 58, 64, 65, 80, 192, 201, 218, 224, 241, 271, 294n10; Zardain Brothers and, 76, 242, 353n22

Obregón, Alvaro, 49, 147, 149, 153

Obreras Guadalupanas Nacionales, 175

Olavarrieta Brothers, 52, 53

Olivares, Francisco T., 247

Olmos, Manuel, 53, 60

oral history, 13–15, 84, 287

organized labor: working-class culture and, 9–13. *See also* labor movement

Orizaba, 5, 22, 27, 53, 58, 72, 80, 118, 192, 238, 240, 241, 244; labor laws and, 147–48; plant production in, 66; unions in, 122, 140–45, 167, 247, 254, 256–57, 264, 271, 277; workers, 86, 87, 88, 100, 200, 201, 215, 219. *See also* textile and garment workers

Ortiz, Amparo, 186

Ortiz Sarmiento, Delia, 202–3

owners, plant. *See* exporters and plant owners

Palacios, Marco, 45

Panabiere, Louis, 41

Pan-American Agreement of 1953, 242

Pan-American Coffee Bureau, 237

Pansters, Wil, 163

parades and bands, 218–26

Pardo Zorrilla, Pedro, 238, 240

Sindicato de Obreras Escogedoras de la Ciudad de Córdoba (*cont.*) 186–87, 355n42; band and parades, 218–26; dances, 200–218; executive committee, 195–96; leadership, 166–82, 187–98, 253–60; militant activism and, 177–83; theatrical productions by, 226–32; workers' rights under 1931 labor law and, 189–98

Sindicato de Obreras Molineras de Nixtamal, 148

Sindicato de Trabajadores del Beneficios de Café, Tabaco, y Cargaduría de la Región de Córdoba, 251

Sindicato de Trabajadores en General de la Industria del Café, 185

Sindicato "Emancipación" de Escogedoras de Café de Orizaba, 167

Sindicato Industrial de Obreras Escogedoras del Café del Distrito de Córdoba (SIOECC), 248–49, 251, 253–54, 268; exclusion of Moya by, 259–60; politics and, 258–59; worker strikes and, 262–68

Sindicato Industrial de Obreras y Beneficios en las Plazas de Xalapa, Coatepec, y Teocelo, 261

Sindicato Industrial de Trabajadores de Café, Tabaco, Maderas, Destiladores de Aguardiente y Comercio del Distrito de Córdoba (SITCTAC), 152, 183–84

Sindicato Revolutionario de Inquilinos, 148–49

SIOECC. *See* Sindicato Industrial de Obreras Escogedoras del Café del Distrito de Córdoba (SIOECC)

Siriaco García, Brígida, 104, 113, 115, 202–3, 270, 272, 275–76

SITCTAC. *See* Sindicato Industrial de Trabajadores de Café, Tabaco, Maderas, Destiladores de Aguardiente y Comercio del Distrito de Córdoba (SITCTAC)

Smith, Stephanie, 140

Snodgrass, Michael, 109

Spanish exporters, 32–34, 59–61, 64, 152

Spanish immigrant culture, 5, 62–63, 280

Soconusco, 25, 67, 241

social revolution, 6–9, 158–59, 281–84; caciquismo and, 162–66; Casa del Obrero Mundial (COM) and, 128–30; labor laws and, 125–28; municipal authority and, 127–28; Veracruz as a laboratory of, 123–28; Veracruz's postrevolutionary caudillos and, 145–49

SODCC. *See* Sindicato de Obreras Desmanchadoras del Café de Coatepec (SODCC)

SOECC. *See* Sindicato de Obreras Escogedoras de la Ciudad de Córdoba (SOECC)

sorters, coffee: alternative working women's culture, 12, 108, 200–201, 232; caciquismo and Córdoba union of, 166–76; collective memory of, 119, 200, 273–78; domestic experiences of, 201–10; formation of unions of, 150–59; gender identity and, 101, 102–3, *108*, 206–7; housing for, 207–8; married, 105–7, 206–7, 209; mobilization of,

working conditions, 100–101, 204, 320–21n42; CSORM and, 131–34

World War I, 50–55, 308n116

World War II, 240, 277, 286

Xalapa, 5, 22, 23, 25, 27, 38, 49, 52, 58, 65, 66, 236, 239, 241, 294n1, 301n64; labor movement in, 136–40; mechanization in, 261, 264–66; workers, 87, 98, 100, 104, 111; unions in, 122, 123, 129, 149, 151, 153, 171, 172, 185, 188

Xalapa-Coatepec region, 38, 53, 76, 80, 105, 182, 192, 281; beneficios of, 62–63; coffee agroindustry in, 38, 45, 49, 50, 52, 67; during the Depression, 68–70; domestic experiences of sorters in, 201; workers, 86, 88, 94, 95–96; working conditions in, 100

Xalapa group, 62, 66, 241, 308n117

Xico, 38, 50; plant production in, 66

Yucatán, 8, 9, 125, 126,

Zardain Monteserín, José, 51, 55–56, 75, 242–43

Zardain Monteserín, Manuel, 55–56, 59, 74–76

Zardain Monteserín, Ventura, 55–56

Zardain Brothers, 51, 55–56, 59–60, 62, 74, 192, 276; consolidation into the Beneficiadora, 74–76; during the Depression, 71, 73

Zongolica, 35, 66, 86

Zuno Hernández, Guadalupe, 148

CPSIA information can be obtained at www.ICGtesting.com
Printed in the USA
BVOW030800030513

319776BV00001B/1/P